Angels and Demons

THOMISTIC RESSOURCEMENT SERIES
Volume 6

———————:———————

SERIES EDITORS

Angels and Demons

A Catholic Introduction

SERGE-THOMAS BONINO, OP

Translated by Michael J. Miller

The Catholic University of America Press

Washington, D.C.

Originally published as Frère Serge-Thomas Bonino, OP,
Les Anges et les Démons: Quatorze leçons de théologie catholique
© Éditions Parole et Silence, 2007

English translation copyright © 2016
The Catholic University of America Press
All rights reserved
The paper used in this publication meets the minimum
requirements of American National Standards for Information
Science—Permanence of Paper for Printed Library Materials,
ANSI Z39.48–1984.
∞

Library of Congress Cataloging-in-Publication Data
Bonino, Serge-Thomas.
[Anges et les démons. English]
Angels and demons : a Catholic introduction / Serge-Thomas Bonino, OP ;
translated by Michael J. Miller.
pages cm. — (Thomistic ressourcement series)
Includes bibliographical references and index.
ISBN 978-0-8132-2799-3 (pbk. : alk. paper)   1. Angels—Christianity—
History of doctrines.   2. Demonology—History of doctrines.
3. Thomas, Aquinas, Saint, 1225?–1274.   4. Catholic Church—Doctrines.
I. Title.
BT966.3.B6613 2016
235—dc23   2015031031

Contents

Contents

Abbreviations

———————:———————

ACT	Ancient Christian Texts
ACW	Ancient Christian Writers
AHDLMA	Archives d'histoire doctrinale et littéraire du Moyen Âge
ANF	Ante-Nicene Fathers
BA	Bibliothèque augustinienne
BLE	*Bulletin de littérature ecclésiastique*
BN	*Biblische Notizen*
CCC	*Catechism of the Catholic Church*
CCL	Corpus christianorum, series latina
CG	*Summa contra Gentiles*
CSEL	Corpus scriptorum ecclesiasticorum latinorum
DBS	*Dictionnaire de la Bible (Supplément)*
DC	*Documentation catholique*
DEB	*Dictionnaire encyclopédique de la Bible*
DS	*Dictionnaire de spiritualité*
DTC	*Dictionnaire de théologie catholique*
Dz-H	Heinrich Denzinger, *Enchiridion symbolorum definitionum et declarationum de rebus fidei et morum*

Abbreviations

DV	Douay-Rheims Bible (Catholic Bible)
ETL	*Ephemerides theologicae lovanienses*
FOTC	Fathers of the Church
JB	Jerusalem Bible
JBL	*Journal of Biblical Literature*
MM	Miscellanea Medievalia
MSR	*Mélanges de science religieuse*
NT	*Novum Testamentum*
PG	Patrologie grecque
PL	Patrologie latine
RAC	*Reallexikon für Antike und Christentum*
RNSP	*Revue néoscolastique de philosophie*
RSPT	*Revue des sciences philosophiques et théologiques*
RSR	*Recherches de sciences religieuses*
RT	*Revue thomiste*
RTAM	*Recherches de théologie ancienne et médiévale*
SC	Sources chrétiennes
TDNT	*Theological Dictionary of the New Testament*
VT	*Vetus Testamentum*
VTB	*Vocabulaire de théologie biblique*
WSA	*The Complete Works of Saint Augustine in English*
ZkTh	*Zeitschrift für katholische Theologie*

Angels and Demons

General Introduction

————— : —————

A legendary but nonetheless tenacious anecdote relates that in May 1453, at the hour when Constantinople was falling into the hands of the Turks, an assembly of theologians had gathered in the very heart of the besieged city to debate about the sex of the angels—a quintessential Byzantine dispute, typical of a theology that was disconnected from reality. All the more reason why today, at an hour when Western culture is sinking inexorably into the night of massive unbelief, one might wonder whether the Christian theologian does not have something better to do than to expound upon an angelic other-world, the very existence of which is problematic in the opinion of some believers and whose relevance to everyday life seems almost nil.

I have no trouble admitting that the teaching about angels and demons is not the heart of the Christian faith. This is a side issue, a marginal teaching about a peripheral truth in the hierarchy of revealed truths.[1] However, the Lord Jesus, after feeding the crowds by the multiplication of the loaves, told his disciples to "gather up the fragments

1. The existence of a hierarchy of revealed truths—that is, of an objective logical order among the truths taught by the church—in no way implies that the secondary truths are optional in the eyes of faith. All of them must be believed with supernatural faith; see Charles Morerod, "Le sens et la portée de la hiérarchie des vérités à Vatican II et chez saint Thomas," *Nova et vetera* 71 (1996): 15–47. That said, a certain doctrinal conservatism that stubbornly insists on defending the most contested points of the faith runs the risk of building a doctrinal and practical edifice in which the objectively secondary truths become central, throwing the Christian faith as a whole out of balance. No doubt it is important to recall the value of devotion to the Blessed Sacrament, to the Blessed Virgin, and to the pope, but one cannot make *"les trois blancheurs"* [the three whitenesses] the objective core of the Christian faith. Similarly, it is not a waste of time to meditate and to preach on the angelic world, but it would be somewhat excessive to center everything on this incidental theme.

1

left over, that nothing may be lost" (Jn 6:12). Nothing in revelation is surplus. And I would like to suggest over the course of these chapters that the present-day stakes of angelology and demonology, while not decisive, are far from negligible for Christian life and for a comprehensive theology. We will have to specify the things that are at stake, but for now, by way of an initial approach, let us note that they are either indirect or direct.

Indirectly, reflection on angels serves in philosophy as a thought experiment that illuminates in particular the idea that one can form of the human condition. Indeed, in order to know exactly what a cat is, there is nothing like comparing it with another feline, such as a lion or a panther. Our ancestors, in order to understand better the specific nature of man, therefore compared and contrasted him with the angel, his cousin in the order of spiritual beings. Today the chimpanzee has replaced the angel in this role, and not to the benefit of the humanities. Comparing how one perfection or another (life, knowledge, language, love) is achieved in a pure spirit and in a human being allows us to determine simultaneously the analogically universal stable nucleus of this perfection and the particular features that it assumes in man. The specificity of the human condition stands out all the more clearly as a result.[2] For example, the study of such an exotic topic as the language of the angels allows us to sort out the fundamental structures of all communication and to identify the things in our experience of language that depend on specifically human modalities. Moreover, an examination of the metaphysical structure of an angel reveals, like a photographic image chemically developed in a darkroom, the fundamental truth of the composition of being and essence in every creature. In short, angelology is a "thought laboratory" that allows the philosopher to distill and refine his metaphysical or noetic concepts and to define further what is properly human.[3]

2. See Jean-Louis Chrétien, "La connaissance angélique," in *Le regard de l'amour* (Paris: Desclée De Brouwer, 2000), 126: "For a long time, in every field, one stated what belongs more specifically to man by stating what distinguishes him from an angel, his double in finitude. To think about one was always to think about the other as well."
3. The expression, which has a Gilsonian flavor, is applied to angelology by Tiziana Suarez-Nani, *Les anges et la philosophie: Subjectivité et fonction des substances séparées à la fin du XIIIe siècle* (Paris: J. Vrin, 2002), 184 and 188. Thus the angelic type allows Michel Serres, in La légende des anges (Paris: Flammarion, 1993), to develop a philosophy

It is the same in theology. Angelology indirectly leads the theologian to refine a great many ideas that are central to his discipline: the meaning of creation, the divinizing plan of the Trinity, the universality of providence, the place of Jesus Christ in the economy of salvation, the nature of the church. As for discourse about Satan and the demonical, no doubt it is not the key to the mystery of evil; yet, on the one hand, it is inseparable from a comprehensive theology of redemption as liberation, and, on the other hand, it brings into play most of the major themes of Christian reflection on evil.[4] Thus, for example, the study of the angel's sin obliges theologians to go to the very heart of the notion of sin, toward the sin that is chemically pure.

However, although the study of angels and demons sheds an extremely valuable light on our philosophical and theological knowledge about God, man, nature, and history, angelology cannot therefore be reduced to a simple appendix to anthropology. It is not just a coded, roundabout way of speaking about man, a crypto-anthropology that any serious hermeneutic would show to be alienating and illusory in the final analysis. It is not the now-empty religious chrysalis in which the modern concept of the human subject was supposedly formed.[5]

of communication, or Stanislas Breton, in "Faut-il parler des anges?" *RSPT* 64 (1980): 225–40, to meditate on the "meta" function that is essential to all "poetics." Rainer-Maria Rilke saw in the figure of the angel the very ideal of the poet. The angel is "the creature in which the transformation of the visible into the invisible that we accomplish is already achieved and evident"; Rilke, letter to Witold von Hulewicz, cited by Johann Michl, "Ange," in *Encyclopédie de la foi* (Paris: Cerf, 1965): 1:94.

4. See Origen, *Contra celsum* IV.65, trans. Henry Chadwick (Cambridge: Cambridge University Press, 1965), 236–37: "No one will be able to know the origin of evils who has not grasped the truth about the so-called devil and his angels, and who he was before he became a devil, and how he became a devil, and what caused his so-called angels to rebel with him. Anyone who intends to know this must possess an accurate understanding of daemons, and be aware that they are not God's creation in so far as they are daemons, but only in so far as they are rational beings of some sort. And he must understand how they came to be such that their mind put them in the position of daemons."

5. In his diptych on medieval angelology, *Les anges* and *Connaissance et langage des anges selon Thomas d'Aquin et Gilles de Rome*, Études de philosophie médiévale 85 (Paris: J. Vrin, 2002), Suarez-Nani showed how modern anthropology has brought down to the human being the properties of the medieval angelic subject so that modern man claims for himself certain features of the ontological or noetic status that medieval thinkers attributed to the angelic subject: "[The angel] appears as a figure playing a fundamental role of mediation: a mediation that, in relation to the past, ensures the assimilation of a vast religious and philosophical tradition and looks out over an elaboration and

Besides, can the angel fully perform his anthropological function if he is just a projection of human subjectivity? Only the ontological reality of the angelic world guarantees the reality of humanity's openness to something greater than itself. We will have occasion to repeat this in every key: taking angels seriously is a way of reestablishing the truth of Christian theocentrism, which was obscured by a certain way of understanding the anthropological revolution of contemporary theology.

Indeed, Christian angelology claims first of all—and this is its immediate concern and most profound purpose—to speak about God. In seeking an understanding in faith of the revealed teaching about the invisible universe, the theologian, as he does every time he turns his attention to creatures, seeks in it some reflection of the divine perfections that opens up for him a better and more delectable knowledge of the Creator.[6] Moreover, by reproducing within himself noetically the intelligible structures of the universe, he participates, however slightly, in the divine wisdom that is their source, becomes assimilated to them, and thus anticipates from afar the eternal life that consists in knowing the one true God (Jn 17:3).

Let us now state explicitly the purpose and the literary genre of the chapters in this volume. They will deal with angels and demons. The English term "angel" literally translates the Latin *angelus*, which is itself a copy of the Greek *aggelos*. In Greek common parlance, *aggelos* meant "envoy, messenger," and the Septuagint employed it to translate the equivalent Hebrew term *mal'ak*, which is derived from the verb *la'ak* (to send) and which, in the Bible, is applied to various categories of earthly or heavenly beings that perform the duty of a messenger.[7] Thus, as Tertullian and later Augustine explain, the term "angel" is initially a name for a function before it is a name for a nature.[8]

---

an emancipation with regard to that same tradition, that modern philosophy was to accomplish not so much by getting rid of the figure of the angel and angelology as by absorbing them" (*Les Anges*, 52). But Suarez-Nani does not succumb to the reductionist temptation. Instead, the real otherness of the angel appears to him necessary in order that anthropology not be "deprived of its impetus and cut off from its prospects" (*Connaissance*, 165).

6. See Thomas Aquinas, *CG* II.2–4.

7. See W. Grundmann, "*Aggelos: Aggelos* in the Greek and Hellenistic World," in *TDNT*, 1:74–76; Gerhard von Rad, "*Aggelos: Mal'ak* in the OT," in *TDNT*, 1:76–80.

8. St. Augustine's intention in distinguishing nature and function is to legitimize the application of the term "angel" to Christ while avoiding the ambiguities of Arianism,

But, since the function of messenger between God and men has often devolved upon a category of intermediary beings, it has come to designate those beings who are of a spiritual nature, yet are creatures.[9] We are going to take a strictly theological look at these beings. Our objective is, on the one hand, to determine the content of the Christian faith relative to the angels and, on the other hand, to demonstrate its intelligibility and to reconstitute it in an organic, synthetic, scientific manner.[10] For the latter project, we will go to the school of St. Thomas Aquinas, as the Second Vatican Council invites us to do.[11]

---

which failed to recognize Christ's divine nature; see Augustine, *Sermon VII*.3, in *WSA* III/1:234: "'Angel' is a word signifying function, not nature. 'Angel' is Greek for the Latin 'nuntius,' English 'messenger.' So 'messenger' is the name of an action: you are called a messenger for doing something, namely for bringing some message" [Angelus enim officii nomen est, non naturae. Nam angelus graece, qui latine nuntius appellatur. Nuntius ergo actionis nomen est: agendo, id est, aliquid nuntiando, nuntius appellatur]. See also Augustine, *Exposition of Ps. 103* 1.15, in *WSA* III/19:125: "The angels are spirits. When they are simply spirits, they are not angels, but when they are sent, they become angels: for 'angel' is the name of a function, not of a nature. If you inquire about the nature of such beings, you find that they are spirits; if you ask what their office is, the answer is that they are angels. In respect of what they are, such creatures are spirits; in respect of what they do, they are angels" [Spiritus autem angeli sunt; et cum spiritus sunt, non sunt angeli; cum mittuntur fiunt angeli. Angelus enim officii nomen est, non naturae. Quaeris nomen huius naturae, spiritus est; quaeris officium angelus est; ex eo quo est, spiritus est; ex eo quo agit, angelus est]. See also Goulven Madec, "Angelus," in *Augustinus-Lexicon* (Basel: Schwabe, 1986–94), 1:303–15 [esp. 304–5, "Nomen officii"]. Augustine finds this idea in Tertullian's writings; see Tertullian, *The Flesh of Christ* XIV.3, in *ANF* 3:534a: Although Jesus Christ is called "the Angel of great counsel," this is "officii non naturae vocabulo" [a term expressive of official function, not of nature]; Johannes Mehlmann, "Tertulliani liber *de carne Christi* ab Augustino citatus," *Sacris erudiri* 17 (1966): 269–89. It would be repeated in a passage by St. Gregory that is appointed today for the Office of Readings on the Feast of the Holy Archangels (September 29)—Gregory the Great, *Forty Gospel Homilies, Homiliae in Evangelia* 34.8, trans. Dom David Hurst (Kalamazoo, Mich.: Cistercian Publications, 1990), 286: "We should know too that the word 'angel' is the name of a service, not of a nature. The holy spirits of our heavenly homeland are always indeed spirits, but they cannot always be called angels since they are only angels when some message is communicated by them" [Sciendum quoque quod angelorum vocabulum nomen est officii, non naturae. Nam sancti illi caelestis patriae spiritus semper quidem sunt spiritus, sed semper vocari angeli nequaquam possunt, quia tunc solum sunt angeli, cum per eos aliqua nuntiantur].

9. Hence the term "angels" applies also to demons, to the "wicked angels," although they are not messengers of God.

10. This is not the place to justify the concept of theology underlying this set of chapters. It is inspired to a great extent by Michel M. Labourdette, "La théologie, intelligence de la foi," *RT* 46 (1946): 5–44.

11. Second Vatican Council, Decree *Optatam totius*, 16, in *Vatican Council II*, vol. 1,

We will consider him not only as the Common Doctor who offers an unequalled synthesis of the teaching of Scholastic theology on angels and demons but also as an original author whose way of giving an account of the theological heritage on angelology cannot be reduced to those of other theologians. Some chapters therefore are presented in the form of free commentaries on the questions from the *Summa theologiae* pertaining to the topic being treated. This literary genre was very deliberately chosen and employed; it follows from a certain idea of theology as a work of tradition that advances by way of infinitesimal development, by the gradual enrichment of the heritage, and never by way of revolution. Of course, since the days of the classical commentators (Cajetan, Bañez, John of St. Thomas) and even since their great twentieth-century heirs (Édouard Hugon, Réginald Garrigou-Lagrange, Jean-Hervé Nicolas), the problem has changed under the influence of several interrelated factors: the renewal of biblical and patristic theology that characterized the twentieth century, the customary internal maturation of Scholastic theology, the multiple provocations coming from general cultural developments. It is necessary to take them into consideration, in other words, to prune the dead branches and to come to terms prudently with new findings and perspectives that ought to be incorporated into their proper place in the Thomistic synthesis.[12] But is not this ongoing task of updating the theological heritage—*vetera novis augere* [supplementing old things with new]—the same one that Scholastic theology has ceaselessly carried out over the ages? If these chapters can serve as a new link in this unceasingly renewed tradition, they will have attained their objective.[13]

We will proceed in four stages. Part 1 presents the teaching of scripture and tradition about angels and demons and, given the fact that this teaching is currently called into question, attempts to provide a justification thereof. Part 2 is a systematic reflection on the an-

---

The Conciliar and Post Conciliar Documents, ed. A. Flannery (Northport, N.Y.: Costello Publishing; Dublin: Dominican Publications, 2004).

12. For example, despite the considerable interest of the question for a history of physics, we have left out a choice bit of the classical treatises of Scholastic angelology: the nature and the modalities of the local movement of angels.

13. On the significance of this preferential citation of St. Thomas Aquinas, the reader may wish to consult Serge-Thomas Bonino, ed., *Thomistes ou De l'actualité de saint Thomas* (Paris: Parole et Silence, 2003).

gelic nature in general, which is common to good and bad angels, in the order of being as well as their natural action (knowledge and love). Part 3 addresses the sacred history of angels: the modalities of their creation, their call to supernatural life, the glorification of good angels, and the emergence of the demonic world as a result of sin. Finally, Part 4 considers the role played by angels and demons in the divine government—in other words, their participation in the activity by which God as Creator guides the universe—and especially human beings—to its fulfillment in God as the end of all things.

In all this work, the theologian cannot do without recourse to other disciplines than his own. But he takes them up and utilizes them instrumentally in light of the object of his own science, the revelation of God. Thus, in order to determine the content of tradition, he turns to biblical studies, to the history of religions, or even to the history of Christian doctrines. In order to offer a certain understanding of it, he employs philosophical and especially metaphysical notions, which in return for this theological application acquire a new depth.[14] By reason of the constant interaction between the Christian faith and the cultures that it encounters, he will benefit also (provided that he independently takes them up the light of theology) from the multifarious contents of the human sciences that take an interest in the repercussions of the belief in angels and demons on psychologies, mentalities, and cultures as well as in the ways in which the latter affect that belief in turn.[15] Even the rich contributions of art are capable of illuminating his reflection here or there.[16]

14. See John Paul II, *Fides et ratio*, 97: "If the intellectus fidei wishes to integrate all the wealth of the theological tradition, it must turn to the philosophy of being.... Set within the Christian metaphysical tradition, the philosophy of being is a dynamic philosophy that views reality in its ontological, causal and communicative structures. It is strong and enduring because it is based upon the very act of being itself, which allows a full and comprehensive openness to reality as a whole."

15. Along this line, see among many other examples, Robert Muchembled, *A History of the Devil: From the Middle Ages to the Present* (Cambridge: Polity Press, 2003); and Alain Boureau, *Satan hérétique: Histoire de la démonologie (1280–1330)* (Paris: Odile Jacob, 2004). The demonic inflation of modern times, a genuine societal phenomenon, has given rise to an extensive literature of social psychology. The angelic world can also hold interest as a transcendent model of the politico-religious order; see, among the recent studies, Daniel Ménager, *Diplomatie et théologie à la Renaissance* (Paris: Presses universitaires de France, 2001), which draws a parallel between the figure of the angel and that of the ambassador.

16. On angels and painting, see the solid Christian meditation by Dominique Ponnau

The chapters that make up this volume were actually presented to theology students as lectures. From this original form they retain a pedagogical concern, a striving for expository clarity, and a style that is sometimes rather casual. Supplementary technical information (references, bibliography, related problems) is generally provided in the footnotes. Such a set of lectures does not constitute a treatise. Although it does intend to offer, like a treatise, a synthetic view of the subject, based on solid documentation, it does not claim to be exhaustive, either with regard to the (inexhaustible) history of angelological doctrines or even with regard to the problems being examined. Nor does it try to settle correctly and in due argumentative form the various disputed points; rather, it aims to give an overall view of the problems and their solutions. As such, there is hardly anything like it in recent theological literature, and, for that reason, it could fill a gap and perform a service in the teaching of theology.

and Erich Lessing, *Dieu en ses anges* (Paris: Cerf, 2000); see also Roland Villeneuve, *Le diable dans l'art* (Paris: Éditions Denoël, 1957); and Rosa Giorgi, *Angels and Demons in Art: A Guide to Imagery* (Los Angeles: J. Paul Getty Museum, 2005), which provides essential iconographical landmarks on this topic. In the cinema there has been much discussion of the beautiful film by Wim Wenders, *Les ailes du désir* [*Der Himmel über Berlin*] (1987), in which some aspects of the Christian doctrine about angels are subtly and profoundly suggested, although the film consists primarily of an ambiguous exaltation of man's precarious, temporal, and carnal condition: the passage from the angelic world to the human world is depicted as a transition from black-and-white to color film—that is, to reality.

PART 1

The Traditional Facts and
Their Interpretation

1

———— : ————

Angels and Demons in the Old Testament

Belief in the existence and activity, whether beneficent or maleficent, of intermediate beings between men and the Supreme Deity—
demigods, angels, demons, genies—is a common religious fact, widespread in different traditional cultures.[1] Biblical revelation assumes,
confirms, and corrects these beliefs.[2] There is nothing more debat-

1. From the perspective of the history of religions, see *Anges, démons et êtres intermédiaires: Colloque de l'alliance mondiale des religions du 13–14 janvier 1968 à Paris* (Paris: Labergerie, 1969); *Génies, anges et démons: Egypte, Babylone, Israël, Islam, Peuples altaïques, Inde, Birmanie, Asie du Sud-Est, Tibet, Chine* (Paris: Éditions du Seuil, 1971);
and Julien Ries and Henri Limet, eds., *Anges et Démons: Actes du colloque de Liège et de
Louvain-la-Neuve, 25–26 novembre 1987*, Homo religiosus 14 (Louvain-la-Neuve: Centre
d'histoire des religions, 1989). The genesis of these fundamental religious notions has
been the object of various hypotheses: are the angels fallen, recycled gods or are they
doubles of God and men? See Gerardus van der Leeuw, *La religion dans son essence et ses
manifestations: Phénoménologie de la religion* (Paris: Payot, 1970), §16: "Figure spéciale de
la puissance: Les anges," 137–42, who thinks that angels are "powers making their way
toward the exterior"—in other words, aspects or properties of the "god" that tend to assume their own autonomy.

2. On angelology in the Old Testament, see William G. Heidt, *Angelology of the Old
Testament: A Study in Biblical Theology* (Washington, D.C.: The Catholic University of
America Press, 1949); Paul van Imschoot, *Théologie de l'Ancien Testament*, vol. 1, *Dieu* (Par-
is and Tournai: Desclée, 1954), 114–30 and 147; D. S. Russell, *The Method and Message of
Jewish Apocalyptic* (Philadelphia: Westminster Press, 1964), 235–62; Johann Michl, "Ange,"
1:83–87; Michael Seemann and Damasus Zähringen, chap. 11, "Le monde des anges et des

able than the (rather Protestant) tendency to define the "true" contents of biblical revelation by the sole criterion of originality in relation to nearby religions. Eliminating a doctrine from revelation on the pretext that one finds beginnings or equivalents of it in nonbiblical religions is the result of an erroneous understanding of the relations between faith and reason, between nature and grace, as though grace by definition had to contradict nature. Yet it is true that the Bible corrects natural beliefs—in other words, interprets them in terms of the articles of its essential creed.

With respect both to the Bible and to Christian tradition I will have occasion to describe the development of ideas about the angelic world. Is it necessary to explain that this development takes place not in the realities themselves but in the notions that believers have had about them over the course of history—notions that the action of the spirit of truth guided and refined in them? For example, when I assert that angels become more plentiful starting with the exile or that Satan becomes the head of the demons in the intertestamental period, clearly this becoming does not concern the reality itself (the number of angels has remained the same since their creation, and Satan has been the head of the demons since his original fall), but rather the human perception of this reality, which came about gradually.

THE ANGELS BEFORE THE EXILE

The angelology of the Old Testament is divided into two major periods: before and after the Babylonian exile (sixth century B.C.). From the start, Israel acknowledges the existence of supra-human beings,

demons," in *Mysterium salutis: Dogmatique de l'histoire du salut* (Paris: Cerf, 1970), 8:153–66; André Caquot, "L'angélologie biblique: L'Ancien Testament," in *Les anges*, edited by Georges Tavard, 11–28, Histoire des dogmes II.2b (Paris: Cerf, 1971); Caquot, "Anges et démons en Israël," in *Génies, anges et démons*, 113–52; Paul-Eugène Dion, "Les deux principales formes de l'angélologie de l'Ancien Testament dans leur cadre oriental," *Science et Esprit* 28 (1976): 65–89; Alexander Rofé, *The Belief in Angels in the Bible and in Early Israel* (Jerusalem: Makor, 1979); Pièrre-Marie Galopin, "Ange," in *DEB*, 59–60; Galopin and Pieree Grelot, "Ange," in *VTB*, 58–60; Charles Fontinoy, "Les anges et les démons de l'Ancien Testament," in *Anges et Démons: Actes du colloque de Liège et de Louvain-la-Neuve, 25–26 novembre 1987*, edited by Julien Ries and Henri Limet. Homo religiosus 14 (Louvain : Centre d'histoire des religions, 1989) 117–34; Henri Cazelles, "Fondements bibliques de la théologie des anges," RT 90 (1990): 181–93.

to which it attributes the status of messengers of God, usually designating them by the term *mal'ak*.[3] This simple functional terminology highlights an essential feature of biblical angelology: the radical subordination of the angels to God, whose servants and envoys they are. The most frequently occurring angelic figure in the pre-exilic period is "the angel of God" or "angel of Yahweh."[4] His identity—particularly his relation to God—is difficult to pin down. Sometimes, especially in the oldest passages, this angel speaks and acts as though he were God in person. For example, the angel of the Lord appears in a dream to Jacob to declare to him, "I am the God of Bethel, where you anointed a pillar and made a vow to me" (Gn 31:13).[5] In contrast, in other passages, he is clearly distinguished from the Lord himself. Thus, when God withdraws somewhat in his relationship to Israel, which can no longer withstand his holiness because of the sin of idolizing the golden calf, the angel of the Lord is presented as a substitute for God, distinct from God:

3. The name *mal'ak* is applied initially to men; see, for example, Gn 32:3, "Jacob sent *messengers* before him to Esau his brother." It is used also to designate the prophets (Is 44:26; Hg 1:13) or even priests (Mal 2:7); see Samuel A. Meier, *The Messenger in the Ancient Semitic World* (Cambridge, Mass.: Harvard University Press, 1988); John T. Greene, *The Role of Messenger and Message in the Ancient Near East: Oral and Written Communication in the Ancient Near East and in the Hebrew Scriptures* (Atlanta: Scholars Press, 1989).

4. On the angel of the Lord, see Marie-Joseph Lagrange, "L'ange de Jahvé," *Revue biblique* (1903): 212–23; Jules Touzard, "Ange de Yahweh," in DBS, 1:242–55; J. Rybinski, *Der Mal'ak Jahwe* (Paderborn: Ferdinand Schoningh, 1930); Fridolin Stier, *Gott und sein Engel im A.T.* (Münster: Verlag der Aschendorffschen Verlagsbuchhandlung, 1934); Walter Baumgartner, "Zum Problem des Yahweh-Engels," in *Zum Alten Testament und seiner Umwelt; Ausgewählte Aufsätze* (Leiden: E. J. Brill, 1959); Hermann Röttger, *Mal'ak Jahwe—Bote von Gott: Die Vorstellung von Gottes Boten im hebräischen A.T.* (Regensburg: Frankfurt am Main, 1978); Fritz Guggisberg, *Die Gestalt des Mal'ak Jahwe im AT* (Neuchâtel: Université de Neuchâtel, 1979); Jesús Luis Cunchillos, "Étude philologique du mal'ak: Perspectives sur le mal'ak de la divinité dans la Bible hébraïque," in *Congress Volume, Vienna 1980*, edited by J. A. Emerton, 30–51, Supplements to Vetus Testamentum 32 (Leiden: E. J. Brill, 1981); Galopin, "Ange de Yahvé," in *DEB*, 62; Edmond Jacob, "Variations et constantes dans la figure de l'Ange de YHWH," *Revue d'Histoire et de Philosophie religieuse* 68 (1988): 405–14; Stephen L. White, "Angel of the Lord: Messenger or Euphemism?" *Tyndale Bulletin* 50 (1999): 299–305.

5. Similarly, the angel of the Lord appears in the fire in the middle of the burning bush, but Yahweh himself is the one who calls to Moses and speaks to him (Ex 3:2); compare Ambroise Montagne, "De l'apparition de Dieu à Moyse sur le Mont Horeb (Exode, chap. III)," *Revue biblique* 3 (1894): 232–47; see also Gn 16:7–13, 22:15; Jgs 2:1.

I will send an angel before you, and I will drive out the Canaanites.... Go up to a land flowing with milk and honey; but I will not go up among you, lest I consume you in the way, for you are a stiff-necked people. (Ex 33:2)[6]

Interpreters are therefore divided.[7] For some fathers of the church, who see the angelophanies of the Old Testament as preparations for the mystery of the Incarnation of the Son, the angel of God is already a manifestation of the Christ-*logos*.[8] For others, the angel of God is truly an angelic creature but vested with divine authority. St. Augustine thinks that both interpretations are legitimate in the eyes of faith.[9]

Some modern exegetes think that the angel of God was originally, so to speak, the external soul of God: God inasmuch as he manifests himself to men in visible form. Resorting to the theme of the angel would then have been a way of safeguarding the transcendence of God.[10] Others think that, precisely because of the development toward a more transcendent concept of God, the expression "angel of

6. See also Is 63:9: "In all their affliction he was afflicted, and the angel of his presence saved them." Concerning another interpretation of this difficult passage, see Jacob, "Variations," note 17. Other ancient texts in which the angel of the Lord is distinct from the Lord: Nm 22:31, where it says that "the Lord opened the eyes of Balaam (who was furious with his donkey), and he saw the angel of the LORD standing in the way, with his drawn sword in his hand"; see also 2 Sm 24:16.

7. Francisco Suarez, *Tractatus de Angelis*, in *Commentarii et disputationes in primam Partem D. Thomae*, chaps. 20–21, Opera omnia 2 (Paris: Vivès, 1866), 765–88, discusses at length the role of the angels in the apparitions of the Old and New Testaments and recapitulates Scholastic reflection on this point. From the start he recognizes that "in Scripture the apparitions of God and of the angels are quite mixed up (*apparitiones Dei et Angelorum in Scriptura valde permixta sunt*)" (ibid., chap. 20, no. 3, 6:766). See also Georges Legeay, "L'ange et les théophanies dans la sainte écriture, d'après la doctrine des pères," *RT* 10 (1902): 138–58, 405–24; *RT* 11 (1903): 46–69, 125–54.

8. See, for example, Justin Martyr, *Dialogue with Trypho*, chap. 128 (PG 6:773–76), trans. Thomas B. Falls, rev. Thomas P. Halton (Washington, D.C., The Catholic University of America Press, 2003), 193: "Christ is the Lord, and God the Son; ... in times gone by he appeared by his power as man, and angel, and in the glory of fire as in the bush"; see also Justin Martyr, *The First Apology* 62–63 (ANF 1:184a): "Our Christ conversed with him [Moses] under the appearance of fire from a bush." For Justin, indeed, God the Father does not address men directly, but the Son "is called Angel and Apostle; for He declares whatever we ought to know, and is sent forth to declare whatever is revealed" (*First Apology*, ANF 1:184a).

9. See Augustine, *Sermon VII*, WSA III/1:233–39; Augustine, *The Trinity* II.7–18 (FOTC 45:66–93).

10. See note on Gn 16:7 in the *Jerusalem Bible*.

the Lord" was introduced later into passages that originally had spoken directly about God (the so-called interpolation theory).

Aside from this mysterious angel of the Lord, angels are rarely found in the texts that reflect the [Old Testament] religion before the exile. In them they have a certain affinity with the stars.[11] And since the peoples of the Near East were fond of adoring the stars as divine beings, it is quite possible that originally the angels (stars) corresponded to pagan deities. But a twofold development took place in the thinking of Israel. First, the gods of the pagans were strictly subordinated to Yahweh, "the God of gods,"[12] then little by little they lost their divine status in Israel's eyes; they were "recycled" and reduced to the rank of servants of the one God, put in charge of one mission or another or assigned to guard this or that nation[13]—a fine example of the demythologization of the surrounding religions and of their integration into the theological vision belonging to biblical monotheism. Second, the angels tended to be distinguished from the stars. However, believers would continue to attribute to them a decisive influence on cosmic phenomena (storm, wind, snow).[14] Indeed, the

11. Angels and stars together make up the heavenly hosts, the "army of the Lord" (see Jgs 5:20: "From heaven fought the stars, from their courses they fought against Sisera [by the rain]"). Similarly, stars and angels are associated in the praise that ascends to the Creator, "who laid [the earth's] cornerstone, when the morning stars sang together, and all the sons of God shouted for joy" (Jb 38:6–7). See also Ps 148: "Praise the LORD from the heavens, praise him in the heights! Praise him, all his angels, praise him, all his host! Praise him, sun and moon"; see also Dn 3:36 ff.

12. See Ps 49:1; 136:2 DV.

13. On the thesis of the demotion of local deities to angels or demons, see, for example, Alfred Koloska, *Gottessöhne und Engel in den Vorexilischen Büchern des AT und in der Ras-Schamaramythologie im Lichte des Biblischen Monotheismus* (Vienna: 1953); Cunchillos, "Cuando los Angelos Eran Dioses," *Estudios Biblicos* 12 (1976): 118–38. Celestin Simbanduku, *Yhwh, les dieux et les anges: Permanence du polythéisme dans la religion de la Bible* (Rome: Urbaniana University Press, 2004), shows nicely how the divine group of the "sons of the gods" that surrounds YHWH and is subject to him gradually was transformed into an assembly of angels, especially with the LXX translation, but he thinks that the "angels" maintain a divine ontological status, which is a more difficult concept. Whatever the case may be, the reduction of the gods of the nations to the rank of angels and the dominion of Yahweh over these angels make it possible to express archetypically, in heaven, the sovereignty of the God of Israel over the whole world. See Caquot, "Anges et démons en Israël," 130: "The universal sovereignty of the national god is affirmed in this way, not only on the historical level, but also on the cosmic level."

14. See, for example, Rv 7:1: "I saw four angels standing at the four corners of the earth, holding back the four winds of the earth"; Jubilees 2:2 (in *The Apocryphal Old*

angels have the mission of enforcing observance of the law decreed by God for the universe: they are the guardians of the cosmic order. God's dominion over the cosmos is then expressed often by the affirmation of his sovereignty over the angels who are put in charge of governing the physical world, as the four living creatures of Ezekiel 1 seem to be.[15]

Before the exile, the angels are scarcely individualized; instead they form a collective, a group: they are *ad intra* God's court and *ad extra* his army. Like any self-respecting sovereign, like the Canaanite monarchs on whom the kings of Israel were modeled, God has a court, which is the assembly or council of the old gods transformed into angels. The prologue of the book of Job describes an audience (held every Wednesday?) on "a day when the sons of God (*beney elohim*) came to present themselves before the LORD."[16] This proximity to God makes the angels "holy ones"—in other words, beings irradiated by the divine holiness.

Let the heavens praise your wonders, O LORD, your faithfulness in the assembly of the holy ones! For who in the skies can be compared to the LORD? Who among the sons of gods is like the LORD, a God feared in the council of the holy ones, great and awesome above all that are round about him? (Ps 89:5–7)[17]

This celestial court has two main functions. On the one hand, it is turned toward God, whose grandeur it exalts and celebrates and, in later Judaism, will evolve neatly into something like a liturgical assem-

Testament, edited by H. F. D. Sparks [Oxford: Clarendon Press, 1984], 14): "For on the first day He created the heavens which are above, and the earth, and the waters and every spirit that serves before him—the angels of the presence, and the angels of holiness, and the angels of the spirit of the winds, and the angels of the spirit of the clouds and of darkness and of snow and of hail and of hoar-frost, and the angels of the depths and of thunders and lightnings, and the angels of the cold winds and the hot *winds* and of winter and spring and autumn and summer"; 1 Enoch 60:11 ff. (ibid., 239ff.). Note that in Gn 1:16 the two great lights are said to "rule" over the day and the night.

15. See Jean Steinmann, *Le prophète Ezéchiel et les débuts de l'exil* (Paris: Cerf, 1953), 171–82.

16. Concerning the divine audience, see also 1 Kgs 22:14–22. On the theme of the divine council, see L. Dequeker, "La cour céleste de Yahweh," *Collectanea Mechlinensia* 52 (1967): 131–40; E. Theodore Mullen Jr., *The Assembly of the Gods: The Divine Council in Canaanite and Early Hebrew Literature* (Chico, Calif.: Scholars Press, 1980). On angels as "sons of God," see Dt 32:8; Ps 29:1, 82:1, 89:7.

17. See also Jb 5:1, 15:15; Dn 4:17; Zec 14:5: "Then the LORD my God will come, and all the holy ones with him." Compare Dequeker, "Les *Qedôsîm* du Ps 89 à la lumière des croyances sémitiques," *ETL* (1966): 469–84.

bly.[18] On the other hand, it assures the connection between God and the world of men, to whom the angels generally manifest themselves under a very attractive human form ("he is as beautiful as an angel!").[19] Thus the angels form the army of God—precisely of the "God of hosts (God Sabaoth)"[20]—who are in charge of carrying out his orders on earth. Jacob, whom the angels have just confronted, calls the place of this encounter "the camps of God" (Gn 32:2–3, DV). Joshua meets a man who introduces himself as "commander of the army of the LORD" (Jo 5:14).[21] And so the angels are called the "mighty ones" (Ps 103:20) or "powerful" (Jl 2:11).

Besides the angel-messengers, strictly speaking, the Hebrews are acquainted with two other categories of heavenly beings that would later arrive at angelic status: the cherubim and the seraphim.[22] The cherubim are well represented in the Old Testament, since they are mentioned ninety-one times.[23] They are often compared with the *karibu*, which are, in Mesopotamia, genies who act as guardians and intercessors, whose name means "those who bless." These Babylonian *karibu* are represented as hybrid creatures, winged quadrupeds (bulls) with human faces. They flank the entrances to palaces and sanctuaries or else support and decorate thrones. In the Bible, they assume this role of guardian and protector of the sanctuary, as we see in the case of the

18. See Ps 103:20 and 148:2, where the angels already celebrate the divine praises.

19. See Gn 18: the three visitors to Abraham at Mamre; Gn 19: the two angels who go down to Lot's house in Sodom arouse the perverse desires of the inhabitants of the city; Jgs 13:6, 10, 11 (announcement of Samson's birth): "A man of God came to me, and his countenance was like the countenance of the angel of God, very terrible"; Ez 40:3: "there was a man whose appearance was like bronze." It is therefore quite natural to compare David's beauty to that of an angel (1 Sm 29:9).

20. See 1 Sm 1:3; Ps 24:10.

21. See also 2 Kgs 6:15–17, where invisible horses and chariots of fire fight for Elisha against the Arameans. Jesus himself alludes to the angelic hosts: "Do you think that I cannot appeal to my Father, and he will at once send me more than twelve legions of angels?" (Mt 26:53).

22. See 1 Enoch 61:10 (*Apocryphal Old Testament*, 242); 71:7 (255).

23. On the cherubim: Édouard Dhorme and Louis-Hugues Vincent, "Les chérubins," *Revue biblique* 35 (1926): 328–56; Roland de Vaux, *Bible et Orient: Les chérubins et l'arche d'alliance, les sphinx gardiens et les trônes divins dans l'Orient Ancien* (Paris: Cerf, 1967), 231–50; Manfred Görg, "Keruben in Jerusalem," *BN* 4 (1977): 13–24; Edouard Lipinski, "Chérubin," in *DEB*, 264–66; Othmar Keel, "Mit Cherubim et Seraphim," *Bibel Heute* 112 (1992): 171–74; Raquel Gilboa, "Cherubim: An Inquiry into an Enigma," *BN* 82 (1996): 59–75.

cherub with "a flaming sword which falls to earth [*qui s'abat sur la terre*] (= lightning)" that God posted at the entrance to the earthly paradise to prevent sinful Adam from having access to the tree of life (Gn 3:24). Within the tabernacle, two cherubim—two massive golden statues—face each other while protecting the mercy seat (Ex 25:17ff.). Similarly, in the Temple of Solomon, the walls of which are covered with cherubim (1 Kgs 6:29), two cherubim, consisting of two large gold-plated wooden figures, protect the sacred ark with their outstretched wings (1 Kgs 6:23–28). The cherubim appear also as the ones who support the royal throne. Thus God is often invoked as the one who "is enthroned upon the cherubim."[24]

The seraphim, whose name means "burning ones," appear in two different contexts.[25] First of all the term designates hostile powers that inhabit the desert: venomous serpents[26] or rather winged dragons.[27] They are found again in the famous vision of Isaiah 6: "Above him stood the seraphim; each had six wings.... And one called to another and said: 'Holy, holy, holy is the LORD of hosts.'" The connection between these seraphim, who very much resemble the cherubim, and the winged serpents is difficult to determine.[28]

ANGELIC INFLATION AFTER THE EXILE

After the exile, the angels, if I may say so, really took off. Angelology, until then rudimentary, became expansive and exuberant. Certainly

24. See 1 Sm 4:4; Is 37:16; Ps 80:1; Ps 99:1. Furthermore, the cherubim are probably the living creatures that make up the "chariot" on which God appears to Ezekiel (compare Steinmann, *Prophète Ezéchiel*, 175–76n9, on the connections between the living creatures of Ez 1 and the cherubim). The cherubim are sometimes likened to the "throne" composed of the great clouds carried by the wind (Ps 18:9–10): "He bowed the heavens, and came down; thick darkness was under his feet. He rode on a cherub, and flew; he came swiftly upon the wings of the wind"; and Ps 68:4; Ps 104:3–4: "You made the clouds your chariot, who ride on the wings of the wind, who make the winds your messengers, fire and flame your ministers."

25. See Jean de Savignac, "Les Seraphim," *VT* 22 (1972): 320–25; Görg, "Die Funktion der Serafen bei Jesaja," *BN* 5 (1978): 28–39; Jacob, *Esaïe, 1–12*, Commentaires de l'Ancien Testament (Geneva: 1987), 99–100; Lipinski, "Séraphins," in *DEB*, 1192.

26. Nm 21:6; Dt 8:15.

27. Is 14:29, 30:6.

28. Jacob, *Esaïe, 1–12*, suggests that the view of the bronze serpent, preserved in the Temple until its destruction by Hezechiah (2 Kgs 18:4) may have inspired Isaiah.

in Jesus' day the Sadducees, who were quite old-fashioned, still regarded it as a dubious innovation,[29] but it was accepted by the Pharisees and aroused the esoteric infatuation of the Essenes.[30] The inflation in angelology bursts onto the scene in the canonical apocalyptic
writings (Daniel, Zechariah)[31] and thrives luxuriantly in the literature
of Hellenistic Judaism—for example, in the book of Enoch.[32] Three
factors contribute to this phenomenon.

The first is of a cultural nature: the Hebrew people undergo the
influence of Persian and then of Hellenistic cultures, which allow a
lot of room for the intermediary world of spirits.[33] The second is of
a theological nature: in Israel a deepening of the sense of God's transcendence has two consequences. First, since polytheism was no longer a real danger, the doctrine on the angels loses all ambiguity and
can develop freely at its own level. Second, believers experience the
need to multiply the intermediaries between the thrice-holy God
and man. This need is expressed both in the growing importance assigned to quasi-divine mediating figures, such as Wisdom, the Word,
the Spirit, and in the development of angelology.[34] The third factor is

29. See Acts 23:8: "For the Sadducees say that there is no resurrection, nor angel, nor
spirit; but the Pharisees acknowledge them all." Indeed, according to Jean Le Moyne (*Les
Sadducéens*, Études bibliques [Paris: Lecoffre, 1972], 131–35), what the Sadducees denied
was not so much the existence of angels, although their angelology remains embryonic,
as it was immortality and the existence of a spiritual and immortal double of man. According to Floyd Parker ("The Terms 'Angels' and 'Spirits' in Acts 23:8," *Biblica* 84 [2003]:
344–65), their denial concerned above all the action of the angels in the service of the
predestination of human beings.

30. Among the Essenes, the postulant must swear "equally [to] preserve the books
belonging to their sect, and the names of the angels"; Josephus, *The Jewish War* II.8.7,
trans. H. St. J. Thackeray, in *Josephus: Works in Nine Volumes*, Loeb Classical Library
(Cambridge, Mass.: Harvard University Press, 1961), 2:377.

31. See D. S. Russell, chap. 9, "Angels and Demons," in *Method and Message*; Mathias
Delcor, "L'apocalyptique juive," in *Encyclopédie de la mystique juive* (Paris: 1977), 2–278.
On the angelology of the book of Daniel, see Delcor, *Le livre de Daniel*, Sources bib-
liques (Paris: J. Gabalda, 1971), 45–47.

32. Harold B. Kuhn, "The Angelology of the Non-Canonical Jewish Apocalypses,"
JBL 67 (1948): 217–32.

33. About this influence, see D. S. Russell, *Method and Message*, 257–62.

34. See Klaus Koch, "Monotheismus und Angelologie," in *Ein Gott allein? JHWH-
Verehrung und biblischer Monotheismus im Kontext der israelitischen und altorientalischen
Religionsgeschichte*, edited by Walter Dietrich and Martin A. Klopfenstein, 565–81, 13.
Kolloquium der Schweizerischen Adamedie der Geistes- und Sozialwissenschafter (Fri-
bourg: Universitätsverlag; Göttingen: Vandenhoeck and Ruprecht, 1994), 565–81.

again of a theological nature: the eschatological fever characteristic of that era increased tenfold the interest in an angelic world, which is perceived as the anticipated fulfillment of the ideal pursued by Israel. The angelic world is the future of the holy people.

The angels appear more than ever as mediators between God and men. On the ladder that Jacob saw set up between earth and heaven, "the angels of God were ascending and descending" (Gn 28:12). They are sent by God on various missions. It may be a punitive expedition[35] or an exploratory mission.[36] But most often the angels guide and protect both individuals (as Raphael protects Tobias) and communities (Michael, according to Daniel 12:1, looks after Israel).[37] Again in the sense of descending mediation, the angels intervene in prophetic revelation.[38] Indeed, being admitted to God's council, they are well suited to transmit divine messages (revealing angel) or else to provide the prophets with the correct exegesis (interpreting angel). In Daniel 9:21–22 we read:

While I was speaking in prayer, the man Gabriel, whom I had seen in the vision at the first, came to me in swift flight[39] at the time of the evening sacrifice. He came and said to me, "O Daniel, I have now come out to give you wisdom and understanding."[40]

But the angels also play a role of ascending mediation. They cause the prayers of human beings to ascend to God. Thus Raphael says, "And so when you and your daughter-in-law Sarah prayed, I brought a reminder of your prayer before the Holy One" (Tb 12:12).[41] And since their own prayers reinforce those of men, they thus become intercessors.[42]

35. See Ex 12:23; 2 Kgs 19:35; Ez 9:1; Ps 78:49.
36. See Zec 1:10.
37. Chapter 13 will return to the biblical teaching about guardian angels.
38. See D. S. Russell, *Method and Message*, 242.
39. So angels do in fact sprout wings.
40. See also Ez 40:3, where an angel ("a man, whose appearance was like bronze") explains the prophet's vision to him; and Dn 8:16, 10:5ff.; Zec 1:8ff., 2:2.
41. Compare Zec 1:12: "Then the angel of the LORD said, 'O LORD of hosts, how long will you have no mercy on Jerusalem'"; see also Jb 33:23: "If there be for him an angel, a mediator [literally, 'interpreter'], one of the thousand, to declare to man what is right for him; and he is gracious to him, and says, 'Deliver him from going down into the Pit, I have found a ransom'"; see also Rv 5:8, 8:4.
42. See D. S. Russell, *Method and Message*, 242. See also 1 Enoch 15:2 (*Apocryphal*

As it increases in abundance—"a thousand thousands served him, and ten thousand times ten thousand stood before him" (Dn 7:10)—the angelic world at the same time emerges from anonymity.[43] Some angels receive precise names. They are, in the canonical scriptures, Michael, whose name means "Who is like God?" and who is "one of the chief princes";[44] Gabriel, the angel who interprets Daniel's visions, whose name means "Man of God" or else "God is my strength";[45] and Raphael, "God heals," the companion of Tobias.[46] As for the pseudepigrapha, they are replete with names, each one more fanciful than the rest.[47]

The internal organization of the angelic world is delineated, too, although it is difficult to propose a standard model. An elite—the archangels—sets itself apart. There are sometimes four, sometimes seven of them.[48] Thus Raphael describes himself as "one of the seven holy angels who ... enter into the presence of the glory of the Lord" (Tb 12:15). The pseudepigrapha distinguish among classes of angels according to their function and mention, for example, the angels of

Old Testament, 203): "And go, say to the Watchers of heaven, ... You ought to petition on behalf of men, not men on behalf of you." The Testament of Levi (3:5–6, Apocryphal Old Testament, 527) goes so far as to attribute to the angels of the Presence the role of interceding "and mak[ing] expiation to the Lord for all the sins committed unwittingly by the righteous; and they offer to the Lord a soothing odour, a spiritual and bloodless offering." In this sense, the angel resembles the priest. See Zec 3:7: "you [the high priest Joshua] shall rule my house and have charge of my courts, and I will give you the right of access among those who are standing here [i.e., the angels]"; see also Mal 2:7.

43. See Talmud of Jerusalem, cited by Caquot, "Anges et démons en Israël," 133: "The names of the angels came with those who returned from Babylon." See also Saul M. Olyan, A Thousand Thousands Served Him: Exegesis and the Naming of Angels in Ancient Judaism (Tübingen: J. C. B. Mohr, 1993).

44. Dn 10:13, 10:21, 12:1.

45. Dn 8:16, 9:21.

46. See Dion, "Raphaël exorciste," Biblica 57 (1976): 399–413.

47. Among the noncanonical names of angels, the best attested in the serious writings is that of Uriel ("Fire or Light of God"), which appears among other places in 4 Esd 4:1 or 1 Enoch 10:1 (Apocryphal Old Testament, 194n2); see also George A. Barton, "The Origin of the Names of Angels and Demons in the Extra-Canonical Apocalyptic Literature to 100 A.D.," JBL 31 (1912): 256–67.

48. 1 Enoch 9:1 (Apocryphal Old Testament, 192) gives the list of four archangels: Michael, Sariel (or Uriel), Raphael, and Gabriel, and 1 Enoch 20 (208–9 with footnotes 7 and 10) lists seven: Uriel, Raphael, Raguel, Michael, Sariel, Gabriel, and Remiel. We find a set of "seven angels who stand before God" in Rv 8:2. Their connection with the seven spirits of God in Rv 4:5 is yet to be explained.

the Presence,[49] who are quite close to God, the angels of the Holiness, who are in charge of the *Sanctus* and so on.[50]

SATAN AND THE DEMONS

The men of antiquity spontaneously denounced the action of maleficent spirits behind the evils that assailed them.[51] And so, among the peoples surrounding Israel, the liturgy abounds in exorcisms and magic formulas aimed at neutralizing these bad in-

49. See Jubilees 2:2, in *La Bible: Écrits intertestamentaires*, edited by André Dupont-Sommer and Marc Philonenko (Paris: Editions Gallimard [Pléiade], 1987], 641–42).

50. On these two categories of angels, see the note in the Pléiade edition of *Jubilés* 1:27, 640.

51. On the demonology of the Old Testament, the reader may consult first an exhaustive work with an extensive bibliography: Walter Kornfeld, "Satan (et démons): Satan dans l'Ancien Testament; Démons dans la Bible hébraïque; Protection contre les demons; Bibliographie," in *DBS*, 12:1–21. Then, see also M. J. Grünthaner, "The Demonology of the Old Testament," *Catholic Biblical Quarterly* 6 (1944): 6–27; Rosa Riwkah Schärf, *Die Gestalt des Satans im Alten Testament* (Zürich: Tschudi, 1948); Edward Langton, *La démonologie: Étude de la doctrine juive et chrétienne, Son origine et son développement* (Paris: Payot, 1951); van Imschoot, *Théologie de l'Ancien Testament*, vol. 1, *Dieu*, 130–41; Stanislas Lyonnet, "Le démon dans l'Ancien Testament," *DS*, 3:142–45; Édouard Dhorme, "La démonologie biblique," in *Hommage à Wilhelm Vischer* (Montpellier: La Faculté Libre de Théologie Protestante de Montpellier, 1960), 41–54; W. Foerster, "*Daimôn, daimonion*: The OT and Later Jewish View of Demons," in *TDNT* (1964), 2:10–16; Foerster and von Rad, "*Diaballô, diabolos*: (B) The OT View of Satan," in *TDNT*, 2:73–75; F. J. Schierse, "Satan: Étude biblique," in *Encyclopédie de la foi*, Cogitatio fidei 18 (Paris: 1967), 4:186–87; Marie-Émile Boismard, "Satan selon l'Ancien et le Nouveau Testaments," *Lumière et vie* 15 (1966): 61–76; Zähringen, "Les Démons: L'existence de Satan et des démons," in *Mysterium salutis: Dogmatique de l'histoire du salut* (Paris: Cerf, 1970): 8:205–8; Meinrad Limbeck, "Les sources de la conception biblique du diable et des démons," *Concilium* 103 (1975): 31–44; Jeffrey B. Russell, chap. 5, "Hebrew Personification of Evil," in *The Devil: Perceptions of Evil from Antiquity to Primitive Christianity* (Ithaca and London: Cornell University Press, 1977); Bernard Teyssèdre, *Naissance du diable: De Babylone aux grottes de la mer Morte* (Paris: A. Michel, 1985); Jean-Baptiste Brunon and Pierre Grelot, "Démons," in *VTB*, 257–59; Peggy L. Day, *An Adversary in Heaven: Satan in the Hebrew Bible* (Atlanta: Scholars Press, 1988); Sydney H. T. Page, *Powers of Evil: A Biblical Study of Satan and Demons* (Grand Rapids: Baker Books, 1995); Patrick Dondelinger, "Satan dans la Bible," in *Encyclopédie des religions*, edited by Frédéric Lenoir and Ysé Tardan-Masquelier (Paris: Bayard, 1997), 2:1463–67; Armin Lange, Hermann Lichtenberger, and K. F. Diethard Römheld, eds., *Die Dämonen: Demons, die Dämonologie der israelitisch-jüdischen und frühchristlichen Literatur im Kontext ihrer Umwelt* (Tübingen: Mohr Siebeck, 2003).

fluences.[52] There is nothing of the sort (theoretically) in Israel. Far from attributing evil to one or more principles that are supposedly independent from God, Israel tends instead to situate in God himself the source of evil as well as of good: "I make well-being and create woe, I am the LORD, who do all these things" (Is 45:7)![53] Monotheism forbids any dualism.

That said, the Old Testament acknowledges evil powers at the edges of existence. Hebrew has no collective term to designate what we today call demons—in other words, wicked superhuman beings. The term demon (*daimon*) therefore comes from Greek. In popular Greek religion, the word "demon" designated a sort of ambivalent "genie," "a being endowed with supernatural powers, capricious and incalculable, present in unusual places at particular times and at work in terrifying events in nature and human life, but placated, controlled or at least held off by magical means."[54] The LXX, the Greek translation of the Old Testament, applies this term *daimon* in a negative sense to various maleficent realities to which the Old Testament bears witness, from the *Qeteb* [destruction] that wastes at noonday (Ps 91:6) to the gods of the nations (Ps 96:5).

These "demons" have only a very vague place in the official religion of Israel, which pushes them back to the peripheries. Their existence is not denied, but one avoids having anything to do with them. Divination and magic are severely prohibited as forms of infidelity to the one Master of our destinies: "Do not turn to mediums or wizards; do not seek them out, to be defiled by them: I am the LORD your God" (Lv 19:31).[55] These prohibitions obviously attest, by way of contrast, the position occupied by demonic realities in popular religion.[56]

---

52. See Georges Contenau, *La magie chez les assyriens et les babyloniens* (Paris: Payot, 1947); Reginald Campbell Thompson, *Semitic Magic: Its Origins and Development* (New York: Ktav, 1971); Dirk C. Mulder, "Les démons dans les religions non-bibliques," *Concilium* 103 (1975): 21–30.

53. Kornfeld, "Satan (et démons)," col. 4: "The experience of a threatening and disturbing presence was either integrated into the image of God (Gn 32:25–33 [Jacob's struggle]; Ex 4:24–26; Amos 3:6), or else transferred to angels and spirits that were subject to the Lord."

54. Foerster, "*Daimôn, daimonion: Daimôn* in the Greek and Hellenistic World," in *TDNT*, 2:8.

55. See also Lv 19:26; Dt 18:11; 1 Sm 28:7.

56. The Bible preserves a residual trace of popular demonological beliefs even in

The demonic world is at the origin of a disparate conglomerate of maleficent realities. We find in it, first of all, the spirits of the dead and of the netherworld, Hades, the "ghosts" that necromancers consult,[57] but Jewish demonology develops in a direction quite unlike that of the demonization of the dead. Then there are the demon-maladies that prowl through the air. Then all the hybrid, shapeless beings— half-animals, half-demons[58]—that crawl in the last remaining vestiges of the initial chaos. There are those who live in the desert—because "When an unclean spirit has gone out of a man, he passes through waterless places seeking rest" (Mt 12:43)—a hostile, menacing place, the lair of all sorts of malevolent beasts:[59] hyenas, jackals, wild dogs, etc. This is the habitat of Azazel, the demon of the desert to whom was sent by lot each year a goat loaded down with the sins of Israel.[60] There the traveler runs the risk of passing not only the furry satyrs, but also Ms. Lilith, a seductive female demon who haunts ruins.[61] There are those too who paddle around in that other remnant of the primordial chaos, that lair of the forces of evil hostile to God, which is the sea: Leviathan, the seven-headed sea monster, "the fleeing serpent";[62] Rahab, the primordial ocean, and the *tanninim* (sea monsters). These maleficent beings, however, are creatures of God—"Leviathan which you formed to sport in it" (Ps 104:26)—and not anti-gods. How can it be that these creatures that issued from the hands of a good God are bad today? The question remains up in the air.

Finally, in a more recent era, the demonical world is enriched by all the gods of the pagans. Indeed, the LXX disdainfully applies the name *daimonia* not only to the beings that we have just described but also to the gods of the pagans. For example, in Ps 96:5, where the He-

its most official texts. For example, the commandment to attach small bells to the high priest's garments reflects a very common belief in the power of bells to drive off demons (Ex 28:33–35); again the reference to the Destroyer (Ex 12:23) refers back to a pre-biblical Passover ritual in which the destroyer is a demon that threatens flocks and family and that blood drives away.

57. See the episode of the sorceress of En-dor in 1 Sm 28; compare Is 8:19.

58. It is difficult to draw the line between maleficent animals (serpents, lions, dogs) and demons.

59. See Is 13:21–22.

60. See Lv. 16:10.

61. Is 34:14. See also Kornfeld, "Satan (et démons)," 13.

62. Is 27:1; compare Ps 74:14, 104:26.

brew reads "All the gods of the Gentiles are naught," the LXX translates, "All the gods of the peoples are demons."[63]

What relations do these demonic beings maintain with the angelic world? The answer is complicated, because the distinction between angel and demon was not made immediately in the theology of Israel. Indeed, the affirmation of God's absolute sovereignty, the source of good and evil, led the Israelites to see in every angel indiscriminately simply a being who carries out the divine decrees, whether they are favorable or unfavorable to mankind. God sends angels who accomplish good, but he also sends angels of woe, destroying angels, who carry out missions of vengeance, admittedly in the service of Israel's welfare.[64] He also sends evil spirits who trouble men (lying spirit, spirit of confusion, spirit of sickness).[65] These spirits are evil with regard to their effects, but there is no indication that they are wicked or hostile to God's plan.

Only gradually—because of their intense reflection on evil connected with the exile—did the Jews take an interest in the moral dispositions of these spirits sent by God. Then the angelic world was cut in two. On the one side were the good, beneficent spirits who kept the title of angels, whereas on the other side the term "demon" took on a negative connotation. This emergence of the demonic world within the angelic world is most clearly evident in the case of Satan.

In the Old Testament, the word *satan* designates in a general way an adversary.[66] More particularly, the *satan* is the adversary who con-

63. Along this same line, the demonic beings are increasingly identified with false gods. See Dt 32:17: "They sacrificed to demons which were no gods, to gods they had never known"; Lv 17:7 where the satyrs actually stand for false gods; 2 Chr 11:15.

64. See Ex 12:23; 2 Sm 24:16; 2 Kgs 19:35; Ps 78:49 (angels of woe responsible for the plagues of Egypt). As Augustin George explains (*Études sur l'oeuvre de Luc*, Sources bibliques [Paris: Gabalda, 1978], 164), in Palestinian Judaism, "divine chastisements were preferably assigned to angels, as though to executors who relieve God of disagreeable lowly tasks, while waiting for the development of demonology."

65. See 1 Sm 16:14: "Now the Spirit of the LORD departed from Saul [and rested upon David] and an evil spirit from the LORD tormented him." See also "the spirit of discord" that God sends between Abimelech and the leaders of Shechem (Jgs 9:23); "the lying spirit" that God places in the mouths of the prophets of Ahab so that he might go to war (1 Kgs 22:19–23); "the spirit of confusion" with which the Lord drives Egypt and its leaders mad (Is 19:14); "a spirit of deep sleep" poured out by God over sinful Jerusalem (Is 29:10).

66. See, for example, 2 Sm 19:23: "What have I to do with you, you sons of Zerui-

ducts himself as the accuser at a trial: a sort of district attorney.[67] A superterrestrial figure takes on this role of "Satan" in the divine court, as two major scripture passages show.

The first is the prologue to Job: "Now there was a day when the sons of God came to present themselves before the LORD, and Satan also came among them. The LORD said to Satan, 'From where have you come?'" (Jb 1:6–7). This Satan is an ambiguous figure, a sort of spy: Orwell's Big Brother.[68] He is clearly subordinate to God, to whom he must ask permission, and does not seem to oppose him. Quite the contrary, he seems to attend to his interests.[69] He has nothing to do therefore with the evil god of dualism. That said, he is merciless with regard to human beings and, therefore, skeptical about the success of God's plan for mankind.

The same rather unsympathetic personage is found in Zechariah 3:1–2: "[The LORD] showed me Joshua the high priest standing before the angel of the LORD, and Satan standing at his right hand to accuse him. And the angel of the LORD [Michael?] said to Satan, 'The LORD rebuke you, O Satan! The LORD who has chosen Jerusalem rebuke you!'"

With 1 Chronicles 21:1, where "Satan" is used without an article—in other words, as a proper name referring to a subject having a will—the figure of Satan clearly becomes a personal, wicked being. Whereas 2 Samuel 24:1, which is the source of this passage, reads, "Again the anger of the LORD was kindled against Israel, and he incited David against them" by causing him to take a census of the holy people, which encroaches on the prerogatives of God, the sole master of fecundity, life, and death, the Chronicler (around 330/250 B.C.). is reluctant to attribute David's bad decision directly to God, and so he

---

ah, that you should this day be as an adversary (*Satan*) to me?" Inasmuch as he opposes God's plan, Peter is treated by Jesus as Satan (Mt 16:23).

67. See Ps 109 [108]:6, an imprecatory psalm: "Appoint a wicked man against him; let an accuser (*satan*) bring him to trial."

68. Naphtali H. Tur-Sinai, *The Book of Job: A New Commentary* (Jerusalem: Kiryath Sepher, 1957), has suggested an analogy between the Satan of the heavenly court and the secret services of the court of Persia.

69. Some authors see in the figure of Satan a sort of crystallization of the pure justice of God disconnected from his mercy: the obscure face of God or God as the sinner sees him.

writes, "Satan stood up against Israel, and incited David to number Israel." Satan thus appears as someone who urges men to sin.

Satan is therefore a morally wicked being, hostile to both man and God. He is so not by nature, but because of a vice, as Wisdom 2:24 declares: "Through the devil's envy death entered the world."[70] This passage identifies the serpent-tempter of Genesis 3 with Satan,[71] emphasizing his malice.

The figure of Satan appears therefore as an original creation of inspired biblical theology. He constitutes a sort of archetype in terms of which the "residual" beliefs in demonic realities are interpreted. Thus the malignant character of Satan gradually is extended to the other demons, which leads to a clearer distinction between the angelic world and the demonic world. In the book of Tobit, for example, the demons, such as Asmodeus,[72] "the evil demon" (3:8), who causes husbands to perish and (jealously?) opposes conjugal union, want to harm human beings (6:7), whereas the angels—in this case Raphael—protect them and fight the demons (8:3). Without ceasing to be dependent on God—something that monotheism requires—the demonic world is increasingly perceived as a hostile perversion of the holy, angelic world.

70. The term *diabolos*—the divider, the one who opposes the *"sym-bolos"* that unites—translates "Satan" in the LXX.

71. This identification appears also in *The Life of Adam and Eve* 16 (*Apocryphal Old Testament*, 150–51), where an angel tempts Adam by planting a vine; and *The Greek Apocalypse of Baruch* 4:8 (*Apocryphal Old Testament*, 906).

72. Concerning Asmodeus, see Kornfeld, "Satan (et démons)," 12.

2

———— ⫶ ————

Angels and Demons in the
New Testament

*Now war arose in heaven, Michael and his angels
fighting against the dragon; and the dragon and his
angels fought, but they were defeated and there was no
longer any place for them in heaven.*

—Revelation 12:7–8

This passage from the book of Revelation sets the scene with two antagonistic, well-structured worlds, and it proclaims the good news of the definitive victory of God and his angels, for the benefit of mankind, over the demonic world: "The accuser of our brethren has been thrown down, who accuses them day and night before our God" (Rv 12:10). This victory is the fruit of the Passover of Jesus Christ, the sacrificed Lamb. In a very significant manner, a painting by Josse Lieferinxe, dating from the early sixteenth century and displayed in the Louvre, depicts this pitiful downfall of the demons in the background of the Crucifixion of Christ: it is the effect thereof.[1] For this fall of the demons should not be confused with the original fall of the apostate angels that marks the emergence of the demonic world. Rather, it is about the end of Satan's tyrannical dominion over men, about the defeat that God, in

1. See Ponnau and Lessing, *Dieu en ses anges*, 164–67.

the course of human history, inflicts on the demons through the action of Jesus Christ. Thus—and this is precisely its distinguishing feature—in the New Testament the action of the angels and of the demons in its entirety is referred to one essential event: the coming of the Kingdom of God in Jesus Christ and in his church.

"I SAW SATAN FALL LIKE LIGHTNING FROM HEAVEN" (LK 10:18)

The world of the New Testament is, to a great extent, a dualistic world—certainly not at the ontological level, but on the moral level. Our world is the battlefield for an eschatological conflict between light and darkness. Every human being is situated between two force fields, two worlds: he "belongs" to one or the other depending on his moral choice and his adherence to their "spirit."[2] Neutrality is not an option: the human person is either under the protection of God, who safeguards his authentic freedom, or else under the tyrannical dominion of the devil, which is a form of slavery.[3]

Satan and his demons are omnipresent in the New Testament.[4] The

2. This dualism takes up the Old Testament theme of the "two ways" (see Dt 11:26–28). It has many points in common with "Qumram's Fundamental Dualism"; see the instruction on the two spirits in the *Rule of the Community* III.13–IV.26, in *The Dead Sea Scrolls: Rule of the Community*, multilanguage ed., edited by James H. Charlesworth et al., 58–60 (Philadelphia: American Interfaith Institute and World Alliance, 1996). See also 1 Jn 4:6.

3. See John P. Meier, *A Marginal Jew: Rethinking the Historical Jesus*, vol. 2, *Mentor, Message and Miracles* (New York: Doubleday, 1994), 414–15: "In the eschatological and apocalyptic view of Jews and Christians around the turn of the era [A.D.], human existence was seen as a battlefield dominated by one or the other supernatural force, God or Satan.... A human being might have a part in choosing which 'field of force' would dominate his or her life, i.e., which force he or she would choose to side with. But no human being was free to choose simply to be free of these supernatural forces. One was dominated by either one or the other, and to pass *from* one was necessarily to pass *into* the control of the other. At least over the long term, one could not maintain a neutral stance vis-à-vis God and Satan."

4. Satan and the demons in the New Testament: Lyonnet, "Le démon dans l'Écriture," in "Démon," *DS*, 3:142–52; Schierse, "Satan: Étude biblique," 4:187–91; W. Foerster and von Rad, "*Diaballô, diabolos*," in *TDNT*, 2:16–19 and 79–81; Foerster and Knut Schäferdiek, "*Satanas*: Satan in the New Testament," in *TDNT*, 7:156–63; Seemann and Zähringen, "Monde des anges et des démons," 8:208–13; Jeffrey B. Russell, chap. 6, "The Devil in the New Testament," in *Devil*; Celsas Spicq, "L'existence du Diable appartient

world that Jesus Christ comes to visit is saturated, so to speak, with demonic presence. Even the air is unhealthy, pestilential: "the spiritual hosts of wickedness in the heavenly places" (Eph 6:12), and Satan is "the prince of the power of the air" (Eph 2:2).[5] Above all, the demons reign and lord it over human beings. They "possess" them. Indeed, by consenting to moral evil at the Tempter's instigation, man delivers himself bound hand and foot over to his tyrannical dominion. The moment he becomes involved in the descending spiral of sin, he falls into "the snare of the devil" (2 Tm 2:26), under Satan's power, for "he who commits sin is of the devil" (1 Jn 3:8). Slaves of sin, human beings then become "sons of the evil one" (Mt 13:38), "son[s] of the devil," as the magician Elymas is called (Acts 13:10), his tools and at the same time his victims: "You are of your father the devil, and your will is to do your father's desires" (Jn 8:44).[6] This servitude means that man is alienated: he acts somehow under the influence of another who manipulates him and thwarts the profound impulse of his nature. He signs on to a demolition project, the purpose of which is death: the demons kill human beings and make them kill one another. Satan solidifies his tyranny by exploiting the consequences of sin: sickness and death,[7] or even the perverse social structures that result from sin: the "world"—of which Satan is the "ruler"[8]—and its institutions of death.[9]

à la révélation du Nouveau Testament," in "Satan 'mystère d'iniquité,'" *Communio* 4, no. 3 (1979): 19–27; Trevor O. Ling, *The Significance of Satan: New Testament Demonology and Its Contemporary Relevance* (Scottdale: Herald Press, 1980); Brunon and Grelot, "Démons," 259–61; Lyonnet, "Satan," in *VTB*, 1196–99; Walter Kirchschläger, "Satan (et démons): Satan et démons dans le Nouveau Testament," in *DBS*, 12:24–47; Kevin P. Sullivan, *Wrestling with Angels: A Study of the Relationship between Angels and Humans in Ancient Jewish Literature and the New Testament*, Arbeiten zur Geschichte des Antiken Judentums und des Urchristentums 55 (Leiden: E. J. Brill, 2004).

5. In the religious cosmology of antiquity, demons inhabit an intermediate place between the earth of men and the ether in which the stars move.

6. See also 1 Jn 3:10 (the children of God and the children of the devil); 1 Jn 3:12 (Cain, being of the Evil One, murdered his brother).

7. Sickness, as a consequence of sin, is sometimes considered as a form of "possession"; see Lk 13:16: "this woman, a daughter of Abraham whom Satan bound for eighteen years." It is often compared to the action of evil spirits; see Lk 7:21: "In that hour he cured many of diseases and plagues and evil spirits, and on many that were blind he bestowed sight." The devil is also called "[the one] who has the power of death" (Hb 2:14).

8. See Jn 12:31, 14:30, 16:11; see also 2 Cor 4:4: "the god of this world."

9. For example, the pagan religions (see 1 Cor 10:20) or perverse political structures.

This dominion of the devil is therefore as universal as sin: "The whole world is in the power of the Evil One" (1 Jn 5:19). Displaying all the kingdoms of the world to Jesus, the Tempter unhesitatingly declares, "To you I will give all this authority and their glory; for it has been delivered to me, and I give it to whom I will" (Lk 4:6).[10]

Mankind's servitude to the devil depicts the "misery of man without God." The "possessed" of the Gospels are a terrifying image of the human condition when man has deliberately broken with God. They live in the unclean spirit—in other words, in an inability to enter into relation with the Holy One. Consequently they are raving, mute, blind, deaf, shut off from any genuine relationship with their neighbor. They live in cemeteries (Mk 5:3), unleash their rage against themselves and against others. They are tormented by the evil spirit who drives them to suicidal acts (Mk 9:22). In short, a possessed person is like a dead man walking.

During the intertestamental period, the rather hazy, fluid world of demonic phenomena solidified and became structured. From now on its undisputed chief is Satan, who unifies it under his authority.[11] This "star fallen from heaven to earth" received "the key of the shaft of the bottomless pit" from which the infernal "locusts" spread to torment mankind.[12] In fact, he has under his orders the demons or unclean spirits that are "legion" (Mk 5:9). Christ speaks about "the eternal fire prepared for the devil and his angels" (Mt 25:41). The demons are indeed "the messengers" or "the angels of Satan";[13] when Jesus Christ is accused of driving out demons by Beelzebul, the prince of

---

For the book of Revelation, the idolatrous cult of the emperor is a satanic enterprise, and the places for its ceremonies are called "Satan's throne" (2:13). The persecuting empire is described as a beast that has some of the same features as the dragon (Rv 13:1), of which it is in fact the instrument.

10. St. Irenaeus remarks that, even here, Satan is a liar, because all creation is by right and in fact in God's power; see Irenaeus of Lyons, *Against Heresies* V.22.2 [ANF 1:551a].

11. The idea of a *chief* of the evil spirits is well attested as early as the book of Jubilees (10:8–11, *Apocryphal Old Testament*, 41–42), where he is called Mastema. For Hans Urs von Balthasar, "Comment en arrive-t-on à Satan?," *Communio* 4 (1979): 4–9, the late appearance of the figure of Satan and the unification of the demonic world around it have theological significance: the absolute "no" could manifest itself only in the presence of the absolute "yes" of Jesus Christ.

12. See Rv 9:1–11.

13. See 2 Cor 12:7; Rv 12:7, 12:9.

demons (Mt 12:24), he is referring to the demonic world as a king-dom that stands due to a certain coherence.[14]

The chief of the maleficent spirits is indiscriminately called Sa-tan (thirty-four times in the New Testament) or the devil—in other words, the "divider" (thirty-three times, as opposed to only once in the Old Testament). He also usurps the names of various malevolent deities, such as Beelzebul, a Canaanite god, whose name means "Baal the prince" or "Prince-god,"[15] or else Belial, a name that occurs very frequently in the Qumram writings.[16]

This same sinister figure is also named in terms of his maleficent activity. He is branded as "the Evil One" (*ho poneros*; twelve occur-rences in the New Testament) and the final petition of the Our Father is a plea to be delivered from him (Mt 5:37, 6:13). He is also the En-emy, the Adversary, the one who sows weeds in the field (Mt 13:39), yet his power is trampled underfoot by the apostles (Lk 10:19). As the Enemy, he is the Antichrist par excellence (1 Jn 4:3), even though that term is applied more often to his human instruments.[17] Depending on the forms that his malice takes, he is described as "a liar and the father of lies" and "a murderer from the beginning," since his lying led man into sin and death (Jn 8:44).[18] Inasmuch as he draws men into evil, he is the tempter (*ho peirazôn*)[19] or the seducer.[20] Finally, Satan recapitulates the figures of evil that are depicted in the Old Tes-tament: he is the enormous dragon, the ancient serpent.[21]

14. Mt 12:25–26: "Every kingdom divided against itself is laid waste, and no city or house divided against itself will stand; and if Satan casts out Satan, he is divided against himself; how then will his kingdom stand?"

15. See Mt 12:24 and parallel passages. The form "Beelzebub" found in the Vulgate is a contemptuous play on words that means "Lord of the flies."

16. See 2 Cor 6:14–15: "What fellowship has light with darkness? What accord has Christ with Belial?" See also Kirchschläger, "Satan: Satan (et démons) à Qumram," in *DBS*, 12:21–24.

17. See 2 Jn 1:7; 2 Thes 2:3–4. Concerning the Antichrist, see Béda Rigaux, *L'An-téchrist et l'Opposition au Royaume messianique dans l'Ancien et le Nouveau Testament* (Gembloux: J. Duculot; and Paris: J. Gabalda, 1932).

18. See Jean Giblet, "La puissance satanique selon l'Évangile de Jean," in Ries and Limet, *Anges et démons*, 291–300.

19. See Mt 4:3; 1 Thes 3:5.

20. See in the DV version Rv 12:9: "Satan, who seduceth the whole world"; Rv 20:9–10; 2 Jn 1:7.

21. The dragon: Rv 12:3; 13:2; the serpent: Rv 12:9, 20:2.

This picture of the universal empire of evil would be rather over-whelming if it were not intrinsically related in the New Testament to the victory of Jesus Christ. Indeed, just as the New Testament reveals the depth and universality of sin only at the precise moment when it is pardoned in Christ, so too it insists so much on demonic domination only to highlight the victorious arrival of the kingdom.

The extent to which these Powers—radiating innumerably from a single central point: "the prince of this world" (Jn 14:30)—dominate and determine the whole of existence will be realised only by the Christian who has learnt from what it is that Christ's victory over the world has delivered him (Jn 16:33).[22]

Our Lord Jesus himself described his mission as a *Reconquista*, an enterprise to wrest man from his servitude to Satan and to restore him to God. He came, after all, to "proclaim release to the captives ..., to set at liberty those who are oppressed" (Lk 4:18). He, Jesus, is the "one stronger" who overcomes the strong, well-armed man—in other words, Satan—and despoils him of his goods.[23] Jesus' mission appears as a colossal and salutary exorcism,[24] a vast clean-up operation, a merciless battle against the "unclean spirits (*pneumata akhatarta*)"[25] that disfigure the image of God. "He went about doing good and healing all that were oppressed by the devil" (Acts 10:38).

22. Von Balthasar, *The Glory of the Lord: A Theological Aesthetics*, vol. 1, *Seeing the Form* (San Francisco: Ignatius Press, 1982), 663.

23. Lk 11:21-22: "When a strong man, fully armed, guards his own palace, his goods are in peace; but when one stronger than he assails him and overcomes him, he takes away his armor in which he trusted, and divides his spoil."

24. See Kirchschläger, "Satan (et démons)," 12:42: "In particular in the Gospel of Mark there is a close connection between exorcism and preaching of the *basileia*. By overpowering the demons Jesus establishes in an exemplary way the fact that God's salvation has been realized for mankind." See also Karl Kertelge, "Jésus, ses miracles et Satan," *Concilium* 103 (1975): 45–53; Kertelge, "Diavolo, demoni, esorcismi in prospettiva biblica," in *Diavolo—demoni—possessione: Sulla realtà del male*, edited by Walter Kasper and Karl Lehmann, 7–44, 2nd ed. (Brescia: Queriniana, 1985) [original German: *Teufel—Dämonen—Besessenheit: Zur Wirklichkeit des Bösen* (Mainz: Matthias-Grünewald-Verlag, 1978)]; John P. Meier, chap. 20, "Jesus' Exorcisms," in *Marginal Jew*, 2:646–77, 404–13.

25. Whatever the popular connotations of the idea of impurity may be, the expression "unclean spirit" in Mark has a specific religious sense: the spirit is impure because he opposes God and his holiness; see also Clinton Wahlen, *Jesus and the Impurity of Spirits in the Synoptic Gospels*, Wissenschaftliche Untersuchungen zum Neuen Testament 185 (Tübingen: Mohr Siebeck, 2004).

To consider only the Gospel of Mark, the first act of Christ's public ministry, after his baptism and the call of the disciples, was to expel the unclean spirit from a possessed man (1:23–28), and the crowds marveled because Jesus "commands even the unclean spirits, and they obey him." Then Jesus was "preaching in their synagogues and casting out demons" (1:39); the unclean spirits, when they see him, throw themselves down at his feet and cry out, "You are the Son of God" (3:11). Jesus cannot go one step without meeting a demon! And he confers on his disciples this power to cast out demons (3:14–15).

"I saw Satan fall like lightning from heaven" (Lk 10:18), Jesus replies to his disciples when, back from their mission, they are so glad that "even the demons are subject to us in your name" (Lk 10:17). The actual coming of the Kingdom of God in Jesus Christ is indeed inseparable from the "fall" of Satan—in other words, from the end of his dominion over mankind. We can even go so far as to say that, with the New Testament, this liberation of mankind from the control of Satan and their transfer to the kingdom of God is a privileged expression of the work of salvation accomplished by Jesus Christ—the first "theory of redemption," if you will.[26] "The reason the Son of God appeared was to destroy the works of the devil" (1 Jn 3:8). Since Satan is the Accuser, his fall signifies the end of the effectiveness of the accusations that he presents to God. From now on we have an intercessor, Jesus,[27] and God shows mercy: he is no longer mindful of the sins that placed us under Satan's power.[28]

26. See Col 1:13: "He has delivered us from the dominion of darkness and transferred us to the kingdom of his beloved Son"; Acts 26:18: Jesus tells Paul that he is sending him to the pagan nations "to open their eyes, that they may turn from darkness to light and from the power of Satan to God." This battle between darkness and light is characteristic of the "dualist" theology of intertestamental Judaism and especially of the Qumram community, but the originality of the New Testament is that this apocalyptic battle is historicized: for or against Jesus of Nazareth.

27. In a way, Jesus fulfills the duty of intercession that belonged to the Archangel Michael in the intertestamental writings; see Foerster and Schäferdiek, "Satanas," 7:157.

28. In the writings of the fathers of the church, redemption theology as victory over Satan (see Gustav Aulen, *Christus victor* [Paris: Aubier, 1949]), as liberation from his control over our lives, sometimes developed along the ambiguous line of a "theory of the demon's rights"; see Jean Rivière, *Le Dogme de la Rédemption: Essai d'étude historique*, 2nd ed. (Paris: V. Lecoffre, 1905), part 5, "La question des droits du démon" (373–486); Rivière, *Le Dogme de la Rédemption: Études critiques et documents* (Louvain:

The victory was not won without combat. Satan stubbornly insists on preventing the coming of the kingdom in Jesus. In archetypal fashion, in the manner of a musical "overture," Satan tries in the desert, from the very beginning of Jesus' public life, to divert him from his mission.[29] Even Peter will do so later, and for that reason he is described as Satan.[30] In contrast to Adam, Jesus resists Satan with his unfailing obedience to the will of the Father: "The whole life and suffering of Jesus are a Yes to God and consequently a No to the Tempter."[31] The Gospel of John underscores the invisible but decisive activity of Satan in the Passion. He is the one who pulls the strings. He puts into the heart of Judas the plan to betray Jesus (13:2);[32] he even enters into Judas (13:27).[33] The Passion is from a certain perspective Satan's hour, his *kairos*—"And when the devil had ended every temptation, he departed from him until an opportune time (*kairos*)" (Lk 4:13). He displays then his homicidal will. But it is much more the hour of Christ: "Now is the judgment of this world, now shall the ruler of this world be cast out" (Jn 12:31).[34] Satan's apparent victory marks his definitive defeat.

The devil, already conquered, then begins a battle to the death

---

Bureaux de la Revue, 1931), part 2, "Tradition patristique" (59–240). This theory assumes various forms. In its juridical form, it maintains that Jesus Christ poured out his blood as a ransom to the devil to redeem mankind, which had subjected itself in strict justice to him by its sins. In its political form, it states that the devil abused his authority by turning his destructive power against an innocent man. In this version, *abusus tollit usum*, the devil lost his right and receives not a ransom but punishment for his unjust act. These often very florid accounts of the work of redemption as a battle between Christ and Satan have sometimes emphasized the supposed "rights" of Satan over humanity. But they have the great merit of highlighting the unity between salvation history and the "justice" of the divine action. Man, conquered by the devil in Adam, had to be the conqueror of the devil in Jesus Christ, the second Adam.

29. On the temptations of Jesus, see the presentation and bibliography by Kirchschläger, "Satan," 28–31; see also Bernard Rey, *Les tentations et le choix de Jésus*, Lire la Bible 72 (Paris: Cerf, 1986), and the profound meditation by Joseph Ratzinger, "Looking at Christ: The Figure of Christ as Reflected in the Gospel Account of His Temptation," in *On the Way to Jesus Christ* (San Francisco: Ignatius Press, 2005), 79–101.

30. See Mt 16:23: "But he turned and said to Peter, 'Get behind me, Satan! You are a hindrance to me; for you are not on the side of God, but of men.'"

31. Foerster and Schäferdiek, "Satanas," 7:159.

32. Compare Acts 5:3 (concerning Ananias): "Why has Satan filled your heart?"

33. See also Jn 6:70: "One of you is a devil."

34. See also Jn 16:11: "The ruler of this world is judged."

with the church, which here below is the seed of the Kingdom of God. He does everything that he can to oppose its growth.

"Now the salvation and the power and the kingdom of our God and the authority of his Christ have come, for the accuser of our brethren has been thrown down, who accuses them day and night before our God.... Rejoice then, O heaven and you that dwell therein! But woe to you, O earth and sea, for the devil has come down to you in great wrath, because he knows that his time is short." And when the dragon saw that he had been thrown down to the earth, he pursued the Woman. (Rv 12:10–13)

For this purpose, Satan exploits the powers of this world—for example, the Roman Empire, which is "the Beast" of Revelation 13. He makes use of the resistance of the "self-styled Jews," who are therefore described as the "Synagogue of Satan" (Rv 2:9). He stirs up persecutions, heresies, and dissensions in the community.[35] He obstructs Paul's missionary activity.[36]

In particular, he claims Christ's disciples in order to sift them.[37] He strives, through temptation, to separate every believer from Christ, to snatch the Word from his heart lest he believe and be saved (Lk 8:12). And so the sacred authors warn Christians to be on guard against diabolical activity: "Your adversary the devil prowls around like a roaring lion, seeking some one to devour" (1 Pt 5:8). But they immediately give the antidote: "Resist him, firm in your faith" (1 Pt 5:9).[38] Then "the God of peace will soon crush Satan under your feet" (Rom 16:20). By the faith that unites them to Christ Jesus and to his power, Christians are preserved from sin and therefore from the devil's control; they have "overcome the Evil One."[39] The gates of hell shall not prevail against the

35. See Rv 2:10: "The devil is about to throw some of you into prison."

36. 1 Thes 2:18: "We wanted to come to you—I, Paul, again and again—but Satan hindered us."

37. Lk 22:31: "Simon, Simon, behold, Satan demanded to have you, that he might sift you like wheat, but I have prayed for you that your faith may not fail."

38. See also Eph 6:11–13: "Put on the whole armor of God, that you may be able to stand against the wiles of the devil. For we are not contending against flesh and blood, but against the principalities, against the powers, against the world rulers of this present darkness, against the spiritual hosts of wickedness in the heavenly places. Therefore take the whole armor of God, that you may be able to withstand in the evil day, and having done all, to stand."

39. See 1 Jn 2:13, 14. Union with Christ gives a share in the power of the Spirit who overcomes Satan; compare 1 Jn 4:4: "He who is in you [i.e., the Spirit] is greater than he who is in the world [Satan]."

church of Christ (Mt 16:18). Conversely, anyone who strays from Christ and the community inevitably falls into Satan's power. So it is that the obstinate sinner is "excommunicated," deprived of the helps of the church, and thereby "delivered to Satan" (see 1 Cor 5:5) until he repents. But this maleficent activity will come to an end[40] with the definitive banishment of Satan into "the eternal fire" (Mt 25:41). "And the devil who had deceived them was thrown into the lake of fire and brimstone where the beast and the false prophet were, and they will be tormented day and night for ever and ever" (Rv 20:10). Death and Hades will follow soon after (Rv 20:14). What will become of the holy angels is quite different.

THE ANGELS WHO SERVE THE ONE MEDIATOR

"He must increase, but I must decrease" (Jn 3:30). The Baptist's statement applies also to the angels in the New Testament.[41]

Indeed, insofar as the mediation of salvation between God and mankind is henceforth perfectly assured by a man, Jesus Christ (1 Tm 2:5), acting by his spirit, the angelic intermediaries vanish and lose the importance that they were able to have in late Judaism: "Christian Christology develops at the expense of Jewish angelology"[42]—hence

40. The book of Revelation give a glimpse of a period of remission for the church (the millennium), followed by a new outbreak of persecutions. See Rv 20:7–9: "And when the thousand years are ended, Satan will be released from his prison and will come out to deceive the nations which are at the four corners of the earth, that is, Gog and Magog, to gather them for battle; their number is like the sand of the sea. And they marched up over the broad earth and surrounded the camp of the saints and the beloved city; but fire came down from heaven and consumed them." St. Paul too seems to announce a temporary victory of Satan, with the apostasy and the manifestation of the man of lawlessness (see 2 Thes 2), who will immediately precede the coming of the Lord. Indeed, is it not profoundly fitting that, at the end of time, the church, in imitation of her Lord, should experience a passion and a death that precede the final victory?

41. Angels in the New Testament: Gerhard Kittel, "*Aggelos: Aggelos in the NT*," in *TDNT*, 1:83–87; Michl, "Ange," 1:87–88; Heinrich Schlier, chap. 11, "Les anges dans le NT," in *Essais sur le Nouveau Testament*, Lectio divina 46 (Paris: Cerf, 1968); Seemann and Zähringen, "Monde des anges et des démons," 8:166–80; Michl, "L'angélologsie biblique: II. Le Nouveau Testament," in *Les anges*, edited by George Tavard, 29–49, Histoire des dogmes II.2b (Paris: Cerf, 1971); Galopin, "Ange," *DEB*, 60–61; Galopin and Grelot, "Ange," *VTB*, 60–62.

42. Spicq, *L'Épître aux Hébreux*, Études bibliques (Paris: J. Gabalda, 1953), 2:55. See

the rarity and above all the sobriety of the references to the angelic world in the New Testament, compared with the intertestamental
writings.

The practical replacement of angelology with Christology explains why the early Christians had recourse to angelological concepts familiar to late Judaism in thinking about the newness of the
mystery of Christ and even about the mystery of the Trinity.[43] Since
they wanted to show that Jesus, the Messiah, was par excellence the
One sent by the Father, a heavenly being who had appeared among
men, as did the Son of man in Dn 7:13, it was tempting to present
him as an angel.[44] Thus Hermas refers to the Word as "glorious angel"
or "most venerable angel"[45] and Justin writes, "He who loves God
with all his heart and all his strength ... will worship no other as God,
but he will, since God desires it, revere the angel who is loved by the
same Lord and God."[46] Sometimes, in the Judeo-Christian writings,
the word of God is even likened to the Archangel Michael.[47] This is
the so-called *Christos angelos* Christology.[48] Even when understood

---

also von Balthasar, *Glory of the Lord*, 1:674: "In the New Testament, however, the angels
can only recede to become the accompanying servants of the Son of man on earth." Von
Balthasar remarks that they intervene only when Christ does not speak or act (infancy,
Resurrection): "The angels are always absent whenever Jesus speaks and acts in the fulness of his own power" (1:675).

43. See Jean Daniélou, chap. 4, "The Trinity and Angelology," in *The Theology of
Jewish Christianity*, trans. John A. Baher (Philadelphia: Westminster Press, 1964), 117–
46; Crispin H. T. Fletcher-Louis, *Luke-Acts: Angels, Christology and Soteriology*, Wissenschaftliche Untersuchungen zum Neuen Testament (Tübingen: Mohr Siebeck, 1997).
Besides the absorption of angelic mediation by Christology, there is also a more sub-
dued pneumatological absorption. Among some Christians, the Holy Spirit is thought
of in terms of ancient angelological concepts (see Daniélou, *Theology of Jewish Christianity*, 141–45) and at the same time takes on functions that formerly belonged to the
angels. The clearest example in the New Testament is found in Acts 8:26: "An angel of
the Lord said to Philip, 'Rise and go toward the south.'" Then a few verses further on we
read, "The Spirit said to Philip, 'Go up and join this chariot.'" The angel and the Spirit
seem to be interchangeable here. George (*Études sur l'oeuvre de Luc*, 178) points out that
in Luke's writings, after Easter, the angels are no longer agents of revelation: from now
on God acts and makes himself known through the Spirit.

44. This theme finds support in the title "Angel of the great design (*megalês boulês
angelos*)" that Isaiah (9:5) gave to the Messiah in the LXX version. Concerning the use
that Christian tradition made of this passage, see Spicq, *L'Épître aux Hébreux*, 2:51n1.

45. See Daniélou, *Theology of Jewish Christianity*, 119.

46. Justin Martyr, *Dialogue with Trypho* II.93.2, trans. Falls, 144.

47. See Daniélou, *Theology of Jewish Christianity*, 121–27.

48. See Joseph Barbel, *Christos Angelos: Die Anschauung von Christus als Bote und*

in the orthodox sense in which the term "angel" designates not the nature but the function of Jesus Christ, its limitations became evident rather quickly.

Indeed, the New Testament insists instead on the difference between the preparatory mission of the angels and the definitive mission of the Son, a difference that corresponds to the one between the Old and the New Covenant.[49] Thus the Letter to the Hebrews, which tries to establish the superiority of the Gospel over the Old Law, bases its reasoning on the absolute primacy of Christ, Mediator of the New Covenant, over the angels, mediators of the Old Covenant. Indeed, the idea that the Law had been given to Moses by the angels is already attested by the LXX or the intertestamental writings,[50] and the New Testament authors consider it as something that goes without saying.[51] The deacon Stephen refers to it positively so as to emphasize the seriousness of disobedience to such a sacred Law: "You ... received the law as delivered by angels and did not keep it" (Acts 7:53).[52] In contrast, St. Paul sees instead in angelic mediation a sign of the im-

---

Engel in der gelehrten und volkstümlichen Literatur des christlichen Altertums, Theophania 3 (Bonn: P. Hanstein, 1941); Wilhelm Michaelis, *Zur Engelchristologie im Urchristentum* (Basel: Heinrich Majer, 1942); Georg Kretschmar, *Studien zur frühchristlichen Trinitättheologie* (Tübingen: Mohr Siebeck, 1956); and the synthesis by Alois Grillmeier, *Christ in Christian Tradition: From the Apostolic Age to Chalcedon (451),* trans. J. S. Bowden (New York: Sheed and Ward, 1965), 52–61.

49. Along this line, in which the angels are connected with the economy of the Old Covenant, which prepared for the coming of the Son, St. Thomas Aquinas, restating a common patristic theme, explains that the angelic manifestations of the Old Testament were like prefigurations of the mystery of the Incarnation; see *ST* I, q. 51, a. 2, ad 1: "[The fact] that angels assumed bodies under the Old Law was a figurative indication that the Word of God would take a human body; because all the apparitions in the Old Testament were ordained to that one whereby the Son of God appeared in the flesh" [Hoc etiam quod angeli corpora assumpserunt in Veteri Testamento, fuit quoddam figurale indicium quod Verbum Dei assumpturum esset corpus humanum: omnes enim apparitiones Veteris Testamenti ad illam apparitionem ordinatae fuerunt, qua Filius Dei apparuit in carne].

50. Dt 33:2 (DV) and Ps 68:17 mention the presence of angels on Sinai; see also Jubilees 1:27–29 (*Apocryphal Old Testament,* 13–14). See also Josephus, *Jewish Antiquities* XV.136 (*Josephus in Nine Volumes,* vol. 8, *Jewish Antiquities, Books XV–XVII,* with an English translation by Ralph Marcus [Cambridge, Mass., and London: Harvard University Press, 1969], 66–67), but the *aggeloi* here could be prophets.

51. See Daniélou, chap. 1, "The Angels and the Law," in *The Angels and Their Mission according to the Fathers of the Church,* trans. David Heimann (Westminster, Md.: Newman Press, 1957), 3–13.

52. See also Acts 7:35, 7:38.

perfection of the Law, "ordained by angels through an intermediary [Moses]" (Gal 3:19).[53] The Letter to the Hebrews reconciles the two perspectives. Angelic mediation confers on the Law—"the message declared by angels" (Hb 2:2)—great value and a formidable aspect, but the Law cannot prevail over the Gospel, which was promulgated directly by Christ, the Son. "The Gospel is to the Law what Christ is to the angels. If the Son is far superior to the heavenly messengers, then the New Covenant prevails indisputably over the Old."[54] The whole economy of salvation is henceforth centered on Christ: "For it was not to angels that God subjected the world to come, of which we are speaking" (Hb 2:5).

However—and the fact must be carefully taken into account— the angels have not been discharged, as though they had become useless. Instead they have been placed at the service of the one mediation of Christ. "Truly, truly, I say to you, you will see heaven opened, and the angels of God ascending and descending upon the Son of man" (Jn 1:51). The angels become *his* angels,[55] his servants. This is why, in the Gospels, whatever difference there may be in their theologies,[56] the angels always appear on mission and in connection with Jesus Christ, which is also a way of testifying to the truth of Jesus' full communion with the celestial world and with God. The angels are particularly active in the infancy narratives: they announce the conception of Jesus (Lk 1:26ff.),[57] as they did earlier that of his Precursor (Lk 1:11ff.), and, in keeping with their liturgical function that the Old Testament already acknowledged, they sing the glory of God at the birth of the Messiah (Lk 2:13–14). Although they are more discreet during Jesus' ministry—they minister to him nevertheless after his victory over the Tempter in the desert (Mt 4:11)—the angels return at the Paschal mystery: one of them strengthens Jesus during his ag-

53. See Ronald Y. K. Fung, *The Epistle to the Galatians*, New International Commentary on the New Testament (Grand Rapids: Eerdmans, 1988), 160ff.; Terrance Callan, "Pauline Midrash: The Exegetical Background of Gal 3:19b," *JBL* 99 (1980): 549–67.

54. Spicq, *L'Épître aux Hébreux*, 2:55.

55. See Mt 13:41, 16:27, 24:31.

56. For example, in his *Études sur l'oeuvre de Luc*, 149–83, George clearly showed the close connections between Luke's angelology and the specific major themes of his theology.

57. In Luke, the role of the messenger angel is compared to that of the apostle and witness. One always comes to faith in Jesus Christ through the mediation of a third party.

ony in Gethsemane (Lk 22:43), then they announce his Resurrection as he had foretold (Lk 24:4: *Resurrexit sicut dixit*) and they are present at his Ascension (Acts 1:10).

Quite naturally, the angels then go on to serve the church militant, which is the body of Christ. "Are they not all ministering spirits sent forth to serve, for the sake of those who are to obtain salvation?" (Hb 1:14). Thus the angels assist the apostles in the work of proclaiming the Gospel: an angel frees from prison the apostles (Acts 5:19) and then Peter (Acts 12:7–11), an angel announces to Paul that he will survive his shipwreck (Acts 27:23). The angels also bring people to the church, as we see in the case of Cornelius (Acts 10:3–7, 22). Do the angels not rejoice over the return of the lost sheep (Lk 15:10)?

But the eschatological day of the Lord is when the activity of the angels will reach its completion. They will accompany Christ "when the Son of man comes in his glory, and all the angels with him."[58] They will gather the elect from the four winds (Mt 24:31) and will be present at the Judgment: "Every one who acknowledges me before men, the Son of man also will acknowledge before the angels of God" (Lk 12:8). Then, in the eschatological kingdom, human beings will share their condition (see Mt. 22:30).[59]

AMBIVALENCE OF THE "POWERS" IN ST. PAUL'S WRITINGS

St. Paul proclaims that all, Jews and pagans both, have free access to the Father through faith in the one Mediator. He therefore emphasizes very forcefully the subordination of any other mediation to the essential mediation that Christ guarantees. Hence his insistence on affirming the supremacy of Jesus Christ over all the heavenly realities that he calls powers (*dynameis*), principalities (*archai*), thrones, virtues, dominions.[60] The precise status of these realities is difficult to

58. Mt 25:31; see also Mt 16:27; 2 Thes 1:7.

59. The tendency to see personal death and "particular judgment" as an anticipation of the end times explains the presence and the role of the angels in the parable of poor Lazarus (Lk 16:19–31).

60. See G. H. C. MacGregor, "Principalities and Powers: The Cosmic Background of St. Paul's Thought," *New Testament Studies* 1 (1954–55): 17–28; George B. Caird, *Principalities and Powers: A Study in Pauline Theology* (Oxford: Clarendon Press, 1956); Schlier,

pin down. Are they astral powers or spiritual beings, properly speaking? Is he talking about good angels or about maleficent beings (demons)? In answer to the first question we can say that St. Paul perceives as a whole the complex reality formed by a spiritual being together with the astral reality that it "animates": the powers are spirits that govern the world through the mediation of the influence of the cosmic powers. The answer to the second question is more delicate.

When they appear in 1 Corinthians 15:24, the powers have a plainly negative connotation, since it says at the end of the passage that Christ will destroy every principality (*arche*), dominion (*exousia*), and power (*dynamis*).[61] In Rom 8:38–39, they are, along with the angels, some of the possible obstacles to union with Christ:

For I am sure that neither death, nor life, nor angels, nor principalities (*archai*), nor things present, nor things to come, nor powers (*dynameis*), nor

---

chap. 10, "Principautés et puissances dans le NT," in *Essais sur le Nouveau Testament*; Jung Y. Lee, "Interpreting the Demonic Powers in Pauline Thought," *NT* 12 (1970): 54–69; Wesley Carr, *Angels and Principalities: The Background, Meaning and Development of the Pauline Phrase "hai archai kai hai exousiai"* (Cambridge: Cambridge University Press, 1981); Pierre Benoît, "Angélologie et démonologie pauliniennes: Réflexion sur la nomenclature des Puissances célestes et sur l'origine du mal angélique chez saint Paul," in *Fede e cultura alla luce della Bibbia* (Turin: Editrice Elle Di Ci, 1981), 217–33; Peter T. O'Brien, "Principalities and Powers: Opponents of the Church," in *Biblical Interpretation and the Church*, edited by D. A. Carson, 110–50 (Nashville: T. Nelson Publishers, 1984); Clinton E. Arnold, *Powers of Darkness: Principalities and Powers in Paul's Letters* (Downer's Grove, Ill.: InterVarsity Press, 1992); Arnold, "Returning to the Domain of the Powers: Stoicheia as Evil Spirits in Galatians 4:3, 9," *NT* 38 (1996): 55–76 [Arnold identifies the *stoicheia* with the demons]; Chris Forbes, "Paul's Principalities and Powers: Demythologizing Apocalyptic?" *Journal for the Study of the New Testament* 82 (2001): 61–88; Forbes, "Pauline Demonology and/or Cosmology? Principalities, Powers and the Elements of the World in Their Hellenistic Context," *Journal for the Study of the New Testament* 23 (2002): 51–73. Note also in 2 Pt 2:10–11: The impious "are not afraid to revile the glorious ones, whereas angels, though greater in might and power, do not pronounce a reviling judgment upon them before the Lord."

61. 1 Cor 15:24–25 (DV): "Afterwards the end: when he shall have delivered up the kingdom to God and the Father: when he shall have brought to nought all principality and power and virtue. For he must reign, until he hath put all his enemies under his feet." Concerning this destruction of the powers and how it may be reconciled with the theology of the Captivity Epistles, see Jean-Noël Aletti, ed., *Saint Paul: Épître aux Colossiens*, Études bibliques 20 (Paris: J. Gabalda, 1993), 170n33. For St. Thomas (*In 1 ad Co*, c. 15, lect. 3 [nos. 938–39]), St. Paul merely means to indicate that at the end of time the angelic hierarchies will no longer perform any activity with respect to mankind.

height, nor depth, nor anything else in all creation, will be able to separate us from the love of God in Christ Jesus our Lord.[62]

The metaphysical and moral nature of these "principalities" and "powers" remains hazy: St. Paul just wants to insist on immediate access to God through Christ. In Gal 4:3 and 4:9, the expression "elements of the world (*stoicheia tou kosmou*)" could be referring to a similar theme.[63]

When we were children, we were slaves to the *elemental spirits of the universe*.... Formerly, when you did not know God, you were in bondage to beings that by nature are no gods; but now that you have come to know God, or rather to be known by God, how can you turn back again to the weak and beggarly *elemental spirits*, whose slaves you want to be once more?

The meaning of the expression is much debated. For some, the elements of the world are "natural principles of conduct, far inferior to life in Christ."[64] But the angelic-cosmological meaning is more likely. The "elements of the world" signify:

the elementary powers of the universe, which are then identified more particularly with the angelic powers through which the Law was promulgated or with the spirits directly connected to the heavenly bodies, the governors of the planetary spheres that were thought to exert some influence and control over the life and destiny of human persons.[65]

Thus the heavenly spirits keep human beings in servitude, both through Jewish Law and through the pagan religions, which compel them to observe religious and dietary practices connected with the calendar—in other words, with the cosmic cycles.

Whatever the case may be with these "elements of the world," we again find teaching about the powers in the captivity letters. The Letter to the Colossians accentuates their creation in Christ:

For in him all things were created, in heaven and on earth, visible and invisible, whether thrones (*thronoi*) or dominions (*kyriotetes*) or principalities

---

62. Should a theological meaning be assigned to the contrast angels/principalities? "Height" and "depth" are terms from astrology.

63. See G. Delling, "*Stoicheion*," in *TDNT*, 8:683–87; Fung, *Epistle to the Galatians*, 189–92.

64. Marie-Joseph Lagrange, *Épître aux Galates*, 4th ed., Études bibliques (Paris: J. Gabalda, 1942), 99–101.

65. Fung, *Epistle to the Galatians*, 190.

(*archai*) or authorities (*exousiai*—that is, powers)—all things were created through him and for him.[66]

Further on, it declares that Christ is not only the creator but also the head of these powers:

See to it that no one makes a prey of you by philosophy and empty deceit, according to human tradition, according to the elemental spirits of the universe, and not according to Christ. For in him the whole fulness of deity dwells bodily… [he] is the head (*kephalê*) of all rule (*arche*) and authority (*exousia*).[67]

But does "head" have the same meaning here (Col 2:9) as when Paul says that Christ is "head of the Church" (Eph 1:22–23)? Certainly not. Here it is only a question of showing that Christ rules over the "powers," so that they cannot prevent Christians from receiving everything from Christ. Moreover, several verses further on, St. Paul declares that Christ "disarmed the principalities and powers and made a public example of them, triumphing over them in him."[68] Note that since the "powers" are created in Christ, they are no longer destroyed as in 1 Corinthians but rather subjected.

The same ambivalence is found in the Letter to the Ephesians. In Ephesians 1:20–21, the author exalts the power of Christ by placing him above these powerful and apparently "neutral" realities:

[God] made [Christ] sit at his right hand in the heavenly places, far above all rule (*archê*) and authority (*exousia*) and power (*dynamis*, sometimes "virtue") and dominion (*kuriotês*), and above every name that is named, not only in this age but also that in which is to come.

But Ephesians 6:12 identifies these "powers" with realities that are hostile to God and "demonic":

66. Col 1:16. "The reader will note that the names of the celestial beings mentioned here all point to an exercise of authority, and this is why the passage mentions them in this way—and not merely as angels. These are beings that could be taken for rivals of the Son"; Aletti, ed., *Saint Paul*, 101.

67. Col 2:8–10.

68. Col 2:15, RSVC. [Translator's note: The French version of the scripture passage portrays Christ as a victorious imperial general: "and presented them to the world as a spectacle, drawing them along in his triumphal procession."] Compare the different interpretations set forth by Aletti, ed., *Saint Paul*, 184–85.

For we are not contending against flesh and blood, but against the principalities (*archai*), against the powers (*exousias*), against the world rulers (*kosmokratoras*) of this present darkness, against the spiritual hosts of wickedness in the heavenly places.

An overall interpretation therefore proves to be hazardous. No doubt we can admit that, in the (rare) passages in which the "powers" are viewed neutrally, St. Paul considers them inasmuch as they are beings created by God in Christ, whereas, in the passages where they are viewed negatively, he considers them as being opposed to God. This presupposes the idea of a rebellion against their Creator that is not explicit in these passages. The later tradition, by identifying some of these terms with the angelic orders and asserting that some angels from each order had become demons by sinning freely, while occasionally keeping the specific name of their order (so that "the powers," for example, sometimes designates good angels and sometimes demons) arrived at a coherent explanatory system, even though the scriptural foundations for it remain fragile.

3

The Developments of Christian Angelology until St. Thomas Aquinas

When the thirteenth-century scholastic theologians, and in particular St. Thomas Aquinas, were elaborating a scientific synthesis that was meant to express optimally the intelligibility of the teachings of the Christian tradition concerning angels and demons, they drew on several sources. No doubt the recently discovered Greco-Arabic philosophies provided them with invaluable conceptual tools, but the decisive criterion in their reflection was the word of God as they received it from the church's living tradition as conveyed by the authoritative corpus of the fathers of the church (*Sancti*) and the speculations of the early medieval theologians. And so the angelological synthesis of St. Thomas Aquinas is largely determined by patristic angelology, much more than by pagan Greek metaphysics, and most especially by the teaching of St. Augustine, [Pseudo-]Dionysius the Areopagite, and even St. Gregory the Great. That is why none of the chapters of this book will be able to dispense with an at least summary presentation of the patristic teaching on the topic in question.[1]

1. The information available to us today about the angelological teachings of the fathers is obviously more extensive than what St. Thomas had at his disposal. Since our

It is nonetheless helpful to point out right away several general characteristics of the angelology of the fathers that are capable of shedding light on the more specific doctrines that we will have to examine subsequently. The contributions of two authors who decisively oriented Christian angelology—St. Augustine and [Pseudo-]Dionysius the Areopagite—deserve a special treatment. Finally, before taking an initial look at the texts of the Thomistic corpus that will serve as the fulcrum of our theological reflection, we will mention several trends specific to medieval angelology.

SOME CHARACTERISTICS OF PATRISTIC ANGELOLOGY

The fathers of the church are pastors concerned with guiding the Christian people along the ways of sanctity.[2] Their teaching therefore does not aim in the first place to establish a theological synthesis of Christian doctrine according to a specifically scientific method.[3] They comment on scripture, the word of life, defend disputed points of the faith against pagans or heretics, chart the paths that lead toward the perfection of the spiritual life. In fact, their doctrine on angels and demons is generally integrated into their practical teaching. This is clear in the case of demonology, which has ascetical literature as its

---

perspective is doctrinal and not merely historical, we will not hesitate to refer, when appropriate, to texts that St. Thomas did not know.

2. Patristic angelology: In the seventeenth century, the Jesuit Denis Petau compiled an initial synthesis of the patristic teaching on the angels in the treatise *De angelis* of his *Dogmata theologica* (Paris: Vivés, 1865), 3:603–712, and (1866), 4:1–121. This presentation is divided into three books. The first deals "in general with the nature and the properties of angels and especially of the good angels"; the second "with the orders and functions of the good angels"; and the third "with the devil and his angels." In the twentieth century, see Georges Bareille, "Angélologie d'après les Pères," in *DTC*, 1:1192–22; Daniélou, *Angels and Their Mission*, trans. David Heimann; Michl, "Engel III (christlich)," in *RAC*, 5:109–200; Michl, "Ange," in *Encyclopédie de la foi*, 1:88–93; Tavard, in *Les anges*, chaps. 2–5; Basil Studer, "Ange," in *Dictionnaire encyclopédique du christianisme ancien* (Paris: Cerf, 1990), 1:124–28; Angelo Amato, "L'Angelologia nella tradizione della Chiesa," in *Angeli e demoni* (Bologna: Edizioni Dehoniane, 1992), 105–50.

3. See Jacques Maritain, chap. 7, "Augustinian Wisdom," in *Distinguish to Unite: The Degrees of Knowledge*, trans. Gerald B. Phelan et al., part 2 (Notre Dame, Ind.: University of Notre Dame Press, 1995), 291–309.

privileged context.[4] The spiritual life appears therein as a life-or-death combat waged by the Christian, supported by the spirit of Christ, through asceticism, fasting, and prayer, against the vices and the spirits or demons who preside over them. This struggle begins as early as the catechumenate, and it takes a decisive step at baptism with the renunciation of Satan and the *pompa diaboli*—in other words, with everything in a given culture that is opposed to the Christian spirit (that is, pagan theater and the circus games in late antiquity).[5] It ends among the holy monks, who left for the desert to confront the demon on his own terrain, with a share in Christ's own victory.

But the spiritual life also finds in the angelic world its concrete ideal, which it has to promote in the ecclesial community and at the same time in the personal life of every Christian.[6] Does the Our Father not ask that God's will be done "on earth as it is in heaven" (Mt 6:10)—in other words, that it be accomplished in the world of men as it is accomplished already in the world of angels?

Along these lines, the fathers insist on the connection between the angels and the liturgy of the church.[7] According to an idea that is certainly already present in the Bible and especially in the book of Revelation, the church's liturgy is not only an anticipation of an eschatological worship that is yet to come; rather, it is an actual participation in the uninterrupted worship, the unceasing praise, and in particular the *Sanctus*, that the angels even now cause to ascend to God.[8] "With the Angels and all the Saints we proclaim your glory, as with one voice we sing," the priest proclaims in the preface of the Mass. As for the Eastern churches, they love to sing, at the moment of the

4. See chapter 14 of this volume.

5. See Hugo Rahner, "*Pompa diaboli*: Ein Beitrag zur Bedeutungsgeschichte des Wortes *pompê—pompa* in der urchristlichen Taufliturgie," *ZkTh* 55 (1931): 239–73.

6. See Daniélou, chap. 8, "The Angels and the Spiritual Life," in *Angels and Their Mission*, 83–94.

7. See the classic study by Erik Peterson, *The Angels and the Liturgy*, trans. Ronald Walls (New York: Herder and Herder, 1964); Immaculata (Soeur), "Les anges dans la liturgie," *Carmel* 99 (March 2001): 19–30.

8. The *Regula Magistri*, an ancestor of the *Rule of St. Benedict*, is so attentive to the presence of the angels in the liturgy that it warns, "The one praying, if he wants to spit or to expel filth from his nose, will not do so forwards, but backwards, behind him, because of the angels who stand in front, as the prophet shows when he says, 'In the presence of the angels, I will sing to you'"; chap. 48, in SC 106:218–21.

great entrance, that the Christian liturgical assembly mystically represents the cherubim who surround the King of kings.[9] And if man thus takes part in the angelic liturgy, the angels, for their part, dwell in the churches and intervene actively in the liturgy of men.[10] More generally, however, the angel is presented as the model of the perfect life, which is *bios angelikos*, the angelic life.[11] Imitation of the various aspects of this angelic life, which is their future (see Lk 20:36), becomes for Christians the concrete path to perfection.[12] It is most especially suited to the monks, who embody the very mystery of the church inasmuch as it is associated with the angelic praise, so that the monastic "order" (*ordo monasticus*) is incorporated into the angelic orders,[13] but all Christians are invited to this imitation.[14]

That said, in exegetical writings, controversial works, and certain more systematic works of the church fathers, such as the treatise *On First Principles* by Origen,[15] the reference to the angels can take a more theoretical form. This angelology is the product of an internal maturation of the understanding of the faith within the church, but it owes much to the stimulus of the wisdom traditions of the cultures in which

---

9. See Adrian Fortescue, "Chéroubicon," in *Dictionnaire d'archéologie chrétienne et de liturgie* (Paris: 1913), 3:1281–86.

10. See Origen, *Homilies on Luke*, Homily 23.8, trans. Joseph T. Lienhard (FOTC 94: 101). Compare the Roman Canon: "Jube haec perferri per manus sancti angeli tui in sublime altare tuum, in conspectu divinae majestatis tuae" (Command that these gifts be borne by the hands of your holy Angel to your altar on high in the sight of your divine majesty); see also Bernard Botte, "L'ange du sacrifice et l'épiclèse de la Messe romaine," *RTAM* 1 (1929): 285–308.

11. See Karl S. Frank, *Angelikos Bios: Begriffsanalytische und begriffsgeschichtliche Untersuchung zum "Engelgleichen Leben" im frühen Mönchtum* (Münster: Aschendorff, 1964); Louis Bouyer, chap. 2, "La vie angélique," in *Le sens de la vie monastique* (Turnhout and Paris: Éditions Brepols, 1950), 43–68.

12. Thus St. Gregory the Great proposes to his listeners that they imitate in their lives the different perfections that define the nine angelic orders; see Gregory the Great, *Forty Gospel Homilies*, Homily 34.11, 289–90.

13. On the medieval continuation of this theme of the angelic life of monks, see Marie-Madeleine Davy, "Le moine et l'ange en Occident au XIIᵉ siècle," in *L'ange et l'homme*, Cahiers de l'Hermétisme (Paris: A. Michel, 1978), 107–27.

14. See Laurence Brottier, *L'appel des "demi-chrétiens" à la "vie angélique": Jean Chrysostome prédicateur; Entre idéal monastique et réalité mondaine* (Paris: Cerf, 2005).

15. On Origen's angelology, see Daniélou, *Origen*, trans. Walter Mitchell (New York: Sheed and Ward, 1955), 220–45, and the notes on the angelological texts by Origen in the series Sources chrétiennes.

Christianity is developing. The necessary inculturation of the faith no doubt leads Christian thought to take on doctrinal elements that are contingent and historically dated, but above all it enriches it. Indeed, insofar as the faith causes the seeds of universal truth contained in these particular cultures to germinate, it in turn makes use of them so as to attain a greater awareness of its own potentialities. No doubt, even though we must not underestimate the influence of more specifically Jewish speculations on their angelological reflection, the fathers were to a great extent conditioned by their immersion in the cultures and the philosophies of late Greco-Roman antiquity. Yet, despite inevitable and sometimes regrettable contaminations, there was overall a homogeneous, critical assimilation, in light of the Gospel, of the best of Greco-Roman thought, of its brightest and most universal teachings.

In the era of the patristic apologists (second century), Christians had to confront the accusations of atheism and irreligion. In this context, it is understandable that they insisted on their belief in angels and on the veneration that they showed to them. Thus St. Justin writes:

We are called atheists. And we confess that we are atheists, so far as gods of this sort are concerned, but not with respect to the most true God.... But both Him, and the Son (who came forth from Him and taught us these things, *and the host of the other good angels* who follow and are made like to Him), and the prophetic Spirit, we worship and adore, knowing them in reason and truth.[16]

But the fight against the Gnostics, who dangerously blurred the boundary between the divine and the created, led the fathers to place the emphasis on a fundamental biblical truth: the angels are mere creatures. They are not demiurges, powers situated midway between God and the world that engender one another. St. Irenaeus could not be clearer on this point. The angels on the one hand are created—"All things, whether Angels, or Archangels, or Thrones, or Dominions, were both established and created by Him who is God over all, through His

---

16. Justin Martyr, *First Apology* 6.1 (ANF 1:164b), André Wartelle, ed., trans., in *Justin Martyr: Apologies* (Paris: Études Augustiniennes, 1987), 244–45. See also Athenagoras, *A Plea for the Christians* 10 (ANF 2:133b–34a), which has the merit of not interposing the angels between the Son and the Spirit: "Nor is our teaching in what relates to the divine nature confined to these points; but we recognise also a multitude of angels and ministers, whom God the Maker and Framer of the world distributed and appointed to their several posts by His Logos, to occupy themselves about the elements, and the heavens, and the world, and the things in it, and the goodly ordering of them all."

Word"[17]—and on the other hand are incapable of creating: "The rule of truth which we hold, is, that ... the Father made all things by [His Word], whether visible or invisible ... ; and these eternal things He did not make by angels, or by any powers separated from His Ennoea [Design]. For God needs none of all these things, but is He who, by His Word and Spirit, makes, and disposes, and governs all things, and commands all things into existence."[18] The same insistence on the creatureliness of the angels would return to confront the accusation of disguised polytheism that the pagan reaction of late antiquity later hurled against Christianity and its belief in angels.[19]

In the related realm of demonology, the fathers are faced with a twofold task: to propose a consistent interpretation of the rather heterogeneous tenets of Judeo-Christianity and to integrate apologetically and critically a luxuriant Greco-Roman demonology.[20] Among the topics they developed, besides those that pertain to the spiritual combat, the question as to the origin of the demons has pride of place. Against any and all dualism, the fathers forcefully assert that the devil and the demons are creatures of God and not principles independent of him. Their wickedness, far from being natural and innate (which would make their Creator responsible for evil), results from a free personal decision, a sin, an apostasy.[21]

17. Irenaeus of Lyons, *Against Heresies* III.8.3 (ANF 1:421b). John Damascene nicely summarizes the teaching of the fathers in *The Orthodox Faith* II.3 (FOTC 37:205): "[God Himself] is the maker and creator of the angels. He brought them from nothing into being and made them after His own image into a bodiless nature."

18. Irenaeus of Lyons, *Against Heresies* I.22.1 (ANF 1:347a).

19. See, for example, Theodoret of Cyr, *Thérapeutique des maladies helléniques* (SC 57:196); see the partial English translation, *A Cure of Greek Maladies*, in *Theodoret of Cyr*, by István Pásztori-Kupán (London and New York: Routledge, 2006), 102–3.

20. The demonology of the fathers: see E. Mangenot, "Démon d'après les Pères," in *DTC*, 4:339–84 [a systematic survey of the patristic writings]; Bouyer, *La Vie de saint Antoine: Essai sur la spiritualité du monachisme primitif* (St. Wandrille: Éditions de Fontenelle, 1950), appendix A, "Cosmologie et démonologie dans le christianisme antique" (181–219); Daniélou, "Démon: Dans la littérature ecclésiastique jusqu'à Origène," in *DS*, 3:152–89; Michl, "Satan: Histoire de la théologie," in *Encyclopédie de la foi*, 4:191–200; Studer, "Démon," in *Dictionnaire encyclopédique du christianisme ancien* (Paris: Cerf, *1990*) (original Italian 1983), 1:644–50; Jean-Marc Vercruysse, "Les Pères de l'Église et Lucifer," *RSR* 75 (2001): 147–74. For a nearly exhaustive overview, see Anastasios Kallis, "Geister (Dämonen): Griechische Väter," in *RAC*, 9:700–15; and Pieter G. van der Nat, "Geister (Dämonen): Apologeten und lateinische Väter," in *RAC*, 9:715–61.

21. See chapter 10 of this volume.

TWO MASTERS OF ANGELOLOGY

The neo-Platonic philosophy that was widespread in late antiquity assigns a decisive place to the intermediate beings between God and man. Plato had already attempted to rationalize spontaneous beliefs by defining the demonical as an intermediate world: demons, which he considers as morally good beings, endowed with a lively intellect, make the connection between the world of men and the world of the gods.[22] Although this demonology is still embryonic in Plato's writings, it would be amplified and become one of the main components of the neo-Platonic religious philosophies of late antiquity.[23] The demons, which sometimes became angels under the influence of the oriental religions,[24] play therein the role of the necessary religious mediators between the inaccessible divinity and mankind. Through a critical dialogue with this popularized neo-Platonism, the last bastion of pagan religion against the true faith, St. Augustine in the West and [Pseudo-]Dionysius in the East would give a decisive orientation to Christian angelology.

St. Augustine

In the writings of St. Augustine, two great later works present a very substantial discussion of angelology: *The Literal Meaning of Genesis*

22. See Plato, *The Symposium* (202e–3a), in *The Collected Dialogues*, edited by Edith Hamilton and Huntington Cairns, 555, Bollingen Series LXXI, 13th ed. (Princeton: Princeton University Press, 1987), 555: "'Spirits, you know, are halfway between god and man.' 'What powers have they then?' I asked. 'They are the envoys and interpreters that ply between heaven and earth, flying upward with our worship and our prayers, and descending with the heavenly answers and commandments, and since they are between the two estates they weld both sides together and merge them into one great whole. They form the medium of the prophetic arts, of the priestly rites.... For the divine will not mingle directly with the human, and it is only through the mediation of the spirit world that man can have any intercourse, whether waking or sleeping, with the gods.'" See also *Cratylus* (398b), in *The Collected Dialogues*, 435: "And therefore I have the most entire conviction that he called them daemons, because they were δαήμονες (knowing or wise)." Compare Léon Robin, *La Théorie platonicienne de l'Amour* (Paris: Presses universitaires de France, 1933), 132–99.

23. See Hans-Jürgen Horn, ed., *Jakobs Traum: Zur Bedeutung der Zwischenwelt in der Tradition des Platonismus* (St. Katharinen: Scripta Mercaturae Verlag, 2002).

24. See, for example, Pierre Hadot, *Porphyre et Victorinus*, Études augustiniennes 32 (Paris: Études augustiniennes, 1968), 1:393–95.

(404–14 A.D.) and *The City of God* (413–27 A.D.). But the bishop of Hippo scattered a rich harvest of reflections on angels and demons throughout his works, as we will have occasion to note as we study each of the particular angelological themes.[25] Some original major themes, however, deserve to be mentioned right away.

In book IV of *The Literal Meaning of Genesis*, St. Augustine discusses God's rest on the seventh day (Gn 2:1–3) and inquires as to the significance that should be assigned to the six days of creation. Since, according to him, all things were created simultaneously, these "days" could not correspond to real, chronological durations. They designate instead a noetic reality: the different glances or acts of knowledge that an angel performs with regard to creatures.[26] The Genesis account does not speak explicitly about the creation of the angels, but St. Augustine, proceeding very cautiously, thinks that it can be discerned in the creation of the mysterious light without any material support that shoots out first of all: "the light that was first made was the formation of the spiritual creation."[27] He had already mentioned this hypothesis in book I, where he had defined this spiritual light as "nothing other than intellectual life,"[28] turned entirely toward God who illumines it. Since he is inspired by Plotinus's concept of the constitution of beings, Augustine sees an angel as the solidifi-

25. Concerning the teaching on angels and demons in St. Augustine: Besides the supplementary notes on the angelological passages in the works of St. Augustine in the French translations of the series Bibliothèque augustinienne, see Mangenot, "Démon d'après les Pères," 4:368–73; Karl Pelz, *Die Engellehre des heiligen Augustinus* (Münster: Aschendorff, 1913); Bernhard Lohse, "Zu Augustins Engellehre," *Zeitschrift für Kirchengeschichte* 70 (1959): 278–91; Jean Pépin, "Influences païennes sur l'angélologie et la démonologie de St. Augustin," in *Entretiens sur l'homme et le diable*, edited by Max Milner, 51–59 (Paris: Mouton, 1965); Odilo Lechner, "Zu Augustins Metaphysik der Engel," *Studia patristica* 9 (Berlin: Akademie-Verlag, 1966): 422–30; Madec, "Angelus," 1:303–15; Jan den Boeft, "Daemon(es)," in *Augustinus-Lexicon* (Basel: Schwabe, 1996–2002), 2:213–22; and Cinzia Bianchi and Christof Müller, "Diabolus," in *Augustinus-Lexicon* (Basel: Schwabe, 1996–2002), 2:381–96; Frederick Van Fleteren, "Angels," in *Augustine through the Ages: An Encyclopedia*, edited by Allan D. Fitzgerald, OSA, 20b–22a (Grand Rapids: W. B. Eerdmans, 1999; also "Demons," 266b–68a; and "Devil," 268a–69a.

26. See Augustine, *The Literal Meaning of Genesis* IV.21.38–IV.25.56, trans., annotated John Hammond Taylor (ACW 41:128–45); see also supplementary note 20 by Aimé Solignac, "La connaissance angélique et les jours de la création" (BA 48:645–53).

27. Augustine, *Literal Meaning of Genesis* IV.21.38 (ACW 41:129): "illam lucem, quae primitus facta est, conformationem esse creaturae spiritualis."

28. Ibid., I.9.17 (ACW 41:29): "ipsa est intellectualis vita."

cation of an emanation (an emanation that is free, according to Augustine) that crystallizes when it turns toward its Origin. The angel knows himself in his own nature, then refers himself to God and, in so doing, completes his formation.[29] The angelic world thus occupies in Augustine's writings a place that is analogous to the one belonging to the *Nous* in the universe of Plotinus. It is the first creature. In *The City of God*, Augustine explains:

[The angels] are made participators of [God's] eternal light, which is nothing other than the unchangeable Wisdom by which all things were made, and which we call the only-begotten Son of God. Thus, the angels, illumined by that Light which created them, became light and were called "day" because they participated in that unchangeable Light and Day which is the Word of God, by whom they and all things were made. For, "the true light that enlightens every man who comes into the world" illumines every pure angel that he may be light not in himself but in God.[30]

If the angel is the "first day," then the other "days" correspond to the different glances of the angel at different sorts of creatures. For each one—for example, the firmament—the angelic consciousness operates in a threefold movement.[31] First, the angel knows things a priori in God, in the Word—that is to say, in the eternal *rationes*: this knowledge is described as *diurnal* or "daytime knowledge." Augustine infers from this that the creature is created first in the angelic intellect, which knows it in the Word, even before being created in its own nature. He thinks that he can discern this twofold creation in the very structure of the biblical verse: "And God said, 'Let there be a firmament made....' And it was so [creation in angelic understanding].... And God made the firmament [empirical creation]." Second, an angel knows the creature as it is objectivized in its own nature as distinct from its Creator: this is his *vesperal* or "evening knowledge,"

29. Ibid., IV.22.39 (ACW 41:130).
30. Augustine, *The City of God* XI.9 (FOTC 14:201): "Profecto facti sunt participes lucis aeternae, quod est ipsa incommutabilis sapientia Dei, per quam facta sunt omnia, quem dicimus unigenitum Dei Filium; ut ea luce illuminati, qua creati, fierent lux et vocarentur dies participatione incommutabilis lucis et diei, quod est Verbum Dei, per quod et ipsi et omnia facta sunt. 'Lumen' quippe 'verum, quod illuminat omnem hominem venientem in hunc mundum,' hoc illuminat et omnem angelum mundum, ut sit lux non in se ipso, sed in Deo."
31. See Augustine, *Literal Meaning of Genesis* IV.24.41 (ACW 41:132ff.).

which is more imperfect than the previous sort, just as the evening, with respect to its light, is more imperfect than midday. Finally, third, an angel does not merely regard the creature in itself but cannot help referring the known creature to the Creator and to his praise: this is his *matutinal* or "morning knowledge."[32] It is clear that, in Augustine's writings, the angelic mind appears as the noetic mirror in which the whole creation is reflected, such as it is in God and in itself.

While wary of attributing to the Angel a creative power, Augustine makes the angelic nature the witness and the privileged witness of creation, to the point of saying that the creature is first made somehow in the angelic mind. The world of angels is perfectly integrated with the universe of creatures, in which it plays a primordial role, not just because the angel is the first and the most exalted of creatures but also because he is the reflection of the creative action and of the created works, as well as the first agent of their return toward God through praise and love. The angelic nature thus becomes the archetype, the awareness, and the ideal of the creaturely condition.[33]

The primacy of the angels in God's creation is echoed by their primacy in the City of God. The first books of *The City of God* (I–X) aim to establish the radical helplessness of paganism with regard to both earthly goods and heavenly goods. They contain invaluable reflections on the decisive role of demons in pagan religions, which also imply a reflection on the exact nature and the extent of their superhuman powers. In books VIII and IX, St. Augustine devotes himself to a critical examination of the neo-Platonic demonology of a certain Apuleius of Madaurus. He identifies all demons as evil, maleficent beings and denies that they could play any mediating role whatsoever between mankind and God. That is strictly reserved to Jesus Christ. In contrast, book X explains the place occupied by the good angels in human history: they are not mediators and claim for themselves no worship but appear as auxiliaries of divine providence.

With book XI the account of the history of the two Cities begins: their origin (XI–XIV), their development (XV–XVIII), and their end

32. These subtle developments by Augustine widely encouraged the intense speculation of the scholastics about angelic knowledge and its properties; see Barbara Faes de Mottoni, "Tommaso d'Aquino e la conoscenza mattutina e vespertina degli angeli," *Medioevo* 18 (1992): 169–202.

33. Solignac, "La connaissance angélique," 653.

(XIX–XXII). Books XI and XII concentrate on angelological themes, since St. Augustine discusses therein the modalities of the creation of the angels and their beatitude, as well as the fall of the demons. Indeed, the history of the two Cities begins in the angelic world with the separation of the light (good angels) and the darkness (wicked angels) following the choice that the angels made for or against God. Since human beings enter in turn into this history, the heavenly City therefore is composed of angels and of men, just like the earthly city juxtaposed to it.

There is no real difficulty or impropriety in speaking of a single society composed of both men and angels; and … therefore, it is right to say that there are not four cities or societies, namely two of angels and two of men, but only two, one of them made up of the good—both angels and men—and the other of those who are evil.[34]

Angels and men belong to one and the same celestial society because they communicate in the grace and glory that come from Jesus Christ:

[Christ is] the Head of the whole city of Jerusalem, in which all believers from the beginning even to the end shall be enrolled; together with the legions and armies of angels, so that there may be one city under one king …, happy in its perpetual peace and salvation, praising God without end and unendingly blissful.[35]

34. Augustine, *City of God* XII.1.1 (FOTC 14:245): "Non inconveniens neque incongrua dicatur esse hominibus angelisque societas, ut non quattuor (duae scilicet angelorum totidemque hominum), sed duae potius civitates, hoc est societates, merito esse dicantur, una in bonis, altera in malis non solum angelis, verum etiam hominibus constitutae."

35. Augustine, *Exposition of Ps. 36*, sermon 3, para. 4 (WSA III/16:131). CCL 38:370: "ut esset et ipse totius caput civitatis Ierusalem, omnibus connumeratis fidelibus ab initio usque in finem, adiunctis etiam legionibus et exercitibus angelorum, ut fiat illa una civitas sub uno rege, et una quaedam provincia sub uno imperatore, felix in perpetua pace et salute, laudans Deum sine fine, beata sine fine"; Xenium natalicium, ed. J. Leemans and L. Jocqué, Corpus Christianorum 1953–2003. See also Augustine, *City of God* XII.9.2 (FOTC 14:262): "Those who share this common good [union with God] are in a holy communion both with Him to whom they adhere and one with another, and they form a single community, one City of God, which is also His living sacrifice and His living temple" (Hoc bonum quibus commune est, habent et cum illo cui adhaerent et inter se sanctam societatem et sunt una civitas Dei eademque vivum sacrificium eius vivumque templum eius).

Thus, in Augustinian theology, angels and demons prove to be fully integrated into salvation history, the center of which is Jesus Christ. Books XV–XVIII, devoted to the contrasting developments of the two Cities, offer a few scattered reflections on the activity of the angels and demons (angelophanies, etc.), but books XIX through XXII are much richer in angelological observations: in them Augustine not only insists on the theme of the one eschatological society of angels and men but also is intent on explaining at length the nature and meaning of the eternal sufferings to which the demons are subjected. Is it necessary to note that these angelological findings are the stock-in-trade for medieval theology and especially for the theology of St. Thomas Aquinas?

Dionysius the [Pseudo-]Areopagite

However, in De substantiis separatis, at the beginning of his presentation on specifically Christian angelology, St. Thomas declares:

> It remains for us to show what the Christian religion affirms about each of these subjects [relative to the angels]. To do this, we will use mainly the texts by Dionysius, who excelled in handing down the things that pertain to the spiritual substances.[36]

Dionysius was a master of angelology. Indeed, the famous eponymous writer is the first Christian author to have dedicated a special treatise to the angelic creature. His work The Celestial Hierarchy, written in the late fifth or early sixth century, went on to have considerable influence.[37] The Dionysian universe is a profoundly Christian-

---

36. Aquinas, De substantiis separatis, in Opuscula philosophica, ed. Raymundi Spiazzi (Rome and Turin: Marietti, 1954), c. 18: "Restat ostendere quid de singulis habeat Christianae religionis assertio. Ad quod utemur praecipue Dionysii documentis, qui super alios ea quae ad spirituales substantias pertinent excellentius tradidit."

37. Denys l'Aréopagite, La hiérarchie céleste, introduction René Roques, study and critical text Günter Heil, translation and notes Maurice de Gandillac (SC 58); see also Endre von Ivanka, "La signification historique du 'corpus areopagiticum,'" RSR 36 (1949): 5–24; Roques, L'Univers dionysien: Structure hiérarchique du monde selon le Pseudo-Denys (Paris: Aubier, 1954). On the Thomistic revival of Dionysius, see Wayne J. Hankey, "Dionysian Hierarchy in Thomas Aquinas: Tradition and Transformation," in Denys l'Aréopagite et sa postérité en Orient et en Occident, Actes du Colloque International, Paris, 21–24 septembre 1994, edited by Y. de Andia, 405–38 (Paris: Institut d'études augustiniennes, 1997).

ized revival of the neo-Platonic worldview, under the form that it had assumed in the writings of Proclus. Dionysius describes a universe of beauty and intelligible harmony that is in the process of being divinized. The Holy Trinity, in its inexhaustible generosity, communicates something of its perfection to creatures, but gradually, according to a "hierarchical" order that involves first the angels (the celestial hierarchies) and then mankind (the ecclesiastical hierarchy). A "hierarchy" denotes the organized set of intermediaries, subordinated one to another, through whose activity divinization is accomplished. Every order (or hierarchy) transmits to the next lower order the knowledge that comes from God (illumination), and by that very fact purifies it of ignorance (purification) and leads it to a more perfect knowledge (ongoing perfection). In this way the return of creatures to God is brought about. "The goal of a hierarchy, then, is to enable beings to be as like as possible to God and to be at one with him."[38] Each rank of the hierarchy receives the divinizing light from the next higher rank and communicates it to the next lower rank, like a fire that spreads by degrees.

Rather arbitrarily—"the best illustration of what can happen when philosophical schemas are transposed into the presentation of revealed truth"[39]—Dionysius imagined that the angelic world is organized into nine choirs divided into three triads or hierarchies. The first triad— seraphim, cherubim, thrones—is in direct contact with God. The second is composed of dominions, virtues, and powers, and the third consists of principalities, archangels, and angels, who come into contact with the ecclesiastical hierarchy. This extensive view of the angelic world, despite certain ambiguities, attracted medieval thinkers and therefore constitutes the framework of classical angelology.

38. Dionysius the Areopagite, *The Celestial Hierarchy*, chap. 3.2, in *Pseudo-Dionysius: The Complete Works*, Classics of Western Spirituality (New York and Mahwah, N.J.: Paulist Press, 1987), 154; see also chap. 7.2 (162): "The aim of every hierarchy is always to imitate God so as to take on his form, that the task of every hierarchy is to receive and to pass on undiluted purification, the divine light, and the understanding which brings perfection."
39. Roques, "Denys l'Aréopagite (le Pseudo-): La doctrine du Pseudo-Denys," *DS*, 3:270.

MEDIEVAL ANGELOLOGY IN THE WEST

The High Middle Ages[40] were a prolongation of the patristic age. Starting with the work of Johannes Scotus (called Eriugena), who in the ninth century translated and commented on *The Celestial Hierarchy*, the Dionysian influence was one of the main driving forces of angelological reflection. In the eleventh century, St. Anselm, in *De casu diaboli*, subtly analyzes the status of the angel before and after sin.[41] In the twelfth century, the school of Chartres, which tried to reconcile the dialogue *Timaeus* with the book of Genesis, integrated Platonic demonology into its Christian view of the cosmos.[42] In that same era, a work such as the *Sentences* of Peter Lombard, which was destined to become a classic, presents, in distinctions 2 through 11 of book II, an angelological synthesis that neatly defines the scholastic problems and their common solutions, although the Lombard also includes some of his own original thinking.[43] The question about the angels

40. See Alfred Vacant, "Ange: Angélologie dans l'Église latine depuis le temps des Pères jusqu'à saint Thomas d'Aquin"; "Angélologie de saint Thomas d'Aquin et des scolastiques postérieurs," in *DTC*, 1:1222–48; George Tavard, André Caquot, and Johann Michl, *Les Anges*, trans. from German by Maurice Lefèvre, Histoire des dogmes II.2b (Paris: Editions du Cerf, 1971), 147–97; Marcia L. Colish, "Early Scholastic Angelology," *RTAM* 62 (1995): 80–109; Faes de Mottoni, "Ange," in *Dictionnaire encyclopédique du Moyen Âge* 1:64–66; David Keck, *Angels and Angelology in the Middle Ages* (New York and Oxford: Oxford University Press, 1998); Suarez-Nani, "Angélologie," in *Dictionnaire du Moyen Âge*, edited by Claude Gauvard, Alain de Libera, and Michel Zink, 56–59 (Paris: Quadrige and PUF, 2002). Among the monographs on the angelology of medieval authors, see, for example, Edmond Boissard, "La doctrine des anges chez saint Bernard," *Analecta Sacri Ordinis Cisterciensis* 9 (1953): 114–35; James McEvoy, *The Philosophy of Robert Grosseteste*, part 2, "The Angelic Light" (Oxford: Clarendon Press; New York: Oxford University Press, 1982), 51–146; Faes de Mottoni, *San Bonaventura e la scala di Giacobbe: Letture di angelologia*, Saggi Bibliopolis 49 (Naples: Bibliopolis, 1995).

41. *De casu diaboli* is cited by St. Thomas in *ST* I, q. 63, a. 3. Concerning this text by St. Anselm, see Anselm of Canterbury, *De la chute du diable*, French trans. R. de Ravinel, introduction and notes Michel Corbin, L'oeuvre de St. Anselme de Cantorbery 2 (Paris: Cerf, 1986), 249–375; Eduardo Briancesco, *Un triptyque sur la liberté: La doctrine morale de St. Anselme, De Veritate, De Libertate arbitrii, De Casu diaboli*, L'oeuvre de St. Anselme, Étude no. 2 (Paris: Desclée De Brouwer, 1982).

42. See L'École de Chartres, Bernard de Chartres, Guillaume de Conches, Thierry de Chartres, and Clarembault d'Arras, *Théologie et cosmologie au XIIᵉ siècle*, trans. Michel Lemoine and Clotilde Picard-Parra, Sagesses médiévales (Paris: Les Belles Lettres, 2004), 16–19 [a text by Guillaume de Conches].

43. Peter Lombard, *Sententiae in IV libris distinctae*, vol. 1, part 2 (Liber I et II), ed.

is addressed within the context of a reflection on creation. Taking his inspiration quite directly from *De sacramentis* by Hugh of St. Victor,[44] Peter Lombard divided the subject matter into three parts: *primo*, "when [the angelic nature] was created, and where, and the qualities it had when it was first made"; *secundo*, "how it was affected by the defection of some and the conversion of others"; and *tertio*, remarks "about their excellence and orders and the difference of their gifts, and their functions and names and several other matters."[45] The first two parts show an Augustinian influence, while the third incorporates the Dionysian contribution.

Three major phenomena modify angelological reflection in the thirteenth century. The first is the development of scholastic methods and of the university as an institution. This leads to a more systematic treatment of angelological questions, generally in the form of *quaestiones disputatae*, whether independently or incorporated into much larger works, such as the commentaries of the *Sentences* and the *summas*.

The second phenomenon is Catharism and, consequently, the resurgence of dualist doctrines.[46] The Fourth Lateran Council (1215) countered it by vigorously affirming that angels and demons are creatures of God and that the demons' malice is in no way a natural attribute:

Firmly we believe and we confess simply that ... [God, the Holy Trinity is the] one beginning of all, creator of all visible and invisible things, of the spiri-

Collegii s. Bonaventurae, Spicilegium bonaventurianum 4 (Grottaferrata and Rome: Editiones Colegii S. Bonaventurae ad Claras Aquas, 1971), 336–83; English ed. *The Sentences, Book 2: On Creation*, trans. Giulio Silano, Mediaeval Sources in Translation 43 (Toronto: Pontifical Institute of Mediaeval Studies, 2008), 8–49; Ermengildo Bertola, "Il problema delle creature angeliche in Pier Lombardo," *Pier Lombardo* 1 (1957): 33–54; Colish, *Peter Lombard*, Brill's Studies in Intellectual History 41 (Leiden: E. J. Brill, 1994), 1:347–53.

44. Hugh of St. Victor, *De sacramentis*, lib. 1, pars 5 (PL 176:245–64).

45. Peter Lombard, *Sentences* II, d. 2, c. 1, n. 1 (8): "De angelica itaque natura haec primo consideranda sunt: quando creata fuerit, et ubi, et qualis facta dum primo conderetur; deinde qualis effecta aversione quorundam et conversione quorundam; de excellentia quoque et ordinibus et donorum differentia, et de officiis ac nominibus aliisque pluribus aliqua dicenda sunt."

46. In the *status quaestionis* on angelology that he draws up in the first part of *De substantiis separatis*, St. Thomas devotes a whole chapter (chap. 17) to the Manicheans, whose error appears to him to be the most serious of all.

tual and of the corporal; who by His own omnipotent power at once from the beginning of time created each creature from nothing, spiritual, and corporal, namely, angelic and mundane, and finally the human, constituted as it were, alike of the spirit and the body. For the devil and other demons were created by God good in nature, but they themselves through themselves have become wicked. But man sinned at the suggestion of the devil.[47]

This reminder about the creation of the angels *de nihilo* would not be superfluous, given the third and perhaps most decisive major event: the progressive dissemination in the West of texts that provided access to Greco-Arabic science and philosophy. The ensuing intellectual revolution first of all acquired for theology extremely valuable conceptual tools in physics, metaphysics, and epistemology, from which angelology benefited greatly. It also fostered the development of a heightened sense of the relative autonomy of the natural order, which made possible some useful clarifications, inasmuch as theologians distinguished more clearly, in the case of the angels, between what depends on nature (which is common to the good angels and the demons) and what depends on their supernatural destiny. Finally, it conveyed to the scholastics a complex set of doctrines concerning "separated substances" (that is, separated from matter), sometimes called *Intelligences*, which were essential components of the cosmological system[48] and, more fundamentally, of the metaphysics of the Greco-Arabic authors. In the *falsafa*, this philosophical speculation on separated substances had already been correlated with the religious belief in angels. Maimonides, for example, purely and simply identified the angels in the Bible with Aristotelian Intelligences:

The angels are incorporeal. This agrees with the opinion of Aristotle: there is only this difference in the names employed—he uses the term "Intelligences," and we say instead "angels." His theory is that the [separated] Intelligenc-

---

47. Denz.-H., no. 800: "Firmiter credimus et simpliciter confitemur, quod ... unum universorum principium: creator omnium visibilium et invisibilium, spiritualium et corporalium: qui sua omnipotenti virtute simul ab initio temporis utramque de nihilo condidit creaturam, spiritualem et corporalem, angelicam videlicet et mundanam: ac deinde humanam, quasi communem ex spiritu et corpore constitutam. Diabolus enim et alii daemones a Deo quidem natura creati sunt boni, sed ipsi per se facti sunt mali. Homo vero diaboli suggestione peccavit."

48. See Suarez-Nani, "Les anges et la cosmologie au Moyen Âge," in *Anges et esprits médiateurs*, Connaissance des religions 71–72 (Paris: Éd. Dervy, 2004), 103–15.

es are intermediate beings between the Prime Cause and existing things, and that they effect the motion of the spheres, on which motion the existence of all things depends. This is also the view we meet with in all parts of Scripture: every act of God is described as being performed by [the mediation of] angels.[49]

Consequently, just as St. Augustine in his day had managed to integrate Platonic demonology into Christian theology, so too thirteenth-century theologians had to take a stance with regard to this speculation on separated substances. Now, in the Christian setting, there was no consensus as to the equivalence of angels and Intelligences. There were many theologians who feared that naturalizing the angels threatened to obscure the essential point of the biblical teaching: angels are spirits "sent forth to serve, for the sake of those who are to obtain salvation" (Hb 1:14).[50] Even St. Albert the Great had reservations. Addressing the question explicitly, he refused to equate the angels of the theologians and the Intelligences of the philosophers: not only does the Christian angel have quite different things to do than to move the celestial spheres, but he exhibits properties that do not square well with neo-Platonism's emanationist system of the world.[51]

49. Moses Maimonides, *The Guide for the Perplexed*, trans. M Friedländer, 2nd ed. (London: Routledge and Kegan Paul, 1956), 2:160. The noncorporeality of angels alluded to here was established in Maimonides, *Guide*, 1:65–66. Maimonides assigns decisive importance to the belief in angels: it depends directly on belief in God and is the basis for the belief in prophecy and therefore in the Law; see Maimonides, *Guide*, 3:355–59): "The belief in the existence of angels is thus inculcated into the minds of the people, and this belief is in importance next to the belief in God's Existence; it leads us to believe in Prophecy and in the Law" (3:356).

50. Faes de Mottoni showed that St. Bonaventure's insistence on making the angels' ministerial role in salvation history the key of his angelology was a response to the naturalism of the Greco-Arabic philosophy of the angels; see Faes de Mottoni, *San Bonaventura e la scala di Giacobbe*.

51. In *In II Sent.*, d. 3, a. 3 (in *Commentarii in II Sententiarum*, edited by Auguste Borgnet, 64–66, *Opera omnia* 27 [Paris: Vivés, 1894]), Albert the Great poses the question "Should we call angels these separated substances that the philosophers call intelligences, as some dare to defend polemically?" (Utrum nos vocemus angelos substantias illas separatas quas philosophi intelligentias vocant, ut quidam contentiose defendere praesumunt?)

He cites Avicenna, Algazel, and Maimonides as favoring the identification of the angels of religion with the Intelligences of philosophy: "Thus Avicenna declared: the Intelligences are what the people and the interpreters of the Law call angels" (Ita dicit Avicenna, quod intelligentiae sunt quas populus et loquentes in lege angelos vocant).

The position of St. Thomas Aquinas is more balanced. Convinced that Christian revelation does not destroy the correct intuitions of the philosophical traditions but purifies them and brings them to their completion, Aquinas to a great extent adopts the philosophical reflection on separated substances. It serves as a support for Christian angelology.[52] But he firmly rejects any reductionism. The philosophical approach to the angels reaches only the surface of the angelic world and leaves what is essential in obscurity.[53] If it were set up as a thorough-

But Albert's own response is quite negative: the properties that the philosophers attribute to the Intelligences are incompatible with Christian dogmatic theology. From this perspective it is understandable that he minimizes the cosmological role of the Christian angel; compare Albert, *In II Sent.*, d. 2, a. 1 (p. 45): "Do the angels serve God by moving the spheres? We have no certainty thereof. On the contrary, we hold with the utmost certitude according to the holy Fathers that not all the angels are occupied with moving the heavens, because tradition teaches us that some remain in the presence [of God] and that some minister to us" (Utrum angeli deserviant Deo in motu orbium, vel non, incertum est nobis: hoc tamen certissime tenemus secundum sanctos Patres, quod non omnes occupantur circa motum coelorum … quia nobis traditur quosdam assistere, quosdam circa nos ministrare). And in Albert, *In II Sent.*, d. 3, a. 2 (p. 61): "We will never fall into the error of saying that the angels are necessary in order to move the spheres, although we would not deny that they could move them, but their number and the reason for their creation does not depend on that" (Nos numquam declinabimus in hunc errorem, quod dicimus angelos esse necessarios ad motum orbium: licet non negamus quin possint movere: sed numerus et ratio creationis non dependet ex illo).

In *Anges*, Suarez-Nani showed that, following the Albertine line of thought, Thierry of Freiberg neatly distinguished the angels of Christian faith and theology from the Intelligences of philosophy. Reflecting on "the intelligences by means of Proclus and the angels by means of Augustine" (151), he defends "the coexistence without interference of these two types of intermediary realities which are by nature radically different" (167). The intelligences of philosophy are nonetheless metaphysically superior to the angels of philosophy. Indeed, they enter into the intrinsic structure of the natural universe, where they exercise an essential mediating causality, which, however, is not on the order of creative action.

52. For example, concerning the existence of angelic knowledge of singulars, St. Thomas asserts repeatedly that this is required by revelation because of the ministry that the angels perform for the benefit of mankind, but secondarily he does not neglect to base it also on the cosmological function of the angel as Aristotle understands it; see CG II.100 (no. 1857); ST I, q. 57, a. 2.

53. As for the number of angels (ST I, q. 50, a. 3), Aquinas states Aristotle's position: the number of separated substances corresponds to the number of first movements, but he immediately denounces it as being contrary to scripture. Likewise, concerning the cosmological role of angels (ST I, q. 110, a. 1, arg. 3 et ad 3), he dismisses the (Platonic) idea that the angelic orders are defined according to the number of corporeal species that they must minister to.

going interpretation, it would subvert the order of the world, the hierarchy of beings, by chaining spirit to matter. Indeed, separated substances
do not exist in dependence on corporeal substances; rather, corporeal substances exist for the service of spiritual substances. The heavenly bodies are only the habitual instruments by means of which the separated intellectual substances communicate with the empirical world
the forms that exist spiritually within them in the form of ideas.[54]

De substantiis separatis, which is one of St. Thomas's late, great
metaphysical works, is exemplary along these lines. It is an exercise in
integrating Platonic and Aristotelian philosophical reflection on separated substances into Christian angelology. Unfortunately St. Thomas did not complete the second part presenting the Christian doctrine on angels and demons (from ch. 18 on), but before that, Aquinas
makes a sort of historical assessment of philosophical angelology
(ch. 1–17).[55] He begins by setting forth and comparing the systems
of Plato and Aristotle (ch. 1–4), then shows how their correct insights became degraded in the writings of their disciples (ch. 5–17).
For Plato, as St. Thomas interprets him, the existence of separated
substances results from the Theory of Ideas, understood as the transcendent causes of the visible world.[56] As a good Aristotelian, Aquinas rejects these hypostatized Ideas, but he salvages the substance of
Platonism by identifying the Platonic Ideas with the divine and an-

54. See the texts compiled by Thomas Litt, "Les corps célestes, instruments de
leurs esprits moteurs," in Les corps célestes dans l'univers de saint Thomas d'Aquin, Philosophes médiévaux 7 (Louvain and Paris: Publications universitaires, 1963), 179–85.

55. St. Thomas also proposes a reasoned summary of the history of philosophical
reflection on separated substances in ST I, q. 110, a. 1, ad 3; Q. de pot., q. 6, a. 6; Q. de
malo, q. 16, a. 1; Q. de spiritualibus creaturis, a. 5.

56. See ST I, q. 50, a. 3: "Plato contended that the separate substances are the species of sensible things" (Plato enim posuit substantias separatas esse species rerum sensibilium); see also ST I, q. 110, a. 1, ad 3. In De substantiis separatis, c. 1, the analysis is
taken further. St. Thomas explains how Platonism is led to acknowledge four types of
intermediate realities between man and God: "It is clear therefore that [the Platonic
philosophers] posited between us and the Supreme God four orders: that of the secondary gods, that of the separated intellects, that of the celestial souls, and that of the
good or bad demons. If these things were true, we would call all these intermediate orders by the name of angels" (Sic igitur patet quod inter nos et summum Deum quatuor ordines ponebant [platonici]: scilicent deorum secundorum, intellectuum sepa-
ratorum, animarum caelestium, and daemonum bonorum seu malorum. Quae si vera
essent, omnes huiusmodi medii ordines apud nos angelorum nomine censerentur).

gelic thoughts.[57] The universe exists in the first place as something thought by God, then by the angels, before existing in its empirical reality. Thus, "in the manner of Platonic Ideas, the Thomistic Angels guarantee the intelligibility of the world above and beyond its phenomenal reality."[58]

For the Aristotelians, the existence of separated substances answers a need that is metaphysical and at the same time cosmological. The changes that we observe in nature are not sufficiently explained by their immediate, univocal causes—in other words, the causes situated at the same level of being as the effect that is produced: a rosebush produces another rosebush, a dog engenders another dog. But what about the form itself—in other words, the intelligible type that represents "roseatude" or "dogginess"? How could this form be produced solely by the agents that share in it (a particular rosebush or dog) and that are therefore its effects? It is absolutely necessary to have recourse to the causality of more universal forms and to equivocal, supra-specific higher agents. The heavenly bodies play this role. Thus, instances of generation and corruption are governed by the movements of the sun: "Man is begotten by man and by the sun as well."[59] But the movements of the heavenly bodies must themselves have a cause. This is found in the unmoved movers, who act upon the heavenly bodies as final causes and are none other than substances separated from matter. Thus the first heaven is moved by the attraction exerted upon it by the Prime Mov-

57. See CG III.24 (no. 2047), trans. Bourke, III/1:94]: "So, all the forms that are in these lower substances, and all their motions, are derived from the intellectual forms which are in the intellect of some substance, or substances.... And on this point, Plato's statement is verified, that forms separated from matter are the principles of forms that are in it. Although Plato claimed that they subsist in themselves and immediately cause the forms of sensible things, we assert that they exist in an intellect and cause lower forms through the motion of the heavens" (Omnes igitur formae quae sunt in istis inferioribus, et omnes motus, derivantur a formis intellectualibus quae sunt in intellectu alicuius substantiae, vel aliquarum.... Et quantum ad hoc verificatur dictum Platonis, quod formae separatae sunt principia formarum quae sunt in materia: licet Plato posuerit eas per se subsistentes, et causantes immediate formas sensibilium; nos vero ponamus eas in intellectu existentes, et causantes formas inferiores per motum caeli).

58. Suarez-Nani, Anges, 142.

59. Aristotle, Physics II.2 (194.b.13), trans. R. P. Hardie and Russell K. Gaye (Oxford: Clarendon Press, 1930); see also Jan Aertsen, Nature and Creature: Thomas Aquinas' Way of Thought, Studien und Texte zur Geistesgeschichte des Mittelalters 21 (Leiden and New York: E. J. Brill, 1988), 302–10.

er, but the other heavenly spheres are also moved by unmoved movers that correspond to them.[60] This metaphysical-cosmological vision provides, so to speak, a philosophical interface with Thomistic angelology, but it does not exhaust its wealth.

ANGELS IN THE WRITINGS OF ST. THOMAS

Besides many incidental teachings about the angels that are scattered throughout his scriptural commentaries or the disputed questions,[61] Aquinas treated angelology systematically four times—first of all, in 1252–56, in the *Scriptum*, when he comments on distinctions 2–11 of book II of the *Sentences* of Peter Lombard. He returns to the topic obliquely around 1261–62 in the *Summa contra Gentiles* where, within the context of the study of creation and a benevolent confrontation with pagan philosophies, he takes an interest in intellectual substances in general.[62] After the treatise on the angels in the *Summa theologi-*

60. See Aristotle, *Metaphysics* XII.8, trans., commentaries Hippocrates G. Apostle (Bloomington: Indiana University Press, 1966), 207–9; Philip Merlan, "Aristotle's Unmoved Movers," *Traditio* 4 (1946): 1–30. Concerning the movers of the heavenly bodies in St. Thomas' philosophy, see Joseph de Tonquédec, *La Philosophie de la nature*, part 1, *La nature en général* (Paris: P. Lethielleux, 1957), 2:148–56; Félix Fernandez de Viana, "Motores de cuerpos celestes y Angeles en S. Tomas de Aquino," *Estudios Filosoficos* 8 (1959): 359–82; Litt, chap. 5, "Les moteurs des corps célestes," in *Les corps celestas*, 99–109; Suarez-Nani, *Anges*, 91–171: "Les anges et les cieux ou la fonction cosmologique des substances séparées."

Are the heavenly bodies endowed with a soul or are they simply moved from without? Medieval thinkers debated this. For St. Thomas, the heavenly bodies belong to a region of the universe entirely different from our sublunary world, and therefore they cannot be moved by nature. Without rejecting outright the thesis of an animated heaven, St. Thomas therefore upholds the idea that a heavenly body is moved by an extrinsic mover with an intellectual nature, which is an angel belonging to the second Dionysian hierarchy, that of the Virtues. The comparison made by Suarez-Nani, *Anges*, 120–34, between the answers that Albert the Great, Robert Kilwardby, and Thomas Aquinas gave to a query by John of Verceil concerning the movement of the heavenly bodies confirms that "the position of Thomas Aquinas is the only one that attributes a cosmological function to the angels and thereby confers on spiritual creatures a philosophical legitimacy" (133).

61. Some disputed questions are quite directly concerned with the angels; see Aquinas, *Q. de veritate*, q. 8–9 (on angelic knowledge and the communication thereof); Aquinas, *Q. de spiritualibus creaturis*; and Aquinas, *Q. de malo*, q. 16 (on demons). Likewise several *quodlibet* questions address angelological themes.

62. CG II, c. 46–55.

ae (around 1266–68), St. Thomas would devote *De substantiis separatis* also to the angels.

The place in which St. Thomas discusses a topic in the *Summa theologiae* is always highly instructive. That said, the question of the plan of the *Summa* is still disputed.[63] Although I cannot prove it here, I personally think that we must take seriously the prologue to question 2 of the *prima pars* in which St. Thomas announces that this first part will deal with God, and then explains, a few lines later, that this *consideratio de Deo* will comprise three parts: the study of the Divine Essence, the study of the distinction of persons, and, starting in question 44, the study of "those things that pertain to the procession of creatures from God (*ea quae pertinent ad processum creaturarum a Deo*)." The classic theory that divided the *Summa theologiae* into two parts (the "theology": *ST* I, q. 2–43, then the "economy," structured by the *exitus-reditus* schema: *ST* I, q. 44 to the end), regards the link between the study of the *exitus* and the study of the mystery of God as nothing but an oversight on the part of St. Thomas. This view sees question 44 as the beginning of the study of creatures and the end of part I as the discussion of their *exitus*. But upon closer inspection it is evident that the second half of part 1 is by no means limited to the study of the *exitus*. In it St. Thomas also considers aspects of the return of the creature to God, beginning with the *reditus* of the angel and his entrance into beatitude or his definitive exclusion from it. The very theme of divine government—the activity by which God guides creatures toward their perfection, their end—concerns the *reditus* more than the *exitus*. I wonder therefore whether the *prima pars* should not be considered as a truly coherent treatise, a whole, the object of which would be, as St. Thomas actually announces, the study of God—*consideratio de Deo*—both in himself and in creatures (as their principle, and as their end). According to this hypothesis, the *prima pars*, a summa within the *Summa*, would already contain all of theology in its most universal principles. Part II and part III would then merely repeat, *for the particular case of man*, and in light of the general principles of part I, the study of the return to God.[64]

63. See the *status quaestionis* in Jean-Pierre Torrell, *Initiation à saint Thomas d'Aquin: Sa personne, son oeuvre*, Vestigia 13, 2nd ed. (Paris: Cerf; Fribourg: Presses universitaires de Fribourg, 2002), 219–28.

64. See *ST* I, q. 2, prol.: "principium rerum et finis earum, et specialiter rationalis

This hypothesis is in partial agreement with the one that insists on the unity of the *prima pars* as setting up the framework within which man's return to God takes place, which is object of the rest of the *Summa*, but it differs from it in its evaluation of the respective importance of the parts of the *Summa*. In contrast to the prevailing tendency to see the heart of the *Summa theologiae* in its moral theology, this hypothesis underscores the primacy of the *prima pars*, which specifically concerns contemplative theology centered on the knowledge of God.

Be that as it may, angelology finds its place in the third section of the *prima pars* dedicated to the "procession of creatures" (q. 44–119), an expression that could in fact designate the whole *exitus-reditus* of creatures, considered generally. St. Thomas proceeds in three phases. First he discusses the production of creatures (q. 44–46: "treatise on creation"), then their distinction—in other words, the diversity of creatures and the theological significance of that diversity (q. 47–102), and finally their conservation and government. The questions on angels are found in the second and third phases. In the second phase, St. Thomas considers the distinction of creatures in general (q. 47), then the quasi-transcendental distinction between good and evil at the metaphysical level (q. 48–49), before dwelling at greater length on the distinction between the two fundamental types of creatures: the spiritual creature and the corporeal creature (q. 50–102). The questions dedicated to "the purely spiritual creature who, in Scripture, is called an angel" (q. 50–64) open this section. We might propose the following outline:

> I. *The substance of the angels*
>   A. As such [*absolute*] (q. 50)
>   B. In its relation to corporeal realities (q. 51–53)
>   1. Its relation to bodies (q. 51)
>   2. Its relation to corporeal place (q. 52)
>   3. Its relation to local movement (q. 53)

---

creaturae ... secundo, de motu rationalis creaturae in Deum." The division of the *Prima secundae* (I-II) and the *Secunda secundae* (II-II) already offers us the example of a division based on the distinction between the general and the particular. Why would it not be the case with the division between the *Prima pars* and the other parts?

II. *Angelic knowledge*
  A. The cognitive power of the angel (q. 54)
  B. The medium of angelic knowledge (q. 55)
  C. The objects of angelic knowledge (q. 56–57)
    1. Immaterial realities [angels, God] (q. 56)
    2. Material realities (q. 57)
  D. The mode [= the properties] of angelic knowledge (q. 58)
III. *The will of an angel*
  A. The will itself (q. 59)
  B. The movement of the will: love (q. 60)
IV. *The creation and the origin of the angels*
  A. In their natural existence (q. 61)
  B. In their existence perfected by grace and glory (q. 62)
  C. How some angels became wicked (q. 63–64)
    1. With regard to the evil of sin: the culpable malice of the angels (q. 63)
    2. With regard to the evil of punishment: the punishment of the demons (q. 64)

At the conclusion of his study of the distinctions among creatures, St. Thomas moves on to the study of their government: how God leads all creatures to their end (q. 103–19). He sets forth the general laws of divine government and, à propos one of the effects of divine government—namely, the transformation of creatures—arrives at the activity that creatures can perform upon one another, while remaining dependent on the divine activity. For this purpose he repeats the tripartite division of creatures. He studies first "how the angels, who are purely spiritual creatures, move"—in other words, the way in which angels exert influence over creatures (q. 106–14), then the action that bodies exert (q. 115–16), and finally the action belonging to human beings (q. 117–19). It is traditional in scholastic treatises on angelology to supplement the commentary on the questions on the nature and origin of the angels (I, q. 50–64) with a commentary on the questions on the role of angels in the divine government (I, q. 106–14). They present the following logical structure:

I. *The action of an angel on other angels*
   A. Angelic enlightenment (q. 106)
   B. Linguistic exchanges between angels (q. 107)
   C. The organization of angels into hierarchies and orders
      (q. 108)
   D. The organization of the wicked angels (q. 109)
II. *The angel's act of governance (praesidentia) over the corporeal
world* (q. 110)
III. *The action of an angel on human beings*
   A. The action of angels on human beings by their natural
      power (q. 111)
   B. The mission of the angels (q. 112)
   C. The guardianship of the good angels and the attacks of the
      demons (q. 113–14)
      1. The guardianship of the good angels (q. 113)
      2. The attacks of the demons (q. 114)

4

———— : ————

Do Angels Exist?
How Is the Problem Framed Today?
The Demystification of the World

Until the onset of the modern era, the real existence of angels and demons was naively taken for granted. Angels were regarded neither as a
symbolic expression of the human psyche nor as a literary device but
simply and unabashedly as personal subjects, autonomous centers of
existence capable of acting and routinely intervening in human history. A whole set of social practices (rituals, popular legends) conferred
a sort of cultural self-evidence on this belief. Our ancestors therefore
would have been less surprised to run into a flesh-and-blood devil at
a bend of a dark alley than we are to meet police cars lying in ambush
alongside a highway.[1] Furthermore, this spontaneous popular belief
found rational confirmation in the philosophical and scientific view of
the world in which angels played a decisive cosmological role. Christian theology, far from having to justify the existence of angels and demons, therefore set out to Christianize this universal belief. That is by
no means still the case today. Belief in the existence of angels has difficulty finding any support outside of sheer adherence to the faith.

1. St. Augustine notes in passing that the most insignificant old lady who is Christian has no doubt about the existence of the diabolical society and "unreservedly detests" it; see *City of God* X.11.1 (FOTC 14:137).

Indeed, a cultural climate that has been intrinsically vitiated by the primacy now assigned to technology has disenchanted our way of looking at the world. Although for the ancients nature was a *cosmos*, a work of wisdom, a word [*logos*] that referred to something more than itself, today it is flattened and reduced to mere material extension, without any other significance than the completely extrinsic one that our subjectivity is willing to confer upon it.[2] This leaves hardly any room for angels, who are therefore obliged to flee the cosmos and take refuge in the human psyche, from which the neurosciences, the final frontier of science, are now hard at work to expel them!

Someone may object to this picture of an inevitable disenchantment by pointing out that belief in the spirit world is not doing that badly, even in the West. Can we not observe a return of the angels in contemporary culture? Yet since postmodernity is the daughter of modernity, the way in which they are making their return tends to confirm the eclipse of the Christian angel. A belief in the reality of spirits is thriving, in fact astonishingly so, and this is no doubt an understandable protest against the reductive character of a techno-logical culture that mutilates reality by cropping it down to the little segment that it has mastered.[3] This belief nonetheless shares the fundamental error of that culture: the one-sided identification of ra-tionality with the sciences. Since any approach resulting from meta-physical reason is deemed null and void a priori, angels find them-selves relegated to the outer limits of rationality. They are doomed to inhabit a hell of an irrational shrine.[4]

2. On the evolution of man's way of looking at nature, see Rémi Brague, *The Wis-dom of the World: The Human Experience of the Universe in Western Thought* (Chicago: University of Chicago Press, 2004).

3. The ontological status of these spirits is difficult to think about in an ametaphys-ical culture, which cannot reach the properly spiritual dimension of reality, so that post-modern angels sometimes look a lot like the Martians and other extraterrestrials that used to be the angelic remnants of scientific materialism.

4. These same remarks apply also to the belief in demons, even though the latter is evidently more deeply rooted in the human psyche and more resistant to skepticism than the belief in the angels (as distinct from belief in God). On the presence of Satan in con-temporary culture and beliefs, see Herbert Haag, *Teufelsglaube* (Tübingen: Katzmann, 1974); Muchembled, *History of the Devil*. People sometimes worry about the rise of sa-tanism. Several national episcopal conferences have had to issue warnings: "Magie et dé-monologie: Lettre pastorale de la Conférence épiscopale de Toscane" (*DC* 91 [1994]: 988–98); "Superstition, magie, satanisme: Note pastorale de Conférence épiscopale de

In these circumstances, some Christians, who rightly disapprove of the dubious rise of an emotional sort of religiosity but continue to tremble reverentially before science, think that the church's teaching on angels and demons has become a very serious handicap for the overall credibility of its preaching. How could a religion so primitive that it still believes in spirits have any credence whatsoever? Therefore, in order to save what is essential, it would be necessary to cut our losses—in other words, quietly to get rid of the excess baggage of angels and demons. The tactic is simple: establish that angelology is an extrinsic element and not part of the substance of revelation itself. In short, it is an option that can be scrapped without damaging the essentials. I beg to differ.

It is therefore urgent for us, before going any further, to make sure of the actual reality of the object that we are proposing to consider. There would be no point in discoursing subtly on the question *quid sit* (what is it?) if the answer to the question *utrum sit* (does it exist?) were to be negative. In that case, on the epistemological level, it would be necessary to forgo all theology of angels—since theology is a science of the real—and to limit ourselves to a history, albeit a fascinating one, of the mental representations thereof, which would be the province of the humanities and no longer of theology. I will argue here in two stages. First, in the present chapter, I will examine the rational credibility of angelology: is it possible from the perspective of philosophical reason to affirm the existence of an intermediate invisible world between God and men? In a second stage—the following chapter—I will consider the relations between angelology and the Christian faith: is it an accidental mythological accretion, which we should get rid of today by an appropriate hermeneutic, or is it an intrinsic article of the faith?[5]

Campanie" (*DC* 92 [1995]: 802–9). On satanism in the limited sense of worship rendered to Satan, see Massimo Introvigne, *Indagine sul satanismo: Satanisti e anti-satanisti dal Seicento ai nostri giorni* (Milan: A. Mondadori, 1994). More specifically, satanism currently designates a trend that started in the United States in the 1960s and regards the experience of evil as a creative power that should be cultivated; see Bruno Borchert, "La seconde venue de Satan," *Concilium* 103 (1975):129–37. But it is not certain that this phenomenon implies a reasoned stance as to the existence of demons, since it is instead the expression of the psychological disarray of a society deprived by materialism. Nevertheless, at another level, the demons are quite capable of exploiting these manifestations of the culture of death for their own purposes.

5. The question of the existence of angels today is posed nicely by Pie-Raymond

As we already noted, in Greek philosophy (once it had been emancipated from mythical thinking) several thinkers—and not the most insignificant ones, since we are talking about Plato and Aristotle, among others—upheld for properly philosophical reasons the existence of "separated substances"—in other words, of spiritual subjects who are ontologically separate from matter. They deemed these realities to be necessary for the intelligibility of the universe, inasmuch as the sublunary world of our experiences does not contain within itself an adequate explanation of the phenomena that occur in it and points to a supraterrestrial causality: that of the heavenly bodies and of the "Intelligences" or separated substances. This conviction was closely connected with a cosmological vision that St. Thomas broadly shared, while taking great care not to reduce the angels to a cosmological power.[6] Now clearly the cosmological system that incorporated the ancient philosophy of the separated substances is out of date. Must we conclude from this that philosophy no longer has anything to say about angels? Nothing could be less certain. The principles of metaphysics and of the philosophy of nature to which this

---

Régamey, chap. 1, "Y a-t-il seulement des anges?" *Les anges au ciel et parmi nous,* Je sais, je crois (Paris: A. Fayard, 1959). See also, but use caution with, Piet Schoonenberg, "Osservazioni filosofiche e teologiche su angeli e diavoli," in *Angeli e diavoli,* Giornale di teologia 60 (Brescia: Queriniana, 1972), 94–128.

6. The theory of the *angeli rectores* still persisted in the writings of the seventeenth-century astronomer Kepler. At the same time, John of St. Thomas (see his *Cursus philosophicus thomisticus,* vol. 2, *Naturalis philosophiae,* Nova editio a B. Reiser [Turin: Marietti, 1933] [*Cursus philosophicus II*], p. 1, q. 1, a. 1 [8b and 16b]) explains that physics must deal indirectly with angels, as well as with God, inasmuch as they are the movers of bodies. Yet, as early as the fourteenth century, John Buridan applied to the movements of the heavenly bodies the theory of *impetus*—in other words, the moving force inherent in the movable object—thus downsizing physics and leaving the Intelligences/first movers unemployed; see Buridan, *Subtilissimae Quaestiones super VIII Physicorum libros Aristotelis* VIII, q. 12 (Paris: 1509) (cited in Pierre Duhem, *Le Système du monde: Histoire des doctrines cosmologiques de Platon à Copernic* [Paris: Hermann, 1958], 8:329): "We do not find in the Bible that there are Intelligences responsible for communicating to the heavenly bodies the movement proper to them; it is therefore permissible to show that there is no need to suppose the existence of such intelligences. One could say, in fact, that God, when he created the World, moved according to his good pleasure each of the celestial orbs; he stamped upon them an *impetus* that has moved them ever since; so that God no longer has to move these orbs, unless by exerting a general influence similar to the one whereby he concurs with all actions that take place." But Buridan leaves the matter to the theologians: "I do not offer all this as certain [*assertive*]; I will simply ask the gentlemen theologians to teach me how all these things can happen."

system tried to do justice have not foundered with all passengers and freight on board, because they were not intrinsically dependent upon it, and we will find them at work again, extracted from their cosmological dross, in the two paths that open up today (perhaps) toward a philosophical affirmation of the existence of the angelic world. The first path, analogous to the *quinque viae* of proving the existence of God, would be the a posteriori way that would prove the existence of the angels starting from certain physical, psychological, or metaphysical effects that are accessible to our knowledge by going back to their cause. Another path, an a priori way, would start from what we know philosophically about God and his creative plan so as to deduce from it the necessary existence of a universe of purely spiritual creatures.

AN A POSTERIORI PROOF OF THE EXISTENCE OF ANGELS?

Some metaphysical properties of reality, in the final analysis, are explained only by the existence of a transcendent First Cause of being. This is the thrust of the Thomistic proofs of the existence of God. Is there something analogous with regard to the angels? Can we identify any facts in our experience that can be explained only as effects of angelic activity?

To answer this question it is necessary first to define, in light of St. Thomas's teaching, what the action of an angel could be in our world, then to verify the possibility in view of certain problems introduced by the modern concept of science. We will then be able to make a pronouncement as to the value of an a posteriori proof of the existence of angels.

Angelic Action in Our World

In his study of the activity of angels in the divine government, St. Thomas considers first the actions that angels perform on one another (*ST* I, q. 106–9), then he goes on to discuss the actions of angels on the physical world, "the corporeal creature" (*ST* I, q. 110), before turning to the actions that they, by means of their natural powers, can perform on human beings (*ST* I, q. 111). These questions 110–11 are the place where we have some chance of finding the effects that we are looking for.

The idea of angels presiding over creatures inferior to them is a commonplace in the Christian tradition. St. Justin, for example, declares that God "committed the care of men and of all things under heaven to angels whom He appointed over them."[7] In particular, the angels preside over corporeal creation,[8] in the sense that they administer it and guide it, either indirectly by assuring the regular movement of the heavens that is the basis for the course of nature, or else immediately by intervening in the play of natural causes.[9] Scripture repeatedly mentions that the angels are set over natural phenomena (winds, fire),[10] and this theme was orchestrated by the fathers, who see angels as administrative officials set over the physical world.[11] For St. Thomas, who also points out the convergence of revelation and philosophy in this regard,[12] this angelic administration of the physical world is based (1) upon the general law of the promotion of the dignity of secondary causes by their effective participation in the divine government, both in the natural order and in the supernatural order of salvation, and (2) upon the related law of hierarchical mediation that characterizes this participation in the divine government. As he explains in the corpus of article 1 of question 110, every particular ac-

7. Justin, *Second Apology* 5.2 (ANF 1:190a).

8. Relying on an allusion by Gregory the Great, *Forty Gospel Homilies* 34.10288, St. Thomas attributed this presidency more specifically to the Virtues (*ST* I, q. 110, a. 1, ad 3).

9. In the background to q. 110 is a problem that had greatly preoccupied the church fathers: the prodigies and miracles performed by angels and demons in salvation history.

10. See chap. 1, note 14, of this volume.

11. In *ST* I, q. 110, a. 1, St. Thomas cites five patristic authorities testifying to this presidency of angels over the cosmos; see Origen, *Homily on Numbers*, Homily 14.2; 9 (trans. Thomas P. Scheck, ACT, 82b–83a); Augustine, Eighty-Three Different *Questions*, q. 79 (trans.David L. Mosher, FOTC 70:200–205) and *Trinity* III.4.9 (FOTC 45:103–4): "But as grosser and lower bodies are directed in a certain order by subtler and stronger bodies, so all bodies are directed by the spirit of life; the irrational spirit of life by the rational spirit of life, the truant and sinful rational spirit of life by the rational, pious and just spirit of life, and the latter by its Creator, from whom, through whom, and in whom it has also been created and established"; cited also in *CG* III.83 [no. 2582]); Gregory the Great, *Dialogues* IV.5.8 (FOTC 39:197–99); John Damascene, *Orthodox Faith* II.4 (FOTC 37:209): Satan originally was set over the earth to guard it.

12. See *ST* I, q. 110, a. 1: "All corporeal things [are] ruled by the angels. This is not only laid down by the holy doctors, but also by all philosophers who admit the existence of incorporeal substances" (Omnia corporalia reguntur per angelos et hoc non solum a sanctis doctoribus ponitur, sed etiam ab omnibus philosophis qui incorporeas substantias posuerunt).

tive power (the active powers of corporeal beings, limited by the po-
tential of matter, are quite particularized, limited to certain effects) is
necessarily governed and directed by a more universal power, that of
a spiritual, angelic being, who fits it into a broader plan.[13] This active
presence of the Intelligences at the very heart of the cosmos testifies
to and expresses the conviction that nature is penetrated by intelligence—that it possesses an intrinsic intelligibility.[14]

13. See *ST* I, q. 110, a. 1: "It is generally found both in human affairs and in natural
things that every particular power is governed and ruled by the universal power; as, for
example, the bailiff's power is governed by the power of the king. Among the angels
also, as explained above (*ST* q. 55, a. 3; q. 108, a. 1), the superior angels who preside over
the inferior possess a more universal knowledge. Now it is manifest that the power of
any individual body is more particular than the power of any spiritual substance; for every corporeal form is a form individualized by matter, and determined to the 'here and
now'; whereas immaterial forms are absolute and intelligible. Therefore, as the inferior
angels who have the less universal forms, are ruled by the superior; so are all corporeal
things ruled by the angels" (Tam in rebus humanis quam in rebus naturalibus, hoc com-
muniter invenitur, quod potestas particularis gubernatur et regitur a potestate universa-
li; sicut potestas ballivi gubernatur per potestatem regis. Et in angelis etiam est dictum
quod superiores angeli, qui praesunt inferioribus, habent scientiam magis universalem.
Manifestum est autem quod virtus cuiuslibet corporis est magis particularis quam virtus spiritualis substantiae, nam omnis forma corporalis est forma individuata per materiam, et determinata ad hic et nunc; formae autem immateriales sunt absolutae et intelligibiles. Et ideo sicut inferiores angeli, qui habent formas minus universales, reguntur
per superiores; ita omnia corporalia reguntur per angelos); *CG* III, 78: "Quod mediantibus creaturis intellectualibus aliae creaturae reguntur a Deo" (That other creatures are
ruled by God by means of intellectual creatures); and the epilogue in CG III.83; *Q de
ver.*, q. 5, a. 8: "Utrum tota corporalis creatura gubernetur divina providentia mediante
creatura angelica?" (Are all material creature's governed by God's providence through
angels?)

14. The idea of an angelic activity that habitually sustains the course of nature in
a constitutive way should not be disregarded; see the suggestive study by Ide, "Anges
dans la nature," 33–50. Karl Rahner ("Angelologie," in *Sacramentum mundi: Theologisches
Lexicon für die Praxis* [Freiburg, Basel, and Vienna: Herder, 1967], 1:146–54) proposed
a theological cosmology in which angels are seen as "free, personal principles who enter
into the structure of the partial orders of the universe." Once the mind observes in the
universe or in history orders or structures or units of meaning that cannot be reduced
to an accumulation of material forces or to human activity, one can legitimately discern
therein the unifying presence of angels. Similarly, Jacques Maritain, who situates the activity of angels at the microphysical level, in the space left free by a certain quantum in-
determinacy (see *Approches sans entraves*, in Jacques Maritain and Raïssa Maritain, *Oeuvres complètes* (Fribourg: Editions universitaires; Paris: Editions Saint-Paul, 1982–95),
13:675–78, enjoys discerning the active presence of angels in the process of the evolution of species.

How is this activity of the angelic mind upon the world carried out? At what point does the activity of a spiritual being enter into the course of the physical world? One might perhaps automatically assume that the pure spirit transforms the natural world at will, by a simple decision, by "telepathy." Not at all.[15] Here, as elsewhere, St. Thomas is staunchly opposed to Platonizing occasionalism and criticizes in particular the Avicennian theory of the Giver of forms, which maintains that a separated substance introduces form into matter once the latter has been adequately disposed by inferior agents. On the contrary, St. Thomas insists on the necessary homogeneity between cause and effect—*omne agens agit sibi simile* [every agent acts in a manner similar to itself]. The production of a being composed of matter and form can, immediately, be the deed only of a being that is itself composed of matter and form.[16]

In fact, the angel's action is carried out through the intermediary of local movement or displacement.[17] In Aristotelian physics, local motion is the most perfect form of corporeal movement inasmuch as it concerns movable things or subjects that are already in act and remain in potency only with respect to the extrinsic accident of place. It is therefore the most spiritual movement, the only kind that is found, for example, in the celestial world, and it proves to be particularly well suited to serve as a connection between the world of spirits and the world of bodies. Consequently, an angel can produce in our world anything that can be caused by local movement, which includes some qualitative effects.[18] By the play of local movement, an angel or a de-

15. See *ST* I, q. 110, a. 2: "Whether corporeal matter obeys the mere will of an angel" (Utrum creatura corporalis obediat angelis ad nutum).

16. Ibid.: "Every informing of matter is either immediately from God, or from some corporeal agent; but not immediately from an angel" (Sic igitur omnis informatio materiae vel est a Deo immediate, vel ab aliquo agente corporali; non autem immediate ab angelo).

17. See *ST* I, q. 110, a. 3: "Whether angels by their own power can immediately produce local motion in bodies" (Utrum angeli sua virtute possint immediate movere corpora localiter).

18. See *ST* I, q. 110, a. 3, ad 2: "The angels, by causing local motion, as the first motion, can thereby cause other movements; that is, by employing corporeal agents to produce these effects, as a workman employs fire to soften iron" (Angeli, causando motum localem tanquam priorem, per eum causare possunt alios motus, adhibendo scilicet agentia corporalia ad huiusmodi effectus producendos; sicut faber adhibet ignem ad emollitionem ferri); *ST* q. 111, a 3: "Whatever can be caused by the local movement of

mon can make corporeal agents concur in the production of an effect that he is unable to produce directly by himself. On his own, a demon cannot directly make matter burst into flames, but he can direct the local displacement of a spark produced by a cardinal's cigarette so as to start a fire in the Vatican gardens.[19]

Similar principles hold true for angelic (and demonic) activity upon the human psyche, which St. Thomas considers in the four articles of question 111. In a very beautiful scene of the film *Ailes du désir / Der Himmel über Berlin*, by Wim Wenders, we see, in a bus in Berlin, a guardian angel put his arm around a discouraged man, whose sad interior monologue we hear in voiceover. Imperceptibly, this interior monologue changes and is directed sincerely toward a healthy moral reaction. According to St. Thomas, God alone acts directly on the spiritual powers of his creation, but an angel can act indirectly on the intellect (art. 1)[20] and on the will of a human being as well (art. 2) by playing on his material psychological conditioning. Indeed, all human knowledge—and the will depends largely on knowledge—derives its material from sensible experience that is then elaborated by the imagination with a view to establishing a source and a constant support for the properly immaterial activity of the intellect. The angel therefore influences the human mind by acting on the imagination (art. 3) and on the senses (art. 4). The simplest but probably the rarest case—even though a naïve reading of the Bible supplies many examples!—is the one in which an angel modifies the sensible data

bodies is subject to the natural power of the angels" (Illa ... quae ex motu locali aliquorum corporum possunt causari, subsunt virtuti naturali angelorum). See also Ide, "Anges dans la nature," 41–42: "The power to intervene immediately on displacement therefore opens the way to mediate intervention on other sorts of change."

19. In *ST* I, q. 110, a. 4, St. Thomas explains that an angel cannot work a miracle in the strict sense—in other words, produce an effect that altogether exceeds the capacities of created nature. He can certainly produce astonishing effects, but these are still within the possibilities of nature, many of which remain hidden from human knowledge. These are miracles from our limited perspective (*quoad nos*) (ad 2); see *ST* I, q. 111, a. 4, ad 3.

20. In the corpus of art. 1 of *ST* q. 111, St. Thomas distinguishes two aspects in the angelic illumination of the human intellect: on the one hand, the angel proposes to the human intellect images adapted to the concepts that he wants to suggest, and, on the other hand, he strengthens (*confortare*) its intellectual light. It is difficult to say whether this strengthening of the intellect in angelic illumination is an action distinct from the presentation of the adapted *species*; see chap. 12 of this volume.

himself (an angelic apparition assuming a body or the transformation of given material). But the angel can also act on the physiological process of external sensation and imagination:[21] he moves the humors and the spirits (today we would say the basic elements of the organic modifications of the brain) in such a way as to present one image or another to the mind.[22] By this intelligent action on the organic conditioning of the psyche, the angel illumines the human intellect by offering it intelligible content under the form of images adapted to its nature. He also acts indirectly on the human will. On the one hand, through the mediation of his indirect action he can present to the will one object or another under an aspect that highlights its attractiveness. On the other hand, he can excite the psychosomatic realities that are termed the sensitive passions and thus bear down on a voluntary decision, without ever being able to compel it:[23] a good angel can stir up a movement of courage, while a demon can ignite concupiscence.

However, it is necessary to ask a question that is logically prior to these processes: are these angelic or diabolical interventions in nature and in the lives of human beings credible or even *possible* in the first place, given what we know or think we know today about the laws that govern nature and about the determinism that they seem to imply? St. Thomas had already stressed, by way of objection, that the necessity of some events seemed to rule out any angelic intervention in the processes concerning them:

21. Faes de Mottoni, "L'illusione dei sensi? Angeli e sensi in Bonaventura e Tommaso d'Aquino," *Micrologus* 10 (2002); Faes de Mottoni and Suarez-Nani, "I demoni e l'illusione dei sensi nel secolo XIII: Bonaventura e Tommaso d'Aquina," in *Jakobs Traum*, 77–94.

22. See *ST* I, q. 111, a. 3, ad 2: "An angel changes the imagination, not indeed by the impression of an imaginative form in no way previously received from the senses (for he cannot make a man born blind imagine color), but by local movement of the spirits and humors" (Angelus transmutat imaginationem, non quidem imprimendo aliquam formam imaginariam nullo modo per sensum prius acceptam [non enim posset facere quod caecus imaginaretur colores], sed hoc facit per motum localem spirituum et humorum).

23. See *ST* I, q. 111, a. 2: "The angels, as being able to rouse these passions, can move the will, not however by necessity, for the will ever remains free to consent to, or to resist, the passion" (Angeli, inquantum possunt concitare huiusmodi passiones, possunt voluntatem movere. Non tamen ex necessitate, quia voluntas semper remanet libera ad consentiendum vel resistendum passioni).

Whatever possesses a determinate mode of action, needs not to be governed by any superior power; for we require to be governed lest we do what we ought not. But corporeal things have their actions determined by the *nature* divinely bestowed upon them. Therefore they do not need the government of *angels*.[24]

Thus the subway in Toulouse needs no conductor because it is entirely computer-programmed. The fact remains that this marvelous mechanism would remain inert without an external energy source. St. Thomas therefore responds to the objection by saying that corporeal beings certainly do have actions determined by their intrinsic nature, but that in order to perform them, in order to pass from potency to act, they need to be moved by a spiritual reality that activates them.[25] Although this physical law is subject to debate, the metaphysical principle that it intends to establish is undeniable: no being can make itself pass from potency to act. This actualization has its source in God, the First Act, but nothing prevents us from thinking that this physical pre-motion should be transmitted by the habitual action of the angels.

But besides necessary events there is the immense realm of contingent events (which might not happen or might not have happened). Here, angelic interventions can play a decisive role. Someone may object that any intervention by a spiritual cause contradicts the fundamental principle of scientific determinism: physical or psychological phenomena must be explained by antecedent phenomena of the same order. Angels have nothing to do with such things. Here we are faced with a particular case of a major philosophical problem: the possibility that a cause of a spiritual order (a human soul, an angel, God) might intervene in the very course of this world's events.

24. *ST* I, q. 110, a. 1, arg. 1: "Videtur quod creatura corporalis non administretur per angelos. Res enim quae habent determinatum modum operandi, non indigent gubernari ab aliquo praesidente, ideo enim indigemus gubernari, ne aliter operemur quam oportet. Sed res corporales habent determinatas actiones ex naturis sibi divinitus datis. Non ergo indigent gubernatione angelorum."

25. *ST* I, q. 110, ad 1: "Corporeal things have determinate actions, but they exercise such actions only according as they are moved, because it belongs to a body not to act unless moved. Hence a corporeal creature must be moved by a spiritual creature" (Res corporales habent determinatas actiones, sed has actiones non exercent nisi secundum quod moventur, quia proprium corporis est quod non agat nisi motum. Et ideo oportet quod creatura corporalis a spirituali moveatur).

This possibility unquestionably contradicts the myth of strict determinism. This myth, which hampers the modern collective unconsciousness, imagines that the present state of the physical universe is the absolutely necessary result of the arrangement of natural forces in a previous state.[26] The idea of contingency is ruled out or serves to cloak the subjective imperfection of our knowledge of causes. In this case—the hypothesis of "Laplace's Demon"—an observer who knew the exact state of the physical forces at moment t$_0$ would be able to predict with certainty the situation of the universe at t$_1$. Or else—this is le Dantec's hypothesis—a "phrenograph" precisely registering my brain waves would make it possible to deduce with the utmost precision all my present and future thoughts. But this strict determinism, besides being unproved (not to mention indemonstrable), is in fact nothing but the projection of the conditions required for a partial scientific description of natural phenomena onto a much more complicated reality. To deny the possibility of spiritual action is to put reality onto the terrible bed of Procrustes. In fact the physical universe, and the psychological universe even more so, are open universes leaving room for initiatives that result from the creativity of certain free, purposeful, and autonomous centers of action.

It is not a matter of disputing the principle of determinism on which the experimental sciences are based, but rather of putting it in its proper place. Picture a snowflake falling slowly. While walking nearby, out of intellectual curiosity or just for fun, or else to attract the attention of the person walking beside me, I blow on the snowflake. The path that the snowflake then follows through space before landing on the ground can certainly be described in terms of the laws of physics. *Post eventum* [after the fact], the physicist can, at least in theory, reconstruct precisely the series of physical causes (including my breath) that led the snowflake to land at this spot rather than an-

26. Compare the definition of determinism by Karl Popper, *The Open Universe: An Argument for Indeterminism* (Totowa, N.J.: Rowman and Littlefield, 1982), 1–2: "The doctrine that the structure of the world is such that *any event can be rationally predicted, with any desired degree of precision, if we are given a sufficiently precise description of past events, together with all the laws of nature.*" Assuming the most difficult position, since I do not want to subscribe to a facile or hasty harmonization of views, I set aside the critique of determinism in the name of quantum physics, even though some philosophers and theologians have seen it as a scientific argument in favor of the possibility of an intervention by spiritual causes in the world of nature.

other. But in the split second that preceded my exhalation, the foreseeable path was quite different. Of course, a consistent materialist would say that an omniscient observer could have foreseen the deviation because he would have known the cerebral processes that were the cause of my decision to blow on the snowflake. That is an utterly gratuitous statement. The cerebral modifications accompanying my decision (if it actually was a deliberate decision and not a simple reflex) are not necessarily the causes: they can just as well have been its effects. A free act as it bursts forth is not susceptible to being predicted scientifically. Once it has entered into the course of phenomena, and only then, can a scientific explanation somehow grasp it: the physicist reconstructs a very partial and narrowly selected series of physical causes that culminates in that event, but the series could have been different if the properly spiritual cause had acted differently. Consequently the events of this world can be interpreted in two ways. After the fact, they can be explained partially by a series of natural causes (the only causes that the experimental sciences can take into account methodologically) but if we also admit the existence of free creatures, nothing prevents us from discerning their activity in those events.

Therefore we cannot rule out the ordinary or extraordinary intervention of free spiritual beings—and therefore of angels—in this world's course of events. Suppose I am driving a car through a deep gorge when an overhanging boulder suddenly breaks loose and comes crashing down on the road a few seconds after I passed by its point of impact with the ground. If I am a materialist, I will say nothing, or, if I give in to a misplaced subjective reaction, I will exclaim, "I was fortunate," "I lucked out," or "that was not my destiny." If I am a Christian, I will recollect myself and say, "Thank you, God; thank you, Guardian Angel," and I will interpret the incident as a message, an invitation to conversion, for example. Is that an infantile reaction? Not necessarily. It is based on a possible and coherent interpretation of the event. Not only was it *subjectively* impossible even for a man equipped with the most precise instruments of observation to foresee the exact moment of the boulder's fall, much less the moment when my car would pass right beneath the boulder, but it was *objectively* impossible, because both the fall of the boulder at point P at 16:03:00

and my passage through point P at 16:02:59 resulted from a multitude
of factors that were strictly speaking contingent, some of them free,
which may have been probable but were per se unpredictable.

A Proof Based on Effects?

Action of angels in the world is therefore possible. But can we affirm
the reality thereof based on a purely philosophical analysis? The difficulty arises from the fact that an angel is not a First Cause but a secondary cause. If, for example, someone discovers a typed manuscript
of which I am the humble author, he can deduce from it with certitude first, the existence of an intelligent author, and second, the existence of a typewriter. But he can neither affirm nor deny the mediation of a secretary who might have typed the text at my dictation.
However, if he happens to know that I employ a secretary, then he
can suppose with some degree of probability that I made use of her
services.

It is somewhat the same in the case of the angels. In the questions
concerning the divine government, St. Thomas rejects any sort of
mediatism, explaining that God does not resort to intermediaries in
order to mitigate an imperfection because he would be incapable of
governing everything directly by himself. God does not need the angels to accomplish his plan on earth in the way that I need a saw and
a hammer to build a shed. God has reasons of the utmost fittingness
for associating the angels in his work, but he is obliged by no necessity. It follows that I cannot prove a posteriori the mediation of such
a secondary cause.[27] The existence of the shed allows me to deduce
the existence of its builder and of the saw because the builder cannot produce by himself the effect belonging to the saw that he uses.
In contrast, God suffices to explain the totality of the effect, even if he
did in fact enlist a secondary cause. Therefore we cannot deduce from
this the existence of the secondary cause.

Action by some spiritual creatures in our world and in the lives of
human beings is therefore possible, but we cannot declare the reality
thereof with absolute certainty until we have proved their existence
in some other way. Then, by virtue of a *reinterpretation*, in light of

27. St. Thomas says, for example, that a man is not necessarily aware of being enlightened by the angels (*ST* I, q. 111, a. 1, ad 3).

what I will know by then about the existence of an angelic world and about the ways of God who loves to associate creatures freely with his activity, I will be able to interpret such and such an effect (a good thought, a chance meeting) as being the result of angelic action.[28]

Someone will object that, in the case of the demons, an a posteriori proof becomes possible: although God can be the cause of every good effect directly, he can never be the cause of a bad effect. Certainly. But in fact it is a matter of determining whether, at the level of rational analysis, the evil that is in the world necessarily points to the existence of demonic causality or whether it can be explained sufficiently, on the one hand, by the play of natural physical causes and, on the other hand, by the unique moral cause that is human freedom.

The second hypothesis has in its favor the effectiveness of modern reductive anthropology: the causality that man attributes to the demonic points in fact to his own unconscious causality. Thus many phenomena in which the ancients spontaneously saw the mark of demons prove to be the result of natural causes that furnish an adequate scientific explanation of them. Not only the depictions of demons but the demons themselves are often projections of the individual or collective human imagination. Man objectifies, in the form of negative, demonic entities, the interior conflicts that gnaw at him or the hostile exterior forces that his intellect cannot analyze or consequently master.[29]

Yet, still more profoundly, it seems that the moral evil committed by man does not per se imply demonic action as a constitutive element or a decisive factor, in such a way that we could deduce from the existence of moral evil the existence of the demon. In adopting the traditional teachings that tend to limit the demon's influence so as not to diminish human responsibility, St. Thomas himself teaches

28. In *ST* I, q. 114, a. 3, arg. 3 et ad 3, St. Thomas declares that the divine aid necessary for all our good actions always passes through the ministry of the angels.

29. We have a good example of this psychoanalytic interpretation of the demonic in Eugen Drewermann, *La parole et l'angoisse: Commentaire de l'Évangile de Marc*, traduit de l'allemand et adapté par Jean-Pierre Bagot (Paris: Desclée de Brouwer, 1995). Legitimate in itself, this interpretation is in this study absolute and reductive, apparently leaving no room for a metaphysical affirmation of the actual reality of demons. Compare, from a Jungian perspective, Anselm Grün, *Aux prises avec le mal: Le combat contre les démons dans le monachisme des origins*, Spiritualité orientale 49 (Bégrolles-en-Mauges: Abbaye de Bellefontaine, 1990), 16ff.

that not all human sin necessarily proceeds directly from the temptation of the devil. Freedom and the corruption of nature following original sin are to a large extent sufficient to explain sin: "All *sins* are not committed at the *devil's* instigation, but some are due to the *free-will* and the corruption of the flesh. For, as *Origen* says (*Peri Archon* III), even if there were no *devil*, men would have the desire for food and love and such like pleasures; with regard to which many disorders may arise unless those desires are curbed by reason, especially if we presuppose the corruption of our *natures*."[30] Certainly, the devil is indirectly the cause of all sins inasmuch as he was the cause of Adam's sin, which places all human beings in a state in which they are inclined to evil. But, apart from the fact that the doctrine of original sin is not directly accessible to reason, one may ask whether satanic temptation was structurally a necessary factor in Adam's sin or whether it was simple factual causation, revealed by scripture, which does not allow us to argue compellingly from Adam's sin to Satan's action.

The Protestant theologian Emil Brunner maintains that a phenomenological analysis of sin necessarily points to some diabolic causality. He says that whereas the Greeks regard sensuality and matter as the cause of evil, the Bible defines the essence of sin as an entirely spiritual revolt against God. In this case, man's sin, inasmuch as it is the sin of a flesh-and-blood creature, cannot come first; it presupposes that a sin of sheer rebellion, the work of a pure spirit, precedes and incites it.[31] The argument is not without interest—even though it overlooks the fact that the first sin of man was a true sin of pride and

---

30. *ST* I, q. 114, a. 3: "Non... omnia peccata committuntur diabolo instigante, sed quaedam ex libertate arbitrii et carnis corruptione. Quia, ut Origenes dicit, etiam si diabolus non esset, homines haberent appetitum ciborum et venereorum et huiusmodi; circa quae multa inordinatio contingit, nisi per rationem talis appetitus refraenetur; et maxime, supposita corruptione naturae." See also *Q. de malo*, q. 3, a. 5; *ST* I, q. 114, a. 1, ad 3. Compare Origen, *On First Principles* III.2.2–3, in *On First Principles: Being Koetschau's Text of the De Principiis*, trans. G. W. Butterworth (New York: Harper and Row, 1966), 213–16, which concludes (216): "From these considerations ... , I think it is clearly apparent that there are some offences which we commit quite apart from the influence of the evil powers, and others which are carried to excessive and immoderate lengths at their instigation."

31. See Emil Brunner, *La doctrine chrétienne de la création et de la rédemption*, French trans. Frédéric Jaccard, Dogmatique 2 (Geneva: Labor et fides, 1965), 160–62.

not of weakness, since in the state of original justice reason's dominion over the senses was complete.[32] But does it amount to more than
an indication or an argument of fittingness within the faith? The same
goes for the argument that deduces the existence of demons from the
observation of certain excesses in the order of moral evil and especially from the terribly efficient way in which evil proliferates, far beyond the subjective intention of those who commit it and beyond
humanity's own abilities to harm. Bernanos put it admirably:

> Either injustice is just another name for Stupidity—and I do not dare think
> so, because it unceasingly sets its traps, plans its moves, now rears up and
> then crawls, and puts on all sorts of masks, even the face of charity. Or else it
> is what I imagine it to be, it has somewhere in creation its will, its awareness,
> its monstrous memory.... Who would dare to deny that evil is organized, a
> universe more real than the one that our senses convey to us ...? Thus injus-
> tice belongs to our familiar world, but it does not entirely belong to it. Its liv-
> id face ... is among us, but the heart of the monster beats elsewhere, outside
> of our world, with slow solemnity.[33]

Thus, although there seems to be no rational proof of the existence of demons,[34] there is no lack of indications that supply the believer, in his reinterpretation of events, with strong arguments of con-
venience in favor of identifying the presence of diabolical action, the
reality of which is already taught him by his faith.

---

32. See *ST* II-II, q. 163, a. 1.

33. Georges Bernanos, *Les grands cimetières sous la lune* (Paris: Plon, 1938), 108–9.
On the theme of the devil, which is central to Bernanos's work, see von Balthasar, *Le
chrétien Bernanos* (Paris: Éditions du Seuil, 1956), 327–42; Jeannine Quillet, "Présence
réelle de Satan dans l'oeuvre de Bernanos," in Milner, *Entretiens sur l'homme et le diable,*
271–85.

34. The ancients saw in certain extraordinary manifestations, such as possession, "experimental" proofs of the existence of demons. In *De substantiis separatis,* c. 2, St. Thomas rebukes Aristotle and his followers, who connect the action of the separated substances strictly to that of the heavenly bodies, for neglecting some sensible phenomena that
cannot be explained by astral influence. According to him, these phenomena transcend
the capacities of nature and point toward a supernatural spiritual cause of a diabolical order. He means phenomena such as true possessions (with xenolalia, speaking in foreign
tongues that were never learned), and demonic prodigies. In the seventeenth century,
J.-B. Gonet considered extraordinary demonic manifestations as true experimental proofs
for the existence of the angelic world; see Gonet, *Clypeus theologiae thomisticae,* vol. 3, *De
angelis* (Paris: Vivés, 1876), 6–7. These "proofs" are based, however, on factual and historical data that should be treated with caution.

NECESSITY IN THE UNIVERSE OF SEPARATED
INTELLECTUAL SUBSTANCES

The impossibility of proving the existence of angels from their action in the world does not mean, however, that all philosophical proof of the existence of the angelic universe is impossible. Indeed, repeatedly in his work, St. Thomas Aquinas discerns the a priori necessity of the existence of intellectual substances separated from matter based on what we are able to know about the logic of the creative plan as it is reflected in the metaphysical structure of the universe. Now, by right, the existence of God and creation are truths accessible to philosophical reason.[35]

For example, Aquinas likes to highlight the general law of medi-

---

35. Concerning these proofs, see M.-V. Leroy, *Les anges*, mimeographed course notes (Toulouse: n.d.), 123–26; Jean-Hervé Nicolas, "De l'existence dans l'univers créé de créatures invisibles," in *Synthèse dogmatique*, vol. 2, Complément (Fribourg and Paris: Éditions universitaires, 1993), 268–76; Suarez-Nani, "Les anges: une réalité nécessaire," in *Les anges et la philosophie*, 27–35.

Do the a priori Thomistic arguments for the existence of angels have demonstrative force? No doubt about it, according to Gilson, *Le thomisme*, 6th ed. (Paris: J. Vrin, 1972), 209, followed by Jean-Marie Vernier, *Les anges chez saint Thomas d'Aquin: Fondements historiques et principes philosophiques*, Angelologia 3 (Paris: Nouvelles Éditions latines, 1986), 77–82. In his *Dogmatik*, however, Matthias J. Scheeben seems to consider them no more than fitting: "Apart from revelation, the existence of angels cannot be proved by 'reason alone' with complete certitude. A priori it would be possible to give only reasons of fittingness" (vol. 3, part 2, section 1, art. 1, no. 140, ed. l'abbé P. Bélet, Bibliothèque théologique du XIXᵉ siècle [Paris: Socicle [Paris: Victor Palme, 1881]) [translated from French; the passage cited is not found in the abridged English edition, *Manual of Catholic Theology*.] So too Louis Jugnet, *La pensée de saint Thomas d'Aquin*, 3rd ed. (Paris: Éditions de la Nouvelle Aurore, 1975), 137: reason can only establish the likelihood or at most the probability, of the existence of angels.

In fact the problem of proving philosophically the existence of angels has assumed in modern thought, apart from Christian faith, a degree of importance that it did not have in medieval thought. In the practice of theological reflection, a medieval thinker like St. Thomas does not always feel the need to make a clear-cut distinction between what depends on philosophical proof and what depends on theological reasoning. It seems, however, that his proofs for the existence of angels mean to be rationally decisive. For example, as the conclusion of CG II.91 indicates, this chapter is entirely devoted to refuting the Sadducees and the materialism of the ancient physicists and establishing the existence of separated substances. That said, in this passage, as in *ST* I, q. 50, a. 1 or in *Q. de spiritualibus creaturis*, a. 5, the proof for the existence of angels is part of a reflection on the incorporeal nature of angels; see D. P. Lang, "Aquinas' Proof for the Existence and Nature of the Angels," *Faith and Reason* 21 (1995): 3–16.

ation or of gradualness that regulates "the order of things." Hence, once we have acknowledged, at the one extreme, the existence of God, Pure Act, and given, at the other extreme, the existence of corporeal substances, Thomistic thought, abhorring a vacuum and disproportion, immediately infers from this the existence of an intermediate category of created spirits.[36] This view of the world is not without foundation in experience, but does the argument based on it go beyond fittingness?

A more decisive proof deduces the existence of angels from the perfection of the universe. This is a two-step argument.[37] Step one: the existence of incorporeal and therefore purely intellectual substances is necessary. Indeed, the purpose of creation is the communication or diffusion of divine goodness. God intends to make other beings share in his perfections. He wants to assimilate them to himself, to make them similar to him.[38] Now "the perfect assimilation of an effect to a cause is accomplished when the effect imitates the cause according to that whereby the cause produces the effect." For example, a student should be assimilated to his Latin teacher according to

36. See, for example, *Q. de spiritualibus creaturis*, a. 5: "We can consider the same thing starting from the order of things, which is such that one passes from one extreme to the other only through intermediaries.... At the highest summit of things there is something absolutely simple and one, namely God. It is therefore impossible that corporeal substance, which is totally composed and divisible, should hold the position immediately after God. Instead it is necessary to allow for numerous intermediaries through which we pass from the supreme divine simplicity to corporeal multiplicity. Some of these intermediaries are incorporeal substances not united to bodies, some are corporeal substances united to bodies" (Secundo potest idem considerari ex ordine rerum, qui talis esse invenitur ut ab uno extremo ad alterum non perveniatur nisi per media.... Est autem in summo rerum vertice id quod est omnibus modis simplex et unum, scilicet Deus. Non igitur possibile est quod immediate sub Deo collocetur corporalis substantia, quae est omnino composita et divisibilis. Sed oportet ponere multa media per quae deveniatur a summa simplicitate divina ad corpoream multiplicitatem; quorum mediorum aliqua sunt substantiae incorporeae corporibus non unitae, aliqua vero substantiae incorporeae corporibus unitae).

37. This two-step structure is clearly shown by the distinction between *ST* I, q. 50, a. 1, which concludes that an incorporeal creature necessarily exists, and *ST* I, q. 51, a. 1, which concludes that an intellectual substance not united per se to a body necessarily exists. It figures also in the parallel passages from *CG* II. In ch. 46, St. Thomas proves that the existence of intellectual substances in general is necessary for the perfection of the universe, and then, after discussing the human soul, an intellectual substance united to the body, he proves in ch. 91 that intellectual substances not united to a body also exist.

38. See *ST* I, q. 44, a. 4.

his knowledge of Latin and not according to his baldness or his lisp. Now the creative act is not a necessary, unconscious effusion of the divine substance. God created all things by a personal act, "by His intellect and will." Consequently there must be in the universe creatures that imitate this aspect of God's perfection—in other words, creatures capable of intellectual knowledge and of love.[39] Now intellection, because it transcends the particular so as to attain the universal, cannot be the act of a particularized, corporeal power as such. The perfection of the universe therefore requires the existence of at least one created substance that is incorporeal and therefore intellectual.[40] Because it is the effect of a pure Spirit, creation must include as its summit a properly spiritual reflection of its Creator, an "image" of God that is capable of intimate union with its Principle.

But, someone will say, there is man! Is he not the image of God par excellence? Does he not have the vocation to be the interpreter of voiceless creation and to make sure that it returns to its beginning? Step two: what is accidental to a given nature is not coextensive with the whole set of subjects that share in that nature.[41] For example, it is essential for an animal to move by itself, but it is accidental for it to have wings. Consequently, all animals move by themselves, but not all animals have wings. Now the very notion of an intellectual substance—in other words, of a substance that engages in the properly

39. *ST* I, q. 50, a. 1: "Necesse est ponere aliquas creaturas incorporeas. Id enim quod praecipue in rebus creatis Deus intendit, est bonum quod consistit in assimilatione ad Deum. Perfecta autem assimilatio effectus ad causam attenditur, quando effectus imitatur causam secundum illud per quod causa producit effectum; sicut calidum facit calidum. Deus autem creaturam producit per intellectum et voluntatem, ut supra ostensum est. Unde ad perfectionem universi requiritur quod sint aliquae creaturae intellectuales." In *CG* II.46, St. Thomas presents the same teaching in dynamic form: the communication of the divine likeness is also what enables creation to make a return to its principle (no. 1230); this return is accomplished not only by a static resemblance but by a dynamic resemblance, in the second act, in the order of action: therefore it was necessary for there to be some creature capable of having God as the object of its specific action, which can be the case only with a spiritual creature. In no. 1235, St. Thomas insists on the necessary existence of creatures that imitate God insofar as he contains spiritually, intellectually, the whole set of creatures. We find again here the idea, so dear to Augustine, of the angel as an intelligible mirror of reality.

40. *ST* I, q. 50, a. 1: "Intelligere autem non potest esse actus corporis, nec alicuius virtutis corporeae: quia omne corpus determinatur ad hic et nunc. Unde necesse est ponere, ad hoc quod universum sit perfectum, quod sit aliqua incorporea creatura."

41. See *ST* I, q. 51, a. 1; *CG* II.91; *Q. de malo*, q. 16, a. 1; *Q. de spiritualibus creaturis*, a. 5.

immaterial activity of thought—does not per se require union with a body. Union with a body, and through the body to the sensible world, is necessary for a human being only by reason of the weakness of his intellect, which is in pure potency and must draw its suitable nourishment from the physical world. Union to a body is therefore accidental for an intellectual substance. Consequently, not all intellectual substances are necessarily united to a body. Let us go further. According to a correct metaphysics of participation, we must affirm that, for the transcendental perfections, if there is an imperfect realization of the perfection, a perfect realization thereof must also exist. The alert Thomist discerns here the thrust of the *quarta via*. The human intellect is imperfect, since it is in potency and destined to acquire its actualizing knowledge only progressively; therefore the mind is led to recognize the existence of a created intellectual power that is fully in act. This is the angel.[42] He therefore accomplishes in act and archetypically that which is the ultimate vocation of all creation: to be pure praise to the glory of the Creator. "Above him stood the seraphim; each had six wings: with two he covered his face, and with two he covered his feet, and with two he flew. And one called to another and said: 'Holy, holy, holy is the LORD of hosts; the whole earth is full of his glory'" (Is 6:2–3).

42. See *ST* I, q. 51, a. 1: "Angeli non habent corpora sibi naturaliter unita. Quod enim accidit alicui naturae, non invenitur universaliter in natura illa: sicut habere alas, quia non est de ratione animalis, non convenit omni animali. Cum autem intelligere non sit actus corporis nec alicuius virtutis corporeae, ut infra patebit, habere corpus unitum non est de ratione substantiae intellectualis inquantum huiusmodi, sed accidit alicui substantiae intellectuali propter aliquid aliud; sicut humanae animae competit uniri corpori, quia est imperfecta et in potentia existens in genere intellectualium substantiarum, non habens in sui natura plenitudinem scientiae, sed acquirens eam per sensus corporeos a sensibilibus rebus, ut infra dicetur. In quocumque autem genere invenitur aliquid imperfectum, oportet praeexistere aliquid perfectum in genere illo. Sunt igitur aliquae substantiae perfectae intellectuales in natura intellectuali, non indigentes acquirere scientiam a sensibilibus rebus. Non igitur omnes substantiae intellectuales sunt unitae corporibus; sed aliquae sunt a corporibus separatae. Et has dicimus angelos."

5

---:---

Do Angels Exist?
How Is the Problem Framed Today?
The Demystification of Revelation

The angelological issues found in the synthesis by St. Thomas would undergo no substantial modifications for the duration of the reign of Scholastic theology. Of course, this theology is anything but monolithic in its conclusions. The diversity of the philosophical tools used by various authors, or even the opposition of their strictly theological insights, produce angelologies with specifically different contents that were quite willing to engage in polemics.[1] A mere glance at the angelological section of the *Defensiones* of Jean Cabrol, written in the first quarter of the fourteenth century, suffices to convince the reader that almost all the particular theses of St. Thomas were disputed by later medieval theologians (Duns Scotus, Durand de St.-Pourçain, Peter Auriol, Gregory of Rimini).[2] Nonetheless, the questions treated within the framework of the Scholastic angelological syntheses

1. Thus the angelology of John Duns Scotus is in many ways opposed to that of St. Thomas Aquinas; see Gilson, chap. 5, "L'ange," in *Jean Duns Scot: Introduction à ses positions fondamentales* (Paris: J. Vrin, 1952); so is William of Ockham's. See Armand Maurer, chap. 8, "Angels," in *The Philosophy of William of Ockham in the Light of its Principles* (Toronto: Pontifical Institute of Medieval Studies, 1999).

2. See Jean Carbol (Capreolus), *Defensiones theologiae divi Thomae Aquinatis , In II Sent.*, d. 2–11, ed. C. Paban and T. Pègues (*Tours*: A. Cattier, 1900–8), 3:119–504.

remained almost identical until the seventeenth century. The only noteworthy—and harmful—development was the "philosophizing" trend of angelology that, during the Late Middle Ages, dangerously detached itself from sacred scripture and sometimes became a pretext for highly refined speculations or "experiments" of more or less religious philosophy. The sophisticated problems in physics posed by the displacement of angels intrigued our university scholars more than the place of angels in the economy of salvation! The delicate balance that St. Thomas had been able to maintain between philosophical speculation and his basic theological aim was disrupted.[3] Angelology was no better off for it.

From the sixteenth century on, however, the elite ceased to be educated in Scholasticism. It was disputed both by humanism and the Reformation and also by the emergence of a new philosophy that was very hostile to Aristotelianism. Reflection on the angels was severely affected by it. On the one hand, humanism and the Reformation joined forces in demanding a return to the biblical and patristic sources,[4] which incidentally had beneficial effects on Catholic theology. Not only were the first systematic treatises of positive theology about the angels published, like the one included in the *Dogmata theologica* (1644–50) by the Jesuit Denis Petau,[5] but the Scholastic treatises themselves proved from then on to be more attentive to positive data.

Much more consequential—to the point of making angels "useless and uncertain"—was the rise of the new rationalistic philosophy, which opposed Scholasticism not only by its hostility to Aristotelianism, but above all by its separatist concept of the relations between faith and reason. Philosophy as such, having rid itself of the speculations on separated substances that foundered with the old cosmology,

3. See Chrétien, "Connaissance angélique," 138: "The patristic doctrine of the angels had a properly theological keynote: it did not lose sight of the fact that angels are God's messengers, and it inquired above all into their role in the order of grace, in light of revelation. With many aspects of Scholastic teaching, one cannot help feeling that they are a philosophical excrescence or incursion into theology rather than vice versa."

4. The Reformation per se was not hostile to the angels; see Tavard, chap. 7, "La théologie protestante," in *Anges*. What Catholics and Protestants debated was not so much the existence or the nature of angels as the veneration due to them.

5. Denis Petau, *Dogmata theologica*, vols. 3–4.

decided that it no longer had very much to say about angels. Descartes, for example, even though he by no means disputed the existence of angels, advocates in his *Entretien avec Burman* (1648) a certain speculative discretion that, in his view, was terribly lacking in St. Thomas. The latter, he says, described the angels

each in particular as though he had been among them, and hence he acquired the name and fame of the Angelic Doctor; yet although he was perhaps never more painstaking in any other field, nowhere is he more inept. Knowledge of the angels eludes us almost entirely, because ... we could not possibly derive it from our mind. Furthermore we do not know anything that is ordinarily asked on the subject: whether they can be united to a body, what those bodies were that they often assumed in the Old Testament, and the like. It is better for us to follow Scripture on this point and to believe that they were young men, that they appeared as such, and the like.[6]

But let us examine instead the radical critique that Thomas Hobbes (d. 1679) elaborates in part 4 of *Leviathan*. There he discusses "The Kingdom of Darkness." Significantly, his critique applies to demonology much more than to angelology as such. In fact, the rationalist thinkers made belief in demonic activity and the practice of exorcism one of their favorite targets.[7] It must be said that, ever since the decline of the Middle Ages and especially during the modern era, the West has been afflicted with severe, obsessive demonophobia. It resulted in part from a pastoral approach generally based on fear, in which Satan occupies center stage,[8] and was expressed in "witch-hunting," which left a deep impression on consciences.[9] The vehemence of the Enlightenment reaction is understandable. Thus, in 1691, a work penned by a Dutch pastor, Balthasar Bekker (1634–91) was published, causing a scandal and (therefore) enjoying great success: *The Enchanted World*, which, based

6. René Descartes, *Entretien avec Burman*, in *Oeuvres et lettres*, Bibliothèque de la Pléiade (Paris: Gallimard, 1953), 1370.

7. See Paul Hazard, *The European Mind, 1680–1715* (Cleveland and New York: World Publishing, 1963), 155–79.

8. See Jean Delumeau, *La Peur en Occident, XIVᵉ–XVIIIᵉ siècle: Une Cité assiégée* (Paris: Fayard, 1978); Delumeau, *Le Péché et la Peur* (Paris: Fayard, 1983); Muchembled, *History of the Devil*. Muchembled thinks that this pastoral approach could not have developed without the demonological systematization of Scholastic theology, which proposed a less folksy view of Satan than in the previous popular traditions.

9. See Julio Caro Baroja, *Les sorcières et leur monde*, Bibliothèque des histoires (Paris: Gallimard, 1971).

on a rational reading of scripture that was supposed to purge surviving pagan beliefs, concluded that the devil, even if he exists, has no real influence in our world.[10]

Thomas Hobbes, for his part, brought about a drastic anthropological reduction: the kingdom of darkness that the Bible speaks about is nothing but "a Confederacy of Deceivers, that to obtain dominion over men in this present world, endeavor by dark, and erroneous Doctrines, to extinguish in them the Light, both of Nature, and of the Gospell."[11] It is paradoxical that these "deceivers" perverted the human race and even the church "by introducing the Daemonology of the Heathen Poets, that is to say, their fabulous Doctrine concerning Daemons, which are but Idols, or Phantasms of the braine, without any reall nature of their own, distinct from humane fancy."[12] Indeed, in chap. 45, with the revealing title "Of Daemonology, and other Reliques of the Religion of the Gentiles," Hobbes, who is willing to accept the existence of "Bodily Spirits," explains that belief in pure spirits is an illusion that results from a wrong interpretation of the functioning of our imagination. Images are mistaken for independently existing realities.

Hobbes's main interest is not in this crude materialistic reductionism but rather in carefully combining his theory with an exegesis of scripture. If demonology, a doctrine of pagan origin, is false, "why … did not our Saviour contradict it, and teach the contrary? Nay why does he use on diverse occasions, such forms of speech as seem to confirm it?"[13] Because, Hobbes replies, "such questions as these, are more curious, than necessary for a Christian mans Salvation."[14] Indeed, scripture has value "onely to shew us this plain and direct way to Salvation." Consequently, anything in scripture that does not correspond directly to this purpose has no particular authority.

A similar method was systematically applied during that same era by Spinoza (d. 1677) in his *Tractatus Theologico-Politicus* (1670). The

10. Balthasar Bekker, *Le monde enchanté, ou examen des communs sentiments touchant les esprits, leur nature, leur pouvoir, leur administration et leurs opérations*, 4 vols., French ed. (Amsterdam: Pierre Rotterdam, 1694).

11. Thomas Hobbes, *Leviathan*, ed. A. R. Waller (Cambridge: Cambridge University Press, 1904), 447.

12. Ibid., 448.   13. Ibid., 474.

14. Ibid., 476.

principle is simple: scripture has no other purpose than to inculcate obedience to God according to the precept of love of neighbor. Consequently, any speculations that do not tend directly toward this precept do not depend formally on revelation, even though they may be found materially in the Bible. In short, the reduction of revelation to a form of orthopraxis (love of neighbor) allows him to relativize the theoretical teachings thereof: "The prophets ... are to be believed only in so far as the matter and purpose of their revelations are concerned, every one in all other particulars being at liberty to believe what he pleases."[15] Even God does not hesitate to adapt to the indifferent or even false beliefs of those whom he addresses, since he can thus promote the true ethical religion. One immediate application of this principle:

When [Christ] says to the Pharisees, for example [Mt 12:26], "And if Satan cast out Satan, he is divided against himself, how then shall his kingdom stand?" he desired nothing more than to convince the Pharisees on their own principles, not to teach that there were devils or any kingdom of Satan.[16]

We have here in principle the critique of the angelic and demonic world by rationalist exegesis, which led, in nineteenth-century liberal Protestantism (David Strauss, Friedrich Schleiermacher), to what Karl Barth calls "the angelology of the weary shrug of the shoulders": the absolute refusal to take angels and demons seriously.[17]

Catholicism put up more resistance. Within Catholic scholarship, challenges to the reality of the angelic world are more recent and apply perhaps more to the devil than to the angels. Not until the 1960s did some theologians call the traditional teaching into question radically.[18]

15. Benedict Spinoza, *Tractatus Theologico-Politicus: A Critical Inquiry into the History, Purpose, and Authenticity of the Hebrew Scriptures*, trans. from Latin (London: Trübner, 1862), chap. 2, at 69.

16. Ibid., 70.

17. See the edifying anthology raked together by Karl Barth, *Church Dogmatics*, part 3, ed. G. W. Bromiley and T. F. Torrance (Edinburgh: T. and T. Clark, 1960), 3:413–18.

18. On the history of this questioning of the reality of the demonic world, see Renzo Lavatori, *Satana, un caso serioso: Studio di demonologia cristiana* (Bologna: Ed. Dehoniane, 1996); Gabriele Nanni, *Il dito di Dio e il potere di Satana: L'esorcismo, Esperienza e fenomenologia mistica* (Vatican City: Libreria editrice vaticana, 2004), 51–69. Exegetes and theologians started by suspending judgment; see, for example, Christian Duquoc, "Symbole ou réalité? (Satan)," *Lumière et vie* 15 (1966): 99–105. Then some went so far as to deny outright the existence of demons; see Henry A. Kelly, *The Devil:*

THE DEMYTHOLOGIZATION OF
SACRED SCRIPTURE

For the ancients, the revealed character of teaching on the angels was directly deduced from the frequent mentions of these creatures in scripture. St. Gregory the Great was able to write:

> I spoke of nine ranks of angels. We know from sacred Scripture that there are angels, archangels, virtues, powers, principalities, dominations, thrones, cherubim and seraphim. Nearly every page of Scripture testifies to the existence of angels and archangels.[19]

But since then we have come to understand better that not everything stated in scripture is formally the object of revelation and therefore does not necessarily call for the adherence of faith.

In order to demonstrate that a doctrine is canonized and has the authority of a truth *taught* by Scripture, it is not enough to heap up passages. It is necessary that it be explicitly asserted by the sacred author: and ... not everything stated in Scripture, even in the form of an affirmative statement [e.g., "Cretans are always liars" (Ti 1:12)], is a statement by the sacred author and, consequently, through him, a statement by God, the first Author of Scripture.[20]

The Christian reading of the Bible is therefore not naïve. It implies a hermeneutical operation that allows the reader to distinguish between the essential content of the biblical teaching—which is binding as a matter of faith—and the extrinsic elements with which this essential content may accidentally be combined. These elements, as such, do not have the authority of revelation.

Demonology and Witchcraft (London: Doubleday, 1968), and above all Haag, *Abschied vom Teufel* (Einsiedeln: Benziger, 1969). Among the specifically theological reactions to the last-mentioned work, see, for example, Joseph Ratzinger's 1973 essay "Abschied vom Teufel?," English translation, "Farewell to the Devil?" in *Dogma and Preaching* (San Francisco: Ignatius Press, 2011), 197–205.

19. Gregory the Great, *Forty Gospel Homilies* 34.7 (285): "Novem vero angelorum ordines diximus, quia videlicet esse testante sacro eloquio scimus angelos, archangelos, virtutes, potestates, principatus, dominationes, thronos, cherubin atque seraphin. Esse namque angelos et archangelos paene omnes sacri eloquii paginae testantur." Likewise, St. Augustine, in *City of God* IX.19 (FOTC 14:107), in the context of his refutation of pagan demonology, asserts that Christians, "relying on the language of Scripture, which is our norm (*secundum quam christiani sumus*), have learned that some of the angels are good and some bad," and that only the latter group should be called demons.

20. Leroy, *Anges*, 101.

First of all, it is necessary to take into account the literary context of the word of God. Indeed, in the Bible we encounter "literary beings" that, as significant as they may be, do not claim to be real entities. Now sometimes angels play a literary role of this sort. For example, in the apocalyptic literature, the angel has the very precise function of introducing a statement that has the force of revelation. The expression "an angel appeared and said to me" means "the following statement comes from God" and not "in the empirical world there was an apparition of an angelic being," even though there is no reason such an apparition could not be real in some cases.[21]

Next and most importantly, it is necessary to take into account the cultural context. The sacred author expresses the revealed message in the cultural categories of his time. This does not rule out the possibility that they may contain universal truths that revelation intends to adopt and corroborate with its own authority, but it may also be that they do not have the guarantee of revelation. To take a common example, the outdated cosmological categories in which the dogma of creation is expressed at the beginning of Genesis are not binding in faith. It is therefore perfectly legitimate to wonder whether the existence of angels and demons depends on a worldview that is accidental with respect to revelation or whether it is the object of a revealed teaching that is normative for the faith.[22]

The essential thing is to make no mistake in choosing the criteria that enable us to carry out this discernment. Now in Catholic theology, this criterion, in the final analysis, can only be the teaching of the magisterium to which Christ entrusted the authentic interpretation of scripture.[23] Certainly, in this task of discernment, the magis-

21. Be careful not to reduce all angelophanies to literary devices. Profound theological reasons sometimes require these appearances to be real events, as in the case of the annunciation to Mary; see *ST* III, q. 30.

22. This is the thesis, for example, of Haag, *Liquidation du diable*, Méditations théologiques (Paris: Desclée de Brouwer, 1971), 65: "The statements of the New Testament about Satan cannot belong to its compelling message; they depend solely on the concept of the world belonging to the Bible, a concept that is by no means binding in faith. These statements purely and simply reflect the ideas that were widespread in the roughly contemporary Jewish writings and that characterized the religious thought of that era."

23. See Vatican Council I, Dogmatic Constitution *Dei Filius* on the Catholic Faith, chap. 2 (Denz.-H., 3007).

terium prudently adopts the findings of the rational reflection of exegesis, but it integrates them into a more comprehensive view that is
better suited to the supernatural character of the matter under consideration—a perspective that takes into account the profound life of
the church animated by the spirit of truth: the teaching of the saints,
liturgical practice. But in no case may the decisive criterion be of a
worldly sort: the "scientific" view of the world at a given moment; the
"current consensus" registered by sociological surveys. We should be-
ware of the formula: "today it is no longer possible to say ... ," which
often serves as an epistemological cloak in theology.

This is the weak point in the campaign of demythologization
launched, archetypally, by Rudolf Bultmann (1884–1976). According to that Protestant theologian, the New Testament is expressed in
mythical terms derived from Jewish apocalyptic literature and Gnosticism. They are "incredible to men and women today because for
them the mythical world picture is a thing of the past."[24] Christianity
cannot possibly ask our contemporaries to acknowledge this mythical world picture as true, when "there is nothing specifically Christian
about [it]." Now the angelic world—like all miracles, the assertion
that death and sin are connected, the spiritual effectiveness of the sacraments, the Resurrection—is part of these mythical representations
whose unreality has been demonstrated by advances in science.

Also finished by knowledge of the forces and laws of nature is faith in spirits
and demons.... We cannot use electric lights and radios and, in the event of
illness, avail ourselves of modern medical and clinical means and at the same
time believe in the spirit and wonder world of the New Testament. And if we
suppose that we can do so ourselves, we must be clear that we can represent
this as the attitude of Christian faith only by making the Christian proclamation unintelligible and impossible for our contemporaries.[25]

The discrepancy between the mythological categories of the Bible and the modern *Weltanschauung* [worldview] demands a campaign of demythologization.[26] Demythologizing, for Bultmann, does

24. Rudolph Bultmann, "New Testament and Mythology: The Problem of Demythologizing the New Testament Proclamation [1941]," in *The New Testament and Mythology and Other Basic Writings*, edited and translated by Schubert M. Ogden, 3 (Min-
neapolis: Fortress Press, 1984).

25. Ibid., 4–5.

26. Along similar lines, an author such as Otto Dilschneider, *Christus Pantokrator*

not consist of bringing faith back within the limits of reason, as some liberal Protestants tried to do by interpreting Christianity as a simple figurative anticipation of modern philosophy, eliminating the mythology and thus doing away with the *kerygma*. Rather, it is a question of paying attention to the cultural gap and seeking the intelligible core of the Christian message (the *kerygma*) so as to interpret in its light the myths adopted by the first Christians. Now, according to Bultmann, who means to Christianize some of the insights of Martin Heidegger, the essential element of Christian faith is a personal decision, the product of grace, in favor of authentic life. Man must adopt an existential attitude of faith by which he "live[s] out of what is invisible and nondisposable [i.e., beyond his control] and, therefore, surrender[s] all self-contrived security."[27] Thus the biblical teaching about the dualist battle between the church and Satan must be interpreted as an image of the ongoing combat that man must wage within himself for the faith against unbelief.[28]

Despite its apparent common sense, the Bultmanian enterprise is seriously deficient with respect to theology.[29] On the one hand, it betrays great naïveté with regard to the secular marvels of modern science. Bultmann capitulates unconditionally to a science that obviously impresses him. Overlooking the possibility of a rational approach to reality other than the superficial one that the sciences offer, he relegates to them the entire explanation of external reality. In this

---

(Berlin: K. Vogt, 1962), proposes a transmythologization of biblical myths such as that of the "Powers." Indeed, a myth cannot die inasmuch as it expresses a fundamental fact about human existence—in this case the distressing awareness of an evil that surpasses us. At the time of the New Testament, this fact was expressed in the theme of enslavement by Satan. Today, by virtue of a sort of proportional analogy, we would have to attribute to the major totalitarian, depersonalizing ideologies what the ancients attributed to the "Powers"; see Gérard Siegwalt, *Dogmatique pour la catholicité évangélique: Système mystagogique de la foi chrétienne*, III: L'affirmation de la foi, (2) Cosmologie théologique: Théologie de la création (Paris: Cerf; Geneva: Labor et fides, 2000), 259–62.

27. Bultmann, "New Testament and Mythology," 17.

28. See ibid., 15: "The task, then, is also to interpret the dualistic mythology of the New Testament in existentialist terms. Thus, when the New Testament talks about demonic powers that rule the world and under whose power we human beings have fallen, is there in such talk a view of human existence that offers even to us today, who no longer think mythically, a possibility for understanding ourselves?"

29. See Maurice Corvez, "Chronique bultmanienne," *RT* 56 (1956): 322–52; Siegwalt, *Dogmatique pour la catholicité évangélique*, 256–59.

domain, anything that is not scientific is necessarily mythical. As for faith, it no longer has a handle on the objective world of nature and therefore takes refuge in pure subjectivity. It is reduced to an existential one-on-one between a soul and her Savior. On the other hand—and this may be the reason for the preceding—faith is falsified by the absence of any appropriately ecclesial criterion in the interpretation of scripture. This method is exactly the opposite of the Catholic theologian's approach: the latter must start by noting the normative teaching of the church about the angelic world so as then to apply a hermeneutic of scripture in that decisive light, while prudently incorporating the findings of modern culture.

THE EXISTENCE OF ANGELS AND DEMONS: A REVEALED TRUTH

Indeed, whatever one may think about its appropriateness or even its necessity at the philosophical level, the existence of angels is in the first place, for a Catholic theologian, an article of faith: *Esse angelos novimus ex fide*.[30] We believe that angels exist because God revealed it in the scriptures as the Catholic Church, aided by the spirit of Christ, receives and understands them. Now, despite the serious objections of which it is not unaware, the magisterium persists in teaching that the existence of angels and demons is an integral part of the word of God and must be believed with divine faith.

Having never really been disputed until quite recently, the very existence of angels has not been the object of a solemn definition. Nevertheless, the *Nicene Creed* (325) already proclaims that God is "Creator of ... all things visible and invisible" (*"pantôn horatôn te kai aoratôn poiêtên"*), whereby the "invisible" refer to angels, among other things. The profession of faith *Firmiter* of the Fourth Lateran Council (1215) explains Nicaea somewhat by stating that God, "creator of all visible and invisible things, of the spiritual and of the corporal, ... by His own omnipotent power at once from the beginning of time creat-

---

30. Augustine, *Exposition of Ps. 103* 1.15 (WSA III/19:125): "But we know from our faith that angels exist, and we read of their having appeared to many people. We hold this firmly, and it would be wrong for us to doubt it" (Tamen esse angelos novimus ex fide, et multis apparuisse scriptum legimus, et tenemus, nec inde dubitare fas nobis est).

ed each creature from nothing, spiritual, and corporal, namely, angel-ic and mundane."[31] Even though the primary objective of the conciliar definition is to combat Catharist dualism, its authority seems to guar-antee also the positive part of the confession of faith: the affirmation that God created spiritual creatures. It is not just mentioned as though in passing but is quite plainly taught.[32] In a more recent era, when doubts were already being voiced, Pius XII, in his Encyclical *Humani generis*, denounced as an example of the "poisoned fruits" of the new theological trends the questioning of the personal character of the an-gels.[33] Most importantly, the *Catechism of the Catholic Church* teaches unequivocally that the real existence of the angelic world is not pro-posed to Christians as an option but is an article of faith.[34]

Similarly, given the speculation questioning the personal exis-tence of demons, the Congregation for the Doctrine of the Faith was prompted, in 1975, to recommend "as a sure basis for reaffirming the doctrine of the Magisterium" the study of an anonymous expert on "Christian Faith and Demonology,"[35] which incidentally relies on a teaching of Paul VI:

Evil ... is an active force, a living, spiritual being that is perverted and per-verts.... Anyone who refuses to acknowledge its existence departs from the

31. Denz.-H., 800: "Creator omnium visibilium et invisibilium, spiritualium et cor-poralium: qui sua omnipotenti virtute simul ab initio temporis utramque de nihilo con-didit creaturam, spiritualem et corporalem, angelicam videlicet et mundanam.... Dia-bolus enim et alii daemones a Deo quidem natura sunt creati boni, sed ipsi per se facti sunt mali." Part of this passage was repeated in Vatican Council I, Dogmatic Constitu-tion *Dei Filius* on the Catholic Faith, chap. 1 (Denz.-H., 3002).

32. See Paul M. Quay, "Angels and Demons, the Teaching of IV Lateran," *Theologi-cal Studies* 42 (1981): 20–45. The contrary opinion is held by Charles Meyer, "Les anges et les démons dans la doctrine de l'Église," *Concilium* 103 (1975): 71–79; Schoonenberg, "Osservazioni filosofiche e teologiche," 108–9.

33. Denz.-H., 3891: "The question is also raised by some whether angels are person-al creatures" (Quaestio etiam a nonnullis agitur num angeli creaturae personales sint).

34. CCC, nos. 328–36: "The Angels"; nos. 391–95: "The Fall of the Angels." See also Bonino, "Le Diable dans le *Catéchisme de l'Église catholique*," *Nova et vetera* 74 (1999): 39–49. The CCC takes as its inspiration a series of catecheses during General Audienc-es by John Paul II in the summer of 1986; see John Paul II, *Catéchèses* sur les anges et les demons, DC 83:797–98 [the creation of invisible beings; the angels, free creatures]; 851–53 [the ministry of the angels; angels in salvation history]; 894–97 [the wicked angels; Christ's victory over the spirit of evil].

35. "Foi chrétienne et démonologie," DC 72:708–18. On the teaching of the magis-terium in relation to demons, see also Nanni, *Il dito di Dio e il potere di Satana*, 69–80.

teaching of the Bible and of the Church ... as does anyone who explains it away as a pseudo-reality, as a mental, imaginary personification of the un-known causes of our misfortunes.[36]

This traditional doctrine is repeated again in the recent *Ritual of Exorcisms* (1998). Now liturgical practice constitutes a major testimo-nial to the ordinary magisterium of the church—*lex orandi, lex cre-dendi.*[37]

The church therefore declares authoritatively that sacred scrip-ture teaches the existence of angels and demons. The theologian re-ceives this declaration in faith, but it is also his duty to seek to justify it at the rational level. In order to do that, correct methodology de-mands that he list the passages and themes from scripture that teach specifically about the invisible world—in other words, the passages and themes that would lose their meaning if he were to suppose that the angelic or demonic world did not exist.

Let us start with the demonic world.[38] An initial argument in fa-vor of the revealed character of the existence of demons comes from the massive and historically very-well-attested presence of exorcisms in Jesus' ministry. Now possession cannot be explained away as ill-ness. Besides, Jesus works cures without proceeding by way of an ex-orcism. In fact, the diagnosis of possession, which is supposed by the evangelists and manifested by the text itself,[39] conveys a specifically

36. General Audience, November 15, 1972, Vatican website [translated here from Italian]; cited in French from *DC* 69:1053–54.

37. An in-depth study of the present liturgy of the church would clearly show that the church intends to remind believers faithfully about the existence of angels and de-mons as well as about their role in the combat of Christian life; see Leroy, "L'enseigne-ment dans la liturgie sur l'existence des anges," in *Anges*, 116–17.

38. Emil Brunner, in *Doctrine chrétienne de la création*, maintains, like a good Prot-estant, that the only solid ground for establishing "an ecclesially justified doctrine of the angelic powers" is "the fact that the testimony of Christ Jesus, the Victor, implies as a negative presupposition the existence of a power of superhuman darkness" (155). This demonological assertion, which is connected with the very heart of revelation—in oth-er words, the redemptive work of Jesus Christ—holds in his opinion a certain primacy over angelology, which is only a derivative logical consequence thereof. Whatever con-clusions he may draw from this, Brunner deserves credit for emphasizing how belief in the demons that were conquered by Christ is intrinsically bound up with the New Tes-tament profession of faith, which in fact insists more on the demons than on the angels.

39. Jesus' attitude toward possessed persons is twofold, reflecting the double per-sonality of a possessed individual: he threatens the demon but shows his mercy to the

theological message that means to give a glimpse into the full depth of Christ's action: Jesus is not simply a healer; he is the redeemer. Not an abstract redeemer who liberates man from alienation and selfishness, but a concrete redeemer who snatches man from the power of a malevolent personal enemy. In so doing he inaugurates the Kingdom of God. "If it is by the finger of God that I cast out demons, then the kingdom of God has come upon you" (Lk 11:20).

The second argument is that it is not possible to reduce the opposition between Christ (and his disciples) and the Prince of this world (and his minions)—an opposition that underlies and structures many New Testament passages—to a mere literary staging of the interior combat waged within each human being by good and evil. The cosmic dimension of this combat, which is not on a human scale, although human beings are decisive actors in it, underscores the absolute necessity of fighting under Christ's leadership. If demons were just fictions, St. Paul's statement would lose all its meaning:

For we are not contending against flesh and blood, but against the principalities, against the powers, against the world rulers of this present darkness, against the spiritual hosts of wickedness in the heavenly places. (Eph 6:12)

Concerning the good angels, it is necessary to note first that it was culturally possible to deny their existence (or at least their action in the world), since the biblical authors attribute this view to the Sadducees. Furthermore, the New Testament authors would have had a certain interest in denying their existence. St. Paul, for example, could have refuted the partisans of the cult of the angels by purely and simply denying their existence. The evacuation of the angels would have made it possible to highlight more the central affirmation that Jesus Christ is the one and only mediator. Now something kept him from doing that. Certainly, the soteriological role of the angels was redefined in terms of Christological faith, but their very existence was not called into question.[40]

---

possessed person. This double personality of the possessed individual is manifested also in the supernatural knowledge that gives him a presentiment of Jesus' identity.

40. See Cazelles, "Fondements bibliques," 181–93, which concludes, "The Bible, while demythologizing the polytheism of the ancient world, did not consider mythological the existence of invisible creatures, whether good or bad, who are more powerful than man."

We should add that, in Jesus Christ's teaching, the reality of the angelic world seems altogether necessary in order to establish the realism of the Christian's dignity. Thus Jesus invites his disciples to respect little children *because* their angels see the face of God (Mt 18:10). This is not a figurative way of saying that little children are worthy of respect, but rather an explanation that claims to give the reason or the efficacious sign of their dignity.

WHAT IS AT STAKE IN AFFIRMING THE EXISTENCE OF THE INVISIBLE CREATED WORLD

One of the major objections to the angelological doctrine of the Catholic Church is its uselessness. What good is it? Whether or not there are angels and demons changes nothing in a Christian's everyday life. But this sort of reflection is paradoxically the sign of the urgent need for an angelological doctrine. Indeed, it starts from the principle—which we already encountered in the writings of Hobbes and Spinoza—that revelation has a purely practical purpose; that it comes down to a form of orthopraxis. Now this reductive approach is unacceptable. Revelation or *sacra doctrina* is an apprenticeship in the eternal life that essentially consists of "knowing you, the only true God" (see Jn 17:3). It is a foretaste of contemplative beatitude, a participation in the knowledge by which God knows himself and knows all things. The knowledge about angels included in revelation is therefore like a fortunate anticipation and a pledge of that total knowledge of the universe in God that will be given to us fully and additionally in the beatific vision.

Yet, even on the existential, practical level, we will not readily concede the uselessness of preaching about angels and demons.[41] It ap-

41. See John Paul II, General Audience, August 6, 1986, DC 4 (1986): 852: "The theme that we just spoke about may seem 'remote' or even 'less vitally important' to the mindset of modern man. However the Church, in frankly proposing the totality of the truth about God, the Creator of the angels as well, is certain that she is rendering a great service to mankind." Concerning the stakes, see Arturo Blanco, "Angeli: Il senso della fede cristiana negli angeli in una cultura scientifica e tecnologica," in *Dizionario interdisciplinare di scienza e fede* (Vatican City: Urbaniana University Press; Rome: Città Nuova, 2002), 1:79–82.

pears, on the contrary, to be an excellent antidote to certain insidious temptations in today's atmosphere that sap the vitality of Christian life.

The angels, as everyone knows, were banished from our daily life by the hegemonic development of a culture in which the success of technological reason has discredited the other dimensions of the life of the mind. A certain brand of Christianity thought that it had to resign itself to this trend by relinquishing the cosmos to the sciences and refocusing the faith anthropologically, essentially on morality. This strategy of compromise overlooks the totalitarian character of the technocratic ideology; today, evidently, it is quite logically turning against man himself so as to reduce him to what it can apprehend and manipulate: his material component.

In this context, the church's preaching on angels has a liberating value, and it is a safe bet (without any risk of someone taking us up on it) that if the nationally approved curriculum called for as many hours in angelology as in earth sciences, the cultural climate would be more favorable to the development of an authentic humanism. By setting the absolute primacy of the spirit in sharp relief against matter, angelology returns man to his true dimension, which depends on his spiritual component. In a certain sense, it protects his dignity and his mystery. "Angels," Peterson writes, "are more than poetic extras from the repertoire of folk-lore. . . . They represent for us a possibility in our own nature, an enhancement and intensification of our being."[42] The angel is man's future. In particular, the consideration of angelic life is, for contemporary man, an invitation to rediscover the fullness of an intellectual life, of which the objectifying rationality and technology are only one very limited aspect.[43]

The reacquisition of a broad, metaphysical, and religious view of reality would also make it possible to break out of the anthropological confinement of a certain brand of contemporary theology. Taking angels seriously means avoiding the risk (which is inherent in the one-on-one between man and God) of favoring anthropological or psychologizing categories exclusively in approaching the mystery of God, even though they are much more narrow and ambiguous than

---

42. Peterson, *Angels and the Liturgy*, 47.

43. See Servais Pinckaers, "Les anges, garants de l'expérience spirituelle selon saint Thomas d'Aquin," *Revue Théologique de Lugano* 1 (1996): 179–92.

the universal categories of metaphysics, which embrace the physical order as well as the spiritual order.

And even our perspective on nature would be re-enchanted by a theology that is attentive to the existence of angels. I do not claim that it is necessary to force oneself to experience psychologically the immediacy of the angelic presence. This type of immediate, naïve relation to the supernatural has become difficult for us, if not impossible. Attention to angels depends instead on a faith-based, reflexive reinterpretation of existence. But our intellect has everything to gain in discerning the presence and the activity of spirit in the overall intelligible structure of the universe.

On the more immediately theological level, two things at stake in angelology are worth highlighting. First, the role played by the angels in salvation history broadens our vision of the communion of saints and reinforces a sense of the social, cosmic dimension of Christian life. Second, the reality of a glorified angelic world—"innumerable angels in festal gathering" (Hb 12:22)—which is the holiest part of the church, testifies that the Kingdom of God is not a utopia. It is the kingdom of heaven, the Kingdom already at work, the created glory of God, which mankind does not so much have to build as it has to receive. It is a matter of entering into the Kingdom prepared for us. And so we pray that the will of our Father may be done on earth as it is already done in heaven by the holy angels.

Now what about preaching on the devil? The stakes here are essentially moral. It recalls three things. First, the moral life of every spiritual being exhibits a dramatic character—with the possibility of eternal damnation, which was concretely realized in the case of the demons. Second, this combat has a social and even a cosmic dimension: the moral and religious adventure of every human life is woven into a story, a drama that extends much farther than the personal stories or even the collective history of mankind. Third, man is not equal to this combat.

Some raise the objection that belief in the devil has a disastrous moral effect, since it dispossesses a human being of his responsibility. Sometimes it exonerates excessively, while other times it paralyzes. It exonerates excessively when responsibility for evil is shifted from human freedom to a strange power. "That wasn't me; that was the devil!" Certainly, everyone recognizes that in many respects evil is prior to my free-will decision. But even there this evil is a human evil. This is the "sin of the world"—in other words, the result of the social objectification of bad personal initiatives. In short, "evil is not something outside of human society: it comes entirely from man. Satan would be a way of escaping culpability. He would shoulder the responsibility that humanity collectively refuses to take. He is the figure who reassures me that my own freedom is not perverse."[44] This would make Satan like the God of Feuerbach: we would be dealing with an illusory idol that feeds on the positive (in God's case) or negative attributes (in the devil's case) that belong by right to humanity as such but that individuals refuse to take upon themselves and instead project on the idol. What is more, belief in the existence of the devil paralyzes moral effort by the suggestion of a disproportion between the power of that wicked personal force and our own moral strength.

To this we reply that the church has always taught that, whatever external factors may incline us to moral evil, not one of them is compulsory: however great the influence of external factors, sin has its origin in the free choice of the human will, which bears the entire responsibility for it. It would in fact be Satan's greatest victory to make us believe that we can unburden ourselves of our moral responsibility for sin by blaming it on him. That said, it is true that there is a spiral of sin, for although it is up to me alone to get on the toboggan, once it is launched I no longer have the power to stop. Every time I consent to sin, I alienate my freedom a little more, without ever losing it, however. In this sense, through sin I make myself a stranger to myself; I allow something like a zone of depersonalization to form, which eludes my genuine spiritual interiority and through which I give Satan a hold on me (see Eph 4:27). He suggests, amplifies, and orchestrates my failings until he makes me the slave of his malevolent design, when "I do not do the good that I want, but I do the very evil that I hate" (see Rom 7:15). For sinful man, therefore, there is a certain disproportion in the spiritual combat. But this is an urgent invitation to employ, with the utmost personal responsibility, the means suited to victory: vigilance over ourselves and above all confident recourse to Jesus Christ, who alone can conquer in us the power of the enemy.

44. Duquoc, "Symbole ou réalité? (Satan)," 100. Duquoc does not say whether he subscribes to this argument that he reports against the personal existence of the demon.

PART 2

———— : ————

Angelic Nature

Once the existence of spiritual creatures called angels is recognized, based on revelation and corroborated by metaphysical reflection, what can we say about them? Karl Barth would have wanted theologians to stick to reflecting on the function and the ministry of the angels as scripture presents them. And so he passes a negative judgment on the development that led the fathers of the church to take an interest in the nature of the angels, their "ontology."[1] Nevertheless, the specific movement of the understanding of the faith is what prompts the Christian to investigate, in a manner that is sober yet resolute, the very nature of these beings, and it is not certain that this legitimate interest is as foreign to scripture as one might want to believe. Moreover, this ontological approach, far from competing with the soteriological approach, provides its best foundations: action is explained by being.

What sort of knowledge of angelic nature can we claim to have?

1. Barth, *Church Dogmatics*, part 3, 3:381: "In the Church fathers there is a whole series of similar conceptions which plainly deviate from the Bible and obviously derive their nourishment from another source. Decisive for all that follows is the emergence and the rapid domination of the assumption that it is possible, legitimate and necessary to seek the existence and nature of the angels elsewhere than in their function as God's heavenly messengers. It was under the sway of an alien interest that there was an increasing desire to know about the nature of the angels and an increasing belief that it was possible to know what these beings are in themselves."

Our intellect, programmed here below to know the essences of the material world, has no direct intuition or knowledge about immaterial substances.[2] Yet, starting from the principle that the angels are purely intellectual substances, metaphysical reasoning enlightened by faith can arrive at a certain indirect knowledge of the generic properties of these substances. We apply analogically to the angel what we know about the general metaphysical properties of a created substance and, more precisely, of an intellectual substance. In order to do this, we rely on the knowledge that we have of our own embodied spiritual life,[3] and we elaborate, through comparison and contrast (withholding from the angel whatever in our own spiritual life is intrinsically connected with corporeality), an idea of what the life of a purely spiritual created subject is like. This procedure by no means arrives at the knowledge of the *quid sit* or "quiddity" of the angels—in other words, of the ultimate explanatory principle that would give an account of the personal properties of each angel—but it does provide a general knowledge of the nature common to the angels.[4]

2. See *ST* I, q. 88. In this question St. Thomas opposes, first, the Platonic philosophies that identify angels with universals, the ultimate objects of our abstract knowledge, and, second, the Averroist theory of union with the separated Agent Intellect. Averroës (see *De anima* III, com. 36) claims in effect that at the end of an intellectual process, man can be united to the Agent Intellect that becomes his very form. He would then participate in the knowledge of separated substances that by nature belongs to the Agent Intellect, which is itself a separated substance.

3. See *ST* I, q. 88, a. 1, ad 1.

4. On the nature of our knowledge of the angelic world, see Thomas Cajetan, *In de ente et essentia D. Thomae Aquinatis Commentaria*, c. 6, q. 15, cura et studio P. M.-H. Laurent (Turin: Marietti, 1934), 196–208): "An intelligentiae sint a nobis quidditative cognoscibiles"; Jacques Maritain, *Les degrés du savoir*, in Maritain and Maritain, *Oeuvres complètes* (Fribourg: Editions universitaires; Paris: Editions Saint-Paul, 1983), 4:660–62; English edition *Distinguish to Unite*, 234–36. The knowledge that we have of the angels is not unlike the knowledge that we have of God. In any case, the rules that govern our knowledge of God often reflect the consequences of God's absolute simplicity and therefore cannot be applied as such to our discourse about the angels. In a certain way we are better equipped to speak about the angels than about God.

6

The Metaphysical Status of the Angel

AN ANGEL IS A PURE SPIRIT

Not until the thirteenth century, in particular in the writings of St. Thomas Aquinas, did Christian theology arrive at the clear and distinct affirmation of the pure spirituality of the angels: the angel is an incorporeal, immaterial subject; absolutely no matter enters into its essence.[1] Indeed, such an affirmation presupposes a rather elaborate philosophical concept of what spirit, matter, and corporeality are and of the relations between them.

The Uncertainties of Tradition

Whatever St. Thomas may think about it,[2] the term *spirit* applied to an angel in the Bible is not a direct affirmation of its incorporeal nature. In the qualitative physics of antiquity, in which there are more or less noble bodies, it only signifies that angels are classified with the most

---

1. The spirituality of the angels, understood in the broad sense, in other words as the negation of corporeality as we experience it, is no doubt an article of the faith, but, understood in the strict sense, the spirituality of the angels was never precisely defined by the magisterium (see Leroy, *Anges*, 119–21). Nevertheless, today it is the common teaching of the magisterium and of theology. The CCC speaks of "spiritual, non-corporeal beings" (no. 328) and explains, "As purely *spiritual* creatures angels have intelligence and will: they are personal and immortal creatures" (no. 330).

2. See *ST* I, q. 50, a. 1, sed contra.

dignified parts of the corporeal world, such as wind or fire.³ Nevertheless, a movement toward spiritualization is manifested when the angels are explicitly exempted from the condition of human corporeality: food, sex, and especially death. In very ancient accounts, the angels do not yet refuse to take part in meals,⁴ but the angel of the Lord who appears to the parents of Samson already refuses the food that they offer to him.⁵ Raphael says to his companions, "All these days I merely appeared to you and did not eat or drink, but you were seeing a vision" (Tb 12:19), and the Vulgate explains, "I use an invisible meat and drink, which cannot be seen by men" [Tb 12:19 DV]. The angels have a celestial food: manna, the bread of angels.⁶ Concerning sexuality, the idea of an illicit union between the angels and the daughters of men (Gn 6), the first form assumed by reflection on the sin of the [fallen] angels, seems to imply a certain corporeal character, but at the same time, by the reprobation that it elicits, it indicates that an angel, per se, should not have sexual activity.⁷ In fact the absence of any sexual life among the angels is confirmed by the teaching of Jesus himself: "For when they rise from the dead, they neither marry nor are given in marriage, but are like angels in heaven" (Mk 12:25).

The teaching of the fathers—down to and including St. Augustine—reflects the same perplexities.⁸ "The Fathers seem to have held

3. See Ps 104:4: "[You] make the winds your messengers, fire and flame your ministers."

4. See Gn 18:1–8; 19:3.

5. Jgs 13:15–16: "Manoah said to the angel of the LORD, 'Please, let us detain you, and prepare a kid for you.' (For Manoah did not know that he was the angel of the LORD.) And the angel of the LORD said to Manoah, 'If you detain me, I will not eat of your food; but if you make ready a burnt offering, then offer it to the LORD.'"

6. Ps 78:25; Ws 16:20; 4 Esd 1:19 (Vulg.). In the *Dialogue with Trypho* 57 (PG 6:605 [88–89]), Justin develops this theme of a hidden food by which the angels are nourished.

7. See 1 Henoch 15:6–7 (online ed., English trans. from Ethiopic by Richard Laurence, 1883): "But you from the beginning were made spiritual, possessing a life which is eternal, and not subject to death for ever. Therefore I made not wives for you."

8. See Petau, *Theologica dogmata*, De angelis I, ch. 2–4, 3:607–31; Bareille, "Ange: D'après les Pères; Nature; Spiritualité," *DTC*, 1:1195–1200; Boissard, "La doctrine des anges," 116–19; Palémon Glorieux, *Autour de la spiritualité des anges* (Tournai: Desclée, 1959); Michl, "Ange," 1:88–89; Johann Michl and Theodor Klauser, "Engel: Geistigkeit," *RAC* 5:119–22. On angelic corporeality according to St. Augustine, see *83 questions*, BA 10, supplementary note 46, "Le corps des anges," 728; *La Trinité*, BA 15, supplementary note 25, "Le corps des anges," 580–81; *La Cité de Dieu*, BA 35, supplementary note 21, "Nature des anges selon saint Augustin," 500–2; Madec, "Angelus, 312–14. See Aquinas,

divergent views on the problem," St. Bernard admits with regard to the corporeality of the angels.[9] Indeed, four principal factors disposed the fathers to attribute to angels a certain corporeal character. The first is of a philosophical order. Ancient Latin theology was in certain aspects affected by Stoic materialism, according to which every substance is necessarily a body.[10] Thus Tertullian declares, "Everything which exists is a bodily existence *sui generis* [of its particular genus]. Nothing lacks bodily existence but that which is non-existent."[11] And so he says about the angels that "their nature [is] of a spiritual substance, although in some sense peculiar to themselves, corporeal; and yet they could be transfigured into human shape, and for the time be able to appear ... [to] men."[12]

The second factor is strictly speaking theological. It was necessary to find for the angels an ontological status that shows at the same time their inferiority in relation to God and their superiority in relation to man. A passage from St. Gregory the Great captures this dilemma well: "As [the angels'] very spirits, in comparison indeed with our bodies, are spirits, but being compared with the Supreme, and Incomprehensible Spirit, they are Body."[13] The assertion of a certain corporeality of the angels appeared to be a necessary means of pre-

---

ST I, q. 54, a. 5, ad 1: "those authorities are speaking according to the opinion of such men as contended that angels and demons have bodies naturally united to them. Augustine often makes use of this opinion in his books, although he does not mean to assert it; hence he says (*De Civ. Dei* xxi) that 'such an inquiry does not call for much labor'" (Auctoritates illae loquuntur secundum opinionem illorum qui posuerunt angelos et daemones habere corpora naturaliter sibi unita. Qua opinione frequenter Augustinus in libris suis utitur, licet eam asserere non intendat, unde dicit, XXI de Civ. Dei, quod "super hac inquisitione non est multum laborandum").

9. Bernard of Clairvaux, *On the Song of Songs*, Sermon V, trans. Kilian Walsh, OSCO, (Spencer, Mass.: Cistercian Publications, 1971), 1:29.

10. See Michel Spanneut, "Stoïcisme," in *Catholicisme* (Paris: 1996), 14:470–71, "Le corporéisme des Pères."

11. Tertullian, *Flesh of Christ* XI.4 (ANF 3:531b). Compare, however, the commentary by J.-P. Mahé in SC 217:372, which attenuates Tertullian's alleged materialism.

12. Tertullian, *Flesh of Christ* VI.9 (ANF 3:527a).

13. Gregory the Great, *Morals on The Book of Job* II.3 (Oxford: John Henry Parker, 1844), 1:70: "Sicut et ipsi illorum spiritus comparatione quidem nostrorum corporum, spiritus sunt, sed comparatione summi et incircumscripti spiritus, corpus." See John Damascene, *Orthodox Faith* II.3 (FOTC 37:205): "Now, compared with us, the angel is said to be incorporeal and immaterial, although in comparison with God, who alone is incomparable, everything proves to be gross and material—for only the Divinity is truly immaterial and incorporeal."

serving God's transcendence over every creature. Incorporeality is a divine privilege; God is the only truly incorporeal being. Thus, for example, St. Ambrose: "We however think that nothing is exempt from material composition, with the sole exception of the substance of the adorable Trinity, which is truly pure and simple and of an unaltered, unmixed nature."[14] The angels therefore have a body. But this body is not of the same sort as the human body, because in corporeality itself there are degrees that reflect the hierarchy of beings.[15] The angelic body is more subtle than the human body, which is only flesh. *Corpus, non caro,* says St. Augustine about the angelic body,[16] which sometimes appears as a spiritual, luminous, ethereal body, such as the bodies of men who have attained eternal happiness will be.[17]

The third factor is theological, too: the biblical angelophanies [apparitions of angels] seem to imply that an angel has a certain corporeality that makes him visible and even tangible, according to the requirements of his ministry among men. Moreover, the fathers of the Second Council of Nicaea (787) approved a text by Bishop John of Thessalonica that relies precisely on this corporeality to justify iconographic representations of an angel.[18]

14. Ambrose, *De Abraham libri duo* II.8.58 (PL 14:506) [trans. from Latin]. See Origen, *On First Principles* I.6.4 (New York: Harper Torchbooks, 1966), 57–58. John Cassian, *Conferences* VII.13 (ACW 57:256–57).

15. See Clement of Alexandria, *Extraits de Théodote* 10.1–2 and 14.1–2 (SC 23:76–79 and 86–87).

16. Augustine, *Sermon 362,* 17 (PL 39:1622). See Irenaeus of Lyons, *Against Heresies* III.20.4 (ANF 1:450b): "The angels are without flesh." For Irenaeus this statement has a Christological resonance: unlike the Word who became flesh, the angels, who have no flesh, cannot save the carnal being that is man.

17. See Augustine, *Eighty-Three Different Questions,* q. 47 (FOTC 70:82): "It is necessary to believe that the bodies of angels, such as we hope to have, are completely full of light and are ethereal" [Angelica corpora, qualia nos habituros speramus, lucidissima atque aetherea esse credendum est]. This is probably the same sense in which we must often interpret the statements of several Greek fathers who do not hesitate to describe the angels as incorporeal (*asomatoi*) or immaterial (*ahuloi*). St. Basil, for example, while using these expressions, nevertheless attributes to the angels a substance made of subtle matter. See Basil the Great, *On the Holy Spirit* XVI.38; English trans. Stephen Hildebrand (New York: St. Vladimir's Seminary Press, 2011), 72: "With the heavenly powers, their substance is ethereal spirit, perhaps, or immaterial fire, as it is written: 'He makes his angels spirits, and his ministers flames of fire' [Ps 104:4]. On account of this they have place and became visible, appearing to those who are worthy in the form of bodies proper to them."

18. See Giovan Domenico Mansi, *Sacrorum conciliorum nova et amplissima collectio* (Graz: Akademische Druck- u. Verlagsanstalt, 1960), 13:163–66.

Finally—and this is a fourth factor—the corporeality of the angels was made more probable by the corporeality of the demons, which seemed more certain and was not per se a consequence of sin but a condition of their angelic nature.[19] Thus St. Augustine, in book 8 of *The City of God*, subscribes to Apuleius's idea that the demons are living beings endowed with an "aerial body,"[20] and, in book 21, he acknowledges that the sufferings that fire inflicts on the demons are more easily explained if they are corporeal.[21] It is true that the body of a demon, after sin, became thicker and heavier.

At the end of antiquity, however, some authors attain the higher idea of a strict and absolute spiritual character of the angels. This is the case, in particular, with Dionysius the Areopagite, who describes them as follows:

Such [intelligent] beings owe their presence and their uneclipsed and undiminished lives to these rays [of the Supreme Good], owe them their purification from corruption and from death, from corporeality and from the process of birth. They owe them too their immunity to motion, to flux and to all that goes with change. They are understood as bodiless and immaterial, and as minds they too understand, although in a supra-mundane way.[22]

Dionysius then explains that the corporeal figures attributed to the angels (human figures, fire, wind) are purely metaphorical and are intended to make us understand symbolically certain truths about the angels.[23]

In the Middle Ages, the situation developed very little until the thirteenth century, and most authors, impressed by the authority of St. Augustine, leave the question open.[24] But the thirteenth-century

19. On the corporeality of demons, see Studer, "Démon," in *Dictionnaire encyclopédique du christianisme ancien*, 1:649.

20. See Augustine, *City of God* VIII.16 (FOTC 14:50).

21. See Augustine, *City of God* XXI.10 (FOTC 24:366–67), and in the French edition supplementary note 35: "Les souffrances endurées par les corps des démons" (BA 37:424–29, 785).

22. Dionysius, *The Divine Names*, chap. 4.1, in *Pseudo-Dionysius: The Complete Works*, 72; cited in part by St. Thomas, *ST* I, q. 50, a. 2, c.

23. Dionysius the Areopagite, *Celestial Hierarchy*, chap. 15, 182–91.

24. Peter Lombard, *Sentences* II, d. 8, c. 1–2 (33–36): "Utrum omnes angeli corporei sunt." In his dialogue with Duke Geoffroy, William of Conches explains the arguments of both sides without trying to settle the issue; see L'École de Chartres, Bernard de Chartres, Guillaume de Conches, Thierry de Chartres, and Clarembault d'Arras, *Théologie et*

Scholastics agree in recognizing that an angel (unlike that other spiritual substance, the human soul) is not destined to be united by nature to a body and has no need of a body. St. Bonaventure explains:

In the past great doctors wavered on this question: do angels have bodies that are united to them by nature? That is why both Augustine and Bernard speak about it hesitantly. But now it is held with sufficient certainty—and Richard [of St.-Victor] asserts it—that the angels are incorporeal by nature.[25]

However, this same Bonaventure, following his master, Alexander of Hales, thinks that in order to preserve the transcendence of the divine simplicity and to account for certain properties of the angel, one must admit that in an angel the form enters into composition with some sort of spiritual matter.[26]

Angelic Immateriality according to St. Thomas

It was left to St. Thomas Aquinas to take the decisive step, thanks to a more in-depth understanding of the metaphysical structure of created being, which enabled him to assert the strict spirituality of an angel without thereby attributing to him absolute simplicity, which belongs to God alone.[27]

---

cosmologie au XII siècle, 59–62. St. Bernard wavers: is the angelic body natural or assumed for the occasion? But the Scholastics of the thirteenth century cite him as an advocate of corporeality; see Bernard, *On the Song of Songs*, Sermon 5, 1:25–31, in *ST* I, q. 51, a. 1, arg. 1; Albert the Great, *In II Sent.*, d. 8, a. 1 (167). See Vacant, "Ange: Angélologie dans l'Église latine depuis le temps des Pères jusqu'à saint Thomas d'Aquin, II. XIIᵉ siècle, Spiritualité des anges," *DTC*, 1:1225; Faes de Mottoni, "Discussioni sul corpo dell'angelo nel secolo XII," in *Parva mediaevalia: Studi per Maria Elena Reina* (Trieste: Universit Maria Elena Reinaangelo, 1993), 1–42.

25. Bonaventure, *In II Sent.*, d. 8, a. 1, q. 1 (204): "Circa istam quaestionem dubitaverunt aliquando magni doctores, utrum scilicet angeli habeant corpora naturaliter sibi unita; unde super hoc dubie loquitur tam Augustinus quam Bernardus. Sed nunc satis certitudinaliter tenetur, et Richardus affirmat, quod angeli sunt naturaliter incorporei."

26. See Bonaventure, *In II Sent.*, d. 3, a. 1, q. 1 (79–82); Faes de Mottoni, chap. 3, "Il corpo dell'angelo," in *Bonaventura e la scala di Giacobbe*, 105–63.

27. On the Thomistic critique of universal hylomorphism and its context, see Erich Kleineidam, *Das Problem der hylemorphen Zusammensetzung der geistigen Substanzen im 13. Jahrhundert, behandelt bis Thomas von Aquin* (Breslau: G. Tesch, 1930); Aimé Forest, *La structure métaphysique du concret selon saint Thomas d'Aquin*, Études de philosophie médiévale 14 (Paris: J. Vrin, 1931), chaps. 4 and 5; Odon Lottin, "La composition hylémorphique des substances spirituelles: Les débuts de la controverse," *RNSP* 34 (1932):

He discusses this controversial problem in *ST* I, q. 50, a. 2, and in many parallel passages: "Is an angel composed of matter and form?" as the Franciscan tradition teaches. The objections that Aquinas addresses go to the heart of the problem. The angel belongs to a genus, that of substance; now everything that belongs to a genus possesses some matter in common with the other subjects that fall under the same genus (obj. 1). An angel is passive—in other words, capable of receiving something—and he also plays the role of subject or suppositum [French: *support*] of certain determinations—all of which are properties of matter (obj. 2). If he were pure form, he would be, like God, a pure act since form is act (obj. 3).[28] He would also be infinite because form is limited only by matter (obj. 4).

In his response, Aquinas sets forth and refutes the theory of the partisans of universal hylomorphism, who claim that an angel, like any creature, is composed of matter and form. He connects them to the teaching that the eleventh-century neo-Platonic Jewish philosopher Ibn Gabirol (Avicebron) propagates in his *Fons vitae*:[29] our intellect discerns in incorporeal substance something that it has in common with corporeal substances and something that belongs to it alone and distinguishes it from them. What is common is "matter," and what is proper plays the role of "form." St. Thomas notes (and critiques) the Platonic basis for this reflection. Avicebron wrongly supposes, because of the Platonic parallelism between ontology and logic that projects the structures of the mind onto reality, that everything

21–41; James D. Collins, *The Thomistic Philosophy of the Angels* (Washington, D.C.: The Catholic University of America Press, 1947), 42–75; Fernand Brunner, *Platonisme et aristotélisme: La critique d'Ibn Gabirol par saint Thomas d'Aquin* (Louvain: Publications universitaires de Louvain; Paris: B. Nauwelaerts, 1965); James Weisheipl, "Albertus Magnus and Universal Hylemorphism: Avicebron," in *Albert the Great Commemorative Essays*, edited by Francis J. Kovach and Robert W. Shahan, 239–60 (Norman: University of Oklahoma Press, 1980); María-Pilar Ferrer-Rodríguez, *La inmaterialidad de las substancias separadas: Santo Tomas versus Avicebron* (Pamplona: Servicio de Publicaciones de la Universidad de Navarra, 1988).

28. "Form is act. What is form only is therefore pure act. Now an angel is not pure act, because that pertains to God alone. Therefore an angel is not form solely but has a form in matter" (Forma est actus. Quod ergo est forma tantum, est actus purus. Sed angelus non est actus purus: hoc enim solius Dei est. Ergo non est forma tantum; sed habet formam in materia [*ST* I, q. 50, a. 2, obj. 2]).

29. See Colette Sirat, *La Philosophie juive au Moyen Âge* (Paris: Éditions du Centre national de la recherche scientifique, 1983), 88–104.

of which we have a distinct concept really exists in a distinct state in reality. In fact, our intellect thinks about things not according to the manner of being of those things, but according to its own manner of being. It is thus legitimately led to distinguish intellectually what is only one in reality, especially when it applies itself to thinking about things that are simpler than it is, like an angel or God.

However that may be, Aquinas makes two radical critiques of universal hylomorphism. First, the idea of a matter common to spiritual beings and corporeal beings is contradictory. It supposes that the corporeal form is received in some other part of this common matter than the spiritual form (since two forms of unlike/contrasting [*opposé*] genus cannot inform one and the same matter). Now what allows some matter to be divisible into parts or portions is the accident quantity that extends the substance in space. Consequently, the spiritual form would have to be quantified—in other words, definitively corporeal.

Second, hylomorphism is incompatible with the intellectual nature of angels. Indeed, for St. Thomas, intellectual being implies immateriality, because to know intellectually is to receive, in a way that is immaterial—that is, not particularized—the universal form of the object known. Now in order for a subject to be apt to receive in an immaterial way, it must exist in an immaterial way. Angels—pure intellects—are therefore necessarily devoid of all matter.

If therefore an angel is a pure form, it remains to be demonstrated—and this is the purpose of the responses to the objections—that this lack of hylomorphic composition does not elevate the angel to the same level of simplicity as God. St. Thomas's solution involves the most profound elements of his metaphysics. It consists of bringing to light a potentiality and therefore an "imperfection" in every creature that is even more radical than the one that results from matter. The composition of matter and form is not the only or even the chief composition of potentiality and act in a subject: there is also in every creature a radical composition of essence and existence. It is worthwhile to cite the *ad* 3.

Although there is no composition of *matter* and *form* in an *angel*, yet there is act and *potentiality*. And this can be made evident if we consider the *nature* of material things which contain a twofold composition. The first is that of form and *matter*, whereby the *nature* [*or* essence *or* substance] is constituted. Such a composite *nature* is not its own *existence (esse)* but *existence* is its act. Hence the *nature* itself is related to its own *existence* as *potentiality* to act. Therefore if there be no *matter*, and supposing that the form itself subsists without *matter*, there nevertheless still remains the relation of the form to its very *existence*, as of *potentiality* to act. And such a kind of composition is understood to be in the *angels*.... But in *God "existence"* and *"what is"* are not different, as was explained above (question 3, article 4). Hence *God* alone is *pure act.*[30]

Essence and existence are the two joint principles of every created being (*ens*).[31] The essence is already an act, a determination, a perfection, in its order. As soon as it is actualized by existence, it enables the being to be this or that, to exist according to such and such an intelligible structure: it is that through which and in which the being has existence. Just as, in a general way, every potentiality receives, limits, and multiplies the act, so too essence receives, limits, and mul-

30. *ST* I, q. 50, a. 2, ad 3: "Dicendum quod, licet in angelo non sit compositio formae et materiae, est tamen in eo actus et potentia. Quod quidem manifestum potest esse ex consideratione rerum materialium, in quibus invenitur duplex compositio. Prima quidem, formae et materiae, ex quibus constituitur natura aliqua. Natura autem, sic composita, non est suum esse; sed esse est actus eius. Unde ipsa natura comparatur ad suum esse, sicut potentia ad actum. Subtracta ergo materia, et posito quod ipsa forma subsistat non in materia: adhuc remanet comparatio formae ad ipsum esse, ut potentiae ad actum. Et talis compositio intelligenda est in angelis.... Unde solus Deus est actus purus."

31. The literature on the subject is vast. The reader may consult Marie-Dominique Roland-Gosselin, ed., *Le "De ente et essentia" de s. Thomas d'Aquin,* Texte établi d'après les manuscrits parisiens, introduction, notes et études historiques par Roland-Gosselin (Paris: J. Vrin, 1948) [the essay on the origin and significance of the thesis that there is a real distinction between essence and existence, 135–205, is still a reference work]; Gilson, chap. 3, "L'être et l'existence," in *L'être et l'essence,* 2nd ed. (Paris: J. Vrin, 1972); Gilson, *Thomisme,* esp. 169–89, "une nouvelle ontologie"; English ed. *Thomism: The Philosophy of Thomas Aquinas* (Toronto: Pontifical Institute of Medieval Studies, 2002), esp. 153–74, "A New Ontology"; Jacques Maritain, *Court traité de l'existence et des existants,* chap. 1, in Maritain and Maritain, *Oeuvres complètes,* 9:21–52 (Fribourg [Switzerland]: Editions universitaires; Paris: Editions Saint-Paul, 1991); Joseph de Finance, *Connaissance de l'être: Traité d'ontologie* (Paris and Bruges: Descleé de Brouwer, 1966), 315–43; Leo Elders, chap. 12, "La distinction réelle entre l'être et l'essence," in *La métaphysique de saint Thomas d'Aquin dans une perspective historique* (Paris: J. Vrin, 1994), 195–216; Alain de Libera and Cyrille Michon, eds., *L'être et l'essence: Le vocabulaire médiéval de l'ontologie,* Deux traités de Thomas d'Aquin et Dietrich de Freiberg (Paris: Éditions du Seuil, 1996); John F. Wippel, *The Metaphysical Thought of Thomas Aquinas: From Finite Being to Uncreated Being,* Monographs of the Society for Medieval and Renaissance Philosophy 1 (Washington, D.C.: The Catholic University of America Press, 2000), chap. 5.

tiplies *esse* [existence]: (1) It is the material cause of the *esse* because it receives it; (2) It limits it: if the *esse* were not received, it would be subsistent and would realize the fullness of the perfection of being, which is true only in the case of God, *Ipsum Esse subsistens*; (3) It multiplies it: if the *esse* were not received, it would be unique. Hence if there are several beings, it is because there are several essences. Since the *esse* is what is analogically common to all the beings, in itself it is not a principle of distinction, even though it alone makes real the distinction that comes from the essences.

As for the *esse*, in actualizing the essence, it brings it into a new dimension, that of the existential order, which is irreducible to the order of essences. The *esse* is therefore not situated at the level of the essence; it is not one last essential determination, a supplementary "form." It is a perfection of a different order. Consequently we must say that the *esse* is really distinguished from the essence: it not a property or an emanation thereof, but comes from somewhere else. The *esse* is therefore, according to St. Thomas, the first act of every being. It is that by which the substance and all its determinations or perfections *are*. It is, according to a famous expression, "the actuality of all its acts and, therefore it is the perfection of all its perfections."[32] Or in other words, "Existence is the most perfect of all things, for it is compared to all things as that by which they are made actual; for nothing has *actuality* except so far as it exists. Hence *existence* is that which actuates all things, even their forms. Therefore it is not compared to other things as the receiver is to the received; but rather as the received to the receiver."[33] In this respect, *esse* [existence] is what is deepest in things, the fundamental, radical perfection that is communicated, if I may say so, to all the forms and imbues them with its existentiality.

The discovery of the composition of essence and existence in an angel allows St. Thomas to dispense with the composition of matter and form without any problem. Thanks to this discovery, he can hold at the same time the pure spirituality of an angel, which indicates his

---

32. Aquinas, *Q. de pot.*, q. 7, a. 2, ad 9: "Esse est actualitas omnium actuum et propter hoc est perfectio omnium perfectionum."

33. *ST* I, q. 4, a. 1, ad 3: "Ipsum esse est perfectissimum omnium, comparatur enim ad omnia ut actus. Nihil enim habet actualitatem, nisi inquantum est, unde ipsum esse est actualitas omnium rerum, et etiam ipsarum formarum. Unde non comparatur ad alia sicut recipiens ad receptum, sed magis sicut receptum ad recipiens."

transcendence over man, and the transcendence of God over the angels, since in God alone, *Ipsum Esse subsistens,* existence and essence are really identified.

The composition of essence and existence in an angel also explains why he is not infinite, even though he is not limited by matter. Since Gabriel's *esse* is really distinct from the essence with which it enters into composition, he is limited by it. However, the angel does possess a certain relative infinity, *secundum quid.*

Any immaterial substance is finite in so far as it has existence limited to its own nature, since no created substance, although immaterial, is its own existence, but participates in existence. Nevertheless, it is infinite by reason of the removal of that limitation by which a form is limited by the very fact of its reception into matter.[34]

Relying on a spatial image taken from the *Book of Causes,* St. Thomas sometimes explains that purely spiritual beings are like cones, finite or limited above, because they receive from God a determinate existence, but infinite or unlimited below, because this existence is neither received nor contracted in any matter.[35] Only God, pure Act, is infinite *absolutely speaking,* because in him alone *esse* is not received in an essence, in a nature, and therefore is realized without limit. That is why his power is infinite and is the only power to be so.[36]

The Relation between an Angel and a Body

Questions 51 through 53 of the first part of the *Summa* discuss in some detail the relations between immaterial angelic nature and bodies and their properties. Despite allusions to the cosmological theme of an-

34. *Q. de ver.,* q. 20, a. 4, ad 1: "Quaelibet substantia immaterialis, est quidem finita in quantum habet esse limitatum ad propriam naturam, eo quod nulla creata substantia, quamvis immaterialis, est esse suum, sed esse participat: est tamen infinita per remotionem illius terminationis secundum quam forma terminatur ex hoc ipso quod in materia recipitur, cum omne receptum sit in recipiente secundum modum recipientis"; cited in English from Aquinas, *The Disputed Questions on Truth,* trans. James V. McGlynn (Chicago: Henry Regnery, 1953), 2:415.

35. See, for example, *ST* I, q. 50, a. 2, ad 4. Compare *Le Liber de causis,* édition établie à l'aide de 90 manuscrits, avec introduction et notes par A. Pattin (Louvain: n.d.), xv (xvi).131, p. 81; Pierre Magnard, Olivier Boulnois, Bruno Pinchard, and Jean-Luc Solère, *La demeure de l'être: Autour d'un anonyme,* Étude et traduction du *Liber de Causis,* Philologie et Mercure (Paris: J. Vrin, 1990), 62–65.

36. See *ST* I, q. 25, a. 2, which is explicitly dependent on I, q. 7.

gels ruling the heavenly bodies, it is primarily a matter of accounting for the "angelophanies" or angelic manifestations in the Bible. Indeed, St. Thomas thinks that some angelic apparitions, in particular those that are seen by several persons, cannot be reduced to interior prophetic revelations.[37] These objective apparitions imply a manifestation of a corporeal order. Since an angel is not a body (like a stone or a tree) and has no body either that is united to him by nature (like man), the remaining possibility is that an angel sometimes *assumes* a body.[38] Not because he needs it in order to be what he is, but out of condescension, so as to carry out a mission among men. According to The Common Doctor, an angel forms for himself an *ad hoc* body by condensing the air, which then assumes shape and color, as clouds do.[39] The angel's union to this body is not of the type of close union between form and matter. It is rather on the order of the operative union between a mover and a thing moved. But not every union of this type is an assumption (we do not say that a child assumes the hoop that he rolls). It is also necessary for the thing moved to represent the mover: the body that is assumed signifies something about the angel who moves it.[40] This body is therefore a sort of sacrament of the angelic presence.

A body assumed by an angel is moved externally, not animated from within, and so it is not a living body. Yet, as the purpose requires, it can artificially imitate certain vital operations, such as displacement or phonation (producing sounds), along the lines of what these operations have in common with the movements of inanimate bodies.[41] But vital activities per se (feeding, reproducing) are impossible for these assumed bodies.[42]

37. See *ST* I, q. 51, a. 2, corpus.

38. St. Augustine poses the question about the body in which angels appear in *Trinity* II.7.13 (FOTC 45:67) and III.1.4–5 (FOTC 45:98–99). He says that he is unable to decide whether, in angelophanies, the angels borrow a material body from inferior beings or transform their own bodies at will. Peter Lombard addresses the question, relying on the Augustinian passages, in *Sentences* II, d. 8, c. 2 (367–68).

39. See *ST* I, q. 51, a. 2, ad 3.

40. See *ST* I, q. 51, a. 2, ad 2.

41. See *ST* I, q. 51, a. 3. This speculation opens up interesting perspectives on the philosophical question about a mechanical man. To what extent can a robot imitate a human being? See *L'Eve future*, by Auguste, comte de Villiers de L'Isle-Adam (Paris: M. de Brunhoff, *1886*).

42. The reader will take *cum grano salis* [with a grain of salt] the ingenious descrip-

It is the nature of a body to be situated in a place. Place, in Aristotelian physics, is a very concrete notion that must not be confused with space, which is a mathematical abstraction. Place is defined as "the limit within which a body is"—in other words, the external surface of a body that immediately surrounds or contains such and such an object. Thus the place of a fish is that portion of the water with which it is in actual contact according to its dimensional quantity.[43] An angel, being incorporeal, cannot be situated in a place in the same way as a body is localized.[44] However, as St. Thomas already explained in reference to God, an incorporeal being is present, by dint of a virtual contact, wherever it acts.[45] Thus an angel (or a demon) is present to the corporeal substance to which he applies his causality, not as though he were contained in that corporeal reality but rather as that which somehow contains it.

Since God is the cause of the universal perfection of *esse*, he is present everywhere. In contrast, since an angel's power of causal action is shared and created, and therefore limited, an angel can act only on a determinate reality that is the subject of his immediate action. If this subject is a composite whole (for example, the people of France), then the angel is in several places, inasmuch as these places are one from a certain point of view.[46] On the other hand, there is no danger of congested traffic! Several angels cannot be in the same place at the same time.[47] Indeed, if God and an angel can act and be in one and the same place, this is because their actions are not competitive: the angel's causality is subordinate to the transcendent causality of the First Cause. In contrast, since the causality of angel A and that of an-

tion of ways in which a real human child can be born from the relations of an incubus demon and a woman (*ST* I, q. 51, a. 3 and 5).

43. About place, see Aristotle, *Physics* IV.4. Compare John of St.-Thomas, "De loco et ubi," in *Cursus philosophicus* II, q. 16, 335–60; Henri-Dominique Gardeil, *Initiation à la philosophie de saint Thomas d'Aquin*, vol. 2, *Cosmologie* (Paris: Cerf, 1953), 67–74.

44. St. Thomas discusses the localization of the angels in the three articles of *ST* I, q. 52. The fundamental text on the question of the localization of angels is John Damascene, *Orthodox Faith* I.13 (FOTC 37:197–201). The subject was debated in the Middle Ages; see the few references to Scholastic authors made by Philip L. Reynolds, *Food and the Body: Some Peculiar Questions in High Medieval Theology*, Studien und Texte zur Geistesgeschichte des Mittelalters 69 (Leiden, Boston, and Cologne: E. J. Brill, 1999), 183n38.

45. See *ST* I, q. 8, a. 1.   46. See *ST* I, q. 52, a. 2.
47. See *ST* I, q. 52, a. 3.

gel B are situated on the same level of categorical causes, it is impossible for both of them to act as an immediate cause on one and the same subject, which is required for angelic presence in a place.

Question 53 addresses a problem that would be debated passionately by the theoreticians of late medieval physics: the displacement of an angel (not of the body that he assumes but rather his own).[48] Since an angel is not in a place in the same manner as a body is, his displacement—his passage from one place to another—is not of the same type as that of a body. In particular, the translation of a body is continuous, in the sense that a moving thing must pass through all the points between A and B, whereas the displacement of an angel is discontinuous, discrete. It designates the successive (causal) contact of the angel with several distinct places.[49] By reason of its successive character, this angelic displacement implies the existence of a time belonging specifically to angels, which is not our cosmic time and does not depend on it any more than angelic movement depends on the movements of celestial bodies.[50]

TWO CONSEQUENCES OF IMMATERIALITY

The immateriality of an angel involves two remarkable properties. First of all, contrary to the rather common opinion that all the angels, or at least all those of a certain order, belong to the same species, Thomas Aquinas asserts that each angel is unique in his species.[51] This Thomistic thesis caused a scandal in his day, so much so that it was condemned by the bishop of Paris in March 1277.[52] It follows inevitably, however,

---

48. See J. J. MacIntosh, "St. Thomas on Angelic Time and Motion," *Thomist* 59 (1995): 547–75.

49. See *ST* I, q. 53, a. 1: "Motus angeli in loco nihil aliud [est] quam diversi contactus diversorum locorum successive et non simul, quia angelus non potest simul esse in pluribus locis."

50. See *ST* I, q. 53, a. 3.

51. See *ST* I, q. 50, a. 4 and the numerous parallel passages. Compare Rega Wood, "Angelical Individuation according to Richard Rufus, St. Bonaventure, and Thomas Aquinas," in *Individuum und Individualität im Mittelalter*, edited by Jan A. Aertsen and Andreas Speer, MM 24, 209–29 (Berlin and New York: Walter de Gruyter, 1996).

52. See *La condamnation parisienne de 1277*, Latin text, trans., introduction, and commentary David Piché (Paris: J. Vrin, 1999), 104: "81 (43). Quod, quia intelligentie non habent materiam, Deus non posset plures ejusdem speciei facere" [That, because

from the encounter between the thesis of the absolute immateriality of an angel and the Aristotelian doctrine of individuation by quantified matter.[53] A species is the most determinate, particularized intelligible type that there is, a sort of intelligible individual (the genus *animal*, for example, is an intelligible type that is capable of being further determined, divided, and specified, precisely by the species). In the corporeal world of generation and corruption, the species is generally realized in a plurality of individuals—*in-dividuum*: that which cannot be further divided—of which the intelligible properties are therefore identical. Consequently, the multiplicity of individuals within a species is not explained by something dependent on the order of the form. If the species is multiplied, it is rather because the same specific form is received in two distinct quantified portions of matter. The cast for the bust of Napoleon is unique, but there are many statues of Napoleon and therefore several individual forms because the model of the cast is received in different portions of matter.

Now the difference between two angelic individuals, Gabriel and Raphael, for example, cannot come from matter, since both are immaterial. Therefore it comes from their form. By his very form, his intelligible type, one angel is distinguished from another. Each angel is, therefore, a unique species unto himself. Gabriel is distinguished specifically from Raphael as dogs are distinguished from cats, and not as Fido is distinguished from Fifi. Indeed, the plurality of individuals in a corporeal species is not in itself a perfection, but rather a trick of nature to mitigate an imperfection: no individual is capable of realizing in himself all the perfection of the species. In contrast, Gabriel fulfills and exhausts this degree of unique being, this unprecedented manner of participating in the divine all-perfection that is gabrielness.[54] For

---

intellects have no matter, God cannot make several of the same species]; and "96 (42). Quod Deus non potest multiplicare individua sub una specie sine materia" [That God cannot multiply individuals of one species without matter]." Compare Wippel, "Thomas Aquinas and the Condemnation of 1277," *The Modern Schoolman* 72 (1995): 239–48, esp. 243–48. On the initial reception of the condemnation of this thesis, see Wippel, *The Metaphysical Thought of Godfrey of Fontaines: A Study in Late Thirteenth-Century Philosophy* (Washington, D.C.: The Catholic University of America Press, 1981), 366–69.

53. On the Thomistic theory of individuation, see Roland-Gosselin, "Le Principe de l'individualité," in *Le "De ente et essentia" de s. Thomas d'Aquin*, 104–26; Wippel, *Metaphysical Thought of Thomas Aquinas*, 351–75, with the bibliography of 352n205.

54. One should not conclude too hastily from this that the angelic subject is identi-

St. Thomas this is one way of exalting the personal dignity of each angel, who was willed directly by God to manifest a definite aspect of his own glory.

The second consequence of an angel's immateriality is his incorruptibility and, therefore, his immortality.[55] Here St. Thomas accounts theologically for a well-established datum of tradition.[56] Cor-

---

cal to his nature. On this question about the relations between the nature and the *suppositum* or concrete subject among spiritual beings, pure forms, St. Thomas's thought underwent a development. In the *Prima Pars* of the *Summa theologiae* (1266–68), the distinction *suppositum-natura* is presented as belonging to corporeal substances, so that St. Thomas deduces immediately from incorporeality the real identity of *suppositum* and nature in all spiritual beings: God is by identity his Deity and Gabriel is his gabrielness. But later on, and especially in the *Quodl.* II, q. 2, a. 2 (later 1269), Aquinas extends to all creatures the distinction between nature and *suppositum*. In the meantime he had understood that this distinction does not result primarily from the composition of form and matter, but, more profoundly, from the composition of essence and existence. There is a distinction between the *suppositum* and the nature in every being in which there is more in the concrete subject than what belongs by right to its essence. This is obviously the case for material beings, in which the shaped matter is added to the essence. But it is also the case for spiritual creatures, because in them existence (*esse*) does not belong per se to their essence. It does not follow from it. Therefore there is more in this subject who is an angel than his mere essence; there is his existence and also a certain number of spiritual accidents (this act of will or that act of intellection). Only God is absolutely identical to his Deity, because in him essence and existence are identified by the fact that he is the Subsistent Being.

55. See *ST* I, q. 50, a. 5.

56. St. Augustine insists on the natural immortality of an angel, which distinguishes him from man. See *City of God* XIII.1 (FOTC 14:299): "God did not endow man with the same nature that He gave to the angels—who could not possibly die even if they sinned." This theological conviction was supported by Apuleius's definition of demons as beings that are "eternal [as to time] (*tempore aeterna*)"; see Augustine, *City of God* IX.8 (FOTC 14:89–90). Some fathers of the church, however, not having a sufficiently clear concept of the distinction between nature and grace, identify immortality with a gift of grace and consequently refuse to attribute it by nature to creatures. See Petau, chap. 5, "De Angelorum immortalitate," in *Theologica dogmata*, De angelis I, 3:631–36. See, for example, Ambrose, *De Fide ad Gratianum* III.3, ed. Otto Faller (CSEL 78:114–16): "The immortality of divine nature is one thing, and that of our nature is something different. For fragile things should not be compared to divine realities. There is only one substance, God's, which cannot die. And so the Apostle, while he knew that the soul and the angel are immortal, preached that 'God alone has immortality.' For the soul dies also.... And the angel is not immortal by nature, since his immortality depends on the Creator's will" (Sed alia est immortalitas suae naturae, alia nostrae. Non sunt fragilia conparanda divinis. Una sola substantia divinitatis est, quae mori nescit. Unde et apostolus, cum sciret et animam et angelos immortales, quod "solus Deus immortalitatem habeat" [1 Tm 6:16] praedicavit. Nam et anima moritur.... Nec angelus immortalis est naturaliter, cuius immortalitas in voluntate est creatoris).

ruption is the disappearance of a substance. In the world of bodies, it occurs when the substantial form no longer succeeds in unifying and actualizing the matter and the dispositions of the latter no longer correspond to the requirements of the form (the material dispositions of a frog under a steamroller no longer allow the exercise of its vital functions). In this case the *esse*, which is the act not of the form as such but of the matter-form composite, as well as the form itself, which had being only as a joint principle, disappear. In the case of an angel, who is a pure form, the *esse* directly actualizes the form and therefore can never be separated from it, except by pure and simple annihilation, if God were to cease communicating its *esse*. The angel is by nature immortal.

THE STATUS OF ACTION IN AN ANGEL

After considering "what pertains to the angel's substance,"[57] St. Thomas Aquinas, from question 54 on, discusses his action. He does not devote a special question to the status of angelic action in general but rather considers right away the two major activities of the angel, which are those of every spirit: intellectual knowledge and love. However, his exposition on knowledge in an angel, like the one on love, includes a metaphysical reflection on the articulation of the principles of being and the principles of action in the angel.[58]

For us, simply to be is one thing, and to act—in other words, to exercise in act an immanent or transitive operation—is something else.[59] For example, I exist in act as a spiritual being even though while asleep I do not exercise any sort of spiritual activity: I do not think, I do not will, but that does not mean that I disappear! Action is therefore something different from being: it is accidental in relation to the subject. But we must not exaggerate this distinction between being and action be-

57. Prologue to *ST* I, q. 54.

58. See *ST* I, q. 54 (especially aa. 1–3) and q. 59 (esp. a. 2). The reader will note that in resolving the first three articles of q. 54, St. Thomas explicitly points out that these conclusions are valid for all creatures and not just for angels.

59. The classic study on this topic is de Finance, *Être et agir dans la philosophie de saint Thomas*, 2nd ed. (Rome: Presses de l'Université Grégorienne, 1960); see also Yves Simon, chap. 2, "Cognition and Activity," in *Introduction to the Ontology of Knowledge* (New York: Fordham University Press, 1990), 39–84.

cause, in the final analysis, to be and to act are two perfections that are inscribed along the same line, the line of act. We are dealing with two degrees of actuality. To be and to act are not two irreducible perfections that develop along nonintersecting lines (as, in the case of a professor, his waistline and his pedagogical competence). On the contrary, the distinction between them results, as we will explain, from the imperfection of the creature. The distinction is reabsorbed in God who is pure subsistent Action; in other words, his very being is to act.

What constitutes a thing in the order of being (we say, "what constitutes it in its first act") is its substantial form, which is itself actualized by the act of being. For example, the soul, the substantial form, is the first act of a human being, that by which he exists purely and simply as a human being. This substantial form is also the source from which proceed the specific capacities to act (*virtues*, powers, faculties) that his vital, animal, and spiritual functions exercise. But once constituted in his first act, the subject remains in potentiality in relation to the operations of these faculties. In order to proceed to an act, in order to act, he must again integrate an additional measure of actuality, which is accidental in relation to the actuality provided by the substantial form. He must pass from the first act to the second act.

Thus, for every being that is not Pure Act, which means in fact for every creature and hence for the angel, action is really distinct from substance.[60] Even if he is always actually thinking, an angel is not identical to his act of thought. If that were the case, he would be pure, subsistent, unique, and perfect intellection. In short, he would be God. If it is not identified with his essence, is the angel's act of thinking or loving then identified with his *esse*?[61] St. Thomas considers that impossible, too, because intellection and volition are operations that can be extended to infinity: by intellection the intellect can know all truth, become every thing, and by volition the will can adhere to all good. Now the *actus essendi* [act of existence] of an angel is determined, limited, finite, because it is received in an essence. Therefore it cannot be identified with the angelic action.[62]

60. See *ST* I, q. 54, a. 1.
61. See *ST* I, q. 54, a. 2.
62. According to an idea that Aquinas is fond of, the ontological limitation inherent in creatures is somehow compensated for by the transcendental openness of their spiritual action. By knowledge and love, the spiritual creature goes beyond his own ontologi-

One consequence of the nonidentity of being and action in an angel is the necessity of acknowledging a certain multiplicity in angelic action: with an angel there are several actions that follow one another. Now, to speak of succession is to speak of temporality. Of course the being of an angel, unlike the being of corruptible substances, is not per se subject to change, nor therefore to time. His action, though, is characterized by a succession of spiritual acts, so that the angel is indirectly subject to time. The duration proper to this type of being is *aevum*.[63] With respect to his being, therefore, an angel is measured by *aevum*, but his action is measured by time, even though that time is not cosmological time.[64]

St. Thomas continues his inquiry into the ontological status of the instances [i.e., stages] of angelic action by showing that the angel's intellect is really distinct from his essence.[65] Indeed, in every creature there is, in the order of action, an intermediary instance that is really and simultaneously distinct from the subject and from its actions: the operative power or faculty—in other words, the stable principle of a determined form of action—for example, the intellect or the will. It is not difficult to grasp that the intellect is really distinct from the act of thinking: a human being permanently has the capacity to think but does not always exercise it. As for the angel, even though he is always thinking, his acts of intellection vary according to their object, whereas the intellective power remains the same—proof that these two instances [stages] can be distinguished. It is perhaps more difficult to

---

cal limits. Moreover, on the supernatural level, is it not through knowledge and love that we "become God"?

63. See *ST* I, q. 10, a. 5 and 6. Answer 6 suggests that the *aevum* of the simplest angel serves as a reference for the *aevum* of all angels. Compare Pasquale Porro, "Aevum," in *Dictionnaire du Moyen Âge*, edited by Claude Gauvard, Alain de Libera, and Michel Zink, 12–14 (with bibliography) (Paris: Quadrige and PUF, 2002).

64. See *ST* I, q. 57, a. 3, ad 2: "Although the angel's intellect is above that time according to which corporeal movements are reckoned, yet there is a time in his mind according to the succession of intelligible concepts; of which Augustine says (*Gen. ad lit.* VIII) that 'God moves the spiritual creature according to time'" (Licet intellectus angeli sit supra tempus quo mensurantur corporales motus, est tamen in intellectu angeli tempus secundum successionem intelligibilium conceptionum; secundum quod dicit Augustinus, VII *super Gen. ad litt.*, quod "Deus movet spiritualem creaturam per tempus").

65. See *ST* I, q. 54, a. 3. Compare Alfred Wilder, "St. Thomas and the Real Distinction of the Potencies of the Soul from its Substance," in *L'anima nell'antropologia di s. Tommaso d'Aquino*, Studia Universitatis s. Thomae in Urbe 28 (Milan: Massimo, 1987), 431–54.

show that every operative power is really distinct from the essence of the subject, although that power necessarily proceeds from it, as a proper accident (as soon as there is an angelic essence there is an angelic intellect).[66] St. Thomas deduces this here from the preceding argument—namely, the distinction between being and operation in an angel. Every power is defined by an act. The act in relation to which essence is defined is *esse* [existence]. The act in relation to which the intellective power is defined is intellection. Now, intellection is really distinct from the act of being. The powers that are defined in relation to these two distinct acts are therefore distinct also: the intellect of an angel is really distinct from the essence of an angel.

What remains to be seen now is the profound reason for these distinctions between substance, operative power, and action itself. In fact this reason manifests the participated, created character of creaturely being. Being, essence, the faculties, and action coincide absolutely in God alone. As they enter into the created order, these instances [steps] are differentiated and multiplied: existence and essence, essence and faculties, faculties and actions. Although the study of *the manner* in which an angel thinks and loves sets him in stark contrast with man, the study of the principles of his action clearly assigns the angel to the position of a creature—in other words, of one who has being by participation, whose *esse* [existence] is distinct from his essence.

66. On the way in which a pure form like an angel can be the subject of an accident, see *ST* I, q. 54, a. 3, ad 2.

7

The Natural Knowledge of the Angels

There are two sides to angelic action. First, the angel exercises an immanent activity—in other words, an activity that perfects and enriches the subject himself. This immanent activity unfolds according to the two irreducible axes/dimensions of all spiritual life: knowledge (this chapter)[1] and love (chapter 8). And so the two highest angelic orders are designated in terms of their excellence in these two activities: the seraphim, or "the burning, the ardent ones," are characterized by the excess of their love, and the cherubim by *plenitudo scientiae*—by the excellence of their knowledge. But then the angel exercises a transitive activity—in other words, an action that aims to transform or perfect a reality external to himself.

Knowledge is a perfection that could be called semi-transcendental. It is one aspect of the perfection of the being that (unlike the transcendentals properly so-called, which are strictly coextensive with being) appears and flourishes within beings only as a result of a certain level of actuality—as is also the case with life, the highest expres-

---

1. Besides the Scholastic commentaries on *In II Sent.*, d. 3 and *ST* I, q. 54–58, see Wilhem Schlössinger, "Die Erkenntnis der Engeln," *Jahrbuch für Philosophie und Theologie* 22 (1908): 325–49, 492–519; 23 (1909): 45–84, 198–230, 274–315; Leroy, *Anges*, 148–59; Nicolas, Connaissance chez l'ange," 289–97; Chrétien, "La connaissance angélique," 125–39; Suarez-Nani, "La connaissance des anges selon St. Thomas d'Aquin," in *Connaissance*, 17–75 [a systematic commentary on qq. 54–58 of the *Prima pars*]. For the parallel passages, the reader may consult especially *Q. de ver.*, q. 8: *De cognitione angelorum*.

sion of which is knowledge. To know is the vital operation by which a subject "becomes the other as other," according to the famous expression of John of St. Thomas. In knowing, the subject participates in the perfections proper to the object. He assimilates them and is enriched thereby. He makes them exist in him in an absolutely original manner, conferring on them an existence different from their natural existence (my brain does not burn when it thinks about fire!), which we call intentional existence.[2]

Thus the knowing subject is like a mirror or a synthesizing center that interiorizes what is real and recomposes in itself the perfections that are otherwise dispersed in the universe. In doing so he pursues a process of becoming like God: he tends to imitate God, in whom the entire set of the perfections that are realized piecemeal in the universe exist in the most perfectly unified manner.[3] And so in every creature—and therefore in an angel—knowledge is a way of expanding oneself, of surpassing the ontological finitude proper to creatures so as to be opened up to the infinite.[4]

2. St. Thomas often points out, following Averroës, that the forms of things are received in different ways in the intellect and in matter (see *Q. de ver.*, q. 2, a. 2). Indeed, the form received in matter is united with it to form with it a *tertium quid*, a third reality, whereas knowledge respects the substantial integrity both of the subject and of the object. If they are now one, it is in some other order than the substantial order. To describe this very special mode of reception that is proper to knowledge, St. Thomas speaks about "immaterial" reception. More precisely, we say that the object's mode of being *sui generis* in the subject is an "intentional" mode of being. Thus, with regard to sensible knowledge, St. Thomas writes that "the form has a different mode of being in the sense and in the sensible reality. In the sensible reality, it has a natural being, whereas in the sense it has a spiritual or intentional being (Alterius modi esse habet forma in sensu et in re sensibile: nam in re sensibile habet esse naturale, in sensu autem habet esse intentionale sive spirituale)" (*In De anima* II.24.169). In the note that accompanies the latter passage, Fr. Gauthier points out that the expression "intentional being," which is of Arabic origin, hardly ever appears at the Faculty of the Arts in Paris until 1250. Intentional being is thus contrasted to natural being. The opposition occurs frequently in the works of St. Thomas. See *In IV Sent.*, d. 44, q. 2, a. 1, qla 3, arg. 2 (1084), and ad 2 (1086); *Q. de ver.*, q. 22, a. 3, ad 4.

3. See *ST* I, q. 80, a. 1: "The soul of man is, in a way, all things by sense and intellect: and thereby, those things that have knowledge, in a way, approach to a likeness to God, 'in Whom all things pre-exist,' as Dionysius says (*Div. Nom.* v)" (Anima hominis [est] omnia quodammodo secundum sensum et intellectum: in quo quodammodo cognitionem habentia ad Dei similitudinem appropinquant, 'in quo omnia praeexistunt,' sicut Dionysius dicit).

4. St. Thomas does not hesitate to speak about knowledge as a "remedy" (*Q. de*

This movement finds its unexpected accomplishment in the supernatural order, in the beatific vision of God. And so the theologian distinguishes two types of knowledge in the good angels:

> There is a twofold *knowledge* in the *angel*. The first is his *natural knowledge*, according to which he *knows* things both by his *essence*, and by innate *species*.... There is another *knowledge* of the *angels*, which renders them *happy*; it is the *knowledge* whereby they see the Word, and things in the Word.[5]

In this chapter we consider only the *natural* knowledge of an angel—in other words, the knowledge that he exercises by virtue of the operative principles of his nature, prescinding from the principles of knowledge that may accrue to him by a supernatural gift.[6]

---

ver., q. 2, a. 2), as though finitude were a sort of "metaphysical evil." The beings endowed with knowledge have, in effect, the privilege of causing to exist within themselves, in an original manner, the perfections of which they are ontologically deprived.

5. *ST* I, q. 57, a. 5: "In angelis est cognitio duplex. Una quidem naturalis, secundum quam cognoscunt res tum per essentiam suam, tum etiam per species innatas.... Est autem alia angelorum cognitio, quae eos beatos facit, qua vident Verbum et res in Verbo."

6. Is there any point to this methodological step? For ultimately, someone might say, an angel exists concretely and thinks in a supernatural state. Nevertheless, a study of the natural structures of angelic knowledge is necessary for at least four reasons. First, the grace of beatitude does not destroy nature, so that natural knowledge is not suppressed by supernatural knowledge and remains even in the beatific vision; see *ST* I, q. 62, a. 7: "After entering glory, did their natural love and knowledge remain?" (Utrum post consecutionem gloriae remanserit in eis dilectio et cognitio naturalis?) Indeed, one can know the same truth by two different methods, one of which is more perfect than the other. For example, I can know the solution to a mathematics problem either by working it out myself or by reading it at the back of the book. Second, grace flows within the structures of nature, so that the supernatural knowledge of an angel embraces some modalities that characterize natural knowledge and are incomprehensible outside of that perspective. Third, if we follow *Q. de malo*, q. 16, a. 4, we must admit that, in the first instant of his creation, even though he was in a state of grace, the activity of an angel consisted in taking possession of the objects that were suited to him by nature. *Quarto*, natural knowledge is still the knowledge that the demons exercise concretely, since their sin did not destroy their nature. Now this question about the knowledge of demons legitimately preoccupied theologians, since it is preliminary to any inquiry into the extent of the demons' power to harm, or into the demonic prophecies of the pagan religions, or again into the practices of divination. In the Middles Ages, these questions about demonic knowledge are discussed mainly in commentaries on the *Sentences* II, d. 7, c. 5–6 (361–62).

THE MEDIUM OF ANGELIC
KNOWLEDGE (Q. 55)

The essential point in the Thomistic teaching about angelic knowledge is the following statement: an angel does not know creatures by
receiving from the known object the form of its knowledge but rather by knowing himself as well as the innate ideas (*species*) that God
placed in him at the moment of his creation, which cause him to participate in the knowledge that God has of creatures.

St. Thomas adopts here, by way of a radical correction required
by the Christian faith, the model whereby the neo-Platonists explained the knowledge that superior substances have of inferior substances, which was neatly summarized in *The Book of Causes*: "Every
intelligence knows what is above it insofar as it is caused thereby and
what is beneath it insofar as it is the cause thereof."[7] A spiritual substance knows other things by knowing itself as their cause or else as
their effect.

Medieval Christianity willingly accepted this model of an internal, causal knowledge in order to account for God's knowledge.[8] It
allowed them to go beyond the *aporia* (difficulties) of Aristotelianism, which denied the divine knowledge of the universe by granting
the principle that God cannot learn anything because he can in no
way be determined by something outside of himself. In reality, God
knows all things by knowing himself as their cause.

Yet, in the case of the angels, this model runs up against a major
difficulty: unlike the neo-Platonic hypostases, a Christian angel exerts
no causality in the order of the communication of being.[9] Therefore it

7. See *The Book of Causes* VII (VIII), 72 (*Liber de causis*, 64); cited in *ST* I, q. 56. a.
2, arg. 2.

8. See *Thomas d'Aquin, De la vérité, Question 2 (La science en Dieu)*, introduction,
trans., and commentary Serge-Thomas Bonino, preface by Ruedi Imbach, Vestigia 17
(Paris and Fribourg: Cerf, 1996), 198–221.

9. St. Thomas is perfectly clear about the opposition that the dogma of creation sets
up between the neo-Platonic theory of the knowledge of separated substances (*philosophi*)
and the Christian theology of angelic knowledge (*nos*). See *Q. de ver.*, q. 8, a. 8, which highlights the opposition on this point between the philosophers and the Christians: "All
knowing takes place by means of assimilation, and likeness existing between two things is
caused by their agreement in a form. Now, since unity in an effect shows unity in a cause,
and, since, in consequence, no matter what genus any form may belong to, one must get

was necessary to find a "resemblance without causality" between the angel and the created object that he reputedly knows.[10] The detour by way of the divine ideas became imperative.

It must be admitted that the angels, at the time of their creation, received from the First Cause and the transcendent Model of all things "a noetic inheritance,"[11] "a dowry of light"[12]—in other words, *species* or ideas that allow them to know all things by knowing themselves.[13] Thus, in knowing himself as the *Ipsum esse subsistens* [subsistent existence itself], the transcendent Source and Model of all possible perfection, God possesses in himself the ideas of all the spiritual and corporeal creatures that are possible and real. These ideas he communicates freely in two ways: on the one hand, by actualizing them in reality; on the other hand, by placing them in the mind of an angel.[14] The idea of a plane tree [*Platanus*, North American syc-

---

back to the one first principle of that form, two things can resemble each other for two reasons only: either one is the cause of the other or both have been caused by one cause that has imprinted the same form upon both. Using this principle, we say that angels know material things in a manner different from that in which philosophers say that angels know them. For we do not say that angels cause material things. God is the creator of all things, visible and invisible. Consequently, a likeness of the things of nature cannot be within an angel unless it comes from Him who is the cause of material things.... Philosophers, however, have asserted that angels are the creators of material things" (Omnis cognitio est per assimilationem; similitudo autem inter aliqua duo est secundum convenientiam in forma. Cum autem unitas effectus unitatem causae demonstret, et sic in genere cuiuslibet formae ad unum primum principium illius formae redire oporteat, impossibile est aliqua duo esse ad invicem similia, nisi altero duorum modorum: vel ita quod unum sit causa alterius, vel ita quod ambo ab una causa causentur, quae eamdem formam utrique imprimat; et secundum hoc diversimode ponimus angelos materialia cognoscere ab eo quod philosophi posuerunt. Nos enim non ponimus, angelos esse causas materialium rerum, sed Deum creatorem omnium visibilium et invisibilium; et ideo non potest in angelo esse similitudo materialium rerum nisi ab eo qui est materialium rerum causa.... Philosophi autem posuerunt rerum materialium esse angelos creatores). The same opposition between the *philosophi* and *nos* [us] can be found in *Q. de ver.*, q. 8, a. 7.

10. *ST* I, q. 56, a. 2, ad 2: "similitudo absque causalitate."

11. Suarez-Nani, *Connaissance*, 32.

12. Jacques Maritain, *Three Reformers: Luther—Descartes—Rousseau* (New York: Charles Scribner's Sons, 1955), 62.

13. Here we meet again the Augustinian insight that sees the angelic mind as a mirror that is always in the act of knowing God.

14. See *ST* I, q. 56, a. 2: "As Augustine says (*Gen. ad lit.* ii), such things as pre-existed from eternity in the Word of God, came forth from Him in two ways: first, into the angelic mind; and secondly, so as to subsist in their own natures" (Sicut Augustinus dicit, II *super*

amore] is at the same time placed from the beginning in the angelic mind and realized in the particular plane trees that line our roads. That is why an angel, without having to bend down outside of himself, can know plane trees.

The *medium*—the objective formal means—of angelic knowledge—in other words, the representative form that informs the angelic intellect—is therefore its own essence inasmuch as it is determined from the beginning by the *species* that God created together with and in it.

Question 55 deals with this *medium*. St. Thomas approaches it by way of a contrast with the properly divine mode of knowledge (a. 1), then by contrast with the properly human mode of knowledge (a. 2). Finally, he presents the hierarchy of angels in terms of the greater or lesser universality of this *medium* (a. 3).

In article 1, Aquinas explains that God alone knows all things by his own substance because only the divine substance, which is infinite, synthesizes perfectly as source, in an absolutely simple manner, all the perfections dispersed among things—somewhat in the way that white light summarizes and contains all colors. An angel, in contrast, suffers from a sort of lag or discrepancy—characteristic of every spiritual creature—between his essence (which is a type of determined and therefore limited being) and his intellect (which, like any intellect, is open to the infinite, the totality of being and of intelligibility). God is self-sufficient: the infinite Divine Essence perfectly actualizes the Divine Intellect; it saturates his cognitive capacity. In contrast, no creature can be satisfied by itself. Despite its exalted perfection, the angelic substance is incapable of fully actualizing an angelic intellect that is open to the infinite. An angel therefore cannot know *everything* in knowing his own substance. Certainly, there is in the angelic substance a generic resemblance to other beings: in knowing himself, an angel can therefore know what a being is, what a living thing is, what an angel is … , but this knowledge remains very general and therefore imperfect.[15] In order to attain a determinate knowledge, he must receive other information besides.

Gen. ad litt., ea quae in Verbo Dei ab aeterno praeextiterunt, dupliciter ab eo effluxerunt, uno modo, in intellectum angelicum; alio modo, ut subsisterent in propriis naturis).

15. See *ST* I, q. 55, a. 1, ad 3.

Will he draw them from the things themselves, as man does? No, in the estimation of St. Thomas, in article 2. The ideas by which an angel thinks are innate ideas; they are connatural to him and exist in him from his creation.[16] In order to manifest the coherence of this theory, St. Thomas proceeds to make a double comparison between human knowledge and angelic knowledge.

The first comparison is based on an analogy of proportionality that occurs very frequently in the treatise on the angels: the relation of angels to men is analogous to the relation of celestial bodies to terrestrial bodies. Now in the corporeal universe, the superior forms inform and totally actualize matter. They saturate it and "anchor it down" [*"l'arriment"*] in such a way that the composite is stable, since the matter no longer tends toward another being. In contrast, the inferior forms do not actualize matter totally, so that it remains susceptible to other forms; this explains the phenomenon of change. To adapt an Aristotelian metaphor, it is somewhat like a wife who is filled with affection for her husband and will no longer seek her happiness elsewhere, while an unsatisfied wife runs the risk of playing fast and loose. Similarly, in the universe of intelligent beings, the capacity of the human intellect, which is the lowest, is not saturated by intelligible forms at the outset. On the contrary, to begin with the possible intellect is *tabula rasa*, and can be compared to a blank but formatted compact disk that is capable of receiving and storing data. The human intellect acquires intelligible forms gradually, therefore, over the course of a *history*, by abstracting them from the physical world, thus constructing its mental universe. In contrast, the angelic intellect is saturated from the start: "In the higher *spiritual substances*—that is, the *angels*—the power of understanding is *naturally* complete by intelligible *species*, in so far as they have such *species* connatural to them, so as to understand all things which they can *know naturally*."[17]

16. The angel's innate ideas are accidents, really distinct from his substance and from his intellective power, but they "are not in juxtaposition to the very form that is the angel's substance, rather they determine and complete it as an intelligible form" (Nicolas, *Synthèse*, 291). They are, in the strict sense, properties of his nature, produced indeed by the same action that created him, as a necessary perfection, as an intrinsic complement of this essence (see M.-V. Leroy, *Anges*, 151a).

17. *ST* I, q. 55, a. 2: "Potentia vero intellectiva in substantiis spiritualibus superioribus, idest in angelis, naturaliter completa est per species intelligibiles, inquantum

The second comparison is based on the different manners of existing of a man and an angel. The human intellect, because it is the faculty of a soul that informs a body, shows a certain affinity with the corporeal world. It is normal that it should draw its intelligible nourishment from its relations with the physical world. In contrast, the angelic intellect is the intellect of a purely spiritual substance, so that it acquires its perfection from its spiritual intake.[18]

But in the final analysis, he who can do what is greater can do what is lesser! The intellectual power of an angel is far superior to that of the agent intellect of a man; why couldn't the angel abstract what is intelligible from what is sensible?[19] St. Thomas replies that abstraction requires more than simply putting an intellectual power into contact with a physical reality. Digestion does not take place immediately by the mere application of a steak to the stomach lining. Similarly, abstraction implies a process of gradual refinement between the purely physical reality and what is intelligible in act; it requires passing through intermediary stages, in particular external and internal sense knowledge. Now an angel, being incorporeal, does not have sense knowledge.[20]

The consequence of this mode of knowing is that the structure of the angelic intellect is not the same as that of our intellect.[21] Since we are not always in the act of thinking, there must be in us a cognitive faculty in potency, which is capable of receiving intelligible *species* or forms (the possible intellect), and a cognitive power capable of producing them starting from sense data in which they exist only in potency (the agent intellect). There is no such thing in an angel,

habent species intelligibiles connaturales ad omnia intelligenda quae naturaliter cognoscere possunt."

18. Moreover, the notion of some dependence of the angel with regard to inferior substances would run counter to the principle that what is superior does not receive from what is inferior, since reception always implies some passivity (see *ST* I, q. 52, a. 2, arg. 4).

19. *ST* See I, q. 55, a. 2, arg. 2.

20. *ST* See I, q. 54, a. 5. Since the absence of sense knowledge in an angel results from his incorporeal nature, it is understandable that the writers who wavered about the ontological status of angels and demons were also tempted to attribute to them a kind of sense knowledge. St. Augustine mentions the possibility thereof; see *Literal Meaning of Genesis* II.17.37 (ACW 41:72).

21. See *ST* I, q. 54, a. 4.

whose intellect is always in act in relation to its natural objects, which are themselves always intelligible species in act. It would therefore be equivocating to speak about an agent intellect and a possible intellect in an angel.

Article 3 of question 55 explains that angelic ideas differ from one angel to another in their universality and simplicity. The higher an angel is in the hierarchy, the closer he is to God and the more he participates in his unity, especially in that property of divine knowledge that consists of being "monoideic"—in other words, of knowing everything by means of one *species*. The superior angels therefore know by means of more universal ideas than the inferior angels. What a superior angel grasps in one glance through the idea "animal," for example, an inferior angel grasps only through several ideas, such as the ideas "bird," "reptile," "amphibian." The intellectual power of angels is, indeed, more or less intense, so that the superior angel is capable of exploiting fully the intelligible content of a general idea that the inferior angel grasps only by breaking it down, in much the same way as a healthy stomach can digest a solid piece of food, whereas it must be cut up into smaller bits to enable a weaker stomach to assimilate it.

We should explain immediately that the universal ideas possessed by angels are not of the same kind as those that we form by abstraction. Indeed, in our case, the more universal the idea is in extension (in other words, the wider the domain of its application), the poorer it is in comprehension (in other words, its intelligible content). The reason for this is that we form our general ideas by disregarding the particular characteristics, which remain at the door, so to speak. Our abstract ideas thus correspond to a sort of lowest common denominator. Consequently, it is necessary for us to multiply our abstract ideas in order to attain a more complete knowledge of reality. On the contrary, the universal ideas of an angel, since they are participations in the divine ideas, contain the internal diversifications of the perfection that they represent. "Their universality," Jacques Maritain writes, "is not the universality of representation due to the process of abstraction, but the universality of causation or activity belonging to the creative ideas, whence things descend into being."[22]

22. See Jacques Maritain, *Three Reformers*, 67.

THE OBJECT OF ANGELIC KNOWLEDGE

St. Thomas Aquinas devotes two questions to the object of angelic knowledge. He examines first what an angel can know about immaterial, purely spiritual realities (q. 56), then what he can know about realities that are material or connected with the material universe (q. 57).

Angelic Knowledge of the Spiritual World (q. 56)

The first object that an angel knows is none other than himself.[23] Moreover, through this knowledge of himself the angel knows also everything that is not himself. For this self-knowledge is immediate and constitutive. If I put a wet firecracker on a hot plate that I have just turned on, the (possible) explosion will occur only after the plate has been reheated and the gunpowder has dried out. In contrast, if I throw a dry firecracker onto a white-hot plate, the deflagration is immediate. The same goes (*mutatis mutandis!*) for the knowledge that a man and an angel have of themselves. The human person has no direct intuition of his deepest reality—namely, his intellective soul.[24] On the one hand, his intelligence is originally in potency and therefore unintelligible unless it is actualized by an intelligible object. Similarly, as long as light does not encounter a body, it is not perceptible to our eyes. On the other hand, human intelligence is programmed to grasp the essences of corporeal realities and can apprehend itself only indirectly—namely, by tracing its acts back to their source. In short, man is "an exodus being [i.e., essentially outgoing], because in order to know ourselves, we cannot stop at ourselves, in other words, at the void, but we must make the detour (if it is a detour) via the world and material things before grasping our acts that grasp them, and ourselves operating in those acts."[25] And the result of this painstaking knowledge of self still remains very imperfect, leaving all sorts of shadowy areas that demonstrate the extent to which we remain strangers to ourselves.

It is quite a different story with an angel. An angel is at the very

23. *ST* I, q. 56, a. 1. See H.-D. Simonin, "La connaissance de l'ange par soi-même," *Angelicum* 9 (1932): 43–62.

24. See *ST* I, q. 87, a. 1, in which St. Thomas makes a comparison between God, an angel, and a man from the perspective of their self-knowledge.

25. Chrétien, *Regard de l'amour*, 127.

same time intelligent in act and intelligible in act. And since he is immediately present to himself, the angelic substance, as the formal medium of knowledge, is always actualizing the angelic intellect. The angel always knows himself in act. Just as an eye cannot not sense the light, the angelic intellect cannot not know in act the angelic substance from which it emanates. An angel is therefore pure self-awareness. He is transparent to himself and sees himself down to his innermost depths. Thus he realizes that perfect noetic self-possession, that spiritual grasp of himself, that is the ideal of every spirit and the highest form of unity and of being.[26]

But, some quarrelsome scholastic will say, an angel is an individual, a singular reality. Now it is a fundamental principle of Aristotelianism that an intellect operates only on the universal, never on the particular,[27] to which St. Thomas replies that the singular as such is not unintelligible, but rather the singular inasmuch as it is individuated by matter, which, being pure potency, is in principle opaque to thought. Now the angelic individual is immaterial and therefore intelligible.[28] What is more, the unintelligibility of the material singular is relative to human abstractive knowledge, in which individual characteristics necessarily remain at the intellect's door, which is not the case in angelic knowledge.[29]

26. However, although an angel knows his nature perfectly, he does not know his supernatural destiny to the extent to which it is not directly inscribed in that nature and depends only on the gracious initiative of God (*ST* I, q. 56, a. 1, ad 1). With regard to the supernatural, an angel surpasses an angel [i.e., his ability to comprehend], just as man surpasses man.

27. See *ST* I, q. 56, a. 1, arg. 2.

28. *ST* I, q. 56, a. 1, ad. 2: "We have no knowledge of single corporeal things, not because of their particularity, but on account of the matter, which is their principle of individuation. Accordingly, if there be any single things subsisting without matter, as the angels are, there is nothing to prevent them from being actually intelligible" (Singularium quae sunt in rebus corporalibus, non est intellectus, apud nos, non ratione singularitatis, sed ratione materiae, quae est in eis individuationis principium. Unde si aliqua singularia sunt sine materia subsistentia, sicut sunt angeli, illa nihil prohibet intelligibilia esse actu).

29. Note also that this knowledge of the angel by himself is productive of a word. No creature, as we saw, identifies himself with his activity, because no creature is identified with his *esse*. Consequently, the intellective activity of an angel that is completed in the production of a mental word—the final act—whereby the angel tells himself to himself as something known, cannot be the angelic substance itself. See Édouard Hugon, *Tractatus dogmatici*, vol. 1, *De Deo uno et trino, Creatore et gubernatore; De angelis et homine* (Paris: P. Lethielleux, 1933), 611.

An angel also knows other angels.[30] He does not know them by
reason of the union of their essence to his intellect—for he is not the
effect of them. Nor does he know them by his essence as such—for
he is not the cause of them, and any knowledge of the other members
of his genus that he can deduce from his essence alone would remain
general and imprecise.[31] He knows them with a determinate knowledge thanks to the connatural *species* that God placed in him from the
beginning and that represent intentionally the other angels in the individual properties of each.

What about the natural knowledge of God in an angel?[32] St. Thomas distinguishes three general types of knowledge. First, a subject can
know an object because the object's essence is really present in the
subject. This is how an angel knows himself. No creature by his natural
resources alone can know God in that manner. Only God knows himself in that way.[33] Second, a subject can know an object through a representation of that object that exists in a separate reality. For example,
I see in a mirror an assassin who is walking toward me, brandishing a
well-sharpened ax. This is the "specular" (from *speculum*, which means
"mirror") manner in which a human being knows God in the mirror
of creatures—in other words, by deducing the existence of God and
of some of his properties based on what is required to explain certain
metaphysical properties of the creatures. Third, a subject can know
an object through a representation of that object that is substantially present to him. In other words, the subject is himself the image
of the object. Now this is the way in which an angel knows God. He

30. See *ST* I, q. 56, a. 2.

31. See *Q. de ver.*, q. 8, a. 7: "Since all knowledge takes place through assimilation,
by knowing his own essence one angel would know only as much about another angel
as his [own] essence resembled the latter's. Now, one angel resembles another only according to their common nature. Hence, it would follow that the knowledge one angel
would have about another would not be complete" (Cum enim omnis cognitio sit per
assimilationem, angelus per essentiam suam non potest de alio angelo plus cognoscere
quam hoc in quo essentiae suae est similis. Unus autem angelus alteri angelo non simi-
latur nisi in natura communi: et sic sequeretur quod unus alium non cognosceret cognitione completa).

32. See *ST* I, q. 56, a. 3.

33. By grace, God can make himself present to the mind, lift up the intellect (by a
lumen gloriae [light of glory]) and unite himself to the intellect as its form, thus communicating to it in a supernatural way a mode of knowledge analogous to the one by which
God naturally knows himself.

knows him by knowing himself as his image. However, since the angel is a creature, and since no creature could possibly represent God adequately, the natural angelic knowledge of God remains very imperfect: it does not reach the Divine Essence itself but apprehends God as the Source and the End of his own being. Unlike the knowledge that the angel has of other angels—which comes about by way of the infused *species* added to the substance and can therefore be both in the second act and also only in the first act—the knowledge that he has of God is necessarily always in act. This knowledge remains objectively mediate, specular, indirect, but it assumes the form of an intuition because—as we will explain later—the angelic intellect does not proceed by deduction but sees right away the cause in the effect.

Angelic Knowledge of the Material World (q. 57)

In question 57, dedicated to the angelic knowledge of material things, St. Thomas begins by affirming the general truth: an angel knows the material world.[34] He deduces this from the place occupied by the angel in the hierarchy of beings, considered in terms of the theory of participation. In each higher degree of being is found, in a synthetic and more perfect manner, the perfections that characterized the lower degrees. Thus the human intellective soul synthesizes in a more perfect manner the perfections belonging to the vegetative soul and the sensitive soul; Dominican life synthesizes in a more perfect manner the contemplative ideal of the Benedictine, the pastoral ideal of the parish priest, the Franciscan's ideal of humility.... The same perfections are encountered on the various levels of the chain of beings, but, in the higher beings, they exist "eminently, with a certain totality and simplicity (*eminenter, per quandam totalitatem et simplicitatem*)," whereas in the lower beings they exist "in a manner that is deficient, partial and multiple (*deficienter, partialiter et multipliciter*)." Corporeal realities that are inferior to an angel must therefore exist in him (although he does not cause them) in the manner proper to the angel, which is an immaterial manner: they are therefore directly intelligible in him.

St. Thomas then proceeds to examine the angelic knowledge of

34. See *ST* I, q. 57, a. 1.

different types of realities, the knowledge of which presents a particular difficulty: singulars (a. 2), the future (a. 3), and the thoughts of
hearts (a. 4).

The question about the angelic knowledge of individual and singular realities (events or things) is of capital importance in the intellectual context of the thirteenth century.[35] Indeed, Greek-Arabic
philosophy was inclined to remove this lower world from the direct
influence and knowledge of God and even of the angels. *De minimis
non curat praetor* [A leader is not concerned about the least things].
This was an attack on the doctrine of the universality of divine providence that is at the heart of the Christian faith.[36] Moreover, the *sed
contra* and St. Thomas's first argument against those who deny that
there is any angelic knowledge of singulars are arguments of faith:
if the angels do not know particular acts, how could they be the
guardians of men, the instruments of divine providence in regard to
them?[37]

Then, in order to establish the very existence of this angelic
knowledge of singulars, St. Thomas invokes the aforementioned principle that higher beings that are closer to the divine simplicity possess
by way of synthesis and unity what the lower beings possess by way
of multiplicity. Consequently, what man knows thanks to a variety of
cognitive powers—namely, intellect and the different senses—an angel knows by intellect alone.

Can we describe in somewhat more detail the manner of this an-

35. See *ST* I, q. 57, a. 2. See Julien Peghaire, "L'intellection du singulier matériel chez
l'ange et chez l'homme," *Revue dominicaine* 39 (1933): 135–44.

36. Concerning what is at stake in the question about the divine (and angelic)
knowledge of singular things in the thirteenth century, see Aquinas, *Disputed Questions
on Truth*, question 2, "God's Knowledge," 1:52–135.

37. See *ST* I, q. 57, a. 2: "Some have denied to the angels all knowledge of singulars.
In the first place this derogates from the Catholic faith, which asserts that these lower
things are administered by angels" (Quidam totaliter subtraxerunt angelis singularium
cognitionem. Sed hoc primo quidem derogat catholicae fidei, quae ponit haec inferi-
ora administrari per angelos). In *Q. de ver.*, q. 8, a. 11, St. Thomas declares at the outset
that "such a position is contrary to faith, denying as it does the custody of angels over
men, as well as opposed to right reason, because, if angels did not know things which we
know, their knowledge would, at least in this respect, be less perfect" (Haec positio et a
fide est aliena, quia removet ministeria angelorum circa homines, et etiam rectae rationi
repugnat; quia si angeli ignorant ea quae nos cognoscimus, ad minus quantum ad hoc
imperfectior est eorum cognitio). See also Aquinas, *Q. de anima*, a. 20.

gelic knowledge of singulars? In fact, an angel knows something singular exclusively through the *species* that God placed in him.[38] Indeed, the angelic *species* are participations in the divine ideas. Now the latter, which are the cause of all that is found in existing things, represent not only the universal but also the singular, since God's creative knowledge is at the same time the most universal and the most concrete and extends as far as the final material determinations. Angelic *species*, unlike abstract human *species*, therefore represent adequately the material singulars and allow angels to know them.[39]

Whereas the first two articles tended to highlight the perfection of angelic knowledge and its superiority in relation to human knowledge, the next three articles (articles 3 to 5) neatly define the limits of that knowledge in such a way as to preserve the unique character of the divine knowledge. I will discuss elsewhere the angelic knowledge of the mysteries of salvation, the object of article 5. For now, let us note that neither the demons nor the angels know the future as such, unlike God, whose exclusive privilege that is.[40] There are, in fact, two ways of knowing the future: either in itself, or in its present causes. God and God alone knows with a perfect certitude the

38. In *Q. de ver.*, q. 8, a. 11, St. Thomas dismisses three erroneous explanations. Angels do not know something singular by abstraction based on what is sensible. Nor do they know it, as Avicenna thought, by cross-checking it with universal causes (see *ST* I, q. 14, a. 11). Finally, they do not know it by the application of universal forms to singulars, because a person can apply one thing to another only if the latter is already known in some way.

39. John Duns Scotus vehemently disputed this thesis, and his critique recapitulates his fundamental opposition to Thomistic angelology; see Scotus, *Ordinatio* II, d. 3, p. 2, q. 3, in *Opera omnia* VII (Vatican City: Typis Polyglottis Vaticanis, 1973), 569–603; Jean Cabrol, *Defensiones, In II Sent.*, d. 3, q. 2, 3:270a–71b, 271b–72b, 312b–13b, 315a–17a; Vacant, "Ange," *DTC*, 1:1233–34; Gilson, *Jean Duns Scot: Introduction à ses positions fondamentales*, Études de philosophie médiévale 42 (Paris: J. Vrin, 1952), 428ff.... According to the Subtle Doctor, an angel cannot know something singular, which is potentially infinite, by *species*, which are necessarily finite in number. Indeed, he does not see how a universal *species* could distinctly represent a plurality of individuals (isn't this once again the opposition between the Scotist concept of univocal being and the Thomist concept of intensive *esse*?), all the more so because, in his view, the singular adds an intelligible determination to the universal. Scotus does not see that the angelic species is not an abstract, impoverished species such as a human *species*, but rather a participation in the divine knowledge. The only alternative, in Scotus's view, is that an angel acquires an experiential knowledge of the singular thanks to the abstractive activity of his agent intellect.

40. See *ST* I, q. 57, a. 3.

future in itself inasmuch as what he sees is realized, since the totality of temporal unfolding is present to the divine eternity. But then
a future event can be in its causes in three ways. First, it results from
them necessarily. The eclipse that saves the day in the graphic novel
Le temple du soleil [Temple of the Sun] is already present, as something programmed in its causes, at the moment when the hero Tintin reads about it in a scrap of newspaper, and nothing could prevent it from happening. Tintin can predict it with certainty. An angel
could, too. Second, the future event results habitually (*ut in pluribus*)
from causes that are presently at work. Generally, standing for even
a short time under a freezing-cold waterfall causes someone to catch
cold, but not the Irish monks of olden times! In this case the angels
(and the demons) can conjecture the future with some probability,
as we do. Their conjectural knowledge is, however, much more perfect than ours inasmuch as they comprehend a wider range of causes.
The physician who has access to the complete test results can foresee with greater exactitude the course of my illness than my neighbor
who has to be content with looking at my appearance. As the fathers
of the church went to great lengths to prove, there can therefore be
correct diabolic predictions (the oracles of the pagans, acts of divination) that seem to human beings (but wrongly) to be supernatural.[41]
Third, the event is totally contingent, the product of pure chance. In
this case, the angels and the demons absolutely cannot know it in advance by virtue of their natural knowledge. This is likewise true about
the movements of human free will, even though sometimes they can
be conjectured on the basis of knowledge about the conditions thereof (character, habits, moral dispositions).[42]

41. See, for example, the *De divinatione daemonum*, by St. Augustine (BA 10).
42. One difficult question tormented the Scholastics with respect to the angelic
knowledge of the future. How does an angel, who previously did not know a future object, know it when it comes to pass? Must we suppose that in angelic knowledge there
is a change caused by events? That would be to attribute to him a misplaced passivity
in relation to lower creatures. In fact, from his creation an angel possesses a *species* that
represents this object that comes to pass. But how does the angel know that the event of
which he has an idea is coming about? For St. Thomas, all novelty, all change is on the
part of the known object: only when the object begins to exist in act and really participates in the nature represented by the *species* does it enter into a new relation (which is
real on its part only) to the *species* that represents it: it becomes similar to the *species* in
act and can effectively be known thanks to it. See Aquinas, *In II Sent.*, d. 7, q. 2, a. 1, ad 4;

But what about the thoughts of the heart—in other words, those spiritual movements that make up the subjective life of a mind?[43] Here again, St. Thomas reserves this knowledge strictly to God. By their nature, angels have no direct access to the secrets of the human heart or to the subjective interior life of other angels. Indeed there are two ways, one direct and the other indirect, of knowing the spiritual movements of someone else. First one can deduce these movements based on external signs that are like the effects thereof. Thus our behaviors reveal our interior dispositions. Or else certain somatic states say a lot about our psychological state: joy and sadness can be read on our faces, and a lie detector can obtain astonishing results. The demons, who are external observers of our somatic changes, can thus know indirectly our psychological dispositions and act accordingly.

As for knowing directly in themselves the movements (*affectiones*) of the will, that is the privilege of God, who alone scrutinizes hearts and loins. Indeed, God alone is present in the intimate sanctuary of the will—the inside of a human being or of an angel, his inner sanctum—by virtue of the fact that he created it and unceasingly activates it. God thereby knows also the actual thoughts of our mind, since the exercise of thought depends in the final analysis on the initiatives of the will. A spiritual subject *freely* engages his intellect in getting down to work, either to learn something new or to use the knowledge that he already possesses. This mediation of free will prevents angels and men from having direct knowledge of someone else's thought. No doubt I may know that my friend Joseph is perfectly fluent in Latin, but I cannot know whether at this moment he is thinking in Latin rather than in English.

The neurosciences have pointed out the existence of a certain parallelism between cerebral states and the states of psychological consciousness. Even though a spiritualist philosophy rejects any interpretation of this parallelism in terms of univocal causal determinism, one may legitimately wonder whether this parallelism does not offer to

---

Q. de ver., q. 8, a. 12, ad 1, I, q. 57, a. 3, ad 3, q. 64, a. 1, ad 5; Q. de malo, q. 16, a. 7, ad 6. On this subtle question, see also John of St.-Thomas, *Cursus theologicus*, vol. 4, *Opera et studio monachorum solesmensium* (Paris, Tournai, and Rome: Typis Societatis S. Joannis Evangelistae, Desclée et sociorum, 1946), disp. 42, a. 2 (4:636–55).

43. See *ST* I, q. 57, a. 4.

an external observer as subtle as an angel or a demon wider access to our subjectivity than medieval authors thought. In fact there is a two-fold leeway between cerebral states and spiritual movements. First, it is possible that cerebral states are to some extent polyvalent—in other words, even though every state of consciousness corresponds to a cerebral state, the same cerebral state can correspond to several different states of consciousness, and vice versa, so that one cannot accurately deduce a state of consciousness from a cerebral state. Second, the relation between states of psychological consciousness and the movements of spiritual subjectivity is not linear, since the life of the mind cannot be reduced to what psychological consciousness grasps of it. A genuine spiritual joy can coexist with a profound psychological sadness. Our spiritual subjectivity is a mystery in our own sight, and this mystery is compounded when we are dealing with the supernatural action of divine grace in us, which to a great extent eludes the grasp of consciousness.

THE PROPERTIES OF ANGELIC KNOWLEDGE (Q. 58)

Angelic knowledge has properties or modalities that clearly distinguish it simultaneously from human knowledge and divine knowledge.[44] St. Thomas explains them in question 58.

The human intellect is sometimes in act, sometimes in potency. Moreover, it presents, as it were, two degrees of actuality and potentiality. Sometimes, having acquired them previously, I possess certain *species* that form a system—constitute a science, in other words, for example, metaphysics—but at the moment I am not exercising metaphysical thought in the second act; I am not presently using the things that I know. We then say that I am in secondary potency. But sometimes I do not even possess metaphysical science. I have only the real capacity to acquire it (which a chimpanzee does not have).

44. Jacques Maritain, who insists on the carnal condition of human spirituality, denounced Descartes's misreading of the mode of knowing that is proper to man, which leads to a pernicious confusion with an angelic-type mode of knowledge (independence with regard to things, innate ideas, intuitiveness). He sees therein the source of many modern philosophical errors, particularly idealism; see Jacques Maritain, "Descartes or the Incarnation of the Angel," in *Three Reformers*, 52–89.

Then we say that I am in first potency.[45] The Divine Intellect, in contrast, is never in first potency or in second potency: it is always in act. God is pure intellection. An angel occupies an intermediary status. He is never in first potency, since his intellect is fully actualized from his beginning and an angel, at least in the natural order, does not acquire new *species*. On the other hand, with regard to second potency, an angel is certainly always in the act of thinking something ("An angel is an intellectual substance, ever in motion," St. John Damascene already declared),[46] but he does not always consider in act all the *species* that he possesses. Hence the possibility of a certain change in an angel: his thought is uninterrupted, but he passes from the consideration of one idea to that of another.[47]

Cannot an angel then think several things at once?[48] Yes and no. The principle is that to each distinct *species* necessarily corresponds a distinct act of intellection. It follows that an intellect can think several things at once only inasmuch as they form one whole and can therefore be represented by one *species* or intelligible form. For example, I can think at the same time about a triangle, a rectangle, and a hexagon insofar as my intellect is presently informed by the notion of "geometric figure" that is common to the triangle, the rectangle, and the hexagon. Now the only *species* that contains everything is the Divine Essence. In the beatific vision, an angel or a man who sees the Divine Essence therefore knows simultaneously all things,[49] but besides this case, which depends on the supernatural order, neither man nor angel can think all things at once, because the *species* that they use are finite. Still, it is true that the more universal the *species* that actualizes his intellect, the more an angel grasps things by one act of thought, and this knowledge is a proper knowledge since, unlike the difference of the abstract human *species*, the angel's universal *species*, which is a noetic participation in the creative ideas, represents in a determinate fashion everything that it contains.

This angelic thought, unlike ours, is purely intuitive.[50] Of course

---

45. This vocabulary "first potency—second potency" is found, for example, in Aquinas, *In De anima* II, lect. 11.

46. John Damascene, *Orthodox Faith* II.3 (FOTC 37:205).

47. See *ST* I, q. 58, a. 1.   48. See *ST* I, q. 58, a. 2.

49. See *ST* I, q. 12, a. 10.

50. See *ST* I, q. 58, a. 3. On the relations between *intellectus* and *ratio*, intuition and

intuition, which is characteristic of intellectuality, envelops in a way and subtends [underlies] the entire life of our intellect: it is at the origin and at the conclusion thereof. But we pass from our initial intuition of the first theoretical or practical principles to our final intuition of the truth contemplated or to our practical decision by the heavy work of rationality. We reason and we think discursively. Starting from truths already known, we painstakingly extract some new bits of truth and, in doing so, we progressively and historically actualize our intellect. Thus man appears as:

> a patient being, because we are what we are only by having to become it, little by little, in lifting ourselves up over time to ourselves.... If we saw at the outset, we would not be these travelers without baggage, wresting from fatigue, pain and adversity each step of their path toward the light, and unable to win the bread of knowledge except by the sweat of their brow, in simple terms: human beings.[51]

In contrast, an angel neither reasons nor thinks discursively; he intuits. He does not seek; he finds. He possesses in a superior way what we attain, for our part, in a discursive manner. In considering a *species*, he immediately grasps all of its intelligible content. He sees at the outset the conclusions in the premises. For example, considering an axiom, he sees immediately in it all the mathematical propositions that can be deduced from it. Thus, man can be compared to a fisherman who, while in his boat, draws a net up from the sea and gradually discovers its contents, whereas an angel can be compared to an undersea diver who, in a single glance, by a sort of panoramic view, sees right away everything that the net contains.

The fact that our intellect, by reason of its weakness, does not immediately grasp all of the intelligible content of its object involves two remarkable properties: our intellect thinks discursively (third operation of the mind), to be sure, but also and more fundamentally, it composes and divides (second operation of the mind).[52] In order

---

discursive thinking, see Peghaire, *"Intellectus" et "ratio" selon S. Thomas d'Aquin*, Publications de l'Institut d'études médiévales d'Ottawa 6 (Paris: J. Vrin; Ottawa: Inst. d'études médiévales, 1936); Cottier, *"Intellectus* et *ratio,"* RT 88 (1988): 215–28.

51. Chrétien, *Regard de l'amour*, 127–28; see also Cruz Gonzalez Ayesta, *Hombre y verdad: Gnoseologia y antropologia del conocimiento en las Q.D. De Veritate*, Filosofica 172 (Pampelune: Ediciones Universidad de Navarra, 2002).

52. See *ST* I, q. 58, a. 4.

to attain reality, it must in effect bring about a synthesis among the different aspects of the one reality that it was able to apprehend only analytically and serially. In order to do this, it affirms or denies in its judgment the union of a subject and a predicate. For example, it separates the notion of spiritual substance from that of spatial localization when it denies that a spirit is contained in a place. An angel, for his part, immediately knows all the truths relative to the object of his consideration, including those that concern its present existence, because he has a direct intellection of its essence. Whereas we work to disengage the one from the many, the angel sees the many in the one.

One major consequence of this: an angel cannot be mistaken, at least on the level of his natural knowledge.[53] In fact, in our case, the error does not reside in the intuitive grasp of principles, because the intellect cannot be mistaken with regard to the proper object that is its intrinsic end (the essence of things) any more than the senses can: the eye knows infallibly when there is light and when there is not. The error, which is a failure in our intellectual activity, occurs only where there is a certain potentiality—in other words, in the work of interpretation, in the judgment or else in the reason. Now, in the angel's case, the totality of his intellectual activity is analogous to what is in our case the mere intuitive grasp of principles. The possibility of an error is therefore removed: the angel knows without any error everything that enters by right into the field of his natural knowledge.[54]

53. See *ST* I, q. 58, a. 5.

54. An angel can, however, be mistaken in the supernatural order. Perfectly in act as to his nature, he remains in effect in potency with regard to supernatural truths that transcend the natural truths. Although he knows everything that belongs naturally to a subject, he does not know, in that subject, that which results from supernatural divine free decisions. Error is therefore possible. But doesn't the supernatural interfere concretely in the natural order? Certainly; this is why a good angel, at the level of his natural knowledge, affirms nothing without making a reservation about this possibility of a supernatural divine action. A demon, in contrast, because of the perversity of his will, absolutizes the judgment based on his mere natural knowledge and can therefore be mistaken—for example, when he judges it impossible for a dead man to rise again. Resurrection is indeed impossible, if one considers only natural causes, but "nothing is impossible with God." The moralist will derive from this doctrine a wealth of applications for a nonnaturalist ethics of the intellect and the need for the mind seeking true wisdom to remain structurally open to superior divine reasons. There is something diabolical in the claim to make a science self-enclosed.

8

---:---

The Affective Life of the Angels

St. Thomas devotes two questions to the affective life of angels on the natural level. The first question defines the nature and the status of the affective power in an angel (q. 59); the second explains the activity of this affective power as well as the objects to which an angel's love is attached (q. 60).[1]

THE AFFECTIVE POWER OF AN ANGEL

The existence of a will in an angel is deduced directly from his intellectual nature, since the will is nothing other than the spiritual dynamic of adhering to the good that results from intellectual knowledge. Nevertheless, in article 1 of question 59, St. Thomas addresses the question from a loftier perspective, considering its higher reasons. All things, he explains, proceed from God's will. Now the divine will has the good as its object. Not the good to be obtained, because God has need of nothing, but the good to be communicated. God creates for his glory, in other words, in order to show forth his goodness, which amounts to

1. Concerning the will in angels, see Schlössinger, "Das angelische Wallen," *Jahrbuch für Philosophie und spekulative Theologie* 24 (1909–10): 152–224. Among modern and contemporary theologians, the most in-depth analyses on love and will in an angel are generally developed within the framework of the debate about the sin of the fallen angels. Here we will stay closer to the letter of St. Thomas's treatment.

making creatures participate in his own perfection by way of assimilation. Consequently, since the end of the passive recipient is the same as that of the agent, every creature tends toward this good that God wants to give him, but each in its own manner. St. Thomas then distinguishes among three ways of pursuing the good, which correspond to three levels in beings.

Beings that are devoid of all knowledge, such as inanimate objects and plants, are inclined or oriented toward the good—in other words, toward their own perfection and their full actualization, by virtue of a natural, intrinsic dynamism, which is called natural appetite, that is placed in them by the Author of nature.[2] Thus fire naturally tends to diffuse itself, a plant to grow, flower, and spread its seed.... Beings endowed with sense knowledge—namely, animals—perceive through this knowledge certain particular goods, and they are programmed to tend instinctively toward them. To the natural appetite that results from their substantial form is added an elicited sensitive appetite that results from the intentional form representing a particular good. So it is that a dog tends toward a bone. Finally, intellectual creatures as such have access to the universal.[3] Therefore they know the very notion of good (*ratio boni*), good in itself. The will is nothing other than the tendency, the dynamism that inclines a spiritual being toward the good that is grasped under the aspect of good.

Since an angel has an intellect, he necessarily has a will, an inclination toward the good as such. Article 2 explains that this will is really distinct from the essence of the angel.[4] In effect, the essence defines a subject in terms of his intrinsic components [*constituants*]. Now, in every creature, appetite brings the subject into relation with external realities that do not enter into his constitution. The angelic will that is directed, for example, toward God or other angels therefore cannot enter into the very essence of the angel. In God and in God alone is there an identity between the essence and the will, be-

2. See Jorge Laporta, "Pour trouver le sens exact des termes: *Appetitus naturalis, desiderium naturale, amor naturalis*, etc. chez Thomas d'Aquin," *AHDLMA* 40 (1973): 37–95.

3. In the response to the first objection, St. Thomas explains that it matters little whether the intellect arrives at the universal by intellectual intuition (angel) or at the conclusion of a reasoning process (man). In either case, the openness to the universal is the basis for the existence of a will.

4. See chapter 6 of this volume: "The status of action in an angel."

cause the divine will is determined only by his own goodness. Similarly, because in God the intellect and the will are directed toward the
same reality—namely, God as universal truth and goodness—they
are really identical, whereas in every creature, and therefore in an angel, intellect and will are necessarily distinct, since the intellect is centripetal, causing intelligible perfections that the subject does not have
to exist within it, and the will is centrifugal, turned toward the external good that the subject does not have.

Since the angel has a will, the question arises of whether he is endowed with free will, because this is nothing other than the will itself considered as capable of self-determination. The affirmation of
the angel's free will, which is well attested in tradition,[5] is obviously
of capital importance inasmuch as it opens up angelology to the moral dimension, strictly speaking. Yielding to his felicitous penchant for
vast perspectives, St. Thomas addresses the existence of angelic free
will by situating the perfection of freedom within a global vision of
the universe.[6] The hierarchy of beings can in fact be ascertained from
the degree of interiority of their activity. Some beings, because they
are deprived of knowledge, have no sort of interiority: they act only
and strictly insofar as they are moved by other beings. A billiard ball
pushes another billiard ball only inasmuch as it transmits an impulse
that it received in the first place. It conveys an energy that it in no way
interiorizes. Other beings—namely, animals—present an embryonic
form of interiority: they act by virtue of an estimation that is proper
to them, but this judgment (*arbitrium*) is not free. It results from in-
stinct; it is totally determined by their nature. Thus the sheep instinctively judges that it must get away from the wolf as quickly as possible.
Finally, intelligent beings act freely. Certainly, they are by nature—a
nature that they did not choose—inclined toward the good in general. But precisely this natural orientation toward the Absolute Good
makes them free in relation to each of the particular goods. They are
capable of stepping back from the immediate solicitations of these
particular goods and of relativizing them, in other words, in the liter-

5. See, for example, John Damascene, *Orthodox Faith* II.27 (FOTC 37:259): "One
should note that, since the angels are rational, they are free."
6. See *ST* I, q. 59, a. 3. On free will in God, see *ST* I, q. 19, a. 10, and in man, see *ST*
I, q. 83.

al sense of putting them in relation to the general notion of good. If this relation is not necessary, then they are free to choose this particular good or not to choose it, to choose this one rather than that one. They determine themselves in the order of means. This is the most perfect way of tending toward the good: not being guided from outside, but determining oneself from within, from the depths of one's personality, in keeping with the dignity of a mind that is fully master of its action.

St. Thomas notes that the perfection of free will is realized in a more excellent fashion in an angel than in a man, quite simply because the angelic intellect is more perfect than the human intellect. Moreover, among the angels themselves, the higher angels, being more intelligent, are also freer.[7] This idea, which is characteristic of Thomistic intellectualism, that a being is freer the more intelligent he is, runs directly counter to the universal notion of freedom that modern thinkers have devised.[8] In effect, if one defines freedom as the power to choose indifferently between good or evil, the logic becomes binary: one is free or one is not free, but one is not more or less free. But for St. Thomas, the absence of constraint, the power to choose either good or evil, is only the bark of freedom. The sap is to be found elsewhere. It is in the spiritual interiority of consent to the good. Now there are degrees of interiority: the more a being has integrated authentic values, the more he is master of his action—in other words, free.

Some object to the idea that an angel is free, arguing that freedom implies a choice, which in turn presupposes a deliberation: it is necessary to weigh the pros and cons before deciding freely. Now, an angel does not deliberate, since he grasps intuitively the conclusion in the principle. This is undeniable, St. Thomas replies, but the connection between choice and deliberation is proper to the human condition, signaling the imperfection thereof. In an angel, choice exists but it does not pass through the meanderings of previous deliberation; it is in a way instantaneous.[9] But in the natural order, the angel exercis-

---

7. See ST I, q. 59, a. 3, ad 3.

8. Concerning the opposition between the Thomistic freedom of excellence or quality and the modern freedom of indifference, and also its origins, see Servais Pinckaers, *The Sources of Christian Ethics*, trans. Mary Thomas Noble (Washington, D.C.: The Catholic University of America Press, 1995), chaps. 14–15, 327–78.

9. See ST I, q. 59, a. 3, arg. 1 and ad 1.

es this free choice only with respect to the realities that are inferior to him, because in the case of those that are superior it belongs to the angel's natural perfection to be determined by nature to will them.[10]

Besides the will, is it necessary to recognize in an angel the existence of two very general forms of appetite: the irascible (the faculty pertaining to the pursuit of difficult goods) and the concupiscible (the faculty pertaining to the pursuit of delectable goods, which are sources of pleasure for the senses)? This is the subject of the final article of question 59. Some patristic texts mentioning sensible passions in angels and especially in demons might be inclined to respond in the affirmative, but St. Thomas's resolute option in favor of the total immateriality of an angel prevents him, of course, from positing in an angel any sensitive power whatsoever. But do not "irascible" and "concupiscible" designate in an angel, analogously at least, two aspects as it were of his spiritual appetite? St. Thomas is unyielding. The powers, he explains, are distinguished not in terms of their material objects but in terms of their formal object. Sight pertains not to white dogs or green trees but to something that is colored as such. Therefore, we do not distinguish one power to see white and another power to see green. Similarly, the will pertains to the good in general, which indifferently includes the delectable good and the arduous good. As for the sensible appetite, it pertains by definition to particular goods, so that there is one form of appetite for the delectable good and another for difficult goods.

If an angel possesses neither an irascible nor a concupiscible appetite, in what sense does tradition attribute to him passions, sentiments, and even the virtues of temperance and fortitude, which in us

10. See ST I, q. 59, a. 3, arg. 2 and ad 2 (see also article 2, corpus). An angel cannot make a mistake in the order of natural knowledge; there is no indetermination in him. Is it not necessary to conclude from this that the same holds true in the volitional order? St. Thomas responds by distinguishing between knowledge and appetite. Knowledge is "centripetal": the object of knowledge is immanent to the subject, so that it enters into the definition of the subject's perfection. An angel that did not have all the knowledge that he can have naturally would therefore be imperfect. In contrast, love is "centrifugal": the object of appetite is outside the subject. In this case, in order for a subject who loves to be perfect, it is enough that his love should be rightly determined with respect to superior realities (here, God and the higher angels), but the angel's relation to inferior creatures is indeterminate: it depends on free will. The existence of an elective love therefore does not contradict the angel's perfection, as the existence of a progressive knowledge would.

human beings serve to regulate the passions of the concupiscible and
the irascible appetites according to the norm of reason and furthermore are seated in those two sensible faculties?[11] St. Thomas refuses to attribute passions, strictly speaking, to an angel. When a passage from tradition speaks about angelic passions, we must interpret
it, as in the case of the divine passions, either to mean the purely spiritual movement that in human beings is incarnated in the passion in
question (spiritual joy, for example), or else in a metaphorical sense,
by virtue of an analogy of proportionality based on a similarity of
effects: the angel is said to be angry when he acts as an angry man
would act—in other words, by punishing the one who is doing evil.[12]
Consequently temperance, in an angel, has a different meaning than
in human beings; it signifies that the angel's will is regulated according to the divine will. The same goes for fortitude: it signifies that the
angel resolutely carries out the will of God.

LOVE IN AN ANGEL

The first act of any will—the act from which all the others flow—is
none other than love or dilection. For if I detest Peter, it is because

11. See *ST* I, q. 59, a. 4, arg. 1–3 and ad 1–3.
12. St. Thomas resorts to the same principle of interpretation as in the case of divine anger; see *ST* I, q. 3, a. 2, ad 2. Compare Augustine, *City of God* IX.5 (FOTC 14:85–
86): "We may well ask the further question whether our liability to passion even in the
performance of duty is not a part of the infirmity of our present life. For the holy angels
punish without anger those whom the eternal law of God has delivered to them for punishment, succor the suffering without suffering compassion, and rescue from peril those
whom they love without sharing their fear. Yet, in our human way, we speak as though
the angels had all these feelings. This is done by reason of the analogy between their actions and ours, not because we attribute to them the infirmity of our own passions—
much as, in Scripture, God Himself is said to be angry without implying the least movement of passion. The word 'anger' is used because God's vengeance is effective, not
because His nature is affective" (Sed adhuc merito quaeri potest, utrum ad vitae prae-
sentis pertineat infirmitatem etiam in quibusque bonis officiis huiusce modi perpeti affectus, sancti vero angeli et sine ira puniant, quos accipiunt aeterna Dei lege puniendos,
et miseris sine miseriae compassione subveniant, et periclitantibus eis, quos diligunt,
sine timore opitulentur; et tamen istarum nomina passionum consuetudine locutionis
humanae etiam in eos usurpentur propter quamdam operum similitudinem, non propter affectionum infirmitatem, sicut ipse Deus secundum Scripturas irascitur, nec tamen
ulla passione turbatur. Hoc enim verbum vindictae usurpavit effectus, non illius turbu-
lentus affectus).

I love Paul more, and Peter is his sworn enemy; if I rejoice that my friend has passed his exam, it is because I love him.... In short, all the movements of the affectivity depend in the last analysis on love.[13]

St. Thomas begins question 60 by distinguishing two general modalities of love in an angel: natural love and elective love.[14] Article 1 is concerned with natural love.[15] Every being is defined by an essence or nature. Now every nature involves a certain inclination toward the good that corresponds to it. This inclination (which must be understood here as a second act) is called natural love. Since an angel is a nature, he too possesses a natural love. But natural love is realized in different ways according to the natures in question. In beings devoid of knowledge, it is a matter of a simple natural dynamism, like the one that conveys a stone downward. In animals, this natural love is embodied in the sensible appetite, such as the one that moves a dog toward its bone. In a spiritual being who is endowed with intellectual knowledge, this natural love is the love that his will has for the good in general, for his final end, the love that defines him.

But is not an affirmation of the existence of this natural love for the good the same as a denial of the angel's freedom?[16] Such an objec-

---

13. See *ST* I-II, q. 25, a. 2.

14. The adjective "natural" is the source of inevitable ambiguities. Here, natural means "by way of nature" and is contrasted to "elective." Yet, at the same time, in *ST* qq. 59–60, St. Thomas is situated within the framework of the natural order as distinct from the supernatural order of grace. Consequently there is such a thing as a natural elective love or even a supernatural natural love!

As we already noted with reference to knowledge, the supernatural order does not destroy the natural order but takes it up and perfects it. Thus the supernatural love of charity, based on the communication by God to an angel of a deeper, more intimate participation in his perfection, which draws the angel toward God as the fully beatifying Good (see *ST* I, q. 60, a. 5, ad 4), does not suppress but takes up and integrates the dynamisms of love in the natural order in the angel, without absorbing them, however. St. Thomas criticizes all supernaturalism that would tend to obscure the natural stratum of a life that is concretely supernatural; see *ST* I, q. 60, a. 1, ad 3. The dynamisms of angelic love in the order natural, described in q. 60, therefore subsist in the supernatural order both in the good angels and also in the demons, in whom they are falsified, however. Furthermore, according to *Q. de malo*, q. 16, a. 4, an angel's first act of love, at the first instant of his creation, was concretely an act pertaining to the object of the angel's natural love.

15. Cajetan's commentary on this passage gives useful clarifications as to the exact meaning to be assigned in this article to the terms *inclinatio, natura, amor naturalis*.

16. See *ST* I, q. 60, a. 1, arg. 2 et ad 2.

tion results from a very erroneous view in which freedom is thought to be, on the one hand, an absolute, a sheer self-assertion, and, on the other hand, opposed to nature. Now, first, it must be admitted that in every creature freedom is exercised within the conditions of a nature that the creature did not give to itself but rather receives from the Creator along with its fundamental dynamisms. Natural love, which is so to speak the inalienable mark of the creature's dependence on God, precedes the choices of free will. It is nonetheless totally spontaneous and in no way imposed as though from outside, since it expresses the inherent nature of the subject. Only in God, and in God alone, is will really identified with nature and consequently moved by nothing but itself; God is all that he wants and wants all that he is. It is necessary, second, to understand that freedom is possible only within the dynamism of natural love, the condition of all freedom. Only the natural love of the end introduces a tension in the will and allows the exercise of choices relative to the means. All of my volitional activity therefore presupposes this basic dynamism that impels me toward the Good in general.

The *will* tends *naturally* to its last end; for every *man naturally* wills *happiness*: and all other desires are *caused* by this *natural* desire; since whatever a man wills he wills on account of the end.[17]

The second type of affective dynamism found in an angel— namely, elective love— the love of choice (*dilectio electiva*), which is discussed in article 2, therefore exists only in dependence on natural love, which thus appears as the permanent condition and the source of elective love. These two modalities of angelic love are therefore not simply juxtaposed, but rather one envelops the other. Indeed, it is a general rule that what belongs to the nature of a being plays the role of a principle in relation to its various activities. Aquinas spells this out in the case of knowledge and love in man. In the order of intellectual knowledge, man progressively actualizes his knowledge starting from the light of the first principles that are naturally known. In the order of love, man loves with an elective love the means that advance

17. *ST* I, q. 60, a. 2: "Unde voluntas naturaliter tendit in suum finem ultimum: omnis enim homo naturaliter vult beatitudinem. Et ex hac naturali voluntate causantur omnes aliae voluntates: cum quidquid homo vult, velit propter finem."

him toward his end—that is, happiness—starting from the natural love of that end. An angel therefore loves with a love of choice the goods inferior to himself that he orders to what he loves with a natural love.

Let us specify now those goods, those objects onto which the natural or elective love of an angel fastens. St. Thomas discerns three types: the angel loves himself (a. 3), he loves the other angels (a. 4), he loves God—and he naturally loves him more than himself (a. 5).

St. Thomas's approach is particularly baffling for a mind formed by the categories of modern thought. This is so for two main reasons. The first has to do with the *objective* character of the Thomistic analysis of love. To be brief, let us say that the modern approach to love is essentially subjective: it is preoccupied with the *subject* who loves and with his psychological and moral dispositions. The Thomistic approach is essentially objective, since a power is defined by its act and its object: it is preoccupied in the first place with the *object* of love—namely, the good as a property of being—and only afterward, in light of this, does it consider the properties of the *subject* who loves. Thus modern spirituality is obsessed, as it were, with the dialectic between egotism and altruism. Which comes first: egotism or altruism? How does one pass from egotism to altruism?[18] Or from love of self, which seems to come first, to the love of another and to the love of God (God being thought of as the Other par excellence)? This is not the set of questions posed by St. Thomas. The value of love is derived from the dignity of the object loved and not directly from the dispositions of the loving subject. So that egotism, in the sense of self-love, is not bad in itself: there is a good egotism when I love what is good in me in proportion to its degree of goodness (and God proves here to be the supreme egotist), and a bad egotism—just as there is a good and a bad altruism.

The second reason for the baffling character of St. Thomas's approach to love has to do with his metaphysical conviction that unity by nature precedes diversity. Otherness is never first. For modern thinkers, every human being is a monad, an island, who more or less

18. This problem is analogous to the problem of the bridge that obsesses modern epistemology: how does one pass from the subjectivity of the thinking subject to objectivity?

effectively constructs footbridges to the other islands. For St. Thomas, creatures understand one another only within a whole that precedes and supports them. Each one in its way has a share in this fundamental unity that proceeds from his common reference to God. It is logical therefore that all should love the common good of that community more than their particular good.

In this perspective, St. Thomas has no scruples about affirming that an angel loves himself simultaneously with a natural love and with a love of choice.[19] He begins by recalling the distinction (originally Aristotelian) between the love of concupiscence and the love of benevolence or friendship.[20] This is derived from the distinction between substantial good and accidental good. Is the beloved a subject, a person? In that case, we are dealing with a love of benevolence: I want the good of that subject; I want such and such a good for this subject. For example, I want my friend Peter to have metaphysical knowledge and to work to that end. Or is the beloved an accident, a quality? In that case the love that I have for that quality is a love of concupiscence: I desire it for such and such a subject (myself or someone else). For example, I love metaphysics for what it can offer my friend Peter. The love of concupiscence is therefore always dependent on a love of benevolence.

Love of self is a metaphysical law inscribed at the heart of beings. Every being desires by nature, consciously or unconsciously, what is good for it, what is capable of leading it to its own perfection, and "this is [what it means] to love self," says St. Thomas. There is nothing morally impure about it, since in seeking its proper perfection—by that I mean its true good—every being tends in fact to glorify God. This love is a natural love, but it is expressed in elective love when the subject himself determines the particular, non-necessary goods that he intends to use in order to attain his end.

Will someone object that love, and especially the love of friendship, always presupposes two subjects, since it has the remarkable property of uniting beings? In that case, the love of self is a pure con-

19. See *ST* I, q. 60, a. 3.
20. See *ST* I-II, q. 26, a. 4: "Whether love is properly divided into love of friendship and love of concupiscence" (Utrum amor convenienter dividatur in amorem amicitiae et amorem concupiscentiae).

tradition,[21] to which St. Thomas replies that unity precedes union. Indeed, if unity is the result or the fruit of love,[22] it is also, under the form of resemblance, the cause, the condition thereof.[23]

This causality of resemblance in love is moreover the beginning of an answer to the following question: at the level of natural love, does an angel love other angels as himself?[24] The answer is affirmative: it is natural for an angel to love other angels inasmuch as he shares with them one and the same nature. This generic resemblance among angels is a cause of love, just as the specific resemblance among human beings is the cause of a spontaneous benevolence. Even the demons love the good angels by reason of this natural similarity, whereas they detest them otherwise by reason of their extreme moral dissimilarity.[25]

Following Aristotle, St. Thomas therefore has love for others proceed from love of self: it is like an extension thereof. "Friendly relations to others ... seem to be derived from our relations toward ourselves."[26] By loving himself, the subject loves what is one with him, that with which he has something in common. St. Thomas also thinks that the intensity of love for another is measured by the degree of unity. But another consequence of this is that an angel loves himself more than he loves other angels.[27]

The question about the angel's natural love for God is more decisive.[28] St. Thomas defends here, for the first time in the *Summa theo-*

21. See *ST* I, q. 60, a. 3, arg. 2 et ad 2.

22. See *ST* I-II, q. 28, aa. 1–2.

23. See *ST* I-II, q. 27, a. 3. Thus, as the book of Genesis explains, if man and woman tend toward one another so as to be one flesh, it is because they were originally one.

24. See *ST* I, q. 60, a. 4.

25. See *ST* I, q. 60, a. 4, ad 3: "Nor can such natural love be stripped from the wicked angels, without their still retaining a natural affection towards the good angels, in so far as they share the same nature with them. But they hate them, in so far as they are unlike them according to righteousness and unrighteousness" (Nec ista dilectio naturalis removeri potest etiam ab angelis malis, quin dilectionem naturalem habeant ad alios angelos, inquantum cum eis communicant in natura. Sed odiunt eos, inquantum diversificantur secundum iustitiam et iniustitiam).

26. Aristotle, *Nicomachean Ethics*, trans. F. H. Peters (London: Kegan Paul, Trench, and Trübner, 1893), 294.

27. See *ST* I, q. 60, a. 4, ad 2.

28. See *ST* I, q. 60, a. 5. See Marie-Rosaire Gagnebet, "L'amour naturel de Dieu chez saint Thomas et ses contemporains," *RT* 48 (1948): 394–446; 49 (1949): 31–102; Thomas M. Osborne, *Love of Self and Love of God in Thirteenth-Century Ethics* (Notre Dame, Ind.: University of Notre Dame Press, 2005).

logiae, a thesis to which he will often return: every creature naturally loves God more than itself. We find it again in *ST* I-II, q. 109, a. 3 with regard to man: if he had not sinned, man would naturally love God more than himself, but in his present state of fallen nature, he needs healing grace in order to restore in him this natural love of God above all. Then in *ST* II-II, q. 26, a. 3, where St. Thomas explains that charity —which makes us love God above all things—only brings to its accomplishment, in a higher order, what is already present in the natural love of every creature for God. Indeed, if love of self were naturally first in relation to love of God, then charity would destroy that love instead of fulfilling it. Once again, grace does not suppress nature but brings it to its perfection.

In framing article 5 of question 60, St. Thomas begins by presenting the position of an early thirteenth-century theologian, William of Auxerre,[29] only to reject it, as did most of his contemporaries. This theologian thought that an angel (and man before the fall) experiences a twofold natural love with respect to God. First he loves him with an ardent love of concupiscence inasmuch as he wants for himself this objectively supreme good that is God, more than he wants for himself the limited good that is himself. Then he loves him with a certain love of friendship inasmuch as the angel desires for God an objectively greater good than he wants for himself: indeed, he wants God to be God and the angel to be an angel. But he desires this objectively greater good for God with less intensity than he desires his own good.

St. Thomas Aquinas, for his part, insists that the creature's natural love for God, far from being an extension of self-love, is on the contrary the source and permanent foundation of the love of self and of others. It is therefore by nature more intense and more powerful than self-love. To prove this, Aquinas has recourse, as is his custom, to an analysis of the physical world, in which the general laws of metaphysics stand out more clearly. Now in the physical world it appears that every subject whose nature depends on another by way of participation is primarily inclined toward that other, more so than toward itself. This orientation is manifested at the level of action by the prior-

29. Guillaume d'Auxerre (William of Auxerre), *Summa aurea*, lib. II, tr. 2, c. 4, ed. Jean Ribaillier, Spicilegium bonaventurianum 16–20 (Paris: Éditions du Centre national de la recherche scientifique; Rome: Editiones Collegii S. Bonaventurae ad Claras Aquas, 1980), 42–43.

ity that is spontaneously given to the common good of all over the
particular good: the part naturally sacrifices itself for the good of the
whole in which it participates. Thus, in the body, the hand exposes itself to harm in order to protect the head; in the animal world, the individual faces its own destruction for the survival of the species.…
This natural subordination of the particular good to the common
good is adopted, intelligently and freely, by spiritual beings. So it is
that the citizen can come to risk his life for the good of the city.

Since God is the cause of all beings, it follows that they all naturally love God more than themselves. This thesis is inseparable from
a theology of participation, the framework for the Thomistic vision
of the world, which obviously must not be confused with any sort of
pantheism. God is not the whole of which creatures would then be
the intrinsic constituent parts. He is the Principle and the End of creatures—in other words, the common separate Good toward which the
whole universe tends and that it searches to imitate. The deficient resemblance that it attains constitutes the immanent common good of
the universe, a created reflection of the Creator's perfection. Since every creature is a part of this whole that is the universe, of which God is
the common Good, it is natural for it to search the common Good before its particular good—in other words, to love God more than itself.

But finally, does not nature itself teach us that the ultimate motive
for all action is self-preservation?[30] St. Thomas does not believe that at
all. The promotion of the common good always wins out because, if a
subject works for his own preservation, it is inasmuch as the good of
the whole is accomplished thereby and therein. There is much more
in the acting subject than his private good: there is everything in him
that participates in the common good.[31] "None of us lives to himself"
(Rom 14:7).

30. See *ST* I, q. 60, a. 5, arg. 3 et ad 3.
31. The primacy of the common good is, for St. Thomas, one of the main foundations for the prohibition of suicide, considered as an attack on the common good. See
ST II-II, q. 64, a. 5: "Every part, as such, belongs to the whole. Now every man is part
of the community, and so, as such, he belongs to the community. Hence by killing himself he injures the community, as the Philosopher declares (*Ethic.* V.11)" (Quaelibet pars
id quod est, est totius. Quilibet autem homo est pars communitatis, et ita id quod est,
est communitatis. Unde in hoc quod seipsum interficit, iniuriam communitati facit, ut
patet per Philosophum, in V Ethic). The community in question is not necessarily the
political community, because the person in certain aspects transcends that community,
but rather the moral community of spiritual creatures.

Another similar objection, which worldly wise observers of human nature might reaffirm: all love is ultimately an interested love of self.[32] If I love something other than myself, it is always inasmuch as this something is for me a means of attaining my own perfection. Thus, I love God because it is good for me. St. Thomas, as we said, does not share this subjective way of approaching the question of love. According to him, just as the eye is drawn by the light, wherever it finds it, so too love is naturally drawn toward the greatest objective good: an angel loves God not for the good that may result from it for himself, but for the good that God is in himself, even though this love of God fully gratifies him, as though in addition.[33] One could find here the foundations for a Thomistic response to the problem of pure love that has so much obsessed modern spiritual writers. But as soon as one becomes trapped in a logic of psychological opposition between egotism and altruism or pure generosity, the problem becomes insoluble. In order to resolve it, it is necessary to start from an objective approach to love as the faculty of objective good. This, unfortunately, does not remove the concrete difficulties that spring from the conflict within us between nature, sin, and grace.

Indeed, true self-love necessarily surpasses itself in the love of God. What I love in myself, when my love is sincere, is greater than myself. Consequently the movement by which I love myself for what I am in truth makes me love God more than myself, because my true me is defined in relation to God. It is only when I become attached to the *bonum privatum*, to my own good cut off from its relation to God—in short, when I take myself for my final end—that I subvert the natural moral order. We then get the love of self to the point of contempt for God that is at the foundation of the City of evil. But this unnatural love of self stops at the most superficial part of myself, so that someone who loves himself apart from God in fact detests himself.

But properly speaking, in the objectivist perspective of St. Thomas, is it possible not to love God above all else?[34] Can one still give an account of sin and of hatred for God? Yes, St. Thomas replies, in-

32. See *ST* I, q. 60, a. 5, arg. 2 et ad 2.
33. On this question, see Thierry-Marie Hamonic, "Dieu peut-il être légitimement convoité? Quelques aspects de la théologie thomiste de l'amour selon le Père Labourdette," *RT* 92 (1992): 239–66.
34. See *ST* I, q. 60, a. 5, arg. 5 et ad 5.

asmuch as a person can fail to perceive explicitly the real identity between the common Good of the universe, which is also his happiness,
and God considered in himself as distinct from everything.[35] In that
case, this person naturally loves the common Good of the universe
(implicit natural love for God) but can place this happiness in something other than God, thus preferring the creature to the Creator,
which is the very definition of sin. One can even come to hate God
explicitly with an elective hatred, while implicitly loving him with
a natural love.[36] What about an angel? Can he, in the natural order,
come to prefer himself to God? The question is openly debated even
within the Thomistic tradition. For some, since the angel was established in all his natural perfection from the moment of his creation, it
is impossible for him not to love God above all things, impossible for
him to sin in the natural order. For others, the perfection of an angel,
even in the natural order, requires not only a natural love of God but
also an act of love that is a free choice and that aims directly at God,
who is grasped as such, in his singularity, and no longer merely under
the veil of the common Good. And so, above and beyond the considerations about the angelic nature that have occupied us in this chapter, this invites us to consider in the following chapter the concrete
historical realizations of that nature, especially in the supernatural order of the call to perfect communion with the Holy Trinity.

35. With regard to God's existence, *ST* I, q. 2, a. 2, St. Thomas rejects the position of
those who cite the natural desire for happiness as proof that every man knows God in-
nately. For him, it is not permissible to pass directly from what is implicit to what is explicit, from confused knowledge to distinct knowledge. The fact that there is some being, some truth, some good (or even a supreme good that one calls happiness) does not
immediately imply the existence of Being, Truth, or Good—in short, the existence of
God. It is still necessary to show that the common being, the common truth, the common good—in other words, the being, the truth, and the good that are encountered in
the world of our experience—require a transcendent cause. The fundamental structure
of reality—namely, the distinction between beings-by-participation and subsistent Being—is not evident at first to the human intellect.

36. Those who are unwilling to see in God anything but the cause of certain particular effects that go against their particular will may hate God. For example, someone
who rebels against an illness that God permits and hates God inasmuch as he permits
that illness, or the demons who hate God inasmuch as he is the principle and the norm
of the supernatural order that they reject.

PART 3

———— : ————

The Angelic Adventure

We are born as human beings while still having to become men and women. Although we possess, by a birthright, the essential principles that define human nature, the perfection of that nature in us is situated at the end of a long process, of a history during the course of which, by our free choices, we apply—or thwart—the potentialities of that nature. Human life therefore exhibits an intrinsic historic dimension, which is true just as much of persons as it is of communities and cultures. Since grace does not destroy nature but rather seeps into its structures, the marvelous work of our divinization also takes on the form of a history. The life of grace, implanted in us by baptism, attains its perfection only at the end of a complex sacred history made up of advances and setbacks, false steps and conversions, during which, under the influence of God's grace, we apply—or thwart—the potentialities of this supernatural life, the purpose of which is full communion with the Trinity in eternal beatitude.

An angel is by nature simpler than a man and consequently less bound to time. However, he too has a history.[1] On the hypothesis of a purely natural destiny, as we mentioned, theologians are divided: some think that the angel would have been without history, perfect from the first moment of his creation; others maintain that he would

1. See Charles Journet, *L'Église du Verbe incarné: Essai de théologie de l'histoire du salut*, in Journet, *Oeuvres complètes* (St.-Maurice, 2004), 4:206–394.

still have had to make a personal choice in order to take God as his final end. But on the supernatural level, which is the only real one, all agree in acknowledging that the angel was led to make a crucial choice, given the call that God addressed to him: "*Duc in altum.* Put out into the deep." This choice was lightning-quick and irreversible, in keeping with the very nature of an angel. It was in a single, decisive act—a concentrated sacred history—that each angel merited his eternal beatitude (chapter 9) or separated himself forever from God so as to become a demon (chapter 10).

9

Creation, Vocation, and Supernatural
Happiness of the Angels

THE CREATION OF THE ANGELS

The production of the angels in their "state of nature" [*"être de na-*
ture"] is the subject of question 61 of the *prima pars*. It is a matter of
faith that an angel is a creature,[1] and St. Thomas effortlessly gives the
intelligible reason for the created status of an angel in his framing of
article 1 by applying to the angel the main themes of the theology of
creation, elaborated in terms of the categories of a metaphysics of
participation.[2] God and God alone is essentially his *esse*: he is the *Ip-*
sum esse subsistens [subsisting existence itself]. In any subject other

1. See Aquinas, *De substantiis separatis*, c. 18: "Concerning the origin of spiritual
substances, Christian tradition teaches very steadfastly that all spiritual substances, like
other creatures, were produced by God. This is proved by the authority of the canonical Scriptures. For it says in the Psalm: 'Praise Him, all His angels, praise Him, all His
powers,' and after the enumeration of the other creatures it adds, 'for He spoke and they
were made, He commanded and they were created'" (Circa spiritualium substantiarum
originem firmissime docet christiana traditio omnes spirituales substantias, sicut et cet-
eras creaturas, a Deo esse productas. Et hoc quidem canonicae Scripturae auctoritate
probatur. In Psalmo enim dicitur: "Laudate eum omnes angeli eius, laudate eum omnes
virtutes eius"; et enumeratis aliis creaturis subditur: "quia ipse dixit, et facta sunt: mandavit, et creata sunt"). St. Thomas no doubt adopts this scriptural authority from St. Augustine, *City of God*, XI9 (FOTC 14:200), who refers to it in the same context.

2. See, for example, *ST* I, q. 44.

than God, who is subsisting perfection and hence necessarily unique, existence is participated; it is distinct from the essence that it actualizes and with which it enters into composition. Now, if existence is participated, it is received. Consequently, the existence of an angel is caused by the First Cause of existence, who is God.

Every subject whose existence is ultimately dependent on the divine influence is a creature, but not every creature comes into existence by way of creation—in other words, by virtue of a divine act that brings it into being directly out of nothingness. Thus Spot is not produced *ex nihilo*; he is drawn from the potentiality of matter by the action of Fido, his sire, whose generative energies dispose matter in such a way that from it emerges the structure that corresponds to the canine form. An angel, in contrast, can come into being only by way of creation. Indeed, his essence is simple—in other words, not composed of parts. Therefore it can only be produced all at once, *ex nihilo*, by an act that brings into being the totality of his angelic substance.

Now creative action belongs exclusively and immediately to God.[3] There is no intermediary in the creative act, no instrumental cause, quite simply because there is no matter to dispose with a view to the form. Therefore it is necessary to discard resolutely the paradigm of emanation characteristic of the various kinds of neo-Platonism, according to which the angels engender one another. Every angel is immediately created by God.[4]

In fact, at the time of St. Thomas, the chief question being debated concerning the creation of an angel was the question as to the moment thereof. The question is subdivided into two.[5] First, article 2 of

3. See *ST* I, q. 45, a. 5.

4. The immediate relation that every spiritual creature maintains with God as his beginning implies an immediate relation with God as his end. Unlike the various sorts of neo-Platonism that situate the happiness of each separated substance in the contemplation of the immediately superior substance that is its immediate origin, biblically inspired creationism asserts that God alone can be the final end of a spiritual substance. Thus St. Thomas explains that man's beatitude cannot consist in the contemplation of the angels because man is not created by an angel but directly by God. See *ST* I-II, q. 3, a. 7 (especially ad 2).

5. I leave aside the opinion of St. Gregory of Nyssa, *On the Making of Man* XVII (NPNF–2 5:407a), which says that angels multiply mysteriously, in succession, coming into existence one after the other. Gregory of Nyssa is trying to prove that a successive spiritual multiplication of an angelic sort would have been possible for man if he

question 61 refutes the idea that the angels were created from all eternity. This thesis enjoyed renewed interest because of the great debate in the thirteenth century over the possibility of an eternal world.[6] For St. Thomas, the creation of the angels in time is a truth of the faith, and consequently to deny it is heresy. Of course, he admits the theoretical, philosophical possibility of an eternal world, since the eternity or non-eternity of the world depends solely on God's will. But, in that case, it can be known only by revelation, which affirms precisely that creatures had a beginning.

Second, article 3 asks, what is the chronological relation between the creation of the spiritual world and that of the material world? Were the angels created before, at the same time, or even after the material world?[7] The question is ancient and is sustained by the silence of Genesis concerning the creation of the angels.[8] It cannot be

---

had not had original sin—all this in order to corroborate the highly debatable thesis that sexual reproduction in man is merely the consequence of sin. The fathers rejected this hypothesis of a successive production of angels; see, for example, Theodoret of Cyr, *Thérapeutique des maladies helléniques* (SC 57:197): "The nature of incorporeal beings was not made in a couple, but rather God created it all at once [*athroan*], in the sense that he created from the beginning all the myriads whose existence he determined. This is why the use of the female sex is superfluous for the latter: inasmuch as they are immortal they have no need of increasing, and inasmuch as they are incorporeal they are not capable of uniting."

6. The arguments in favor of an eternal creation of the angels that are set forth in this article repeat in their own way the "classic" arguments in favor of the eternity of the world. See *ST* I, q. 46. God is the cause of the world by his existence; now his existence is eternal. Therefore, if the cause is eternal, the effect is also (arg. 1). Creation in time would imply a change in God (arg. 2). The angels are necessary beings, and therefore eternal (arg. 3). On the debate over the eternity of the world in the thirteenth century, see, among the more recent works, Josef B. M. Wissink, ed., *The Eternity of the World in the Thought of Thomas Aquinas and His Contemporaries*, Studien und Texte zur Geistesgeschichte des Mittelalters 27 (Leiden, New York, and Cologne: E. J. Brill, 1990); Richard C. Dales, *Medieval Discussions of the Eternity of the World*, Brill's Studies in Intellectual History 18 (Leiden, New York, and Cologne: E. J. Brill, 1990); Cyrille Michon, Olivier Boulnois, and Nathanaël Dupré la Tour, eds., *Thomas d'Aquin et la controverse sur "L'Éternité du monde": Traités sur "L'Éternité du monde" de Bonaventure, Thomas d'Aquin, Peckham, Boèce et Dacie, Henri de Gand et Guillaume d'Ockham* (Paris: Flammarion, 2004).

7. See Journet, *L'Église du Verbe incarné*, IV: 396–409, "La simultanéité de la création."

8. See Augustine, *City of God* XI.9 (FOTC 14:199): "When Scripture speaks of the creation of the world, it does not indicate clearly whether, or in what order, the *angels* were created" (Ubi de mundi constitutione sacrae Litterae loquuntur, non evidenter dicitur, utrum vel quo ordine creati sint angeli). St. Augustine then sets forth several hy-

resolved, Aquinas thinks, by scripture alone.[9] Moreover, the "holy doctors" are divided on this point. The question seems to have been raised by Origen. According to him, all spiritual creatures were created before the material world for the simple reason that the appearance of the material world is a consequence of their fall.[10] This argument is obviously unacceptable because the material world was not willed by God to make the best of a bad situation. That being said, most of the church fathers did admit that the spiritual creation was prior to the material creation.[11] St. Thomas mentions, as holding this

---

potheses: the creation of the angels is implicitly signified by Gn 1:1: "In the beginning God created the heavens [= the angels] and the earth [= the material world]," or else, in Gn 1:3, the mention of the creation of "light" on the first day to mean the spiritual light that is an angel. In *ST* I, q. 61, a. 1, ad 1, and also in *De substantiis separatis*, c. 17, St. Thomas cites, as the reason for this concealment of the creation of the angels, the "uncultured" character of the Hebrew people to whom Moses was speaking; they were incapable of lifting their minds to the spiritual level and inclined to idolatry.

9. See *De substantiis separatis*, c. 17: "It is impossible to tell clearly from the canonical Scriptures when the angels were created" (Non potest ex scripturis canonicis expresse haberi quando creati sunt angeli). As St. Augustine had noted, *City of God* XI.9 (FOTC 14:200–1), scripture excludes only the possibility that the angels were created after the material world, because of Jb 38:6–7: "Who laid its cornerstone, when the morning stars sang together, and all the sons of God shouted for joy?" In the opinion of St. Thomas, *De substantiis separatis*, c. 17, a later creation of the angels would be unfitting anyway: the most perfect always comes first. As for the noncanonical texts, see *Jubilees* 2:2, which says that the angels were created on the first day: "For on the first day he created the heavens which are above, and the earth, and the waters, and every spirit that serves before him—the angels of the presence, and the angels of holiness, and the angels of the spirit of the winds" (*Apocryphal Old Testament*, 14). An editor's note on page 641 of the Pléiade edition of *La Bible: Écrits intertestamentaires* points out that the rabbis would have combated this doctrine "so that no one would believe that God had had associates at the time of the creation of the world."

10. In any case, this is how St. Augustine presents Origen's position in *City of God* XI.23 (FOTC 14:222): "They also claim that *souls* ... have *sinned* by withdrawing from the Creator and, according to the gravity of their *sins*, have been imprisoned in bodies ranging, by degrees, from heaven down to earth, and that such souls and bodies constitute the cosmos. Thus, they, too, explain creation by saying that it was not for the sake of producing things that were good but merely for imprisoning things that were sinful. *Origen* has been rightly reproved for holding and expressing such views" (Animas dicunt ... peccasse a Conditore recedendo et diversis progressibus pro diversitate peccatorum a caelis usque ad terras diversa corpora quasi vincula meruisse, et hunc esse mundum eamque causam mundi fuisse faciendi, non ut conderentur bona, sed ut mala cohiberentur. Hinc Origenes iure culpatur). See Origen, *On First Principles* III.5.4–5 (1966), 239–42.

11. St. Thomas divided the two theories along cultural lines: the Greeks held that

opinion, St. Jerome, St. John Damascene, and especially Gregory of Nazianzen, "who has great authority in Christian doctrine."[12] On the other hand St. Augustine, after some hesitation, opts for simultaneous creation.[13]

St. Thomas, like most of the Scholastics, prudently sides with the simultaneous creation of the visible universe and the invisible universe.[14] Indeed, according to him, the spiritual creation and the vis-

---

the angelic world existed beforehand (ad 1: "sententia doctorum graecorum, qui omnes hoc concorditer sentiunt, quod angeli sunt ante mundum corporeum creati") and the Latins that it was created simultaneously with the material world. But in reality several fathers among the Greeks (St. Epiphanius, Theodore of Mopsuestia, Theodoret of Cyr) are opposed to the prior existence of the angelic world and, among the Latins, some do hold this opinion. See John Cassian, *Conferences* VIII.7 (ACW 57:295): "before the founding of this visible creation God made the spiritual and heavenly powers.... For we must not think that God first began his creation and his work with the establishment of this world, as if he did not exercise his providence and the divine superintendence during those innumerable previous ages, and as if it should be believed that he had no one upon whom to confer the benefits of his kindness, being alone and a stranger to bountifulness." Cassian's argument is, at the very least, unreliable, because it concludes that an eternal creation is highly fitting. For a presentation of the patristic opinions on the question, see Bareille, "Angélologie d'après les Pères," 1:1193–95. In *De substantiis separatis*, c. 17, St. Thomas suggests an additional explanation for this division: those who opt for a historical interpretation of the six days tend to posit the priority of the angels, whereas the others (St. Augustine) logically favor their simultaneity.

12. See Gregory of Nazianzen, *Oration* 38.9–11 (SC 358:120–27); Jerome, *Commentarii in epistolam ad Titum* 1.2 (PL 26:594); John Damascene, *Orthodox Faith* II.3 (FOTC 37:208): "Now, some say that the angels were made before all creation, as Gregory the Theologian says: 'First He conceived the angelic and heavenly powers, and His conception was an accomplished work.' But there are others who say that they were made after the creation of the first heaven. However, they all agree that it was before the formation of man. For my part, I agree with the Theologian, because it was fitting for the spiritual substance to be created first and then the sensible and then finally man himself from both." Another passage in favor of the priority of spiritual creation that we might mention is Basil, *Homilies on the Hexaemeron* I.5 and II.5 (FOTC 46:8–10, 29–30).

13. See Augustine, *City of God* XI.9 (FOTC 14:199–201). His position is "canonized" by Lombard, *Sententiae* II, d. 2, c. 3 (10).

14. The Fourth Lateran Council in 1215 (Denz.-H., no. 800) defined as an article of faith that God, "by His own omnipotent power at once from the beginning of time created each creature from nothing, spiritual, and corporal, namely, angelic and mundane" (simul ab initio temporis utramque de nihilo condidit creaturam, spiritualem et corporalem, angelicam videlicet et mundanam). But the interpretation of *simul* is debated. The adverb *simul* does not necessarily refer to the phrase *ab initio temporis*; it can mean that God *willed* angels and corporeal creatures at the same time, contrary to the theory of Origen, who saw the material world as an accident. See Aquinas, *In Decretalem I Expositio*, Leonine edition, vol. 40, E 34–E 35: "Origen's error was different: he supposed

ible creation form one universe in which angels and material creatures maintain multiple ties. This relation of the parts within the whole greatly contributes to the unity and therefore to the perfection of the universe. The universe is therefore more perfect when these two parts exist together and interact with one another. Something would have been lacking in the angelic world without the physical world and in the physical world without the angelic world. Now the God of St. Thomas, who is not that susceptible to the charm of a gradual, Teilhardian genesis, produces nothing imperfect.[15]

THE SUPERNATURAL VOCATION
OF THE ANGELS

By a special effect of the "exceedingly great love" of God, which goes well beyond what the angelic nature requires, yet accomplishes its deepest desire, every angel was called to enter by grace into a personal communion of knowledge and love with the Holy Trinity. He has a vocation to divinization—that is, to become "a partaker of the divine nature" (see 2 Pt 1:4), an adoptive son of the Father. But the modalities of this call and the manner in which the angels responded to it remain very mysterious. St. Thomas discusses these questions about

---

that in the beginning God created only the spiritual creatures and then, after some of them sinned, he created bodies so that the spiritual substances might be bound by them as though with chains, as though corporeal creatures had not been produced by God's original intention because it was good for them to exist, but only in order to punish the sins of the spiritual creatures, whereas Gn 1:31 says: 'God saw everything that he had made, and behold, it was very good.' Therefore, in order to rule out this opinion, he says, 'he created both creatures at the same time, the spiritual and the corporeal, in other words the angels and the world'" (Alius fuit error Origenis ponentis quod Deus a principio creavit solas spirituales creaturas, et postea quibusdam earum peccantibus, creavit corpora, quibus quasi quibusdam vinculis spirituales substantiae alligarentur, ac si corporales creaturae non fuerint ex principali Dei intentione productae, quia bonum erat eas esse, sed solum ad punienda peccata spiritualium creaturarum, cum tamen dicatur Gn I:31: "vidit Deus cuncta quae fecerat, et erant valde bona." Unde ad hoc excludendum dicit quod "simul condidit utramque creaturam, scilicet spiritualem et corporalem, angelicam videlicet et mundanam").

15. *ST*, article 4 of q. 61 deals with the "place" of the creation of the angels: the angels were created in the empyrean heaven—the heaven of heavens, not inasmuch as they are said to be bound up with matter but inasmuch as the empyrean heaven is the place from which they can best exercise their influence on the physical world.

"the perfection of the angel in the order of grace and glory" in question 62 of the *prima pars.*

In article 1, St. Thomas distinguishes in the case of an angel a twofold beatitude, a twofold fulfillment. The first is the one that he can attain by the exercise of his own natural resources. It consists in a certain natural knowledge of God as First Cause, accompanied by a natural love of God, and we can describe it in a certain sense (*quodammodo*) as beatitude. Aquinas asserts that the angel possesses this natural beatitude from the very instant of his creation by reason of the dignity of his simple nature. In this sense the angels were created blessed.

But for every spiritual being, St. Thomas says, "Above this *happiness* there is still another, which we look forward to in the future, whereby 'we shall see God as He is.'"[16] This beatitude is beyond the natural capacities of any creature whatsoever for the simple reason that it is natural to God alone and belongs only to him.[17] God, however, can communicate it to whomever he wills by way of graced participation.[18] In relation to this supernatural beatitude, the angels were not created blessed.[19] Besides, if that had been the case, then how could they have lost that beatitude, turned away from God, torn themselves from the beatific vision of Absolute Good? Now faith teaches us that, in fact, some angels did turn away from God. Angels therefore were created as *viatores*, in the state of wayfarers; they attained this supernatural beatitude only at the conclusion of a history, of a progress implying an act of spiritual choice.

16. *ST* I, q. 62, a. 1: "Sed super hanc felicitatem est alia felicitas, quam in futuro expectamus, qua videbimus Deum sicuti est."

17. See *ST* I, q. 62, a. 4: "Perfect beatitude is natural only to God, because existence and beatitude are one and the same thing in Him" (soli Deo beatitudo perfecta est naturalis, quia idem est sibi esse et beatum esse).

18. Without going here into the difficult and controversial question about the connections between nature and the supernatural, we emphasize nevertheless that supernatural beatitude, although inaccessible by right to the unaided powers of created spiritual nature, is not just an extrinsic addition in relation to that nature: it corresponds to the profound wish of every spiritual nature, to his natural (ontological) desire to see God. Certainly, this desire does not constitute a strict requirement of the supernatural—a purely natural destiny for an angel is not a contradiction in terms and the supernatural really is a gratuitous gift—yet the elevation of an angel to supernatural life is highly fitting.

19. See *ST* I, q. 62, a. 1, sed contra.

Grace

This history springs from a divine initiative, which has its source in eternity (election and predestination) and is translated into time by the gift of the grace of the Holy Spirit. Indeed, an angel can effectively turn toward God as the object of his supernatural beatitude only by means of grace.[20] Every creature, St. Thomas explains, is naturally inclined toward an end that is proportioned to it—in other words, that corresponds to its nature, to what its interior dynamism can attain and accomplish. But when it is a matter of attaining an end that surpasses what a nature is programmed or equipped to do, then the active powers of the subject must be elevated. It is necessary for a supernatural principle to come and be grafted onto its nature so as to be in that subject the source of a dynamism that is itself supernatural. Now the beatific vision of God is a good that is radically disproportionate in relation to any created spirit. To know oneself in one's essence is natural only to God. It is necessary therefore that a supernatural agent insert into the mind of an angel an intrinsic principle that elevates its being as well as its powers of action and orients them toward that end which is beatitude. This principle is sanctifying grace (or *gratia gratum faciens*). In the wayfaring state—in other words between the instant of their creation and the instant of the definitive entrance into supernatural beatitude or of their definitive exclusion from it—all the angels (including the future demons) therefore received at a given moment

20. See *ST* I, q. 62, a. 2. The angels are not saints by nature: they need grace in order to merit supernatural happiness. This thesis is traditional in Christianity. See Origen, *On First Principles* I.5.5, with respect to the angels: "To be stainless [immaculate] is a quality which belongs essentially to none except the Father, Son and Holy Spirit; for holiness is in every created being an accidental quality, and what is accidental may also be lost" (1966), 50. See also Basil the Great, *On the Holy Spirit* XVI.38, 70–72; in this passage, which intends to prove that the Spirit is fully God and cooperates with the Father and the Son in the work of the sanctification of creatures, Basil presents the sanctifying action of the Spirit among the angels: "The pure, intelligent, and other-worldly powers both are and are called holy because they have acquired holiness as a gift given to them by the Holy Spirit.... The ministering spirits exist by the will of the Father, they are brought into being by the energy of the Son, and they are perfected by the presence of the Spirit. Now the perfection of the angels is holiness and abiding in holiness.... There is no holiness without the Spirit. The heavenly powers are not holy by nature; if it were so they would not differ from the Holy Spirit.... Still, holiness is extrinsic to their substance and brings perfection to them through the communion of the Spirit."

sanctifying grace, the seed of true beatitude, and (at least by right of a habit) the virtues that result from it, such as faith and charity.[21]

In St. Thomas's day, the Scholastics wondered when, more precisely, the angels had received that initial grace.[22] St. Thomas presents two hypotheses that, according to the theologians of the thirteenth century, could both be legitimately supported since, as he explains in the parallel article of the *Scriptum*, the moment of an angel's sanctification depends on the divine will alone.[23]

The first position, which was more common at the time, claimed that angels had been created *in naturalibus*—in other words, in a state of pure nature in which they possessed only the resources proper to their nature. Only at the end of a certain period of time were they said to have been raised by God to the supernatural order. This was the opinion of Hugh of St. Victor:[24] the angels certainly were created good, but with a goodness that was quite natural. They were created just, in the sense of not-unjust, happy in the sense of not-miserable, but they in no way possessed the justice or the beatitude that come from grace and merit.[25]

21. See *ST* II-II, q. 5, a. 1, where St. Thomas establishes that an angel before his fall or his confirmation and man before original sin both had faith. We will have to return to the object of this faith in discussing angelic knowledge of the Incarnation. St. Augustine wavered a great deal about the initial status of the angels (is there in the first instant a difference between angels and [future] demons? See the supplementary note "La chute du diable," BA 49:545–53, especially 548–51 and 552–53). Later he inquired about the knowledge that the angels and the (future) demons could initially have had of their lot. These inquiries, popularized by Peter Lombard, *Sententiae* II, d. 4 (18–21), made medieval thinkers anxious to know whether the angels had furthermore received any lights on the mystery of their personal predestination. See Thomas Aquinas, *In II Sent.*, d. 4, q. 1, a. 2, which rules out such foreknowledge.

22. See *ST* I, q. 62, a. 2.

23. See *In II Sent.* D. 4, q. 1, a. 3: "On this point there are two opinions. Some say that the angels were not created in grace but only with their natural resources. This opinion is the more common. Others say that the angels were created in grace. One cannot tell by an effective argument which of these opinions is truer, for the beginning of creatures depends on the simple will of the Creator, which is impossible for reason to investigate" (Circa hoc est duplex opinio. Quidam enim dicunt, quod angeli non in gratia, sed in naturalibus tantum creati sunt; et haec opinio est communior. Alii vero dicunt, angelos in gratia creatos esse. Harum autem opinionum quae verior sit, non potest efficaci ratione deprehendi, eo quod creaturarum principium ex simplici creatoris voluntate dependet, quam ratione investigare impossibile est).

24. Hugh of St. Victor, *De sacramentis* I, p. 5, c. 19 (PL 176:254).

25. This solution was adopted by Peter Lombard, *Sententiae* II, d. 3, c. 4 (14–18).

According to the second position, angels were directly created in a state of grace; in other words, there was no interval between their creation and the gift of sanctifying grace.[26] As he did earlier in the *Scriptum*, St. Thomas leans here in favor of this hypothesis. He explains in a not very convincing analogy that just as, according to St. Augustine, the "seminal reasons," principles of all the unfolding of effects of creatures, were implanted in material creatures from the beginning, so too it was highly fitting that sanctifying grace, the seed of glory, should also be given from the beginning. But, above all, St. Thomas thinks that this opinion is most in keeping with the assertions of the church fathers and especially of St. Augustine, who in book XII of *The City of God* declares—in passing—concerning the angels, that God "at the same time (*simul*) created their nature and enriched it with grace."[27]

Unfortunately, Lombard confuses two problems: that of the interval between the creation of the angels and their supernatural choice and the problem of the necessity of this supernatural choice; therefore, he wrongly connects the impossibility of admitting that the demons were created bad by nature and the necessity of an interval (*morula*). In the thirteenth century, the thesis of a gift of grace deferred until after creation is defended by William of Auxerre (Guillaume d'Auxerre), *Summa aurea* II.2.1, 33: "I prefer the common solution, namely that they did not have the gratuitous gifts" (Nobis magis placet via communis, scilicet quod non habuerunt gratuita); Bonaventure, *In II Sent.*, d. 4, a. 1, q. 2 (124–26).

26. This position is defended by Praepositinus of Cremona, *Summa III*; Alexander of Hales, *Summa theologica fratris Alexandri*, lib. I, p. 1, inq. II, tract. 1, q. un., c. 2, ad 1 (Quaracchi: Editiones Collegii S. Bonaventurae 1928), vol. II, no. 100, 125); Albert the Great, *In II Sent.* d. 3, a. 12 (82–85). The *rationes* [arguments] advanced by St. Albert stress, and rightly so, that there is no plainly evident reason for this time lapse *in naturalibus* in the angels.

27. Augustine, *City of God* XII.9.2 (FOTC 14:261): "simul eis et condens naturam et largiens gratiam," cited in the *sed contra* of the article. Bonaventure, *In II Sent.*, d. 4, a. 1, q. 2, ad 1 (125–26). According to him, *gratia* does not mean sanctifying grace here. Along the same lines as Augustine, see Basil the Great, *On the Holy Spirit* XVI.38, 73: "Thus, in creation the Holy Spirit is present to those [angels] who are perfected not by their making progress but at the moment of their very creation, as he introduces his grace to complete and fulfill their existence"; *Homilia in Ps 32* (PG 19:333), cited by Journet, *L'Église du Verbe incarné* IV, 209: "The angels were not created as little children so as to become perfect gradually by practice, and thereupon worthy to receive the Spirit; but from the moment when they were first established, the gift of sanctity was poured out into them, as though combined with their substance."

Merit

Once established in grace, the angels were capable of meriting their beatitude by a good moral action.[28] Moreover, this was the reason the angels were created as *viatores*: they had to be able to merit beatitude—in other words, to be not only the passive beneficiaries but also, in some way, the active cause thereof. This active collaboration of the creature in the work of his own salvation is a higher good that manifests more fully the glory of God.

There are two ways, St. Thomas explains, of attaining an end by one's own operation. First, I achieve this end by producing it myself. In this case it is necessary that the end be proportioned to the active capacities or powers of the subject. So it is, for example, that I assure my physical self-preservation by cultivating the plot of potatoes by which I earn my living. Second, I attain that end by meriting that someone else should give it to me. For example, being a poor, penniless student, I absolutely cannot pay for my dream trip to Tahiti, despite the tutoring that I do on the side, yet by the efforts that I make in another area, that of my course work, I merit that my parents, who are more well-to-do, should offer me this trip. This meritorious moral causality is the only one that can operate when the end being pursued surpasses the active powers of the subject. This is the case in the supernatural order. Thus, by his meritorious action, the free being really participates in obtaining his supernatural end, and we know that St. Thomas likes to emphasize how much more worthy of God it is to create from active causes than from entirely dependent ones.[29]

The idea that the angels merited their supernatural beatitude supposes that they were at first in a state of grace (whether from the first instant of their creation or later on) before entering into beatitude, because in order to merit, in order act morally in a way pleasing to God, grace is absolutely necessary. St. Thomas therefore dismisses

28. See *ST* I, q. 62, a. 1. St. Thomas rules out the opinion of certain theologians (*quidam*) who think that the angels did not have grace but rather the beginning of glory. Such an idea directly contradicts the notion of reward that is included in the idea of beatitude. See also Aquinas, *In II Sent.*, d. 5, q. 2, a. 2.

29. On the notion of merit in the writings of St. Thomas, see Joseph Wawrykow, *God's Grace and Human Action: "Merit" in the Theology of Thomas Aquinas* (Notre Dame, Ind.: University of Notre Dame Press, 1995).

two limping explanations of angelic merit. Some actually claimed that
an angel merits his happiness by anticipation, so to speak, by virtue
of the acts that he will accomplish in God's service once he is blessed, rather like a soldier who by his acts of valor merits the salary that
he has already drawn.[30] But how can anyone merit what he already
has without contradiction? Merit leads to beatitude and therefore
must be logically prior to it. Others thought—and in the *Scriptum*
St. Thomas himself adopted this hypothesis[31]—that the act by which
an angel merits beatitude and the act by which he grasps the Divine
Essence are one and the same act—namely, the act of turning toward
God (*conversio ad Deum*), but considered from two different view-
points. Inasmuch as it proceeds from freedom, this act is meritorious,
and inasmuch as it apprehends the end, it is eternal enjoyment (*frui-
tio*). In the *Summa theologiae*, St. Thomas objects to this model, saying that grace, which is necessary in order that a free act be meritorious, cannot coexist with glory, because these are two distinct and
more or less perfect states of one and the same reality (a fowl cannot
be a chick and a chicken at the same time). It is necessary therefore to
hold that the act by which an angel merited beatitude was prior to the
act of beatitude itself.[32]

30. This example is found in Aquinas, *In II Sent.*, d. 5, q. 2, a. 2 (153–54): "Others
claim that they merit the beatitude that they have already received by the works that
take place after their confirmation and by which they serve us as though a soldier merited the present that the king has given him by fighting afterward" (Alii dicunt, quod per
opera quae sunt post confirmationem, quibus nobis ministrant, merentur beatitudinem
quam prius acceperunt, sicut aliquis miles meretur munus sibi a rege collatum, poste-
rius militando). The hypothesis of merit that is chronologically later than beatitude is
mentioned already in Peter of Poitiers, *Sententiae* II.4, ed. Philip S. Moore, Joseph N.
Garvin, and Marthe Dulong, Publications in Medieval Studies 11 (Notre Dame, Ind.:
University of Notre Dame Press, 1950), 9.

31. See Aquinas, *In II Sent.*, d. 5, q. 2, a. 2 (p. 154): "And so one and the same movement of conversion is preparation for grace, inasmuch as it comes from free will, and
meritorious of glory, inasmuch as it is informed by grace; and also an act of fruition
inasmuch as it is accomplished by the habit of glory" (Unde unus et idem conversio-
nis motus est praeparatio ad gratiam secundum quod est ex libero arbitrio, et meritorius gloriae, secundum quod est gratia informatus: et iterum fruitionis actus, secundum
quod completur per habitum gloriae). St. Thomas assumes here, however, that the angels were not created in grace.

32. See also *ST* I, q. 62, a. 5, ad 2. Concerning the impossibility that an angel's meritorious act and his entrance into beatitude should be identical, see John of St. Thomas, *Cursus theologicus*, disp. 44, a. 1 (4:768–73). Jean Cabrol, *Defensiones, In II Sent.*, d. 5,

Article 5 addresses the process by which the angel merited beat-itude. This topic, directly connected with the theme of the sin of the fallen angels, is intensely debated even within the Thomistic tradi-tion, first of all because the possible consistency of the passages writ-ten by St. Thomas is not immediately evident. The teaching in the *pri-ma pars* of the *Summa theologiae* does not correspond exactly with the slightly later teaching in question 16 of the *Q. de malo.*

In *ST* I, q. 62, a. 5, Aquinas establishes that the angels obtained beatitude thanks to a sole and unique meritorious act: an act of su-pernatural love of God above all things. Indeed, the divinization of the creature comes about in conformity with its nature: *Gratia per-fecit naturam secundum modum naturae.* Now, on the natural level, an angel is initially placed in a state of actual perfection by his very na-ture.[33] Likewise, St. Thomas affirms, on the supernatural level, an an-gel obtains beatitude immediately after having placed a single act in-formed by charity.

There are therefore (at least) two instants—in other words, two distinct acts—in the scenario of angelic history: the instant of the mer-itorious act and the instant of the reward.[34] But—and here is the crux of the commentators!—does the instant of merit coincide with the in-stant of creation in grace, or is it distinct and later? Is it by his very first act, placed at the very instant of his creation in grace (for the angel is created actually acting), that a good angel merited eternal glory?

In *ST* I, q. 63, a. 5, within the context of reflection on the sin of

___

q. 1, a. 1, secunda conclusio, 3:361–63, had already pointed out the development in Aqui-nas's thought on this point.

33. See *ST* I, q. 62, a. 5: "Now it is proper to the *angelic nature* to receive its *natural* perfection not by passing from one stage to another; but to have it at once *naturally*" (Est autem hoc proprium naturae angelicae, quod naturalem perfectionem non per dis-cursum acquirat, sed statim per naturam habeat).

34. In the case of an angel, we call an act or an operation "instants." See *ST* I, q. 62, a. 5, ad 2: "The various instants regarding the *angels*, are not to be taken except as reckon-ing the succession of their acts" (Instantia diversa in his quae ad angelos pertinent, non accipiuntur nisi secundum successionem in ipsorum actibus). See H.-F. Dondaine, "Le premier instant de l'ange d'après saint Thomas," *RSPT* 39 (1955): 220: "The moments of angelic life are pure spiritual acts, independent of the continuous time of the cosmos in which our experience is engaged. Between two moments of an angel, that is, between two acts, there is no continuous, measurable interval; the rhythm of angelic life is pure number, and not an ever-divisible continuum. There are simply two acts, one after the other: that is all."

the fallen angels, St. Thomas holds that in the very instant of his creation in grace, an angel absolutely cannot sin, but can, on the other
hand, merit. Indeed, some subjects can act in the very instant in which
they begin to exist. For example, as soon as a light bulb is lit (in other words, begins to exist in terms of a certain accidental existence), it
emits light and heat. However, in this first instant, this action, which
is thoroughly the action of the subject (the glowing light bulb), is directly caused by the cause that is at the origin of the subject's existence
(the person who throws the switch), which is no longer the case afterward (the person can go away and the bulb continues to illuminate).
The point is that in the first instant, the actuality of an acting potency
cannot come from itself but only from an external cause that is already
in act.

Now an angel was in fact created acting (thinking and loving),
and he was created directly by God, who is perfect. It follows that the
angel's first operation (in the natural or supernatural order) absolutely cannot be deficient, without making God the direct cause of moral evil. Therefore it is impossible—and the Johannine statement that
Satan "was a murderer from the beginning" (Jn 8:44) cannot be understood in this sense—that an angel should sin in the first moment
of his creation, inasmuch as scripture seems to describe this sin clearly as a "fall" (Is 14:12; Ez 28:13–17), which implies a change of state, a
passage from a positive state to a negative state.[35] If I hold a bird cap-

35. For St. Thomas, this thesis is a matter of faith. See *Q. de malo*, q. 16, a. 4: "That
the angel did not sin in the first instant of his creation ... is held to be based on the
authority of the canon of Scripture.... But it is necessary, even though difficult, to assign the reason why the devil could not have sinned in the first instant of his creation"
(474) (Quod angelus non peccaverit in primo instanti suae creationis ... dicitur expresse haberi ex auctoritate canonicae scripturae.... Sed quare non potuerit in primo instanti suae creationis peccare, assignare quidem oportet, etsi difficile sit).

St. Augustine wavered. As St. Thomas summarizes it in *Q. de malo*, q. 16, a. 4: "Augustine takes up this question in Book XI of *The Literal Commentary on Genesis* [XI.13–
26, ACW 42:145–58] and in Book XI of *City of God* [XI.13–14, FOTC 14:207–10]. In neither place, however does he come to a definite conclusion on this matter, although in
Book XI of the *Literal Commentary on Genesis* he appears to incline more to the opinion
that the angel sinned in the first instant of his creation; on the other hand in Book XI *On
the City of God* he seems to incline more to the contrary opinion" (474) (Hanc quaestionem tractat Augustinus XI super Genes. ad litteram, et in XI de Civit. Dei; in neu-
tro tamen loco aliquid super hoc assertive determinat, quamvis in XI super Genes. ad
litteram, magis videatur in hoc declinare quod in primo instanti suae creationis pecca-

tive in my hand and then throw it toward the sky, in the very first moment the bird will orient itself in the direction of my throw, inasmuch
as it corresponds to his natural, spontaneous impetus. Only in a second moment can the bird eventually change his direction.[36]

Although in his first moment an angel cannot sin, he can on the
other hand merit. To do good is natural to the will, and to act wrongly is contrary to its nature. Now what is natural is given from the
start, whereas what is contrary to nature can come only in a second
phase.[37] The very first voluntary act of an angel in a state of grace was
therefore a spontaneous act of charity that was meritorious of eternal
life. But, someone will object, how could it be meritorious if it was
impossible for the angel to sin? It is an impoverished view of freedom
that reduces it to the power to choose indifferently between good and
evil, whereas true freedom is fulfilled in the choice of the good. Certainly, for St. Thomas the angel's first act was necessary as to its specification—in other words, as to the type of object chosen—because
in that first instant his will could not *not* will what his intellect infallibly identified as his true good. But he was free as to the exercise of
that will, for the act of willing itself remained a particular good with
respect to which the angel's will was not per se determined and therefore depended formally on free will.[38]

---

verit; et in XI de Civit. Dei videatur magis declinare ad contrarium). These Augustinian
vacillations explain why some medieval thinkers supported the thesis of sin in the first
moment of creation, but it was condemned by the Parisian masters.

36. For a Scholastic discussion supported by reasons why it was impossible for
an angel's first act to be bad, see John of St. Thomas, *Cursus theologicus*, disp. 43, a. 2
(4:708–31): "Utrum angelus potuerit peccare in primo instanti?"

37. See *ST* I, q. 63, a. 5, ad 3: "All that is in *merit* is from *God*; and consequently an
angel could *merit* in the first instant of his creation" (Quidquid est in merito, est a Deo:
et ideo in primo instanti suae creationis angelus mereri potuit). See *ST* III, q. 34, a. 3,
ad 1 (the question is whether Christ was able to merit from the first instant of his conception): "Free-will does not bear the same relation to *good* as to *evil*: for to *good* it is
related of itself, and *naturally*; whereas to *evil* it is related as to a defect, and beside *nature*.... Therefore the *free-will* of a creature can be moved to *good* meritoriously in the
first instant of its creation, but not to *evil* sinfully; provided, however, its *nature* be un-
impaired" (Liberum arbitrium non eodem modo se habet ad bonum et ad malum, nam
ad bonum se habet per se et naturaliter; ad malum autem se habet per modum defectus,
et praeter naturam.... Et ideo liberum arbitrium creaturae in primo instanti creationis
potest moveri ad bonum merendo, non autem ad malum peccando, si tamen natura sit
integra).

38. If I open my eyes, I cannot *not* see the sky (the necessity of specification refer-

This scenario, which became a rallying point for the classic commentators, poses several serious problems, however.[39] First, it implies, rather astonishingly, that in a first moment the demons placed an act of charity that was meritorious of eternal life, only to take a step backward—immediately afterward, without delay—and to recant. It was in a second moment that some angels, by their sin, freely annulled and thwarted the merit of the first moment. Thus they deprived themselves of the beatitude that they merited and that the other angels obtained by virtue of the same meritorious act of the first instant, which they did not retract.[40] Second, even though one must acknowledge a certain freedom in that first act, it seems imperfect, as does the merit that is inherent to it.[41] It is necessary therefore to wait until the angel adopts or confirms this first act with full personal freedom in order for him to obtain beatitude.[42] Along these lines, Jacques

ring to the object, which gives to the act its species), but I can decide not to open my eyes (freedom of exercise).

39. John of St. Thomas, *Cursus theologicus*, disp. 43, a. 2 (4:721, no. 37) asserts that it is necessary to read and correct the other passages by St. Thomas, in particular Q. *de malo*, q. 16, a. 4, in terms of the teaching in the *prima pars*. Among recent treatments of the subject, see Hugon, *Tractatus dogmatici* 1:678–80; Aquinas, "Les Anges," in *Summa Theologica I, Questions 50–64*, edited by Charles-Vincent Héris, Éditions de la Revue des jeunes (Paris: Desclée, 1953), 463–73.

40. See *ST* I, q. 63, a. 5, ad 4: "All were *created* in *grace*, all *merited* in their first instant. But some of them at once placed an impediment to their beatitude, thereby destroying their preceding *merit*; and consequently they were deprived of the beatitude which they had *merited*" (Omnes, in gratia creati, in primo instanti meruerunt. Sed quidam eorum statim impedimentum praestiterunt suae beatitudinis, praecedens meritum mortificantes. Et ideo beatitudine quam meruerunt, sunt privati).

41. This difficulty has not escaped the commentators. See, for example, Charles René Billuart, *Tractatus de angelis*, in *Summa sancti Thomae*, 10 Vol. (Paris: 1874–76), 2:43b: "Although they merited glory by that act, it does not follow that they obtained it immediately after that act, because that meritorious act was not free in all respects: it was free as to its exercise but not as to its specification, for it came from God alone who moved and applied [their will] in a special manner" (Neque etiam sequitur quod, quamvis per illum actum meruerint gloriam, eam immediate post illum sunt consecuti, quia iste actus meritorius non erat ex omni parte liber; erat siquidem liber quoad exercitium, non quoad specificationem, quia era a solo Deo specialiter movente et applicante).

42. The classic Thomists were divided on the question of whether or not, in the case of a good angel, the fully meritorious act is identical to the first act elicited at the instant of creation. Scholars distinguished therefore between supporters of three instants of the good angel (Bañez, John of St. Thomas) and supporters of two instants (Jean Cabrol, Salmanticenses) who thought that the act of charity of the second instant was the prolongation of the first act, this time adopted freely. "Quam voluerit sententiam eligat

Maritain, followed by Charles Journet as often happens, took up the question again and proposed an original solution.[43] According to Maritain, the act on which the angel's moral destiny hinges requires a perfect freedom of choice. Therefore this cannot be the first act of his will. That is the product of a general supernatural movement of God who causes the angel's will to tend spontaneously toward its own good and indirectly toward God insofar as he is the universal Good of the supernatural order. This movement is free only in the inchoate and very narrow sense that it conforms to the angelic nature and is not prevented by free will. It is not an act of charity, strictly speaking, and its meritorious character is therefore ineffective. This first act must still be ratified by a choice of the free will. "The angel's free will comes positively into play only with his first act of choosing (with regard to his final end), in other words, in the second instant."[44] To the instant of nature (which includes a certain freedom) must be added therefore the instant of the mind in its own dignity, the instant of the moral choice, of the act of charity as preferential love of friendship.

Maritain's reinterpretation, born of dissatisfaction with the texts and their traditional interpretation, means to take up the question again and to propose an original theoretical solution in the light of more fundamental Thomist principles than the ones employed by St. Thomas, principles that are derived from a preferential attention to the personalist potentialities of Thomism. However, when it is a question of bringing the thought of St. Thomas up to date, nothing is more valuable than a historical exegesis of the Thomistic corpus that traces the possible development in the master's thought and thus points the way to a well-founded updating. Now in 1955 Father H.-F. Dondaine provided us with a fine historical study on St. Thomas's development on the question of the angelic history.[45] He showed that St. Thomas, aware of the shortcomings of his first explanation, had

lector" [The reader may choose whatever opinion he wants]; Billuart, *Tractatus de angelis*, 2:48a.

43. Jacques Maritain, "Le péché de l'ange: Essai de ré-interprétation des positions thomistes," in *Le Péché de l'ange: Peccabilité, nature et surnature*, edited by Journet, Jacques Maritain, and Philippe de la Trinité, 41–86 (Paris: Beauchesne, 1961); Journet, *L'Église du Verbe incarné*, IV, 207–37.

44. Jacques Maritain, "Péché de l'ange," 75.

45. Dondaine, "Le premier instant de l'ange d'après saint Thomas," 213–27.

changed his position between the *prima pars* and article 4 of question 16 of the *Q. de malo*, which, being chronologically a later work, also represents a more finished state of his reflection and therefore should serve as a point of reference for Thomists. The new solution in *De malo*, which incidentally includes many elements from the *prima pars*, results from a better grasp of the structures of angelic psychology and from a clearer sense of the distinction between the natural order and the supernatural order. St. Thomas resolutely distinguishes in an angel, even though he is created immediately in the state of grace, the moment of natural knowledge, and the later moment of supernatural knowledge.[46] An angel's natural knowledge is knowledge of himself and, consequently, of God as the "author of nature."[47] His supernatural knowledge is knowledge of God as "author of grace" and source of beatitude. Now these two sorts of knowledge, St. Thomas insists, cannot be simultaneous. They presuppose two very distinct acts resulting from two *species* or intellectual forms that are necessarily distinct, because the *species* relative to the supernatural mysteries cannot be reduced to the *species* that is the basis for the knowledge of natural realities. Therefore it is necessary to distinguish a first instant, in which every angel takes possession of his natural knowledge, accompanied by an act of love for God (not meritorious, because it is on the natural order)—no sin can occur here—and then a second instant in which the angel places an act of supernatural knowledge and freely determines himself in relation to God's call to eternal life.[48]

---

46. Journet (*L'Église du Verbe incarné*, IV, 229–30) interprets this distinction between natural and supernatural as a distinction between what is spontaneous and what is elective, which is not the question as framed by the Thomistic passage.

47. *Q. de malo*, q. 16, a. 4, ad 14.

48. See *Q. de malo*, q. 16, a. 4: "Therefore the angel in the first instant of his creation must have turned to the natural knowledge of himself, according to which he could not sin … ; but afterwards he could turn toward that which is above nature or turn away from it. And therefore the angel in the first instant of his creation was neither blessed by completely turning toward God nor a sinner by turning away from Him" (476) (Et ideo oportuit quod angelus in primo instanti suae creationis converteretur ad naturalem sui cognitionem, secundum quam non potuit peccare … ; postmodum vero potuit converti in id quod est supra naturam, vel ab eo averti. Et ideo angelus in primo instanti suae creationis non fuit neque beatus per conversionem perfectam in Deum, neque peccator per aversionem ab ipso). The supporters of an angel's natural impeccability rely strongly on this passage.

Reward

In those passages of the *Summa theologiae* that are properly speaking angelological, St. Thomas says little about questions connected with the beatific vision. In truth, he discussed thoroughly the vision of the Divine Essence by creatures in general in question 12 of the *prima pars*.[49] The subject was a delicate one, however, for some years after the Parisian condemnation in 1241, in which Bishop Guillaume d'Auvergne had clearly rejected the tendencies of a certain theology of Dionysian inspiration, which denied that creatures could have the vision of the very essence of God; instead, the glorified intellect would see only theophanies, the radiance of God through his created intermediaries, but never the inaccessible light of the Divine Essence.[50] St. Thomas holds, on the contrary, that the Divine Essence unites itself without intermediary to the created intellect, which is elevated by a supernatural created *habitus*, the *lumen gloriae* [light of glory], which proportions it to the uncreated form that it receives.

Indeed, the last few articles of question 62 present some remarkable properties of the glory proper to the angels: it is given in proportion to their nature (a. 6); as we already emphasized, it suppresses neither the natural knowledge nor the natural love in an angel (a. 7); the blessed angel cannot sin (a. 8), nor progress in an essential way in his beatitude (a. 9).

In article 6, St. Thomas justifies an idea conveyed by Peter Lom-

49. On the contrary, question 8 of the *Q. de ver.*, dedicated to angelic knowledge, begins with five important articles on the beatific vision in an angel.

50. The list of condemned propositions is found in *Chartularium Universitatis pariensis*, no. 128, ed. Heinrich Denifle and Emile Chatelain (Paris: Ex typis fratris Delalain, 1889), 1:170–72. The first condemned error states that "the Divine Essence in itself will be seen neither by angels nor by men" (Divine essentia in se nec ab homine nec ab angelo videbitur). See Dionysius the Areopagite, *Celestial Hierarchy*, chap. 4.3.157: "Someone might claim that God has appeared himself and without intermediaries to some of the saints. But in fact it should be realized that scripture has clearly shown that 'no one has ever seen' or ever will see the being of God in all its hiddenness. Of course God has appeared to certain pious men in ways which were in keeping with his divinity. He has come in certain sacred visions fashioned to suit the beholders." On the controversies concerning the beatific vision that explain the 1241 condemnation, see Dondaine, "L'objet et le medium de la vision béatifique chez les théologiens du XIIIe siècle," *RTAM* 19 (1952): 60–130, and Christian Trottmann, *La Vision béatifique: Des disputes scolastiques à sa définition par Benoît XII*, Bibliothèque des écoles françaises d'Athènes et de Rome 289 (Rome: Ecole française de Rome, 1995).

bard, that grace and glory are given to the angels in proportion to the dignity of their nature.[51] The angels who are superior by nature received from the beginning more abundant grace and, if they were faithful to it, enjoy a more perfect glory. This is not about a necessity, as though the nature were a proximate disposition to grace, but entirely about a free decision of the divine wisdom that freely chooses to give more to those who are greater. At first glance, the idea is startling: could the God of the *Magnificat*, the God who makes the last first and the first last, have a different strategy with regard to the angelic world and raise up the powerful to a greater extent? It is traditional and reasonable, however. For example, St. Basil writes, "The heavenly powers are not *holy* by nature; if it were so, they would not differ from the *Holy Spirit*. Rather, they have a measure of holiness from the Spirit *according to their relationship of pre-eminence with each other.*"[52] St. Thomas explains that the intensity of one's conversion to God merits for the created person (a greater grace at first, in the case of a human being, and finally) a greater glory. Now angelic nature, unlike human nature, is all of a piece, not composed. There is nothing to prevent the spiritual movement of the conversion from being total immediately, whereas in a human being it is curbed by the inherent sluggishness of the sensible part. If the straw does not immediately catch fire, it is because it is mixed with moisture. If it were absolutely dry, the fire would immediately be that much larger, the more abundant the straw. In an angel, the grace received therefore has its entire effect immediately: a greater grace necessarily entails a greater glory.

God, who created the angels with the intention of divinizing them, therefore in his wisdom created superior by nature those angels whom, in the mysterious plan of his predestination, he wanted to be superior in the order of grace, in much the same way that the fact that an artisan hews and polishes certain stones more implies that he

51. See Peter Lombard, *Sentences* II, d. 3, c. 2, 3 (13): "For those [angels] who were created finer in their nature and more far-seeing in their wisdom, also were endowed with greater gifts of grace" (Angeli qui natura magis subtiles, et sapientia amplius perspicaces creati sunt, hi etiam maioribus gratiae muneribus praediti sunt); cited in the *sed contra* of *ST* I, q. 62, a. 6.

52. Basil the Great, *On the Holy Spirit* XVI.38, 71, emphasis added; see also John Damascene, *Orthodox Faith* II.3 (FOTC 37:206): "All angels were created by the Word and perfected by the sanctification of the Holy Ghost, and *in accordance with their dignity* and rank they enjoy brightness [i.e., illumination] and grace" (emphasis added).

will put them in a place where their beauty will be more prominent. Once he has acquired beatitude, the angel's situation is unchangeable. As St. Thomas explains it in article 8, he can no longer fall by sin. This statement was not accepted at first by the Christian tradition. Although Origen's position that, by virtue of the intrinsic changeability of free will, the good angels can still fall and the demons can still convert, had no followers,[53] several fathers thought that the good angels who had successfully passed the original decisive test had nonetheless not obtained full and perfect beatitude and had to continue to advance toward it. Moreover, citing Job 4:18,[54] "Even in his servants [God] puts no trust, and his angels he charges with error," some of them allowed for a certain culpability among the good angels and the need for them to seek God's pardon.[55] But St. Augustine, for whom the idea of a provisional beatitude is a sheer contradiction in terms,[56] clearly affirms that the good angels are absolutely assured of their beatitude, unchangeably blessed, and therefore incapable of falling by sin. The borders between the angelic world and the demonic world are not porous: "For, there is no Catholic who does not *know* that a good *angel* can no more turn into a devil than a bad one can return to the ranks of the angels who are good."[57]

53. See "The Demon's Punishment" in chap. 10 of this volume.

54. See also Jb 15:15 or Rv 2, where the angels of the Christian communities are reproached.

55. See Cyril of Jerusalem, *Lenten Lectures (Catecheses)* II.10, trans. Leo P. McCauley, SJ, and Anthony A. Stephenson, FOTC 61:102 (1969; repr. Washington, D.C.: The Catholic University of America Press, 2005).

"For we relate in some measure what has been written of the mercy of God towards man, but we do not know how much He forgave the angels as well. For He pardoned them also, since there is only one without sin, Jesus, who cleanses us from our sins. But of the angels, enough." [In the French text, the last sentence reads, "To the angels too He grants the appropriate pardon."—Trans.]

56. See Augustine, *City of God* XI.13 (FOTC 14:207): "The beatitude desired by an intelligent being as its proper end will result only from the combination of an uninterrupted enjoyment of that immutable good which is God with deliverance from any doubt or deception concerning the eternity of its continuance. With holy confidence, we believe that the angels of light possess this kind of blessedness" (Utroque coniuncto effici beatitudinem, quam recto proposito intellectualis natura desiderat, hoc est, ut et bono incommutabili, quod Deus est, sine ulla molestia perfruatur et in eo se in aeternum esse mansurum nec ulla dubitatione cunctetur nec ullo errore fallatur. Hanc habere angelos lucis pia fide credimus).

57. Ibid., FOTC 14:208: "Quis enim catholicus christianus ignorat nullum novum

For St. Thomas, the impeccability of the blessed angels can be deduced from the very nature of the beatific vision. No mind that sees the Divine Essence as such can turn away from it. Indeed, the Divine Essence is subsistent Good, utterly satisfying Good. Now the will, any will, by nature has as its end the absolute Good. It cannot *not* desire it, any more than it can, *in via* [in the wayfaring state], not want the good in general. St. Thomas is diametrically opposed to a vision of the will that is centered on the freedom of indifference and that would cause some later theologians to allow that a spirit placed in the presence of God, perceived as the absolute Good, can still freely reject him.

Immutably fixed on God, the blessed angel nonetheless does not thereby lose his free will. He exercises it in relation to all the particular goods that are presented to him, especially in carrying out his ministry: my guardian angel freely chooses this solution rather than that one in order to get me out of a scrape. But he always does so while adhering unwaveringly to his beatifying final end. The exercise of his free will therefore goes hand in hand with his impeccability, thus revealing the true nature of freedom as the faculty of personally consenting to what has value:

Hence it belongs to the perfection of its liberty for the free-will to be able to choose between opposite things, keeping the order of the end in view; but it comes of the defect of liberty for it to choose anything by turning away from the order of the end; and this is to *sin*. Hence there is greater liberty of will in the angels, who cannot sin, than there is in ourselves, who can sin.[58]

However, does an angel not run the risk of committing a venial sin—in other words, of making a bad choice relative to the means yet without calling into question his fundamental attachment to God as his final end? St. Thomas deems this impossible, for just as the nature of an angel causes him to see theoretical conclusions in the principles, so too he wills the practical means inasmuch as they are actually ordered to the end. All volition in him is an explicit willing of the end.

---

diabolum ex bonis angelis ulterius futurum, sicut nec istum in societatem bonorum angelorum ulterius rediturum?"

58. *ST* I, q. 62, a. 8, ad 3: "Unde quod liberum arbitrium diversa eligere possit servato ordine finis, hoc pertinet ad perfectionem libertatis eius: sed quod eligat aliquid divertendo ab ordine finis, quod est peccare, hoc pertinet ad defectum libertatis. Unde maior libertas arbitrii est in angelis, qui peccare non possunt, quam in nobis, qui peccare possumus."

Only an act that turned him away from the end, therefore, could lead to a disordered choice in the order of means.[59]

Although an angel cannot regress, he cannot progress in beatitude, either: he has ceased to journey because he is at his destination; he has ceased to merit because he possesses his reward.[60] Certainly, there are degrees: not in beatitude in its formal constituent—the vision of the Divine Essence itself, resulting in an unchangeable adherence to the Supreme Good—which is the same for all, but rather in the mode or manner of the vision, in its greater or lesser intensity or depth. God alone sees himself perfectly, comprehends himself. Every blessed spirit participates in that vision according to a fixed measure that is proper to him and that God has freely determined.[61] But, someone will object, the blessed angel carries on until the Last Judgment an intense charitable activity, both by illumination and by the various ministries that he performs with regard to human beings. Does this not merit an increase in beatitude? In fact, St. Thomas deems that this outpouring of charity is rather on the order of reward than of merit. The characteristic deed of a being that has already attained its end or perfection is to make it shine upon others.[62] Consequently, the accidental increase of joy that angels experience when they progressively accomplish the divine plans with which they are associated—"There is joy before the angels of God over one sinner who repents" (Lk 15:10)—is not the effect of a merit either but rather the extensive flourishing of the joy of beatitude.[63]

59. *ST* I-II, q. 89, a. 4; *Q. de malo*, q. 7, a. 9. On the impossibility of an angel committing a venial sin, see John of St. Thomas, *Cursus theologicus*, disp. 43, a. 3 (4:732–33, nos. 5–7).

60. See *ST* I, q. 62, a. 9. St. Thomas, as we can see in the parallel passage in *In II Sent.*, d. 11, q. 2, a. 2 (281–83), rejects the idea that an angel reaches his ultimate perfection only at the Last Judgment.

61. Some blessed angels see more profoundly the Divine Essence and the *rationes* that it contains. Hence there is the possibility of a progressive communication of knowledge by the higher angels to the lower angels; this illumination may increase the extent of the lower angel's knowledge, but it does not change the mode or the degree of his beatific knowledge.

62. See *ST* I, q. 62, a. 9, ad 2: "The angelic ministerings are useful for the beatified angels, inasmuch as they are a part of their beatitude; for to pour out acquired perfection upon others is of the nature of what is perfect, considered as perfect" (Ministeria angelorum sunt utilia angelis beatis, inquantum sunt quaedam pars beatitudinis ipsorum: diffundere enim perfectionem habitam in alia, hoc est de ratione perfecti inquantum est perfectum).

63. See *ST* I, q. 62, a. 9, ad 3.

10

How Angels Became Demons

The one God created everything out of nothing and, as he contemplated his work, declared that all that he made is good and even very good (Gn 1:31). Where then do the malevolent spirits come from? Who sowed those weeds in the Master's field? By meditating on the mystery of evil, Christian dogmatic theology arrived at the conviction that the source of evil, in the case of spiritual beings, could be found only in the wrong choice made by their freedom. There is no evil prior to sin. Therefore there can be no question of explaining the origin of the demons by regarding them as beings who are bad by nature;[1] that would be either to profess a dualism that restricted the universality of the Creator's action or else to assign to him the moral responsibility for their malice.[2] The demons, who were originally created good, made themselves bad as a result of a moral fall. An expert in the demonological sciences sums this up as follows:

First, then, let us understand this: demons were not always called "demons" and did not come into being as demons, for God made nothing bad. No, they

1. See, for example, the arguments compiled by St. Thomas against the hypothesis of the natural evil of demons in *ST* I, q. 63, a. 4; *De substantiis separatis,* c. 20.

2. In *Literal Meaning of Genesis* XI.20–23 (ACW 42:152–55), St. Augustine mentions and refutes some undoubtedly Christian authors (Lactantius?) who thought that the devil had been created by the good God in a state of malice; see the supplementary note "La chute du diable," in St. Augustin, *La genèse au sens littéral* VIII–XII, BA 49: 550–51.

too came into being good, but when they fell from heavenly wisdom, from that time on they wandered the earth. The Greeks they deceived through apparitions.[3]

This teaching incidentally offers a unified view of the world of spirits—angels and demons—that was still a long way from being achieved at the beginning of Christianity. If only the perverse choice of the will makes the demon, then the demons must originally have been angels quite similar to the other angels.[4] Anything that might distinguish them by nature from the other angels could indeed be invoked as the more or less immediate explanation for any moral difference, which would thereupon cease to be decisive.[5]

3. St. Anthony the Great, as represented by Athanasius of Alexandria, *The Life of Antony: The Coptic Life and the Greek Life*, trans. Tim Vivian and Apostolos N. Athanassakis, Sec. 22 (Kalamazoo, Mich.: Cistercian, 2003), 109, 111. See also, among many others, Cyril of Jerusalem, *Catechetical Lectures* II.4 (FOTC 61:98): "Nor did [the devil] sin because by nature he was of necessity prone to sin—else the responsibility for sin would reflect upon Him who created him thus—but after being created good, he became a devil by his own free choice, receiving that name from his [personal] action"; Theodoret of Cyr, *Thérapeutique des maladies helléniques* (SC 57:199–200): "As for us, we do not say that the demons were created wicked from the beginning by the God of the universe, nor that they received as their lot a nature of that sort, but that through the perversion of their mind they fell from a better state into a worse state."

4. See Augustine, *City of God* XII.1 (FOTC 14:245): "There is no reason to doubt that the contrary dispositions which have developed among these good and bad *angels* are due, not to different natures and origins, for God the Author and Creator of all substances has created them both, but to the dissimilar choices and desires of these angels themselves" (Angelorum bonorum et malorum inter se contrarios appetitus non naturis principiisque diversis, cum Deus omnium substantiarum bonus auctor et conditor utrosque creaverit, sed voluntatibus et cupiditatibus exstitisse dubitare fas non est).

Barth, *Church Dogmatics*, Section 51, part 3, 3:522, explosively challenges this traditional doctrine. He absolutely rejects the idea that there is an affinity between the angels and the demons, who are by definition their implacable adversaries. "What is the origin and nature of the devil and demons? The only possible answer is that their origin and nature lie in nothingness." The demons never were angels, and the doctrine of the fall is an invention with no real foundation. This "nothingness," which has some kind of consistency and an ambiguous relation to God, poses more problems than it resolves.

5. Thus the hypothesis claiming that the fallen angels were angels belonging by nature to lower orders could endanger the purely moral character of the division between angels and demons. We still find echoes of this inquiry about a possible difference between angels and demons before their fall in St. Augustine; see *Cité de Dieu* XI, supplementary note, "Les mauvais anges, ont-il été dès l'origine différents des bons?" (BA 35, 481–82). Conversely, Origen's theory about the origin of the various forms of spiritual beings takes to the extreme this initial identity and the role of moral choice, since, ac-

THE DATUM OF TRADITION

The idea of an original fall of celestial beings who had been tempted by hubris to make themselves equal to the gods runs through many mythologies—think of the unfortunate Icarus.[6] It can be found in intertestamental Judaism.[7] During that period, some thought that they could discern an allusion to that fall in an extremely curious passage from Genesis that describes the situation right before the Flood. "The sons of God saw that the daughters of men were fair; and they took to wife such of them as they chose" (Gn 6:2). From these illegitimate unions between heaven and earth, which confound the cosmic order and draw the wrath of God, were born species of arrogant giants, the *Nephilim*.[8] For intertestamental Judaism and the first ecclesiastical writers, these "sons of God" designate lying angels, and 1 Enoch, which relates in great detail their incursion on earth, deplores the disastrous consequences of their lust[9]—in short, an anticipation of the 1987 film *Les Ailes du désir* [*Der Himmel über Berlin*]!

Some prophetic texts, such as Isaiah 14 on the fall of the king of

---

cording to him, the spiritual beings who were created equal sinned in a more or less serious manner and were condemned to a more or less heavy bodily state: thus they became angels, men, or demons. See Origen, *On First Principles* I.8 (1966), 120–28.

6. Concerning the general religious context that may have affected some aspects of the biblical doctrine of the fall, see Teyssèdre, chap. 4, "L'origine du Mal ou la chute des Egrégores," in *Naissance du diable*; Adolphe Lods, "La chute des Anges: Origines et portée de cette spéculation," *Revue d'histoire et de philosophie religieuses* 7 (1927): 295–315.

7. On the biblical and intertestamental basis for the fall of the angels, see D. S. Russell, Method and *Message*, 249–57; Delcor, "Le mythe de la chute des anges et de l'origine des géants comme explication du mal dans le monde dans l'apocalyptique juive, Histoire des traditions," *Revue de l'histoire des religions* 190 (1976): 3–53; Archie T. Wright, *The Origin of Evil Spirits: The Reception of Genesis 6:1–4 in Early Jewish Literature*, Wissenschaftliche Untersuchungen zum Neuen Testament 2. Reihe 198 (Tübingen: Mohr Siebeck, 2005).

8. Gn 6:1–4: "When men began to multiply on the face of the ground, and daughters were born in them, the sons of God saw that the daughters of men were fair; and they took to wife such of them as they chose. Then the LORD said, 'My spirit shall not abide in man for ever, for he is flesh, but his days shall be a hundred and twenty years.' The Nephilim were on the earth in those days, and also afterward, when the sons of God came in to the daughters of men, and they bore children to them. These were the mighty men that were of old, the men of renown."

9. See 1 Enoch 6–16 (*Apocryphal Old Testament*, 188–205); see also Jubilees 5 (*Apocryphal Old Testament*, 25–27).

Babylon or Ezekiel 28 on the fall of the king of Tyre,[10] which borrow many features from the Near Eastern mythology of the fall of the angels/heavenly bodies, were also spontaneously understood as descriptions of this original sin of the angels.[11] Isaiah intones a taunt song (*mâshâl*) against a king of Babylon who has just died, underscoring the striking contrast between his past ambitions and his present state:

How you are fallen from heaven, O Day Star,[12] son of Dawn! How are you cut down to the ground, you who laid the nations low! You said in your heart, "I will ascend to heaven; above the stars of God I will set my throne on high; I will sit on the mount of assembly in the far north;[13] I will ascend above the heights of the clouds, I will make myself like the Most High." But you are brought down to Sheol, to the depths of the Pit.[14]

Several passages from the New Testament echo these traditions. The fathers of the church would make much of John 8:44 (Vulgate/DV), in which Christ says that the devil "has not stood in the truth."[15]

10. See Ez 28:2–18: "Son of man, say to the prince of Tyre, Thus says the LORD GOD: Because your heart is proud, and you have said, 'I am a god, I sit in the seat of the gods, in the heart of the seas,' yet you are but a man, and no god, though you consider yourself as wise as a god.... Therefore thus says the LORD GOD: Because you consider yourself as wise as a god, therefore, behold, I will bring strangers upon you, the most terrible of the nations; and they shall draw their swords against the beauty of your wisdom and defile your splendor. They shall thrust you down into the Pit, and you shall die the death of the slain in the heart of the seas.... Son of man, raise a lamentation over the king of Tyre, and say to him, Thus says the LORD GOD: You were the signet of perfection, full of wisdom and perfect in beauty. You were in Eden, the garden of God.... With an anointed guardian cherub I placed you; you were on the holy mountain of God; in the midst of the stones of fire you walked. You were blameless in your ways from the day you were created, till iniquity was found in you. In the abundance of your trade you were filled with violence, and you sinned; so I cast you as a profane thing from the mountain of God, and the guardian cherub drove you out from the midst of the stones of fire. Your heart was proud because of your beauty; you corrupted your wisdom for the sake of your splendor. I cast you to the ground; I exposed you before kings, to feast their eyes on you."

11. See in the early Christian literature: Origen, *On First Principles* I.5.4–5 (1966), 47–51; Tertullian, *Adversus Marcionem*, ed., trans. Ernest Evans (Oxford: Clarendon Press, 1972), II.10.1–6 (1:115), V.11.11 (2:583–85), and V.17.8 (2:617); Augustine, *City of God*, XI.15 (FOTC 14:210–11).

12. In Latin: *Lucifer*.

13. This is a sort of Mount Olympus where the gods gather.

14. Is 14:12–15.

15. See Augustine, *City of God* XI.13 (FOTC 14:208).

We should mention also 2 Peter 2:4, to which the *Catechism of the Catholic Church* refers in this context: "God did not spare the angels when they sinned, but cast them into hell[16] and committed them to pits of deepest darkness to be kept until the judgment,"[17] and the related passage, Jude 6: "And the angels that did not keep their own position but left their proper dwelling have been kept by him in eternal chains in the deepest darkness until the judgment of the great day."[18] The book of Revelation refers to "a star fallen from heaven to earth" to whom "was given the key of the shaft of the bottomless pit"[19] (Rv 9:1)—in other words, of the place where the rebellious angels are detained while awaiting their final judgment in the pool of fire.[20]

Since we will find again in the writings of St. Thomas an echo of the main speculations of the church fathers concerning the exact nature of the sin of the angels, it is useless to attempt a hazardous summary of them here.[21] We merely emphasize that St. Augustine, although he vacillated as to the exact scenario of the angelic history, gave to theological reflection about the fall of the devil its almost definitive form.[22] It corresponds to the principles of his general "theodicy": the origin of evil is not to be sought in the nature of the fallen angels, which is good, but rather in their bad will that is the absolutely

16. In Greek, "Tartarus," which for the Greeks was the place where the wicked are punished after death. It is a terrible place that is not unlike hell as medieval Christians viewed it.

17. St. Augustine already saw in this passage the scriptural evidence for the doctrine of the fall of the demons; see *City of God* XI.33 (FOTC 14:240). See CCC, no. 392.

18. Understand: in order to unite with the daughters of men.

19. "*Tehom*" = the subterranean waters, the abode of the dead.

20. The demons have an ambiguous status as "prisoners on conditional release." They are punished by being bound in the nether regions of the world yet can act for a limited time in the world of men. See Mt 8:29: The demoniacs "cried out, 'What have you to do with us, O Son of God? Have you come here to torment us before the time?'"

21. See Petau, *Theologica dogmata, De angelis*, liber III, ch. 2, 4:62–74; Mangenot, "Démon d'après les Pères," DTC, 4:339–84; Daniélou, "Démon," DS, 3:152–89.

22. St. Augustine systematically treated the fall of the devil in *Literal Meaning of Genesis* XI.14–26; *City of God* XI.11–15 (FOTC 14:205–11), XII.1–8 (FOTC 14:245–59), XXII.1 (FOTC 24:415–17); *De correptione et gratia* X.27. See also Mangenot, "Démon d'après les Pères," 4:368–73; Gérard Philips, *La raison d'être du mal d'après saint Augustin* (Louvain: Éditions du Museum Lessianum, 1927), 202–4; Bianchi and Müller, "Diabolus: Wesen und Fall des d.," 2:385–88; and especially the well-documented summary note "La chute du diable," in St. Augustin, *La Genèse au sens littéral VIII–XII*, BA 49:545–53.

first, deficient cause of evil. In coming to know his perfection, the devil, out of pride and love of his own good and of his own excellence, neglected to refer it to God, the common God of creatures. This love of self unto the contempt of God is the principle of the City of evil, inaugurated by the sin of the angel. In 561, the Council of Braga in Portugal canonized this doctrine.[23] It was solemnly reaffirmed by the great medieval Fourth Lateran Council (1215), where the fathers declared, "The devil and other demons were created by God good in nature, but they themselves through themselves have become wicked."[24]

THE SIN OF THE ANGEL

The nature and the process of the angel's sin give theologians a lot of trouble.[25] But they are very rich in lessons for the moral theologian,

23. See Denz.-H., no. 457: "If anyone says that the devil was not first a good angel made by God, and that his nature was not a work of God, but says that he came forth from darkness, and does not have any author of himself, but is himself the origin and substance of evil, as Manichaeus and Priscillian have said, let him be anathema" (Si quis dicit, diabolum non fuisse prius bonum angelum a Deo factum, nec Dei opificium fuisse naturam eius, sed dicit eum ex chao et tenebris emersisse nec aliquem sui habere auctorem, sed ipsum esse principium atque substantiam mali, sicut Manichaeus et Priscillianus dixerunt, anathema sit).

24. Denz.-H., no. 800: "Diabolus enim et alii daemones a Deo quidem natura creati sunt boni, sed ipsi per se facti sunt mali." In 1241, the bishop of Paris, William of Auvergne, condemned the thesis that the angels were wicked from the first moment of their creation; see Chartularium Universitatis parisiensis, vol. 1, no. 128, prop. 5: "That the wicked angel was wicked from the beginning of his creation and that he was never anything but wicked. We condemn this error. We firmly believe that he was good at one time and not wicked and that then by sinning he became wicked" (Quod malus angelus in principio suae creationis fuit malus et nunquam fuit nisi malus: hunc errorem reprobamus. Firmiter credimus quod aliquando fuit bonus et non malus, et postea peccando factus est malus).

25. Bibliography: Besides the scholastic commentaries on ST I, q. 64,I, q. 63, see Jacques de Blic, "Saint Thomas et l'intellectualisme moral à propos de la peccabilité de l'ange," MSR (1944): 241–80 [St. Thomas is said to hold contradictory theses concerning the peccability of an angel]; Henri de Lubac, Surnaturel: Études historiques (Paris: Éditions Montaigne, 1946), part 2, "Spirit and Freedom in the Theological Tradition," 186–321 [Against the hypothesis of an impeccable spiritual creature]; Philippe de la Trinité, "Du péché de Satan et de la destinée de l'esprit," in Satan: Études carmélitaines (Paris: Desclée de Brouwer, 1948), 44–85; Héris, commentary on Thomas d'Aquin in "Les Anges," in Summa Theologica I, questions 50–64, Éditions de la Revue des jeunes, 454–73; Pierre-Ceslas Courtès, "La peccabilité de l'ange chez saint Thomas," RT 53 (1953):

since we are dealing with a chemically pure sin, in that the malice is not masked by any antecedent error, there is no weakness resulting from carnal sluggishness, and we find none of those countless attenuating circumstances that occur in the case of our poor human sins. And so, before inquiring about the specific nature of this angelic sin—is it a sin of lust? of pride? of envy?—it is necessary to explain how a sin is possible at all in an angel, this superior creature that is perfect in its order.

Peccability

Everyone agrees that an angel is *peccabilis*—that is, capable of sinning, since in fact some angels did sin and all that is real is possible! It remains to be seen whence comes this peccability. No doubt from their status as creatures: drawn from nothingness, every creature has within it something like a natural tendency to return to nothing; it is marked by this potentiality whereby privation and evil can be introduced.[26] St. Thomas, who often examined the question,[27] actually ex-

---

133–63 [The author defends the natural impeccability of a pure spirit]; Journet, "L'univers antérieur à l'Église," *RT* 53 (1953): 439–87 [reprinted in "Essai de théologie de l'histoire du salut," 183–368]; Courtès, "Le traité des anges et la fin ultime de l'esprit," *RT* 54 (1954): 155–65; Dondaine, "Le premier instant de l'ange d'après saint Thomas," 213–27; Edward Montano, *The Sin of Angels: Some Aspects of the Teaching of St. Thomas* (Washington, D.C.: The Catholic University of America Press, 1955); Jacques Maritain, "Le péché de l'ange: Essai de ré-interprétation des positions thomistes," *RT* 56 (1956): 197–239 [reprinted in Journet, Maritain, and Philippe de la Trinité, *Péché de l'ange*]; Philippe de la Trinité, "Réflexions sur le péché de l'ange," *Ephemerides Carmeliticae* 8 (1957): 44–92; Philippe de la Trinité, "La pensée des carmes de Salamanque et de Jean de Saint-Thomas sur le péché de l'ange," *Ephemerides Carmeliticae* 8 (1957): 315–75; Philippe de la Trinité, "Évolution de saint Thomas sur le péché de l'ange dans l'ordre naturel?" *Ephemerides Carmeliticae* 9 (1958): 338–90 [reprinted in Journet, Maritain, and Philippe de la Trinité, *Péché de l'ange*]; Journet, "L'aventure des anges," *Nova et vetera* 33 (1958): 127–43 [reprinted in "Essai de théologie de l'histoire du salut," 183–254]; Journet, Maritain, and Philippe de la Trinité, *Péché de l'ange*; R. E. Marieb, "The Impeccability of the Angels regarding their Natural End," *Thomist* 28 (1964): 409–74 [Defense and illustration of the thesis of natural impeccability against the recent reinterpretations]; Michel-Louis Guérard des Lauriers, *Le Péché et la durée de l'ange*, Collectio philosophica lateranensis 10 (Rome: Desclée, 1965); Nicolas, *Synthèse dogmatique*, vol. 2, *Complément*, 365–70: "The evil that some angels chose"; René Mougel, "La position de Jacques Maritain à l'égard de *Surnaturel*, Le péché de l'ange, ou 'esprit et liberté,'" in *Surnaturel: Une controverse au coeur du thomisme au XXe siècle*, Actes du colloque organisé par l'Institut Saint-Thomas d'Aquin les 26–27 mai 2000 à Toulouse, *RT* 101 (2001): 73–98.

26. See *Q. de ver.*, q. 24, a. 7.

27. *In II Sent.*, d. 5, q. 1, a. 1; d. 23, q. 1, a.1; *Q. de ver.*, q. 24, a. 7; *CG* III.108; *Q. de malo*,

plains in the response of article 1 of question 63 that every rational, moral creature is by nature capable of sinning. For such a creature, impeccability can only be a super-natural gift. The reason for this is the following: a morally good action is an action in conformity with the rule of morality that defines the deep-seated finalities of every being and therefore the conditions for its fulfillment. This rule is in the final analysis the eternal law, the wise and loving will of God. To sin is to stray from this rule. God absolutely cannot sin because he himself is the rule of his action. In contrast, no creature is identical to the moral law. Indeed, since no creature is his own origin, no creature is his own end either: it must regulate its action according to an extrinsic principle, which implies the possibility of departing from it. Therefore every spiritual creature can sin. The usual example in the writings of St. Thomas is that of the craftsman who plans to cut a board. If the craftsman's hand were the rule itself, if the rule were incorporated into his hand, then the cuts would always be perfect. But since that is not the case, if he wants to cut the board correctly, he must use a rule that guides his work, but he can also decide not to use the rule and consequently cut a crooked line.

However, there is no lack of arguments in favor of the impossibility of an angel ever sinning. Some object that evil is a privation, a lack, and that a privation affects only a being in potency—in other words, a being that can either have or not have such and such a perfection. Now an angel is always in act. Certainly, Aquinas replies, an angel, unlike a man, does not have to become what he is, for from the start he is in act with regard to his natural being, but his spiritual faculties, and especially his free will, while always in act, remain in potency in relation to one or another object, and thereby the possibility of sin is introduced.[28]

But doesn't every sin presuppose an error? It requires the intellect to present to the will as something good an object that in fact is only an apparent good. Now, properly speaking, an angel cannot be mistaken. No error, no sin! St. Thomas grants that an angel, unlike a man,

---

q. 16, a. 2; Aquinas, *Expositio super Iob ad litteram*, Leonine edition, vol. 26 [*In Iob*, c. 4, 31–32].

28. See *ST* I, q. 63, a. 1, arg. 1 et ad 1. Therefore it is necessary to distinguish clearly the angels from the heavenly bodies (arg. 2 et ad 2). The latter, which are always in act and governed by necessity, can never fail. In contrast, an angel can fail by reason of his free will.

cannot choose a really bad object, because that always presupposes an error. Indeed, nothing intervenes to trouble the angel's intellect: he has neither passions nor antecedent bad habits that would falsify his practical judgment. He can desire only that which he knows to be good. On the other hand, an angel can *make badly* a choice pertaining to a good object. He chooses an objectively good act (love of self in this case), but his choice—and his choice alone—is not good because it lacks something that ought to exist—namely: consideration of the higher rule. The evil does not come from the object but rather from the nature of the choice. For example, to pray is a good act, but to pray without observing the liturgical regulations of the church (e.g., to recite Night Prayer in the early morning) becomes something bad. This is the case with the angel's sin: the angel loved his own good without considering the fact that God's will was calling him to something else.

Someone will retort that that is impossible, since an angel, as was already explained, naturally loves God more than anything else. How then could he turn away from God? St. Thomas responds by making an invaluable distinction between God as the principle of the angel's natural being and God as the object of supernatural beatitude. An angel cannot *not* love God naturally as the source of his being, but he can reject God as the object of a friendship that the latter proposes to him by grace.[29] Sin actually becomes possible for an angel when he is called to go beyond himself in the supernatural order.

In the mid-twentieth century a controversy arose among the interpreters of St. Thomas over this point. The common opinion among Thomists was that God absolutely cannot create a subject who by nature would be incapable of sinning both against the natural law and against the supernatural order (absolute impeccability). On the other hand, if God had not raised the angels to the supernatural order, they would have possessed a relative impeccability in the state of pure nature. The angels would then be, on the natural level, impeccable, incapable of straying from the natural law. But God did call the angels to the supernatural life, which implied, for them as for us, passing the test of the incomprehensible obscurity of faith. This invitation unbalanced the angels, placing them in a situation where sin became possi-

29. See *ST* I, q. 63, a. 1, arg. 3 et ad 3.

ble at the same time as the higher good of the trinitarian friendship.[30] A religious who is a model of regularity in his peaceful monastery routine governed by the sound of the bells can lose his grip as soon as he is placed in a living situation that is a bit more complicated.

This position, which was vigorously defended by Pierre-Ceslas Courtès, was no less vigorously criticized by Henri de Lubac and Jacques Maritain. In their opinion, the idea that an angel is naturally impeccable and would have been unable to sin had he not been raised to the supernatural order is very problematic. On the one hand, it leads to the conclusion that it would have been better for God not to call the angels to a supernatural life, since it caused some of them to lose their impeccability. On the other hand, and most importantly, it disregards the fact that, even on the natural level, a spiritual being is perfected only by a free moral choice that inevitably presupposes the possibility of failure. When a person settles on his end in the moral order, he always does so by a freely chosen love. Someone may reply that the call to the supernatural life does not destroy a natural property in an angel (impeccability) but rather actualizes, by accident and with a view to a greater good, a real possibility of his nature that had no occasion to manifest itself in the natural order. But the basis of the debate—which we dare not enter into—concerns the manner in which one thinks about the perfection of created freedom, as it is manifested in adherence to God as the final end: is it an act of free choice, implying the possibility of sinning, or is it an infallible and spontaneous consent to the good?

What Sin?

However that may be, some angels, concretely, did sin. What is the specific nature of this sin that is at the origin of the emergence of the

---

30. See *Q. de malo*, q. 16, a. 3: "All the angels were so created that they had immediately from the moment of their creation whatever pertains to their natural perfection; nevertheless they were in potency to supernatural goods which they could obtain through God's grace. Hence it remains that the sin of the devil did not consist in anything that pertains to the order of nature but in something supernatural" (466) (Angeli autem omnes sic conditi sunt ut quidquid pertinet ad naturalem perfectionem eorum, statim a principio suae creationis habuerint; tamen erant in potentia ad supernaturalia bona quae per Dei gratiam consequi poterant. Unde relinquitur quod peccatum diaboli non fuerit in aliquo quod pertinet ad ordinem naturalem sed secundum aliquid supernaturale).

demonic world?[31] There have been several successive theories in the history of Christian doctrines. The hypothesis of a sin of lust, based on Genesis 6, had its proponents in the early decades of the church,[32] but it has been critiqued as a rule since the patristic period.[33]

The hypothesis of an original sin of envy or jealousy with regard to men also had its hour of glory. Was it not "through the devil's envy" that "death entered the world" (Ws 2:24)? This idea is found already in the Latin *Life of Adam and Eve*: the devil and his angels were driven from paradise for having refused to venerate man created in the image of God.[34] St. Irenaeus of Lyons adopts it:

> The devil ... , becoming envious of man, was rendered an apostate from the divine law: for envy is a thing foreign to God. And as his apostasy was exposed by man, and man became the means of searching out his thoughts, he has set himself to this with greater and greater determination, in opposition to man, envying his life.[35]

31. See *ST* I, q. 63, aa. 2–3.

32. See, for example, Justin, *Second Apology* 5.3 (ANF 1:190a): "God ... committed the care of men and of all things under heaven to angels whom He appointed over them. But the angels transgressed this appointment, and were captivated by love of women, and begat children who are those that are called demons"; Tertullian, *On the Veiling of Virgins* VII.4–7 (ANF 4:29a–32a): see 1 Cor 11:10, where St. Paul recommends that women be veiled "because of the angels," which some have related to Gn 6); Lactantius, *Divine Institutes* II.14 (FOTC 49:152–54).

33. See, for example, John Chrysostom, *Homilies on Genesis* XXII (FOTC 82:74). Hilary of Poitiers (*Tractatus super psalmos, In Ps.* 132, no. 6 [PL 9:748–49]) and especially Augustine (*City of God* XV.23 [FOTC 14:470–75]) dispute this theory and the canonical value of the writings on which it is based. Concerning the patristic interpretation of this passage, see Charles Robert, "Les fils de Dieu et les filles des hommes," *Revue biblique* 4 (1895): 340–72.

34. See *Vita Adae et Evae* XII–XVI, ed. Wilhelm Meyer (Munich: G. Franz, 1879); English trans. in *Apocryphal Old Testament*, 149–51.

35. Irenaeus of Lyons, *Against Heresies* V.24.4 (ANF 1:553a). See also *Against Heresies* IV.40. 3–41.2 (ANF 1: 524a): "Hence we learn that this was the apostate angel and the enemy, because he was envious of God's workmanship, and took in hand to render this [workmanship] an enmity with God. For this cause also God has banished from His presence him who did of his own accord stealthily sow the tares, that is, him who brought about the transgression"; Irenaeus of Lyons, *Proof of the Apostolic Preaching* 16 (ACW 16:57). See also Cyprian, *On Jealousy and Envy* (FOTC 36:291–308, cited in Augustine, *On Baptism* IV.7.11 [NPNF–1 4:451a–b]); Gregory of Nyssa, *The Great Catechism* VI (NPNF–2 5:480a–81b). Tertullian speaks about a sin of impatience that strongly resembles jealousy; see Tertullian, *On Patience* 5.5–7 (FOTC 40:200).

Along these lines, St. Bernard explains that the angel rebelled against the elevation of man to the same rank of glory as his: "To him [Satan] they [men] were by nature both lower and weaker, unworthy to be fellow-citizens, to share an equal glory."[36] Some even think that he envied man most especially for the distinguished grace of the hypostatic union, which gives a Christological connotation to the fall of Satan,[37] but one may hesitate, from a Thomistic perspective in which the Incarnation is connected with Adam's sin, to attribute to the angels *in via* a knowledge of the mystery of the redemptive Incarnation.

But little by little the idea emerged that the original sin of the angel was at its root a sin of pride: this idea became prevalent with the writings of St. Augustine.[38] Pride is the disordered love of my own excellence—in other words, of my good, not because it is a good but because it is mine and distinguishes me from others. Pride is therefore love of the *bonum privatum* to the point of contempt for the *bonum commune*—it is love of self to the point of contempt for God. Its effect is to deprive us of the good of others, whereas love of the common good makes us rich with the good of all:

With good reason Scripture has said, *Pride is the beginning of all sin* (Ecclesiasticus 10:15, DV).[39] This testimony is supported also by the statement of St. Paul, *Avarice is the root of all evils* (1 Tm 6:10), if we understand "avarice" in the general sense of the word, that is, the attitude by which a person desires more than what is due by reason of his excellence, and a certain love of one's own interest, his private interest, to which the Latin word *privatus* was wisely given, a term that obviously expresses loss rather than gain. For every privation (*privatio*) diminishes. Where pride, then, seeks to excel, there it is cast

36. See Bernard of Clairvaux, *On the Song of Songs*, XVII.5–6, 1:129: "Because of his lofty endowments of wisdom and grace, [Satan] could have foreseen that members of the human race would one day be raised to be his equals in glory. And if he did foresee this, it was because it was revealed to him in the Word of God. Then, stung by a wild impulse of envy, he plotted to maintain as subjects those whom he scorned as companions. To him they were by nature both lower and weaker, unworthy to be fellow-citizens, to share an equal glory."

37. See Suarez, *Tractatus de Angelis*, lib. VII, ch. 13, 880–91; John of St. Thomas, *Cursus theologicus*, disp. 43, a. 3 (4:746–48).

38. The identification of the angelic sin as an original sin of pride can boast of scriptural support in 1 Tm 3:6: "[A future bishop] must not be a recent convert; or he may be puffed up with conceit and fall into the condemnation of the devil."

39. Concerning pride as the first, fundamental sin, see *ST* I-II, q. 84, a. 2; *ST* II-II, q. 162, a. 7.

down into want and destitution, turning from the pursuit of the common god to one's own individual good out of a destructive self-love.[40]

St. Thomas aligns himself with the Augustinian tradition: he defines the sin of the angel as a sin of pride and interprets the other hypotheses in terms of this principle.[41] It is clear, first of all, that the angel's sin corresponds to his nature—in other words, that it is of a purely spiritual order. Now in this realm there is no fear of excess: one never loves spiritual goods too much, for, unlike material goods that diminish when they are shared, spiritual goods can be held in common. On the other hand, one can love them wrongly if one becomes attached to them apart from the moral norm that emanates from someone superior to us. Now this contempt for the norm pertains to the sin of pride, which is the rejection of all dependence out of an unbridled love for one's own excellence.[42]

From the poisoned spring of the sin of pride immediately flows the sin of envy or jealousy. Envy, like any movement of sadness, is never primary. It always presupposes a thwarted love. In effect, an envious person is saddened by the good of another inasmuch as he thinks that it overshadows his own excellence. The presence of good in another threatens my superiority, and that is why I am saddened by it and seek to disparage and to destroy it. And so the angel wounded by pride was jealous of man and even of God. St. Augustine had already grasped the logic of this sequence:

40. Augustine, *Literal Meaning of Genesis* XI.15.19 (ACW 42:146–47): "Merito initium omnis peccati superbiam Scriptura definivit, dicens: 'Initium omnis peccati superbia.' Cui testimonio non inconvenienter aptatur etiam illud quod Apostolus ait: 'Radix omnium malorum est avaritia'; si avaritiam generalem intellegamus, qua quisque appetit aliquid amplius quam oportet, propter excellentiam suam, et quendam propriae rei amorem: cui sapienter nomen latina lingua indidit, cum appelavit privatum, quod potius a detrimento quam ab incremento dictum elucet. Omnis enim privatio minuit. Unde itaque vult eminere superbia inde in angustias egestatemque contruditur, cum ex communi ad proprium damnoso sui amore redigitur."

41. See *ST* I, q. 63, a. 2.

42. See *ST* I, q. 63, a. 2: "There can be no sin when anyone is incited to good of the spiritual order; unless in such affection the rule of the superior be not kept. Such is precisely the sin of pride—not to be subject to a superior when subjection is due. Consequently the first sin of the angel can be none other than pride" (In spiritualibus autem bonis non potest esse peccatum dum aliquis ad ea afficitur, nisi per hoc quod in tali affectu superioris regula non servatur. Et hoc est peccatum superbiae, non subdi superiori in eo quo debet. Unde peccatum primum angeli non potest esse aliud quam superbia).

Some say that [the demon] fell from the heavenly abode because he envied man made to the image of God. Envy, indeed, does not precede pride but follows it: envy is not the cause of pride, but pride is the cause of envy. Since, therefore, pride is the love of one's own excellence, and envy is the hatred of another's happiness, it is easy to see that vice begets the other. For a person who loves his own excellence envies his peers because they are equal to him, his inferiors because he fears that they may become his equals, and his superiors because he is not their equal. It is by pride, therefore, that one becomes envious, not by envy that one becomes proud.[43]

In article 3, St. Thomas explains somewhat the object of this diabolical pride. The king of Babylon mused, "I will ascend to heaven.... I will make myself like the Most High" (Is 14:13–14), and he was a figure of Lucifer. The diabolical suggestion whispered to Eve—"You will be like gods" (Gn 3:5)—is like an echo of the angel's sin of pride.[44] That said, we must not make the angel stupider than he is. He is too lucidly intelligent to delude himself and desire the impossible. Now it is simply and utterly impossible for a creature to cease being a creature so as to become equal to the Creator in all respects.[45] Satan therefore wanted to be like God, not by nature and as an equal, but *by resemblance*. In what way is that blameworthy? Isn't that the end that God assigns to his creatures: to become similar to him? Isn't this resemblance what God wants to communicate to them? In fact there are certain aspects of the divine perfection that are communicable and that a spiritual creature can legitimately aim to attain (to be wise and good), but there are others that are proper to God and incommunicable (such as being the Creator of heaven and earth) and that it would be sinful to desire. Now the angel wanted something of this second type. Not, as some have thought, to

43. Augustine, *Literal Meaning of Genesis* XI.14.18 (ACW 42:146): "Nonnulli enim dicunt ipsum ei fuisse casum a supernis sedibus, quod inviderit homini facto ad imaginem Dei. Porro autem invidia sequitur superbiam, non praecedit: non enim causa superbiendi est invidia, sed causa invidendi superbia. Cum igitur superbia sit amor excellentiae propriae, invidentia vero sit odium felicitatis alienae, quid unde nascatur satis in promptu est. Amando enim quisque excellentiam suam, vel paribus invidet, quod ei coaequentur; vel inferioribus, ne sibi coaequentur; vel superioribus, quod eis non coaequetur. Superbiendo igitur invidus, non invidendo quisque superbus est."

44. See *ST* II-II, q. 163, a. 2, where Adam's sin is also presented as the desire to be like God.

45. St. Thomas explains moreover that no being can seriously want to be another species than his own, because that would be to desire its own destruction. For proof, look at the frog in La Fontaine's fable who wanted to become as big as an ox!

be similar to God inasmuch as he depends on absolutely nothing, since the angel knows very well that he can exist only by receiving existence from the *Ipsum Esse*. But he wanted to be similar to God inasmuch as God is, by nature, an end unto himself.[46] Therefore he determined for himself in a disorderly fashion, as his final end, one that he could attain by his own natural resources, which virtually implied contempt for the divine offer of supernatural beatitude.

Certainly, the angel knew the objective value of the divine proposal. But supernatural beatitude was proposed to him under certain intrinsic conditions that he refused. First, it could not be obtained by way of a natural requirement but had to be received as a grace through abandonment to God in the obscurity of faith.[47] Second, this beatitude was proposed to everyone, which had the effect of relativizing natural inequalities. Now Satan considers these conditions humiliating and chooses to cling to the possession of his natural perfection, insofar as (1) it distinguishes him from others and (2) it belongs to him by a natural right as though he were the master thereof. He preferred to remain the first in an inferior order rather than to become one among others in a superior order.[48]

The moral theologian will observe here how plainly Satan's sin reveals the profound nature of pride as the will to control one's own life alone. Indeed, the angel preferred to cling to what he controlled rather than to be open to the divine call to "put out into the deep"—in other words, to let go of his destiny so as to receive from another its meaning and fulfillment.[49] Therefore there is something demonic in

46. This desire to be self-subsistent (rather than to exist by opening oneself to others) naturally leads to the desire to lord it over others, for what is self-subsistent is the principle of what exists through something else. In this, too, the demon wanted to resemble God.

47. See the remarks of Héris, in *Summa Theologica I, questions 50–64*, Éditions de la Revue des jeunes, 462–63: "He wanted to possess this God in clarity, to embrace him in the light, without undergoing the test of faith. For an angel, indeed, who is all pure spirit, the scandal of a God offering himself to him in the incomprehensibility of mystery is infinitely more serious than the scandal for man of the suffering and the evil in this world.... No trial could be more severe for an angel, because it meant renouncing himself, proclaiming that God is the incomprehensible Most High."

48. See John of St. Thomas, *Cursus theologicus*, disp. 43, a. 3: "Quo genere peccati, et circa quod objectum, peccaverit angelus" (4:731–54).

49. In *ST* III, q. 8, a. 7, St. Thomas explains that the rejection of God was willed by the demon "under the guise of freedom (*sub specie libertatis*)"—in other words, of nondependence (*non serviam*).

the naturalism that promotes man's fulfillment at the purely human level, to the point that one makes it a virtue—modesty, it seems— to refuse the solicitations of the supernatural: "Most fully man when nothing more than that." A deeply anti-religious culture is then set up in which man, nipping in the bud any aspiration to transcendence, chooses to cultivate his garden [as Voltaire put it in *Candide*], to make himself the master and owner of nature as well as the sole maker of his own personal and communal destiny. This self-mutilation leads to death. In a completely different, more subtle order, there is therefore also something demonic in the temptation lying in wait for the Christian: to stop at a particular stage of his spiritual journey. Certainly, this attitude owes much to the spirit of routine and to that vital reflex that aims to protect from novel disturbances the psychological equilibrium that one has laboriously acquired. It therefore proceeds more from the sluggishness of nature (and age) than from a spiritual movement of pride. But one cannot rule out the subtle presence of pride in this refusal to leave familiar, clearly marked terrain in order to follow the calls of grace and to set out on the obscure paths of purification.

The Sin of Satan and That of the Other Demons

This sin of the angels is at first that of Satan, but the proposed analysis of it applies identically to all the demons. For a long time Christian authors had difficulty unifying the rather heterogeneous nebula of demonic powers and, in particular, articulating coherently the history of Satan and that of the demons.[50] But at the time of St. Thomas, the situation is almost clear. Taking up a theme that was already classic in the Lombard's writings and was attributed to St. Gregory, the Latin specialist in the cartography of the angelic universe,[51] Aqui-

50. Lactantius, for example, presents first the apostasy of Satan and then explains how he corrupted the angels whom God had sent to defend mankind against him, by seducing them through the daughters of men. From these hybrid unions were born the "terrestrial" demons. See Lactantius, *The Divine Institutes* II.14 (FOTC 49:152–54); Emil Schneeweis, *Angels and Demons according to Lactantius*, Studies in Christian Antiquity 3 (Washington, D.C.: The Catholic University of America Press, 1944).

51. See Peter Lombard, *Sententiae* II, d. 6, c. 1 (24). The Lombard, who is inspired by the *Summa sententiarum* II.4 (PL 171:1110–11), invokes the authority of St. Gregory. See Gregory the Great, *Morals on The Book of Job* XXXII.23–24, edition 3/2, 528–29. St. Gregory, who sees in Behemoth the figure of Satan, relies on the biblical statement that he was the first of God's works, "the beginning of the ways of God (*principium*

nas maintains from the very start that the first of the sinful angels was the most exalted of all the angels in the natural order.[52] It is necessary to consider two aspects in sin, Aquinas explains: the inclination (*pronitas*) to sin and the motive of the sin. As for the first aspect, the higher angels were less inclined to sin than the angels of lower rank, since they were by nature drawn more to God. That is why it is understandable, St. Thomas admits, that some fathers thought that the angels who sinned were the inferior angels, who were set over the lower, terrestrial regions of the world to govern them.[53] But this opinion could dangerously favor the theory that tends to explain the sin of some angels by a natural inferiority prior to the choice of their will.[54] It is necessary to affirm, rather, that the intensity of one's inclination to the good and therefore the inversely proportional degree of the ontological *pronitas* to sin do not play a decisive role in the sin of the angels, since it depends only on their free will.[55] But as for the motive of the sin—namely, pride—it is clear that there is more occasion (but not reason) to become proud among the higher angels because

viarum Dei)" (Jb 40:14), in order to describe Satan as the first of the angels in the order of creation, who transcended all the others. See also Gregory the Great, *Forty Gospel Homilies* 34.7.286.

52. See *ST* I, q. 63, a. 7.

53. See John Damascene, *Exposition of the Faith* II.4 (FOTC 37:209). See also *ST* I, q. 63, a. 9, ad 3. Raïssa Maritain relied on this tradition to develop the idea that Satan, first in the hierarchy assigned to care for the universe, was already by right of creation, "by an original title," "the Prince of this world": "If sin had not affected him, he would have governed this universe in gladness and love." See Raïssa Maritain, "Le Prince de ce monde," in Maritain and Maritain, *Oeuvres complètes*, 14:205–15.

54. In *ST* I, q. 63, a. 9, ad 3, St. Thomas points out that in the hypothesis that the angels who sinned belonged to all the angelic orders, "the liberty of *free-will* is more established; which in every degree of creature can be turned to *evil*" (Comprobatur libertas liberi arbitrii, quae secundum quemlibet gradum creaturae in malum flecti potest). In a beautiful miniature from the medieval manuscript *Les Très Riches Heures du duc de Berry*, the artist depicted the fall of the angels. The celestial choirs are symbolized by monastic stalls surrounding God, some of which are occupied while others are being vacated or are already vacant; see Giorgi, *Anges et démons*, traduit de l'italien par D. Férault, Guide des arts (Paris: Hazan, 2004), 237.

55. See *ST* I, q. 63, a. 7: "The angels' sin did not come of any proneness, but of free choice alone" (Peccatum angeli non processit ex aliqua pronitate, sed ex solo libero arbitrio). See also ad 3: "However great was the inclination towards good in the highest angel, there was no necessity imposed upon him: consequently it was in his power not to follow it" (Quantacumque inclinatio ad bonum fuerit in supremo angelo, tamen ei necessitatem non inducebat. Unde potuit per liberum arbitrium eam non sequi).

of their greater natural perfection. It is therefore consistent to think that Satan was absolutely the first of the angels in the natural order, even though the contrary opinion is not heretical. Hence, by reason of the very perfection of his nature, Satan became the worst, because he turned to evil with all his strength, which was great.[56]

The book of Revelation declares that "[The dragon's] tail swept down a third of the stars of heaven and cast them to the earth" (Rv 12:4).[57] Satan's sin involves the sin of many other angels,[58] not through the influence of efficient causality or of constraint but by virtue of exhortation to evil—in other words, the moral causality of bad example. The manifestation of Satan's perverse will immediately incited the free consent of some angels. They joined his rebellion and placed their revolt in the wake of his inasmuch as they counted on Satan's natural action in order to attain, without further reliance on God, the natural end on which they, imitating Satan, had perversely set their sights.[59] St. Thomas sees the sign of Satan's influence on the sin of the other angels in the present submission of the demons to Satan as to their chief: one is the slave of him to whom one has surrendered.

As for determining the percentage of the rebellious angels and

56. See *ST* I, q. 63, a. 8, ad 3: "An angel has nothing in him to retard his action, and with his whole might he is moved to whatsoever he is moved, be it good or bad. Consequently since the highest angel had greater natural energy than the lower angels, he fell into sin with intenser energy, and therefore he became the greater in malice" (Angelus non habet aliquid retardans, sed secundum suam totam virtutem movetur in illud ad quod movetur, sive in bonum sive in malum. Quia igitur supremus angelus maiorem habuit naturalem virtutem quam inferiores, intensiori motu in peccatum prolapsus est. Et ideo factus est etiam in malitia maior).

57. In the literal sense, these stars seem to be the faithful who fall because of persecutions, but a venerable interpretation sees in them the demons dragged down by Satan's fall. See Arethas of Caesarea, *Commentarium in Apocalypsin*, c. 33 (PG 106:661–64). One of the sources could be 1 Enoch 86 (*Apocryphal Old Testament*, 277–78), which is about the fall of a star and then of several more after it.

58. See *ST* I, q. 63, a. 8.

59. But, someone will say, how could the wicked angels, in their pride, subject themselves to Satan rather than to God, since a proud person judges it less humiliating to submit to the First in Command than to the Second (*ST* I, q. 63, a. 8, arg. 2)? In fact, this submission allowed them to remain in the natural order and to obtain their happiness by themselves, which they wanted even more than independence (ad 2). Albert the Great, *In II Sent.*, d. 6, a. 1 (128), offers a caustic example: "It is like some canons who promote an unworthy candidate so that his promotion might raise them up too" (Sicut aliqui canonici promovent unum indignum, quo promoto etiam ipsi exaltentur).

the extent of the ruin of the angelic city, St. Thomas takes an optimistic view. For him, sin is profoundly contrary to nature. Now what is contrary to nature is rare.[60]

THE DEMONS' PUNISHMENT

To every sin, to every moral evil, corresponds a punishment that has the objective of bringing some good from the evil that was committed by reestablishing the order of justice that was violated by the sin and, possibly, by setting the culprit back on the right path.[61] In the case of man, this punishment may consist in a diminution of some of his natural goods (physical integrity, freedom of movement), but for a pure spirit, whose nature is not composed of parts, such an amputation is impossible. The punishment inflicted on the angels for their sin therefore destroys nothing of their nature. According to a formula derived from Dionysius, "their natural gifts remain intact" ("*dona naturalia in eis manent integra*").[62] The demons therefore do not cease to be angels possessing all the natural perfections that define that type of being.[63]

60. See *ST* I, q. 63, a. 9. See the earlier discussion by Augustine, *City of God* XI.23.1 (FOTC 14:222): "The great majority of those in heaven preserve the integrity of their nature" (Cum bonorum longe maior numerus in caelestibus suae naturae ordinem servet).

61. On the demons' punishment, see *ST* I, q. 64. On the notion of punishment, see Jacques Maritain, *Neuf leçons sur les notions premières de la philosophie morale*, Leçon 9, "La notion de sanction," in Maritain and Maritain, *Oeuvres complètes*, 9:923–37; Philippe Besnier, *Faute et peine chez saint Thomas d'Aquin* (Montsûrs: Editions Résiac, 1989).

62. See Dionysius, *The Divine Names*, 4.23, in *Pseudo-Dionysius: The Complete Works*, 91: "And I would claim that the angelic gifts bestowed on them have never been changed inherently, that in fact they are brilliantly complete." See also Bernard Quelquejeu, "Naturalis manent integra: Contribution à l'étude de la portée, méthdologique et doctrinale, de l'axiome théologique 'Gratia praesupponit natura,'" *RSPT* 49 (1965): 640–55.

63. The devil is therefore a person in the metaphysical sense of the term—in other words, an individual subject with a personal nature, a center of being and acting. However, contrary to the vocation of the person, this ontological perfection does not flourish, in him, in communion with other spiritual beings and with God. Instead, the demon works to ruin any authentic relationship between persons so as to reduce them to his own imprisonment. One can understand therefore, without entirely sharing their scruples, why some authors who understand the term *person* only in the full and even supernatural sense of the word, hesitate to describe the demon as a person, without denying his reality; see Ratzinger, "Farewell to the Devil?," 204: "If someone asks whether the devil is a person, we would probably have to answer more accurately that he is the

This is how the darkening of the demonic intellect after sin must be correctly understood.[64] St. Thomas distinguishes three types of knowledge of the truth: first, natural knowledge. It remains intact in the demons: every demon knows himself and naturally knows God in knowing himself.[65] However, since this natural knowledge is not referred to the praise of God, it must be described as nocturnal knowledge.[66]

Then comes, second, purely speculative supernatural knowledge. It results from the revelation that God gives to the angels of certain mysteries of the Kingdom. On the one hand, the supernatural knowledge that they were able to possess on the journey ("*in via*") is not withdrawn from the demons. On the other hand, the demons can still learn certain truths on the supernatural order, either by the revelatory action of the good angels or by their own experience.[67] This supernatural knowledge remains quite inferior to that of the blessed angels. The demons do not see very clearly into God's designs! We will return to this.

Finally, third, it is necessary to deny that the demons, who have turned away from their final end, have an affective and delectable supernatural knowledge of the mystery of God, which is founded on charity and pertains to the gift of wisdom.[68] It is above all in relation to this sort of knowledge that we say that the demon's mind is darkened: it is totally deprived of the light of wisdom.

After their first sin, the free will of the demons stubbornly persists forever in evil, which is to say that it is fixed irremediably in their bad choice, so that their chastisement is eternal.[69] For the demons no re-

---

Un-person, the disintegration and collapse of personhood, and that is why he characteristically appears without a face." Compare the balanced reflection by Karl Lehmann, "Il diavolo, un essere personale?" in *Diavolo*, 79–111.

64. See *ST* I, q. 64, a. 1.   65. See *ST* I, q. 64, ad 1 et ad 2.
66. See *ST* I, q. 64, ad 3.
67. This knowledge by experience, which tradition attributes to the demons (Augustine, *Literal Meaning of Genesis* II.17.37 [ACW 41:72]), must be understood according to the general theory of angelic knowledge. See *ST* I, q. 64; I, q. 64, a. 1, ad 5. This is the accomplishment in the empirical world of the events of salvation history, of which the angel has within himself from the beginning the *species*, which causes the angel to know henceforth as being present that which he formerly knew as being future. But the whole change is on the part of the object.
68. *ST* See II-II, q. 45.
69. *ST* See I, q. 64, a. 2; *Q. de malo*, q. 16, a. 5.

demption is possible.[70] On this subject, the church, relying on scripture (Mt 25:46), has clearly pronounced against Origen's theory that the demons' punishment will be temporary, so that at the end of time all creation will be thoroughly restored in Christ.[71]

But it is up to theologians to determine the exact reasons the demon's bad choice is irrevocable. They distinguish two of them, one extrinsic and the other intrinsic. The extrinsic reason is that God ceases to offer to the demons the grace that could per se convert them. The hour of choice is past. Does this mean that God arbitrarily blows the whistle, declares the game over, and decides that there will be no extra innings? No, because in fact God merely respects the angel's nature.[72] Unlike man, whose free will can change its object because his choice depends on intellectual activity that is discursive, progressive, and changing,[73] an angel, by reason of his purely intellectual nature, is situated from the start in the presence of all that he can know, so that his free will is also fixed from the start, unchangeably, totally, and ir-

---

70. See, for example, Tertullian, *Flesh of Christ* XIV.1, in ANF 3:533a: "Man had perished; his recovery had become necessary. No such cause, however, existed for Christ's taking on Him the nature of angels. For although there is assigned to angels also perdition in 'the fire prepared for the devil and his angels,' yet a restoration (*restitutio*) is never promised to them. No charge about the salvation of angels did Christ ever receive from the Father."

71. See Origen, *On First Principles* I.6.3 (1966), 56–57; see SC 252:202–5 and notes at SC 253:97–100; *On First Principles* II.3.3 (85–87). Origen asserts the possibility of a free change in the will of an angel or a demon; this doctrine on the one hand results from his erroneous reduction of freedom to the univocal capacity to choose at any instant between good and evil, and on the other hand is the prerequisite for his theory of the *apokatastasis* claiming that God ultimately will save every creature. St. Augustine, who could not allow the monstrous idea of a provisional beatitude, severely criticized the "merciful" Origen, whose theory in fact ends up abolishing the beatitude of the saints; see Augustine, *City of God* XXI.17 (FOTC 24:378–79). Origen's theory was condemned. See the anathemas leveled against Origen in A.D. 543 (Denz.-H. no. 411): "If anyone says or holds that the punishment of the demons and of impious men is temporary, and that it will have an end at some time, that is to say, there will be a complete restoration (*apokatastasis*) of the demons or of impious men, let him be anathema."

72. St. Thomas admits that *de potentia absoluta* God could convert the demons, but then he would be acting—unimaginably—against his wisdom, which determined the nature of each being; see *Q. de malo*, q. 16, a. 5, ad 13.

73. Mutability is per se accidental in relation to the perfection that is freedom, just like the possibility of choosing either good or evil. It proceeds from the imperfection of the subject in whom the perfect of freedom is actualized. In God, who is perfectly free, freedom tends always and immutably toward the good. See *Q. de malo*, q. 16, a. 5.

reversibly, on the object of his choice—this is the intrinsic reason for the demon's obstinacy. As long as iron that has been heated in the fire is malleable, the blacksmith can give it one form or another, but once it has solidified, it no longer changes. Now the angelic will solidifies instantaneously.

The cause of the demons' obstinacy in evil is therefore not to be sought in the objective seriousness of the sin committed—no sin per se is too great for God's infinite mercy—but rather in the very nature of the angelic being:

> It is the *irrevocable* character of their choice, and not a defect in the infinite divine mercy, that makes the angels' sin unforgivable.[74] "There is no repentance for the angels after their fall, just as there is no repentance for men after death."[75]

The immutably perverse orientation of their mind is for the demons the source of terrible, continual suffering.[76] I will not linger over the scholastic speculations aimed at explaining how immaterial beings like the demons (or the separated souls) can be chained in a physical place and tortured by the fire of hell.[77] The chief suffering of the demons is of a spiritual order. Certainly, the demons do not

74. See *ST* I, q. 64, a. 2, ad 2. No more than the divine omnipotence is limited by something that is self-contradictory (in other words, cannot exist) is the divine mercy limited by the demons' obstinacy: it quite simply has no material to work on since it is the nature of the demon to be unable to convert and do penance.

75. *CCC* 393. Citation from John Damascene, *Orthodox Faith* II.4 (FOTC 37:210): "The fall is to the angels just what death is to men. For, just as there is no repentance for men after their death, so is there none for the angels after their fall."

76. See *ST* I, q. 64, a. 3.

77. See Aquinas, *In IV Sent.*, d. 44, q. 3, a. 3, qla 3 (*Suppl.*, q. 70, a. 3). The debate very much preoccupied the thinkers of the thirteenth century, and one of the articles condemned in March 1277 bears precisely on this question. See *La condamnation parisienne de 1277*, prop. 19 (210), 84–85; Kurt Flasch, "Die Seele im Feuer: Aristotelische Seelenlehre und augustinisch-gregorianische Eschatologie bei Albert von Köln, Thomas von Aquino, Siger von Brabant und Dietrich von Freiberg," in *Albertus Magnus und der Albertismus: Deutsche philosophische Kultur des Mittelalters*, edited by Maarten J. F. M. Hoenen and Alain de Libera, 107–31, Studien und Texte zur Geistesgeschichte des Mittelalters 48 (Leiden: E. J. Brill, 1995). Journet, "Essai de théologie de l'histoire du salut," 369–94, proposes a reflection on how to understand today the punishment of fire with which the demons are afflicted. It resides in the inversion of the relations between the cosmos and the (fallen) angels: whereas the angel has the vocation to preside over the cosmos, the demon is wounded by the reality of a cosmos that permanently thwarts him but from which he cannot escape. The harmony has changed into conflict.

experience any sort of contrition; they are not afflicted by their sin as such: that would be the sign of an impossible rectification of their will.[78] But they are torn by the discrepancy between their perverse will—that is, definitively, their desire for a world that suits them, instead of the real world, and reality such as it is. Their spiritual suffering, says Aquinas, is "the resistance of the *will* to what is, or to what is not."[79] The demons are allergic to reality, like a man who happened to be allergic to oxygen. This atrocious suffering is really a punishment, because the privation that the demons suffer goes contrary to their will, either their deep-seated will (their natural desire for happiness) or else their perverse will (their desire for the ruin of mankind, which is thwarted and frustrated by God's mercy). By their inability to open themselves up to mercy, the demons eternally give testimony, in spite of themselves, to the aspect of the infinite goodness of God that is his retributive justice.

But their usefulness does not stop there. The last article of question 64 treats a theme that is peculiar from our perspective, which employs a very medieval analogy between one's locality in the cosmos and one's moral situation. In it, St. Thomas explains that after their sin, the demons, having been expelled from the empyrean heaven, are by right consigned to hell by way of chastisement—hell being a repugnant subterranean place to which the demonic will is attached in spite of itself. But, until Judgment Day, God allows them to abide in the lower strata of the atmosphere, the cloudy air that is laden with vapors.[80] This is why the demons in the Gospel ask Jesus not to send them into the abyss, or not to "torment them before the time" (see Mt 8:29). In order to give an account of this scriptural data, St. Thomas Aquinas takes a loftier perspective and contemplates the plan of providence. God leads men to their end through the agency of angels. He procures our good directly by the ministry of the good angels, who encourage us to do good and turn us away from evil. But

78. See *ST* I, q. 64, a. 3, ad 3.

79. Ibid., corpus: "renisus [= the act of struggling against] voluntatis ad id quod est vel non est."

80. See *ST* I, q. 64, a. 4. Compare Eph 2:1–2 and 6:11–12; Augustine, *Literal Meaning of Genesis* III.10, 14–15 (ACW 41:83–84). This theme adopts a common religious notion in late antiquity that regards the demons as aerial beings; the fathers of the church tried to Christianize it, being unable to liberate themselves from it.

he also procures our good indirectly by the trials and the battles that he allows us to undergo in this life. Now, "it was fitting for this procuring of man's welfare to be brought about through the wicked spirits, lest they should cease to be of service in the natural order."[81] The rebellion of the demons is, in spite of them, placed at the service of the plan of divine mercy. Thus, in keeping with a literary device that he customarily uses, St. Thomas, at the moment when he finishes the treatise on the angels, discreetly announces a theme that he will develop in greater depth when he will have to treat the role of the angels in the divine government.

81. *ST* I, q. 64, a. 4: "Et hanc procurationem boni humani conveniens fuit per malos angelos fieri, ne totaliter post peccatum ab utilitate naturalis ordinis exciderent."

PART 4

Angels and Demons in the History of Our Salvation

Neither in the natural order nor in the supernatural order are the world of angels and the world of men two sets of objects that are merely juxtaposed and hermetically sealed off from one another. Angels and men form one and only one universe, a structured, ordered plurality whose members by their activity weave among themselves multiple interpersonal connections that reinforce their unity. This moreover is the reason, according to St. Thomas, that the creation of the angels and the creation of men were simultaneous.[1] Everything that happens in the world of angels has repercussions on the world of men, and vice versa, even though these are two asymmetric types of influence because of the difference in ontological dignity between angels and men.

The action of the angelic world on the world of men takes place within the context of the divine government.[2] Indeed, the *Catechism*

---

1. See *ST* I, q. 61, a. 2.

2. The divine government must be distinguished from providence. Providence is the plan that God conceives from all eternity to lead creation to its end, whereas the divine government is the temporal execution or implementation of that plan. Some properties of providence do not apply to the divine government and vice versa. In particular, providence is immediate (*ST* I, q. 22, a. 3). God alone works out, down to the least detail, the providential plan by which he foresees how to put the universe and every being on the way toward its end; he does not need counselors. In contrast, in the implementa-

of the Catholic Church, paragraph 306, which is an excellent digest of Thomistic theology, explains that "God is the sovereign master of his plan. But to carry it out he also makes use of his creatures' cooperation. This use is not a sign of weakness, but rather a token of almighty God's greatness and goodness. For God grants his creatures not only their existence, but also the dignity of acting on their own, of being causes and principles for each other, and thus of cooperating in the accomplishment of his plan." Let us just add that the closer a creature is to God—in other words, the higher and more perfect it is in the hierarchy of beings—the more important is its participation in the execution of the benevolent designs of providence. The angels, who occupy the created summit of the ontological scale, therefore play an eminent role in the divine government.

The finality of the divine government is to lead creatures to their perfection. Concretely, in the case of spiritual creatures, to whom merely corporeal creatures are ordered, this end is supernatural, consisting of the happiness of communion with the Divine Persons. Angels and men are the common beneficiaries of this action of divine government, which subsumes the natural finalities by bringing them to their unexpected perfection. But they are also actors and cooperators in it, each in his own way.

The sacred history of each angel played out in an instant, in a unique, decisive, and definitive personal choice, so that henceforth angels have arrived at their destination, confirmed in beatitude or definitively deprived of it. In contrast, the supernatural adventure of men unfolds in time, according to the rhythm of an economy of salvation, the center of which is the redemptive Incarnation of the word of God. But this sacred history of men is no less concerned with the pure spirits. On the one hand, the sin of man—starting with Adam's sin, which earned for us so great a Redeemer—is preceded and somehow instigated by the revolt of the demons, so that it is like the deleterious prolongation thereof. On the other hand, the essential events of the history of men's salvation—and most especially the mystery of the Incarnation—have repercussions on the life of the angels and of

---

tion of his plan God can act together with secondary causes (see *ST* I, q. 103, a. 6). Incidentally, in the structure of the *Summa theologiae* the study of providence and the study of the divine government are situated in different places.

the demons. Whatever may be the answer to the controversial question about the Christological character of angelic glory, it is certain that the activity displayed by angels and demons is related to the salvation of men, whether it is to collaborate in it or to oppose it.

From this perspective it is understandable that, in the *Summa theologiae,* of the seventeen questions that make up the treatise on the divine government, St. Thomas Aquinas devotes no fewer than nine to the participation of the angels in the divine government (*ST* I, q. 106–14). Is it necessary to recall that the *prima pars* is not a treatise on philosophical theology but rather reiterates in its first principles the whole divine action not only in the natural but also in the supernatural order? St. Thomas divides up these seventeen questions according to the respective objects on which the angelic government is exercised. The angels act first of all upon one another (qq. 106–9). This action consists essentially in the communication of their supernatural knowledge of the divine plans. Although it is true that the illuminating action that the angels perform for one another weaves the fabric of a veritable angelic society, we must not forget that this action belongs above all to the order of the communication of the mysteries of man's salvation.

The angels preside then over the corporeal world (q. 110). We have already discussed this active presence of the angels in the cosmos apropos the question of their very existence (chapter 4 of this volume). We will not return to this topic, inasmuch as its finality is altogether determined by their action upon a third domain: the life of men (qq. 111–14).

In part 4, we consider first of all the influence of the Son's Incarnation on the glorious life of the blessed angels (chapter 11, "Jesus Christ, Head of the Angels"), then the manner in which the angels know the mysteries of salvation and communicate this knowledge to each other, an activity that accounts for the internal structuring of the angelic world (chapter 12, "Celestial Hierarchies and Knowledge of the Mysteries of Salvation"). This knowledge is at the foundation of the activity that the good angels, as instruments of the divine government, carry out in the service of the communal and personal salvation of men in Jesus Christ (chapter 13, "The Good Angels, 'Ministering Spirits'"). This action is opposed by that of the demons who strive, in vain, to thwart God's benevolent designs (chapter 14, "The Enemy's Attacks").

11

————— : —————

Jesus Christ, Head of the Angels

The Incarnation of the Word is the decisive event in the history of mankind. Since Adam's fall, any grace granted to us passes through Jesus Christ as the meritorious cause and, since the Incarnation, as the efficient cause. This grace that comes from Christ and leads to Christ makes all of us whom it sanctifies members of the body of Christ that is the church. What about the angels? Is their supernatural life touched by the Incarnation of the Word, and if so, how?[1]

St. Thomas addresses this set of problems directly in the Christological part of the *Summa theologiae* in connection with the capital grace of Christ: "Whether Christ is the Head of the angels" (as he is of men).[2] The affirmative response is based on the authority of St. Paul: "You are filled in him [Christ], who is the head of all principality and power" (Col 2:10, DV). To account for this, St. Thomas

1. Among the strictly theological studies that discuss the relations between Christ and the angels, see Paul Benoît d'Azy, "Le Christ et ses anges dans l'oeuvre de saint Thomas," *BLE* 44 (1943): 93–117 and 121–36; Journet, "L'essai de théologie de l'histoire du salut," 287–343; Lawrence Johnson, *Christ Sanctifier of the Angels* (Rome: Pontificia Università San Tommaso, 2000); François Daguet, *Théologie du dessein divin chez saint Thomas d'Aquin: Finis omnium Ecclesia*, Bibliothèque thomiste 54 (Paris: J. Vrin, 2003), esp. 259–93.

2. *ST* III, q. 8, a. 4; see also *In III Sent.*, d. 13, q. 2, a. 2, qla 1; *In IV Sent.*, d. 9, a. 2, qla 5; *Q. de ver.*, q. 29, a. 4 (body and ad 5); *In 1 ad Co.*, c. 11, lect. 1 (no. 357); *In ad Ep.*, c. 1, lect. 8 (no. 69); *Comp. theol.*, c. 214. A similar set of problems appears in connection with the power to judge the angels, which belongs to Jesus Christ; see *ST* III, q. 59, a. 6 and parallel passages.

starts from a traditional premise: angels and men belong to one and the same spiritual society, one and the same church; they commune in one charity while waiting to commune in one and the same beatitude.[3] This teaching is particularly explicit in the writings of St. Augustine, who likes to recall that the church is made up of two parts united under one head: the pilgrim church of men and the celestial church of the angels.[4] Based on this conviction, St. Thomas explains:

Where there is one body we must allow that there is one head. Now a multitude ordained to one end, with distinct acts and duties, may be metaphorically called one body. But it is manifest that both men and angels are ordained to one end, which is the glory of the Divine fruition. Hence the mystical body of the Church consists not only of men but of angels.[5]

Jesus Christ is the one head of this one body because of the fullness of grace that resides in him due to the fact that, by the hypostatic union, his humanity is substantially united to the Person of the eternal Word. Being thus closest to God, Christ's humanity participates most perfectly in his gifts and, consequently, according to the prin-

3. See the earlier passage, sed contra 3 of *In III Sent.*, d. 1, q. 2, a. 2, qla 1: "The one Church is made up of angels and of men. Now there are not two heads of one body. Christ is therefore head of the angels also" (Ecclesia una est constituta ex angelis et hominibus. Sed unius corporis non sunt duo capita. Ergo Christus etiam est caput angelorum). St. Thomas takes this integration between angels and men rather far; see *ST* I, q. 108, a. 8, in which he rejects the idea that in Heaven men will form a separate order, whereas in fact they are associated with all the angelic choirs. Indeed, according to St. Augustine (see *City of God* XII.9 [not translated in FOTC 14:262; translated here from the Latin]), "there will not be two societies of men and angels, but only one; because the beatitude of all is to adhere to God alone" (Non erunt duae societates hominum et Angelorum, sed una, quia omnium beatitudo est adhaerere uni Deo). Compare Daguet, *Théologie du dessein divin chez saint Thomas d'Aquin*, 94–114: "A society of creatures destined for one beatitude."

4. See, for example, Augustine, *Enarrationes in Ps 149:5* (CCL 40:2182): "Ipsa nos genuit, ipsa est ecclesia sanctorum, ipsa nos nutrivit; ex parte peregrina, ex magna parte immanens in caelo. Ex parte qua immanet in caelo, beatitudo angelorum est; ex parte qua peregrinatur in hoc saeculo, spes est iustorum." See Émilien Lamirande, *L'église céleste selon saint Augustin* (Paris: Études augustiniennes, 1964) [esp. chap. 4, "L'église angélique"]; Journet, "L'enseignement de saint Augustin: Les anges font partie de l'église," in *L'Église du Verbe incarné*, 4:296–99.

5. *ST* III, q. 8, a. 4: "Ubi est unum corpus, necesse est ponere unum caput. Unum autem corpus similitudinarie dicitur una multitudo ordinata in unum secundum distinctos actus sive officia. Manifestum est autem quod ad unum finem, qui est gloria divinae fruitionis, ordinantur et homines et Angeli. Unde corpus Ecclesiae mysticum non solum consistit ex hominibus, sed etiam ex angelis."

ciple of the causality of the maximum, it exerts its influence of grace upon all those who participate in the divine life—in other words, to angels and men all at once.

In other passages in which he examines the same problem, Aquinas recalls that all "headship" ["*capitalité*"] requires three conditions: a conformity of nature between the head and the members; a superiority of the head over the members; and the exercise of an influence of the head over those same members. The first condition is satisfied only imperfectly in the case of Christ and the angels. Indeed, "surely it is not with angels that he is concerned but with the descendants of Abraham" (Hb 2:16). Christ assumed a specifically human nature and therefore has only a weak, generic conformity with the angels. That is why although Christ must be called head of the angels, it will be in a less proper sense than when he is called head of men.

The second condition—superiority, excellence—is perfectly satisfied in Christ Jesus, who surpasses the angels in dignity, "having become as much superior to angels as the name he has obtained is more excellent than theirs" (Hb 1:4). This superiority is strikingly manifested on the day of the Ascension when Christ in his humanity is exalted far above the angelic choirs.[6]

The third condition—the exercise of an influence or causality of Jesus Christ in the order of grace—is satisfied, but differently in respect to angels and in respect to men. Theologians are divided on this point, depending on the way in which they understand Christ's place in the overall divine plan. In the line of thought of John Duns Scotus, some advocate a Christocentric view of God's design: Jesus Christ is from all eternity the center and summit of God's plan. As he was creating, God already intended as his objective to work this miracle at the proper time: a God-man. And so, if Adam had not sinned, the Word would nevertheless have become incarnate. From this perspective, all grace bestowed on creatures is directly connected with the mystery of Christ. The Jesuit Francisco Suarez took the logic of this system to its

---

6. See Eph 1:19–23 (DV): "according to the operation of the might of his power, which he [God] wrought in Christ, raising him from the dead and setting him on his right hand in the heavenly places. Above all Principality and Power and Virtue and Dominion, and every name that is named, not only in this world, but also in that which is to come. And he hath subjected all things under his feet and hath made him Head over all things for the Church, which is his Body and the fulness of him who is filled all in all."

limit: all the graces from which the angels have benefited, including the grace of their elevation to the supernatural order and the grace of their free adherence to God, their supernatural end, were merited for them by Jesus Christ. Although he is not the angels' redeemer, Jesus Christ is nonetheless their savior inasmuch as the good angels were preserved from sin by the grace that he merited for them on Calvary.[7]

St. Thomas sees things differently. For him, the Word became incarnate in the first place to redeem mankind from original sin.[8] He is not, in his humanity, the savior of the angels. In no way did he merit for the angels the grace of their elevation to the supernatural order or the grace that enabled them to respond positively to this call and to receive in reward the vision of God.[9] The Word as God was the one who conferred this grace and this glory on the angels.[10] What, then,

7. See Suarez, In IIIam, q. 19, a. 4, disp. 42, in Commentarii et disputationes in tertiam Partem D. Thomae. Opera omnia 18 (Paris: Vivès, 1860), 378–87:"De iis quae Christus meruit angelis." For a vindictive defense of the traditional character of the Scotist position, see Jean-François Bonnefoy, "Christ the Sanctifier and Saviour of the Angels," in Christ and the Cosmos, trans. Michael D. Meilach, OFM (Paterson, N.J.: St. Anthony Guild Press, 1965), 282–308.

8. See ST III, q. 1, a. 2–3.

9. See Aquinas, In II Sent., d. 13, q. 2, a 2, qla 1: "Christ did not exercise his influence on the angels by removing an obstacle or by meriting grace or by praying for them, for they are already blessed. But he exercised it in matters pertaining to the hierarchical acts by which one angel illumines, purifies and perfects another.... The angels receive this in a much more eminent manner from Christ" (Non influit angelis removendo prohibens, aut merendo gratiam, aut orando pro eis, quia jam beati sunt; sed in his quae ad actus hierarchicos pertinent, secundum quod unus angelus illuminat alium, purgat, et perficit ... ; hoc enim multo eminentius a Christo recipiunt); Q. de ver., q. 29, a. 7, ad 5: "Now angels are not wayfarers with reference to the essential reward [i.e., beatitude], and so Christ did not merit for them in this respect. But they are in some sense wayfarers with reference to the accidental reward, in so far as they minister to us. In this respect, then, Christ's merit is of value to them as well. It is accordingly said in the Epistle to the Ephesians (1:10) that through Him are re-established all things that are in heaven and on earth" (Angeli autem non sunt viatores quantum ad praemium essentiale; et ideo quantum ad hoc nihil eis meruit. Sunt autem aliquo modo viatores respectu praemii accidentalis, in quantum nobis ministrant, ad quod valet eis meritum Christi: unde dicitur Ephes.1:10, quod per eum restaurantur quae in caelis et quae in terra sunt).

10. See ST III, q. 59, a. 6, in which St. Thomas explains in what sense the angels are subject to Christ's judgment: "As to the essential reward of the good angels, which is everlasting bliss; and as to the essential punishment of the wicked angels, which is everlasting damnation. But this was done by Christ from the beginning of the world, inasmuch as He is the Word of God" (Quantum ad praemium essentiale beatorum angelorum, quod est beatitudo aeterna, et quantum ad poenam essentialem malorum, quae est damnatio aeterna. Sed hoc factum est per Christum inquantum est verbum Dei, a principio mundi).

is the causal influence at the basis of Christ's headship with respect to the angels? It is twofold. On the one hand, adopting an idea from Dionysius,[11] St. Thomas thinks that Christ in his humanity illumines the angels—in other words, communicates to them something of his surpassing knowledge of the divine designs. Indeed, Christ's soul, by reason of its union with the word of God, is "full of truth." It knows much better than the most exalted angels the deepest plans of God and thus it is capable of revealing it to them.[12] It does so as an instrument of his divinity.[13] On the other hand, by way of merit, Christ has an influence on the accidental glory of the angels. In fact, the blessed angels take up a ministry of salvation among men, the success of which has not yet been achieved. From this perspective, the angels are still somehow wayfarers as long as the history of mankind lasts. Now the happy outcome of their ministry depends entirely on the grace that Jesus Christ merited for men and that he communicates to them.[14] This is why Christ is the cause of the increase of joy—"accidental" joy as opposed to the "substantial" joy of the beatific vision—that accrues to

11. See Dionysius the Areopagite, *Celestial Hierarchy*, chap. 7.3, 164: "Others [i.e., other lower angels], as they puzzle over the nature of Jesus, acquire an understanding of his divine work on our behalf and it is Jesus himself who is their instructor, teaching them directly about the kindly work he has undertaken out of love for man."

12. See *ST* III, q. 59, a. 6: "Christ's soul is more filled with the truth of the Word of God than any angel: for which reason He also enlightens the angels, as Dionysius says (*Coel. Hier.*, vii)" (Anima Christi magis est repleta veritate verbi Dei quam aliquis angelorum. Unde et angelos illuminat, sicut Dionysius dicit, VII cap. *Cael. Hier*); *In ad Ep*, c. 1, lect. 8 (no. 69): "Christ, even as man, illumines the angels and exercises his influence on them, as Dionysius proves from the words of Is 63:1: 'Who is this that comes from Edom ...,' saying that these are the words of the higher angels. And he says that what follows, 'It is I, announcing vindication,' are the words of Christ answering them directly. This gives us to understand that Christ illumines not only the lower angels but also the higher" (Christus, etiam secundum quod homo, angelos illuminat et in eis influit, ut Dionysius probat ex verbis Is. LXIII, 1 scilicet: 'quis est iste, qui venit de Edom,' etc., dicens haec verba esse supremorum angelorum. Quod autem sequitur: 'ego qui loquor iustitiam,' dicit esse verba Christi eis immediate respondentis. Ex quo datur intelligi quod non solum inferiores, sed etiam superiores angelos Christus illuminat); Aquinas, *Super Evangelium s. Ioannis lectura*, ed. Raphelis Cai (Turin and Rome: Marietti, 1952) [*In Ioan.*, c. 1, lect. 3 (no. 98)].

13. See *ST* III, q. 8, a. 4, ad 3: "The humanity of Christ, by virtue of the spiritual nature, i.e., the Divine, can cause something not only in the spirits of men, but also in the spirits of angels, on account of its most close conjunction with God, i.e. by personal union" (Humanitas Christi, ex virtute spiritualis naturae, scilicet divinae, potest aliquid causare non solum in spiritibus hominum, sed etiam in spiritibus angelorum, propter maximam coniunctionem eius ad Deum, scilicet secundum unionem personalem).

14. See *Q. de ver.*, q. 29, a. 7, ad 5.

the angels when men attain salvation. "Just so, I tell you, there is joy before the angels of God over one sinner who repents" (Lk 15:10).[15]

This angelic joy is all the more intense because the salvation of the just is at the same time a reconciliation between the world of men and the world of angels, since Christ "reconcile[d] to himself all things, whether on earth or in heaven, making peace by the blood of his cross" (Col 1:20). Along a similar line of thought, which highlights the repercussions of the salvation of men on the angelic world, a venerable tradition that is common among the fathers of the church claims that men were created, or at least called, to the supernatural order so as to fill the void left in the angelic choirs by the desertion of the fallen angels.[16] Thus the redemption of men themselves, as an indirect effect,

15. The Thomistic position on the question of Christ's headship with respect to the angels is nicely summarized by Domingo Bañez, In IIIam, q. 8, a. 4, in *Comentarios inéditos a la Tercera parte de santo Tomas*, ed. Vincente Beltran de Heredia, vol. 1, *De Verbo Incarnato* (Madrid: 1951), 190–93. Humbert Bouëssé endeavored to refute the testimonies cited by the Scotists in support of the traditional character of the Christic nature of the grace of the angels; see Bouëssé, *Le Sauveur du monde*, vol. 1, *La place du Christ dans le plan de Dieu*, Doctrina sacra 4 (Chambéry-Leysse: Collège Théologique Dominicain, 1951), 246–81.

16. Among the Latin fathers who defend this theory we may cite Augustine, *Enchiridion on Faith, Hope, and Love*, IX.29 (ed. Henry Paolucci, trans. J. F. Shaw [Chicago: Regnery Gateway, 1961], 35–36): Mankind "should be in part restored, and should fill up the gap which the rebellion and fall of the devils had left in the company of the angels. For this is the promise to the saints, that at the resurrection they shall be equal to the angels of God [Lk 20:36]. And thus the Jerusalem which is above, which is the mother of us all, the city of God, shall not be spoiled of any of the number of her citizens, shall perhaps reign over even a more abundant population" (ex eius parte reparata quod angelicae societati ruina illa diabolica minuerat suppleretur. Hoc enim promissum est resurgentibus sanctis, quod erunt aequales angelis Dei. Ita superna Hierusalem mater nostra, civitas Dei, nulla civium suorum numerositate fraudabitur, aut uberiore etiam copia fortasse regnabit). See also supplementary note no. 17, "Remplacement des anges déchus," *Cité de Dieu* XXII.1.2 (BA 37:529). The idea is treated at length by Anselm of Canterbury, *Pourquoi un Dieu-homme* [*Cur Deus homo*] I.16–18, French trans. Michel Corbin, in *L'oeuvre de saint Anselme de Cantorbery*, vol. 3 (Paris: Cerf, 1988).

Gregory the Great proposes a different, more positive view of the relation between the number of angels and the number of elect human beings, which dispenses with the notion of replacing the fallen angels. Certainly, man was created tenth, after the nine angelic orders, "[so] that the number of the elect might be complete" (ut compleretur electorum numerus) (*Forty Gospel Homilies*, 34.6.285, but man was willed from the beginning and not merely to make the best of a bad job. Gregory thinks that there are as many men among the elect as there are angels who remained faithful. See ibid., 289: "The heavenly city is made up of angels and human beings. We believe that as many of the human race ascend to there, as there were chosen angels who happened to remain there. As Scripture

restores the integrity of the angelic world and heals that loss of sub-stance. St. Thomas is not entirely opposed to this view of the matter. But he refuses to reduce man to an interchangeable part meant to re-pair the damage done by angelic stupidity. The creation and the super-natural vocation of man were willed for their own sake; only indirect-ly, in addition, does man fill the gaps in the angelic city.[17] To sum up, in one way or another, Christ's work had repercussions on the angelic world, and, by that very fact, Christ can be called head of the angels. However, St. Thomas explains, this influence of Christ on the angels is not the purpose of the Incarnation. It is a consequence thereof.[18]

Some Thomistic theologians are not satisfied with this minimal solution of an accidental influence, which offends their Christocen-tric sensibility.[19] Thus Journet, on this point relying on the Carmel-ite theologians of Salamanca (*Salmanticenses*), thinks that, although the grace initially offered to the angels was not Christic, the Incarna-tion nevertheless profoundly modified the nature of angelic glory.[20]

---

says: 'He fixed the bounds of the peoples according to the number of the angels of God' [Deut 32:8]" (Quia enim illa superna civitas ex angelorum et hominibus constat, ad quam tantum credimus humanum genus ascendere, quantos illic contigit electos angelos reman-sisse, sicut scriptum est: "Statuit terminos gentium secundum numerum angelorum Dei").

17. See Aquinas, *In II Sent.*, d. 1, q. 2, a. 3; *In ad Ep.*, c. 1, lect. 3 (no. 29): "Not that Christ died for the angels, but that in ransoming mankind he repaired the ruin of the angels" (Non quod pro angelis mortuus sit Christus, sed quia redimendo hominem, re-integratur ruina angelorum). The reaction against the theory that sees man as a replace-ment angel goes back, it seems, to Rupert of Deutz (d. 1129); see Rupert of Deutz, *De glorificatione Trinitatis* III, c. 16–22 (PL 169:67–73). "Man," he says, "was made not so much to replenish the number of the angels as angels and men were made for one man, Jesus Christ" (Non tam homo propter supplendum angelorum numerum; quam et an-geli et homines, propter unum hominem Jesum Christum) (c. 21, 72–73). See also Ma-rie-Dominique Chenu, "Cur homo? Le sous-sol d'une controverse," in *La théologie au XIIᵉ siècle*, Études de philosophie médiévale 45 (Paris: J. Vrin, 1957), 52–61; Jean Gribo-mont, "Introduction," in *Les Oeuvres du saint-Esprit*, by Rupert of Deutz, SC 31:40–43.

18. See *Q. de ver.*, q. 29, a. 4, ad 5: "The Incarnation ... was carried out principally for the sake of man's liberation from sin; and so Christ's humanity is ordained to the influ-ence which He exercises upon men, as to the end intended, whereas His influence upon the angels is not the end of the Incarnation but a consequence of the Incarnation" ([In-carnatio] principaliter facta est propter hominum liberationem a peccato; et sic humani-tas Christi ordinatur ad influentiam quam facit in homines, sicut ad finem intentum; in-fluxus autem in angelos non est ut finis incarnationis, sed ut incarnationem consequens).

19. The *Catechism* seems to adopt this Christocentric angelology: "Christ is the cen-ter of the angelic world. They are *his* angels" (CCC 331).

20. See Journet, "L'essai de théologie de l'histoire du salut," 319–43.

From the first moment of the Incarnation, Jesus Christ "finalizes the substantial glory of the angels (he becomes the object or end of their knowledge and love) and becomes the productive efficient cause of this substantial glory. Christ, so to speak, takes the baton from God in relaying glory to the angels, since by virtue of the principle of "the causality of the lesser by the maximum," all grace henceforth passes through the humanity of Jesus Christ.

At the moment in which the Incarnation is accomplished, Christ's humanity becomes, with regard to the whole order of grace, a principle of universal efficacy. From now on the grace and glory that the good angels hitherto received directly from the divinity will come to them only through the sacred humanity of Christ.[21]

Thus the grace by which the angels live became at a particular moment a Christic and Christ-conforming grace, a grace that comes from Christ and leads to Christ. By virtue thereof, the angels are fully incorporated into the church as a fruit of this Christic grace. The fact remains that, as Journet admits, St. Thomas did not speak explicitly about this efficient causality of Christ on the grace of the angels.[22]

And so recently François Daguet took up the question again to dispute Journet's theses, which in his opinion show excessive signs of the influence of crypto-Scotist Christocentrism.[23] Daguet considers it more in keeping with St. Thomas's thought to distinguish God's plan, on the one hand, from the various economies implemented by God to carry out that plan, on the other. God's plan is to form, out of angels and men, a community of glory assembled and constituted by the trinitarian grace coming from the Son. This has actually happened in the case of the angels. But in the case of men, because of Adam's sin, God set up another arrangement to achieve the same end: the redemptive Incarnation that makes the incarnate Son, in his humanity, the Head of the human beings who are saved by him. As God, Jesus Christ is the source of the grace and substantial glory of the angels, but as man he is the source only of the accidental glory of the angels, the glory that flows indirectly from the salvation of mankind.

Also dependent on the place that one assigns to Jesus Christ with

21. Ibid., 332.
22. See ibid., 334.
23. See Daguet, *Théologie du dessein divin chez saint Thomas d'Aquin*, 283–85.

respect to the angels is the way in which one understands the queen-ship of the Virgin Mary over the angels, as it is often expressed in the liturgy and in the piety of the Christian people.[24] Two theses can be held in this connection.[25] The first is that the Virgin Mary was exalted above the angels by grace. This truth, chanted in every tone by the lit-urgy and preached extensively,[26] is so well established that St. Thom-as does not hesitate to describe as heretical the contradictory posi-tion that human nature always and necessarily remains of an order inferior to the angels.[27] However, this subversion of the natural order is worth elucidating. We must distinguish between the natural hier-archy of beings (which is unchangeable) and the supernatural hierar-chy that is based on one's degree of participation in grace and glory. Grace and glory are given to the angels depending on their place in the natural hierarchy, so that a higher angel always receives a greater grace.[28] In contrast, grace and glory are given to men depending on God's good pleasure alone. It follows that a human creature can attain a degree of supernatural glory equal or superior to that of the angels. Thus, by virtue of the grace of union, Christ's humanity—his body it-self—is exalted above the purely spiritual creatures.[29] Likewise, the Virgin Mary was filled with the highest grace that a creature could ever receive—to be the mother of God—and this places her in an or-der of sanctity above all the angels.[30]

24. The so-called Litany of Loreto invokes Mary as "Queen of Angels (*regina ange-lorum*)"; the antiphon *Ave regina coelorum* as "Lady of the Angels (*domina angelorum*)."

25. On the relations between Mary and the angels, see Gabriele M. Roschini, "De B. M. Virgine Matre Angelorum," in *Mariologia* (Rome: A. Belardetti, 1947), 2:197–99, which takes a maximalist position.

26. See, for example, the Introit to the Mass of the Vigil of the Assumption: "Glo-riosa dicta sunt de te, Maria, quae hodie exaltata es super choros angelorum"; or the Sermon by Peter Damian on the Assumption of Mary (*Sermo 40*, PL 144:717–22).

27. See Aquinas, *In II Sent.*, d. 9, q. 1, a. 8: "But this position is contrary to statements by the saints, and it seems to smack of heresy, for certainly the Blessed Virgin Mary was exalted above the choirs of angels" (Sed haec positio est contraria dictis sanctorum, et vi-detur sapere haeresim, cum etiam beata virgo super choros angelorum exaltata sit).

28. See *ST* I, q. 62, a. 6.

29. See *ST* III, q. 57, a. 5: "Whether Christ's body ascended above every spiritu-al creature?" (Utrum corpus Christi ascenderit super omnem creaturam spiritualem?)

30. See the sermon of St. Thomas on the Ave Maria: "The Blessed Virgin has a three-fold superiority over the angels. First, as to the fullness of grace that is greater in the Blessed Virgin than in an angel. It was to suggest this that the angel showed respect to

The second thesis concerns Mary's causality on the grace and glory of the angels, which is the basis of her royalty and of her spiritual maternity with regard to them.[31] It depends directly on the way in which one understands Christ's causality on the angels. For those who hold that Christ is the meritorious and efficient cause of angelic grace and glory, Mary, as mother of Christ, is also mother of the supernatural life of the angels. For those who limit Christ's action on the angels to their accidental glory, Mary appears instead as the cause of the joy that they experience from the salvation of men.[32]

---

her in saying 'full of grace.' It is as though he said: I show respect for you because you surpass me in fullness of grace.... Second, she surpasses the angels in familiarity with God. Alluding to this, the angel said, 'The Lord is with thee.' It is as though he said: I show respect for you because you are more familiar with God than I, because the Lord is with you.... Third, she surpasses the angels in purity, because the Blessed Virgin was not only pure in herself, but she also obtained purity for others" (Unde beata virgo excessit angelos in iis tribus. Et primo in plenitudine gratiae, quae magis est in beata virgine quam in aliquo angelo; et ideo ad insinuandum hoc, angelus ei reverentiam exhibuit, dicens, "gratia plena," quasi diceret: ideo exhibeo tibi reverentiam, quia me excellis in plenitudine gratiae.... Secundo excellit angelos in familiaritate divina. Et ideo hoc designans angelus dixit: "dominus tecum"; quasi dicat: ideo exhibeo tibi reverentiam, quia tu familiarior es Deo quam ego, nam dominus est tecum.... Tertio excedit angelos quantum ad puritatem: quia beata virgo non solum erat pura in se, sed etiam procuravit puritatem aliis); In Is, c. 7: "As for the expression, 'Behold, a virgin,' it should be noted that he says 'Behold' because of her singular eminence.... She is above all the angels because of the dignity of her offspring. This is why he says, 'and [she will] bear a son.' 'For nowhere doth he take hold of the angels: but of the seed of Abraham he taketh hold' (Hb 2:16)" (Notandum super illo verbo, "ecce virgo," quod dicitur, "ecce" propter eminentiam singularem.... Supra angelos omnes propter fructus dignitatem: unde dicit: "pariet filium." Hebr. 2: "nunquam angelos apprehendit, sed semen Abrahae apprehendit").

31. The Encyclical of Pius XII, Ad caeli Reginam (October 11, 1954) repeatedly mentions Mary's queenship over the angels, without going into the question of its specific theological foundations.

32. See two passages from the Divine Office. St. Sophronius: "On your account joy has not only graced men, but is also granted to the powers of heaven" (PG 87:3242: Liturgy of the Hours, 1:1332, Common of the B.V.M.); Anselm of Canterbury, Oratio 52: "Through the fullness of the grace that was given you, dead things rejoice in their freedom, and those in heaven are glad to be made new. Through the Son who was the glorious fruit of your virgin womb, ... the angels are glad at the restoration of their shattered domain" (in Orationes, PL 158:955; Liturgy of the Hours, 1:1228, Office of Readings, December 8).

12

---:---

Celestial Hierarchies and Knowledge
of the Mysteries of Salvation

Collaborators with God in the work of the salvation of mankind, the holy angels are not passive instruments but carry out their missions personally—in other words, consciously and freely. It is appropriate therefore that they should know, at least in part, the providential designs that they are trying to promote. This knowledge of God's plans is per se inaccessible to the natural knowledge of any creature whatsoever.[1] It is not even contained explicitly—and we will have to explain why not—in the vision of the Divine Essence as such. It requires therefore, within the beatific vision itself, a further revelation. In the angelic world, this revelation of the mystery "hidden for ages in God" (Eph 3:9) follows the hierarchical pathway: the higher angels receive it immediately from God so as to communicate it from rank

---

1. See *ST* I, q. 57, a. 5: "For these mysteries depend upon the pure will of God: and if an angel cannot learn the thoughts of another angel, which depend upon the will of such angel, much less can he ascertain what depends entirely upon God's will. The Apostle reasons in this fashion (*1 Cor 2:11*): 'No one knoweth the things of a man, but the spirit of a man that is in him.' So, 'the things also that are of God no man knoweth but the Spirit of God'" (Haec enim mysteria ex pura Dei voluntate dependent: si autem unus angelus non potest cognoscere cogitationes alterius ex voluntate eius dependentes, multo minus potest cognoscere ea quae ex sola Dei voluntate dependent. Et sic argumentatur Apostolus, I Cor. 2,11: Quae sunt hominis, nemo novit, nisi spiritus hominis, qui in ipso est. Ita et quae sunt Dei, nemo novit nisi Spiritus Dei).

to rank, like a cascade of light, down to the lower angels. The angelic world thus appears like an immense university in the French style, in which the magisterial current surges from top to bottom.

This enlightenment (which conditions an angel's affective movements and *ad extra* activity) is, according to St. Thomas Aquinas, the main action by which an angel cooperates in the divine government with respect to his fellow members of the same genus. In fact, of the four questions in the treatise on the divine government in [part I of] the *Summa theologiae* that consider the action of one angel upon another (qq. 106–9), the first deals with this enlightenment as a hierarchical communication of knowledge coming from God and leading to God (q. 106). In the further elaboration of this problem, we will consider more precisely what the angels were able to know about the central mystery of the economy of our salvation: the redemptive Incarnation. The second question, which arises in elaborating the first, concerns the angelic speech (*locutio*) that encodes any transfer of information among the angels (q. 107).[2] This activity of communicating knowledge finds its best theoretical foundation in the traditional internal classification of the angelic world into orders and hierarchies (q. 108); St. Thomas presents also, by way of addendum, the distorted survival of this order in the demonic world (q. 109).[3]

ANGELIC ENLIGHTENMENT (Q. 106)

Unlike his distant cousin—the angel of Greco-Arabic neo-Platonism—the Christian angel does not produce much. He seems devoid of any causal activity pertaining to the very sources of being. He does not create, since creation is an action strictly reserved to God.[4] Nor does he reproduce, since as simple, immaterial substances the angels come into existence not by way of generation starting from preexisting matter but rather by way of creation.[5] Is the Christian angel therefore irremedia-

2. In *Q. de ver.*, q. 9, St. Thomas treats the enlightenment and the language at the same time, under one heading: "The Communication of Angelic Knowledge."
3. We will examine the teaching of this q. 109 in chapter 14 within the context of reflection on demonic activity.
4. See *ST* I, q. 45, a. 5.
5. In truth, the fact that an angel is incapable of engendering another angel is in no way an imperfection in comparison with the ability of a corporeal individual to produce

bly sterile? Is he deprived of the perfection of causality that is the distinguishing mark of the dignity of a substance? Certainly not. First of all, an angel exerts a certain action on the corporeal world: through the local movement that he impels, he can even originate transformations of a qualitative order, strictly speaking. But in the opinion of the Angelic Doctor, the angel's fecundity, his "paternity"—for, according to St. Paul, there is a "paternity in heaven" (Eph 3:15, DV), in other words, among the angels[6]—is exercised in the first place in the order of instruction (*doctrina*). It consists of the communication of the superior form of life that is true knowledge, an activity that has received the name of enlightenment, since light is a rather common image to designate knowledge. The light of knowledge that springs from the "Father of lights" (Jas 1:17) is poured out in intelligible cascades, through the angelic hierarchies, down to the last of the intellects, the human intellect. The main source of this theory is *The Celestial Hierarchy* of Dionysius.[7] By enlightenment, in a free movement prompted by love, a higher angel turns toward a lower angel so as to manifest to him in an adapt-

---

another individual of the same species. Indeed, the corporeal individual (the dog Fido) does not produce another self (another Fido) but rather produces another dog (the dog Spot), a proof that he acts as an instrument of a nature (doggyness) that requires the generation of new individuals in order to assure its perpetual existence. The reproduction of individuals in corporeal species is a trick of nature to assure the permanence of species despite the corruption of their individual members. There is nothing of the sort among angels. Each angel is a species unto himself—in other words, he represents a unique degree of perfection and is incorruptible. Consequently there is no need of generation.

6. In Eph 3:15 St. Paul says that "all paternity in heaven and on earth is named," i.e., derives its name from God the Father. For St. Thomas, the "paternity in heaven" is the one that belongs to the angels, which can only be on the order of engendering knowledge. See *In ad Ep*, c. 3, lect. 4 (no. 168); *ST* I, q. 45, a. 5, ad 1. This is the sense in which we must understand those passages from the theological or philosophical tradition that seem to attribute a creative activity to the angels.

7. The doctrine is commonly accepted; see John Damascene, *Orthodox Faith* II.3 (FOTC 37:207): "They illuminate one another by the excellence of their rank or nature. Moreover, it is evident that the more excellent communicate their brightness and their knowledge to them that are inferior." In *In II Sent.*, d. 9, q. 1, a, 2, ad 3, St. Thomas severely criticizes the "occasionalists" who argue in favor of a direct enlightenment by God and reject the idea of any enlightenment among angelic creatures: "They deny everything that Dionysius handed down about the angels, which is proved by the authorities of Sacred Scripture and consistent with the teaching of the philosophers" (Negantes totum hoc quod Dionysius de angelis tradit auctoritatibus sacrae Scripturae probatum, et consonum philosophorum doctrinae).

ed way the knowledge that he himself knows.[8] In doing so, he makes him share in his own perfection, causes him to resemble himself, and, by that very fact, leads him closer to God, as a teacher causes his disciple to resemble himself and, moreover, leads him to the truth. This dynamic vision of things fits perfectly into the framework of the Thomistic theology of the diffusion of good and the divine generosity:

Because of His goodness, God communicates His perfections to creatures according to their capacity. Consequently, He shares His goodness with them, not only so that they will be good and perfect themselves, but also so that they can, with God's help, give perfection to others. Now, to give perfection to other creatures is the most noble way of imitating God. Hence, Dionysius says: "The most God-like of all actions is to cooperate with God." On this principle rests the ordering (*ordo*) of angels, according to which some illumine others.[9]

But what, more precisely, is enlightenment?[10] What model can be proposed that, on the one hand, accounts for the intersubjective transmission of some knowledge yet respects the privilege whereby direct access to a person's metaphysical and noetic interiority is reserved strictly to the Creator?[11]

8. Dionysius attributes to the angels a threefold hierarchical operation: enlightening, purifying, and perfecting. But St. Thomas reduces purification and perfecting to two aspects or components of enlightenment. All enlightenment purifies an angel of a certain "ignorance" and dissimilarity with respect to God. Moreover, through enlightenment, the angelic intellect emerges from a certain indetermination so as to become firmly fixed on the truth, thus approaching the perfection of the divine model; see Aquinas, *In II Sent.*, d. 11, q. 1, a. 2, ad 2; I, q. 106, a. 2, ad 1.

9. *Q. de ver.*, q. 9, a. 2: "Dicendum, quod ex bonitate divina procedit quod ipse de perfectione sua creaturis communicet secundum earum proportionem; et ideo non solum intantum communicat eis de sua bonitate, quod in se sint bona et perfecta, sed etiam ut aliis perfectionem largiantur, Deo quodammodo cooperando. Et hic est nobilissimus modus divinae imitationis; unde dicit Dionysius, cap. III *Caelestis hierarchiae*, quod omnium divinius est Dei cooperatorem fieri; et exinde procedit ordo qui est in angelis, quod quidam alios illuminant"; see also *ST* I, q. 106, a. 4.

10. The main passages by St. Thomas on enlightenment in the angelic world are: *In II Sent.*, d. 9, q. 1, a. 2: "Utrum unus angelus purget alium"; d. 11, q. 2, a. 2: "Utrum angeli inferiores illuminantur a superioribus"; *Q. de ver.*, q. 9, a. 1–3; *Comp. theol.*, I, c. 126; I, q. 106, a. 1, 3 et 4. See also Bonino, "L'ange et le prophète: Un aspect de l'angélologie de saint Thomas d'Aquin," in *Le Retour des anges*, Actes du Colloque tenu à Rome les 15 et 16 avril 2005, *RT* 108 (2008): 531–71.

11. See Bernard of Clairvaux, *On the Song of Songs*, V.8.1:29–30. "No created spirit can of itself act directly on our minds. This means that without the mediation of a bodily

Knowledge, which is intentional assimilation, presupposes an object and a subject—in other words, information and a cognitive power capable of integrating that information. The objective content—that is, the intelligible information—is generally made present to the cognitive power thanks to intentional forms (*species*). It is assimilated thanks to the light of the cognitive power (*lumen sub quo*) that makes this objective content its own and judges as to its meaning and its truth.[12] The communication of knowledge between two subjects can therefore be accomplished along two different lines. The one who transmits knowledge can act on the cognitive power itself and/or on the information or objective content.[13]

Along the line of transmitting objective content, the enlightening angel of course cannot create or infuse anything into the mind of the enlightened angel, but he does an instructor's job of arranging within himself and then manifesting to the angel who is being enlightened a meaningful complex of intellectual forms adapted to the latter's cognitive capacity. There is in fact a correspondence between a subject's

instrument it cannot make contact with or infuse itself into our minds, so that thereby we either acquire knowledge or increase it, acquire virtue or improve on it. No angel, no created spirit has power to influence me in this way, nor can I influence them. Even the angels lack this power over each other. That is a prerogative reserved to that supreme and infinite Spirit."

12. See, for example, in the context of the angelic enlightenment of man, *Q. de malo*, q. 16, a. 12: "The intellectual operation of man is achieved in accordance with two things, namely, the intelligible light and the intelligible species, yet, in such a way that the intellect's mental grasp of the things takes place in accordance with the species, and the judgment of the things mentally grasped is effected in accordance with the intelligible light" (532) (Intellectualis hominum operatio secundum duo perficitur; scilicet secundum lumen intelligibile, et secundum species intelligibiles; ita tamen quod secundum species fit apprehensio rerum; secundum lumen intelligibile perficitur iudicium de apprehensis).

13. See Aquinas, *In II Sent.*, d. 9, q. 1, a. 2, ad 4: "Just as man arrives at the sense knowledge of color thanks to two things: the visible object and the light under which it is seen, so also two things are required for intellectual knowledge: the intelligible thing itself and the light by which it is seen. This is why there are two ways of saying that someone teaches: either he proposes something intelligible, or else he furnishes the light by which to understand" (Sicut autem in cognitionem coloris sensibilem pervenit homo ex duobus, scilicet ex visibili objecto, et ex lumine sub quo videtur ... , ita etiam ad cognitionem intellectualem duo exiguntur; scilicet ipsum intelligibile, et lumen per quod videtur; et ideo dupliciter dicitur aliquis docere: vel sicut proponens intelligibile, vel sicut praebens lumen ad intelligendum).

cognitive power and the degree of universality of the *species* that he utilizes. The greater the intellectual power, the more rarefied and universal are the angelic *species* utilized. A man who has good digestion can indulge (at least physically, if not morally) in swallowing big bites that he will digest without trouble, whereas someone whose digestion is weak needs to chew for a long time before being able to assimilate his food. This is why a higher angel particularizes the universal forms so as to place them within the reach of the lower angel. He minces the material for him, in a way, like a professor who uses particular examples that are within the ken of his students, so as to enable them to grasp and to express to themselves in their own way the truths that he himself knows in a more universal manner.

Along the line of action on the cognitive power, St. Thomas keeps repeating that the enlightening angel consolidates or fortifies (*confortare*) the intellectual power of the angel being enlightened. Placed in contact with a superior intellect that is more in act and therefore more perfect, the inferior intellect gains thereby in actuality and is thus rendered more vigorous. This reinforcement enables him, in particular, to grasp higher ideas and to judge more perfectly about them.[14] St. Thomas ordinarily illustrates this action of reinforcing by examples drawn from physics: thus, when a heated body draws near to another body, it communicates to it an increase of heat.[15] Now, in the spiritual order,

14. See *Q. de ver.*, q. 11, a. 3: "As regards the light, although he cannot infuse the intellectual light, as God does, [an angel] can strengthen the infused light to make man see more perfectly. For that which is imperfect in a given genus has its power intensified when it is brought in contact with that which is more perfect in that genus" (Ex parte enim luminis, quamvis non possit intellectuale lumen infundere, ut Deus facit, potest tamen lumen infusum confortare ad perfectius inspiciendum. Omne enim quod est in aliquo genere imperfectum, quando continuatur perfectiori in genere illo, magis confortatur virtus eius); *Comp. theol.*, I, c. 126, with regard to the action of the higher angels on the lower angels: "They enlighten them insofar as they fortify with their light the intellects of the lower angels so that they grasp something higher" (Illuminare vero, inquantum suo lumine inferiorum intellectus confortant ad aliquid altius capiendum); *Q. de malo*, q. 16, a. 12.

15. See *Quodl.* IX, q. 4, a. 5: "Since our minds are proportioned and in proximate potency to receive the action of the angels, the latter can act on our minds in two ways. First, by strengthening our intellect, as in the corporeal world a body that is less warm is strengthened by a warmer body" (quia mentes nostrae sunt proportionatae et propinquae ad recipiendam actionem angelorum, ideo in mentes nostras agere possunt dupliciter. Uno modo, confortando intellectum nostrum, sicut in corporalibus corpus minus calidum confortatur per magis calidum); *ST* I, q. 111, a. 1. We find another example

what corresponds to the local drawing-near is conversion—in other words, the spiritual movement that consists of turning toward and directing one's spiritual activity toward a particular subject. The enlightening angel, by turning toward the angel who is being enlightened, makes him intellectually stronger.

To tell the truth, the exact modalities of this fortification of the enlightened intellect have given rise to serious differences of opinion among the commentators of St. Thomas inasmuch as the master's texts on this matter are ambiguous.[16] Indeed, sometimes the fortification is presented as an action distinct from the adapted presentation of some intelligible content, and sometimes it is identified with it.

In many passages, enlightenment seems to consist solely of the extrinsic proposal of some objective intelligible content in a manner that is adapted to the intellectual capacities of the recipient. Indeed, there could be no question of some other direct action of an angel on the mind of another creature.[17] Yet, since the intelligible content offered to the knowledge of the angel being enlightened participates in the light of the superior intellect that thinks and transmits it, the assimilation of this content indirectly reinforces the light of the enlightened angelic intellect.

The illuminating angel does not make a new light of grace or of nature; he merely shares his light. For, since whatever is known is understood by means

---

in Q. de ver., q. 11, a. 3: "Thus, in bodies, we see that the body which is given position is strengthened by the body giving it position, which is related to it as actuality to potentiality, as is said in the *Physics* [book IV]" (Sicut etiam videmus in corporibus, quod corpus locatum confortatur per corpus locans, quod comparatur ad ipsum ut actus ad potentiam, ut habetur IV Physic).

16. Modern Scholastic commentators on *ST* I, q. 106, generally present the different theories concerning the process of enlightenment. See, for example, John of St. Thomas, *Cursus theologicus*, disp. 45, a. 2 (4:829–35).

17. An angel can neither create a new light (a thesis described as heretical in Aquinas, *In II Sent.*, d. 9, q. 1, a. 2, arg. 6), nor transfuse its own light into another (see *In II Sent.*, d. 9, q. 1, a. 2, ad 6: "Since the intellect of a lower angel is in potency in relation to some things, it can be led by a higher angel, who is more perfectly in act, to a similar act, not by the creation of a new light, nor by the fact that the same light that is in the higher angel is received by the lower" [cum intellectus inferioris angeli sit in potentia respectu quorumdam, poterit per superiorem angelum, qui est in perfectiori actu, reduci in actum similem, non per creationem alicujus novi luminis, nec per hoc quod idem numero lumen quod est in superiori, recipitur ab inferiori]), nor even intensify directly an already existing light.

of an intellectual light, the known as known includes in its notion a shared intellectual light that has the power to strengthen the intellect. This is evident if we consider the teacher who gives his pupil a medium of demonstration in which the light of the [teacher's] active intellect is contained as in an instrument; for, as the commentator says, first principles are quasi-instruments of the active [agent] intellect;[18] and the same is true of all second principles that contain their own means of demonstration. Consequently, when a higher angel shows his knowledge to another angel, the intellect of the latter is strengthened so that it knows what it previously did not. Hence, no new light of nature or of grace comes into existence in the enlightened angel, but the light that was there previously is strengthened by the light contained in the higher angel's knowledge.[19]

Thus the process of angelic enlightenment is somewhat like a physician who builds the skeletal strength of his patient, not by bone grafts, but by recommending that he consume milk products containing calcium.

In this model, the second aspect of enlightenment—namely, the reinforcement of the enlightened intellect—is not a different action from the one that defines the first aspect of enlightenment—namely, the proposal of some objective content adapted to the intellect being enlightened. Since Durandellus at least,[20] the Thomist tradition has heavily sided with this theory of enlightenment by an altogether extrinsic way of artificial teaching: the enlightening angel, like a good professor, explains his thought in such manner as to present it in a way

18. Averroès, *In De anima* III, com. 36 (*Aristotelis libri omnes ... cum Averrois Cordubensis variis in eosdem commentariis*, vol. 6 [Venice: 1574], f.172 v ss.). See also Aquinas, *In II Sent.*, d. 28, q. 1, a. 5; *Q. de ver.*, q. 10, a. 13; q. 11, a. 3; q. 12, a. 3; *Q. de anima*, q. 5.

19. *Q. de ver.*, q. 9, a. 1, ad 2: "Ab angelo illuminante non fit novum lumen gratiae vel naturae nisi ut participatum. Cum enim omne quod intelligitur, ex vi intellectualis luminis cognoscatur; ipsum cognitum inquantum huiusmodi includit in se intellectuale lumen ut participatum, ex cuius virtute habet intellectum confortare; sicut patet quando magister tradit discipulo medium alicuius demonstrationis, in quo participatur lumen intellectus agentis ut in instrumento. Prima enim principia sunt quasi instrumenta intellectus agentis, ut dicit Commentator in III *de anima*; et similiter etiam omnia principia secunda quae continent propria media demonstrationum. Unde per hoc quod superior angelus suum cognitum alteri angelo demonstrat, eius intellectus confortatur ad aliqua cognoscenda, quae prius non cognoscebat; et sic non fit in angelo illuminato novum lumen naturae vel gratiae; sed lumen quod prius inerat, confortatur per lumen contentum in cognito percepto a superiori angelo."

20. See Nicolaus Medensis (Durandellus), *Evidentiae contra Durandum* II.26 (Tübingen: Francke, 2003), 499–512. See also Cajetan, *In Iam*, q. 106, a. 1, no. 5.

that can be assimilated by the one whom he is enlightening, whose intellect he thus strengthens.[21]

There are, however, other passages by St. Thomas in which the distinction made about the twofold action of the enlightening angel—one that is exercised on the cognitive faculty, the other on the intelligible content—seems to refer back to a real distinction.[22] And so the drastic reduction of the fortification of the enlightened intellect to the mere external proposal of an intelligible object adapted by the enlightening intellect has not won all the votes in Scholasticism. Hervé de Nédellec, in the fourteenth century, argues for an intensification of the natural light of the enlightened intellect under the ac-

21. The interpretation of John of St. Thomas, *Cursus theologicus*, disp. 45, a. 2 (4:829–33), would become classic among later Thomists until the twentieth century.

22. For example, in *Q. de ver.*, q. 11, a. 3, St. Thomas defines angelic enlightenment with respect to man in contrast with the divine illumination, on the one hand, and human enlightenment, on the other. God gives man at the very same time the light of reason (subjective aspect) and knowledge of the first principles (objective aspect). The human teacher, in contrast, exerts no direct action on the intellectual light of his disciple, but through a system of external signs proposes to him means that are adapted so that he can derive further conclusions from the objective knowledge that he already possesses. As for the angel, "since by nature an angel has intellectual light more perfectly than man, he can cause man to know *in both ways*, in a manner lower than God, but higher than man" (Angelus vero, quia naturaliter habet lumen intellectuale perfectius quam homo, ex utraque parte potest homini esse causa sciendi; tamen inferiori modo quam Deus, et superiori quam homo). The enlightening angel therefore proposes some intelligible content (a concept in the case of enlightening another angel, or an image in the case of action on a human being), but the very logic of the text suggests that he also acts, in parallel, it seems, on the enlightened intellect itself. Likewise, in *Comp. theol.*, I, c. 129, it seems that the two actions must be distinguished: "Since an angel's natural light is by nature higher than man's natural light, a man can be helped by an angel to understand, not only by way of the object that is proposed to him by the angel, but also by way of the light that is strengthened by the angel's light. However, man's natural light does not come from the angel, for the nature of the rational soul, which received existence by creation, was established by God alone. But God helps man to think not only by way of the object which is proposed to man by God, or by an additional light, but also by the fact that man's natural light, by which he is intellectual, comes from God" (Quia lumen naturale angeli est secundum naturam sublimius naturali lumine hominis, homo ab angelo potest iuvari ad intelligendum non solum ex parte obiecti quod ei ab angelo proponitur, sed etiam ex parte luminis, quod per lumen angeli confortatur. Non tamen lumen naturale hominis ab angelo est, cum natura rationalis animae, quae per creationem esse accepit, non nisi a Deo instituta sit. Deus autem ad intelligendum hominem iuvat non solum ex parte obiecti, quod homini proponitur a Deo, vel per additionem luminis, sed etiam per hoc quod lumen naturale hominis, quo intellectualis est, a Deo est). The logic of the passage seems to attribute to the angel an "*additio luminis.*"

tion of the enlightening angel.[23] Jean Cabrol mentions the possibility that the higher angel communicates to the lower angel an active power or efficacy that possesses an intentional being, comparable to the efficacy that runs through an instrument, rendering it capable of a broader action.[24] As for Domingo Bañez, he thinks that "the higher angel's light is united with the lower angel's light and somehow becomes one principle with him in regard to the knowledge of the revealed truth."[25]

Whatever the case may be as to the exact noetic/epistemological model that accounts for the enlightenment, the question remains concerning the object thereof. To what does the enlightenment pertain? What can the lower angel actually have to learn from the higher angel?[26] Is it not true that every angel knows immediately everything that he can know by nature?[27] As for supernatural knowledge,

23. See Hervé de Nédellec, *In quatuor libros sententiarum Commentaria* (Paris: 1647), Livre II, d. 9, q. 1, a. 2 (229–31).

24. See Jean Cabrol, *Defensiones theologiae divi Thomae Aquinatis de novo editae cura et studio* [*In II Sent.*], d. 11, q. 2, conclusio 2, ed. Ceslai Paban and Thomae Pègues [Tours: Alfred Cattier, 1902], 3:501–3.

25. See Bañez, *In Iam*, q. 106, dubium 2, in *Scholastica Commentaria super caeteras primae partis quaestiones* (Venice: 1602), 1145–50: "Therefore, as for me, I am of the opinion that St. Thomas' idea, both in this article and in q. 9 *de veritate* and *In II Sent.*, is that in the enlightenment of a lower angel, his light is fortified not only by way of teaching, as was explained, but also in a more efficacious way, namely by the conjunction and intelligible union by which the higher angel's light is united with the lower angel's light and somehow becomes one principle with him in regard to the knowledge of the revealed truth" (Igitur quantum ego opinor mens sancti Thomae et in hoc articulo et in quaestione 9 de veritate citata et In 2 d. 9, q. 1, a. 2 est quod in illuminatione angeli inferioris eius lumen confortatur non solum per modum magisterii jam expositum sed alio modo efficaciori, scilicet per conjunctionem et unionem intelligibilem qua lumen angeli superioris unitur cum lumine angeli inferioris et efficit unum principium quodammodo cum illo ad cognitionem illius veritatis revelatae) (col. 1149).

26. See the objection at Aquinas, *In II Sent.*, d. 11, q. 2, a. 2, arg. 1.

27. In *ST* I, q. 109, a. 3, ad 2, St. Thomas, in order to rule out any enlightenment of one demon by another, asserts that in the natural order an angel possesses from the outset all that he can know, so that enlightenment is useless: "According to what belongs to *natural knowledge*, there is no *necessary* manifestation of the *truth* either in the *angels*, or in the *demons*, because, as said above ... they *know* from the first all that belongs to their *natural knowledge*" (Secundum ea quae ad naturalem cognitionem pertinent, non est necessaria manifestatio veritatis neque in Angelis neque in Daemonibus, quia ... statim a principio suae conditionis omnia cognoverunt quae ad naturalem cognitionem pertinent). The same teaching is found in *Q. de ver.*, q. 9, a. 1, ad 9, which explicitly denies that enlightenment pertains to natural knowledge. However, in *ST* I, q. 106, a. 1, ad 2, St.

it is necessary to hold, contrary to the temptations of a certain Eastern theology, that all the blessed angels see directly, without any intermediary, the Divine Essense itself, and not only its external fulgu-
rations.[28] And this immediate vision is not, as such, communicable.[29]
In fact, St. Thomas explains, enlightenment pertains essentially to
the "notions of the Divine works" (*rationes divinorum operum*).[30] It
concerns the intimate and transcendent plans of God for the world.[31]
In the beatific vision, indeed, it is necessary to distinguish the Object,
which is none other than the very Essence of God, one and the same
as itself, and the light of glory—in other words, the subjective capacity to receive this Object intellectually. All the blessed angels immediately see the entire Divine Essence (it has no parts!), but not all
have the same degree of the light of glory, so that not all exploit this

---

Thomas seems to admit that the truths communicated by enlightenment concern not
only the *status gratiae* and the *status gloriae* but also the *status naturae*. Commentators
account in different ways for this possible enlightenment in the natural order. Bañez,
In Iam, 1151–52, asserts that it is not about the revelation of a hitherto unknown natural
truth but rather about participation in a more perfect form of knowledge of a truth already known. John of St. Thomas, *Cursus theologicus*, disp. 45, a. 2 (4:833–35), explains
that the angels certainly know from the start all the quiddities and properties of natural
things but can learn, in the natural realm, what happens, either in a purely contingent
way or by God's explicit will.

28. See Aquinas, *In II Sent.*, d. 9, q. 1, a. 2, ad 3. In *ST* I, q. 106, a. 1, ad 1, St. Thomas
cites along these lines Jer 31:34: "And no longer shall each man teach his neighbor and
each his brother, saying, 'Know the LORD,' for they shall all know me, from the least of
them to the greatest."

29. See Aquinas, *In II Sent.*, d. 11, q. 2, a. 1, ad 3: "One angel does not enlighten another about what concerns the essence of beatitude but about something else" (Angelus non illuminat alium … de his quae ad essentiam beatitudinis pertinent, sed de aliis).

30. See *ST* I, q. 106, a. 1, ad 1; *ST* I-II, q. 5, a. 6, ad 3: "A happy angel enlightens the
intellect of a man or of a lower angel, as to certain notions of the Divine works: but not
as to the vision of the Divine Essence, as was stated in the I, 106, 1: since in order to
see this, all are immediately enlightened by God" (Angelus beatus illuminat intellectum hominis, vel etiam inferioris Angeli, quantum ad aliquas rationes divinorum operum non autem quantum ad visionem divinae essentiae, ut in primo dictum est. Ad eam
enim videndam, omnes immediate illuminantur a Deo).

31. This discovery of God's designs on the world, and most especially God's ar-
rangements for the salvation of the elect, lasts until Judgment Day (see *ST* I, q. 106, a.
4, ad 3). Certainly, on Judgment Day, everything will be revealed, all ignorance in angels will be suppressed: nevertheless a lower angel, without learning anything more, will
take from the higher angel the knowledge that he has of these mysteries. See *ST* I, q. 108,
a. 7, ad 2. This is something like the gift of being, in which we distinguish creation (the
acquisition of being *ex nihilo*) and preservation.

inexhaustible treasure with the same depth. Thus, a higher angel sees more perfectly the Divine Essence than a lower angel—furthermore, without ever arriving at an understanding of it—in other words, without ever exhausting its intelligible content.[32] Similarly, one and the same landscape is offered to the view of all the mountain climbers who have arrived at the summit, but the one who has better eyesight perceives it better, although he does not perceive anything different from the one who is nearsighted. Now anyone who sees the Divine Essence sees in it the universe and its whole history, since God is the universal First Cause thereof and the effect is present in its spiritual cause in an intelligible manner.[33] Yet, given the fact that there are degrees in the glorious knowledge of the angels, there is more or less extensive and profound knowledge of the universe and of its history in God. A higher angel knows therefore in God secrets of the world and of history that a lower angel does not, or at any rate not as explicitly. This higher knowledge of the divine mysteries is what the enlightening angel communicates to the angel being enlightened.[34] From this perspective, we easily understand that only an angel who is higher (by nature and therefore by glory) and endowed with a more perfect knowledge can enlighten a lower angel, and never vice versa.[35]

This enlightening action explains why a higher angel can act indirectly on the will of a lower angel.[36] There are indeed two ways for one subject to act on the will of another. First, he can act directly on the will itself by inclining it, from within so to speak, toward this or that good. But this type of action is reserved strictly to God who, as creator of the will and closer to it than it is to itself, can act in it so as to make it will freely what he wants it to will. Second, he can act indirectly on the will by manifesting to the intellect an object whose goodness will attract the will. But, since an angel cannot give the Absolute Good, God

32. See Aquinas, *In II Sent.*, d. 9, q. 1, a. 2, ad 3 et ad 5; d. 11, q. 2, a. 2; I, q. 12, a. 6.
33. See *ST* I, q. 12, a. 8.
34. Like St. Paul, who in his ecstasy heard "things that cannot be told, which man may not utter" (2 Cor 12:4), the enlightening angel cannot transmit his actual vision of the Divine Essense, but "translates" his knowledge of the mysteries, drawn from the beatific vision, into appropriate *species*, which he then proposes to the enlightened angel; see John of St. Thomas, *Cursus theologicus*, disp. 45, a. 2 (4:834, no. 23).
35. See *ST* I, q. 106, a. 3. The ad 1 explains that, on this point, the ecclesiastical hierarchy imitates the celestial hierarchy only imperfectly.
36. See *ST* I, q. 106, a. 2.

seen in his essence, he proposes to the other angel's mind only relative goods (for example, a mission to be accomplished on behalf of mankind). In this sense the angels stimulate one another to do good. This action—the *persuasio* or incitement to good—is the exact opposite of temptation.

Finally, St. Thomas points out, in an article that is spiritually very rich, that this enlightening activity is without reservations.[37] Indeed, in keeping with the law of the generosity of being, the better a being is, the more he radiates and tends to communicate his goodness. "I learned without guile and I impart without grudging; I do not hide her wealth" (*"Quam sine fictione didici, et sine invidia communico, et honestatem illius non abscondo"*) (Ws 7:13). This is eminently the case with God. But it is also the case with the holy angels who, far from claiming for themselves the good of which they have been made beneficiaries, communicate freely, out of love and without jealousy, all that they receive from God: "The *holy angels*, who enjoy the plenitude of participation of the Divine *goodness*, impart the same to those below them."[38] This unreserved sharing, the ideal of charity, does not however lead to the leveling of the angelic hierarchies, because what a higher angel shares is received by a lower angel according to his own mode, which can never equal that of the higher angel.

ANGELIC KNOWLEDGE OF THE MYSTERY OF THE REDEMPTIVE INCARNATION

At the heart of God's plan is the redemptive Incarnation. When and how did the angels know it? As the Lombard had already brought to the attention of medieval scholars,[39] the fathers of the church are divided on this point, especially because of the difficulty presented by the interpretation of certain New Testament passages.[40] Thus St. Paul declares that the mystery "was hidden for ages in God who created all

37. See *ST* I, q. 106, a. 4.

38. *ST* I, q. 106, a. 4: "Sancti angeli, qui sunt in plenissima participatione divinae bonitatis, quidquid a Deo percipiunt, subiectis impartiuntur."

39. See Peter Lombard, *Sententiae* II, d. 11, c. 2 (47–49).

40. See Michl, "Engel III (christlich)," 143–44, and the note by Maurice de Gandillac in Denys l'Aréopagite, *Hiérarchie céleste*, SC 58, 113–14.

things; that through the Church the manifold wisdom of God might now be made known to the principalities and powers in the heavenly places. This was according to the eternal purpose that he has realized in Christ Jesus our Lord" (Eph 3:9–11), and St. Peter speaks about "the things which have now been announced to you by those who preached the good news to you … , things into which angels long to look" (1 Pt 1:12). Apparently these passages and several others mean that the angels learned something from the preaching of the apostles and of the church. St. Jerome did not hesitate to acknowledge this.[41] But St. Augustine had endeavored to neutralize these texts,[42] and the authority of Dionysius reinforced the conviction that the angels had known the mystery before men did.[43] No need to be a great Thomistic scholar to guess that such a subversion of the order of things could not win approval in Aquinas's view: he even devotes an article in the *Summa theologiae* to a proof that men can never enlighten angels.[44] The first text in which St. Thomas explicit addresses the problem is *In II Sent.*, d. 11, q. 2, a. 4: "Did the angels learn from men about the mystery of the Incarnation?" We find in it almost all the elements of the position that the Angelic Doctor would maintain throughout his works:[45]

On this point, it seems that there is a debate among Jerome, Augustine and Dionysius. Jerome supposes two things: (1) The angels did not know the mystery of Christ's humanity before the Incarnation. On this point, Augustine seems to oppose him when he says that they knew this from the ages, in other words, since the beginning of the world. (2) They learned it from men. On this point, Dionysius seems to oppose him when he states that men were instructed about this mystery by the angels according to the inviolably established order of divine law.[46]

41. See Jerome, *Commentarii in epistolam ad Ephesios II* (PL 26:514 C–15 B).
42. See Augustine, *Literal Meaning of Genesis* V.19.38–39 (ACW 41:169–70).
43. See Dionysius the Areopagite, *Celestial Hierarchy*, 4.4, 158–59.
44. See *ST* I, q. 117, a. 2.
45. The main texts by St. Thomas on the knowledge that the angels had about the Incarnation: *In II Sent.*, d. 11, q. 2, a. 4; *In III Sent.*, d. 3, q. 3, a. 2, qla 2, ad 2; d. 25, q. 2, a. 2, qla 2, ad 1; *Q. de ver.*, q. 8, a. 4, sc 1; a. 9, ad 2; q. 14, a. 11, ad 4; *ST* I, q. 57, a. 5, ad 1; *ST* q. 64, a. 1, ad 4; *ST* q. 106, a. 4, ad 2; *ST* q. 117, a. 2, ad 1; *ST* II-II, q. 2, a. 7, ad 1; *In ad Ep*, c. 1, lect. 3 (no. 162); *In 1 ad Tim*, c. 2, lect. 3 (no. 133).
46. Aquinas, *In II Sent.*, d. 11, q. 2, a. 4: "In hoc videtur esse quaedam controversia inter Hieronymum et Augustinum et Dionysium. Hieronymus enim ponit duo: scilicet angelos ante incarnationem mysterium humanitatis Christi nescivisse: et quantum ad hoc videtur Augustinus, sibi obviare, dicens, eos a saeculis, idest a principio mundi, co-

The debate therefore pertains simultaneously to the time and the manner of this angelic knowledge about the Incarnation, the two being connected, in fact. Good Scholastic that he is, St. Thomas sets out to reconcile these opinions—*diversa sed non adversa*—by making a certain number of distinctions and by looking for that portion of truth that each doctrine contains. An initial distinction relative to the content of the angelic knowledge about the Incarnation allows him to resolve the question of the moment of this knowledge:

To find out how there can be some truth to each position, it is necessary to distinguish—as to the first problem—two possible ways of considering the mystery of the Incarnation. As to the substance of the fact (the Incarnation, the Passion and things of this sort), they all knew it from the beginning. As to the conditions and the circumstances of the mystery (that it should take place under this political authority, or at that particular hour, and things of this sort), they did not know it from the beginning.[47]

In other passages, St. Thomas explains more precisely that it is necessary to distinguish two stages, so to speak, in the initial revelation made to the angels of the "substance" of the mystery. The first stage consists of the instant in which they came to know their supernatural vocation and had to respond to it. At that moment, the angels—all the angels, both the future demons and the future blessed—had faith, without that implying an explicit knowledge of the mystery of Christ.[48] The second stage is the moment of their entrance into glo-

gnovisse. Secundo ponit Hieronymus quod hoc per homines didicerunt: et quantum ad hoc videtur sibi obviare Dionysius, ponens homines de hoc ab angelis edoctos esse, secundum ordinem divinae legis inviolabiliter constitutum."

47. Ibid.: "Ut autem sciatur qualiter unumquodque veritatem habere possit, distinguendum est quantum ad primum, quod mysterium incarnationis dupliciter potest considerari: vel quantum ad substantiam facti; et sic omnes a principio cognoverunt, scilicet incarnationem, passionem, et hujusmodi; vel quantum ad conditiones et circumstantias mysterii, scilicet quod sub tali praeside, vel tali hora, et hujusmodi; et hoc a principio non cognoverunt. His etiam modis differenter enarrant propheta et Evangelista: quia propheta annuntiavit substantiam facti; sed evangelista recitat expletionis modum."

48. About the content of this initial angelic faith, see *ST* I, q. 64, a. 1, ad 4: "All the angels had some knowledge from the very beginning respecting the mystery of God's kingdom, which found its completion in Christ; and most of all from the moment when they were beatified by the vision of the Word, which vision the demons never had" (Mysterium regni Dei, quod est impletum per Christum, omnes quidem angeli a principio aliquo modo cognoverunt; maxime ex quo beatificati sunt visione Verbi, quam daemones

ry. Then only the good angels had a more explicit revelation of the Incarnation in general, insofar as it constitutes the pivotal point of this
economy of salvation that they are called to serve as collaborators.[49]

As for the second problem, it is also necessary to make a distinction. There
are two ways for the angels to receive the knowledge of some things. First, by
enlightenment. Angels receive nothing in this way from men, but the lower angels are enlightened by the higher and the higher immediately by God.
This is the way in which they are instructed about many reasons for the mysteries of the Church. Second, by way of the fulfillment of things. This is the
way in which they know future contingencies when they are fulfilled in act,
by the fact that their causes are determined to the effects, so that they can
be known in them. And so certain things about the mystery of the Incarnation that they did not know, they came to know when they were fulfilled by
the preaching of the apostles, yet they were not instructed by the apostles.[50]

---

nunquam habuerunt). The qualification "which found its completion in Christ" does not
necessarily mean that the angels knew the mystery of Christ's Incarnation. They knew
the divine plan to establish his kingdom among men, about which we know that Christ
is the founder. Advocates of a radical sort of Christocentrism obviously hold that all angels already had in that moment of faith a broad knowledge of the mystery of Christ; see
Suarez, "Quae mysteria fidei cognoverunt angeli in via, seu quos fidei articulos explicite
crediderint" (chap. 5), in *Tractatus de Angelis*, 5:590–601). On this question see also the
commentators on *ST* I, q. 57, a. 5.

49. See *ST* I, q. 57, a. 5, ad 1: "One can speak in two ways of the mystery of the Incarnation. First of all, in general; and in this way it was revealed to all from the commence-
ment of their beatitude. The reason of this is, that this is a kind of general principle to
which all their duties are ordered. For 'all are ministering spirits, sent to minister for
them who shall receive the inheritance of salvation' (*Hb 1:14*); and this is brought about
by the mystery of the Incarnation. Hence it was necessary for all of them to be instructed in this mystery from the very beginning" (De mysterio incarnationis Christi dupliciter contingit loqui. Uno modo, in generali: et sic omnibus revelatum est a principio suae
beatitudinis. Cuius ratio est, quia hoc est quoddam generale principium, ad quod omnia eorum officia ordinantur: "Omnes enim sunt administratorii spiritus," ut dicitur Hb.
1,14, "in ministerium missi propter eos qui haereditatem capiunt salutis"; quod quidem
fit per incarnationis mysterium. Unde oportuit de hoc mysterio omnes a principio com-
muniter edoceri). On this point St. Thomas corrects the thesis of Peter Lombard, who
was right to admit a progressive enlightenment of the lower angels by the higher angels
but wrongly thought that it pertained to the very fact of the Incarnation, known by the
higher angels but unknown to the lower angels, whereas in reality it concerned only the
modalities of the Incarnation, since all the angels knew the substances of the Incarnation from the moment of their entry into beatitude; see *ST* I, q. 106, a. 4, ad 2; *In ad Ep*,
c. 1, lect. 3 (no. 162).

50. *In II. Sent.*, d. 11, q. 2, a. 4: "Quantum etiam ad secundum distinguendum est,
quod angeli dupliciter accipiunt cognitionem aliquarum rerum: aut per illuminationem;
et sic angeli per homines nihil recipiunt, sed inferiores a superioribus illuminantur, et

More explicit knowledge of the conditions for the fulfillment of the mystery of the Incarnation is essentially the product of an enlightenment that goes from God—from Christ—to the higher angels and, through them, to the lower angels. This is altogether Dionysian. St. Thomas mentions also the (very external) modification of angelic knowledge brought about by the fulfillment in time of events already known in the Word and by angelic enlightenment. Angelic knowledge thereby becomes more complete. He thus adopts as his own the Augustinian neutralization of the New Testament passages that seemed to suggest an (impossible) dependence of angelic knowledge on temporal realities.[51]

THE SPEECH OF THE ANGELS (Q. 107)

Sacred scripture mentions, quite incidentally, several linguistic exchanges among the angels,[52] and a somewhat literal reading led theologians to inquire about this mysterious angelic speech.[53] The theme

---

superiores immediate a Deo, per quem modum multas rationes mysteriorum Ecclesiae edocentur: aut per modum expletionis rerum; et sic futura contingentia cognoscunt quando actu complentur, per hoc quod eorum causae ad effectus determinantur, ut in eis cognosci possint; et ita quaedam quae circa incarnationis mysterium nesciebant, quando explebantur praedicantibus apostolis cognoverunt, non tamen ab apostolis edocti."

51. In the passages in which he discusses this problem of exegesis, St. Thomas often refers back to the two main themes of the Augustinian solution. First, the church that teaches the angels is not the church here below but the church in Heaven—in other words, the higher angels who see from all eternity the mystery and communicate it to the lower angels. Second, at the moment when the events of salvation occur thanks to the preaching of the apostles, the angels observe by their evening knowledge that things are indeed in reality as they saw them already by their morning knowledge in the Word.

52. See Is 6:3; 1 Cor 13:1; and the commentary by St. Thomas on this passage, in *Lectura super epistolas s. Pauli* [*In 1 ad Co*], c. 13, lect. 1 (nos. 762–63), ed. Raphaelis Cai, 2 vols. (Turin: Marietti, 1953).

53. Concerning the angelic language in St. Thomas: Faes de Mottoni, "'Enuntiatores divini silentii': Tommaso d'Aquino e il linguaggio degli angeli," *Medioevo* 12 (1986): 189–228; Faes de Mottoni, "Thomas von Aquin und die Sprache der Engel," in MM 19:140–55; Chrétien, "Le langage des anges selon la scolastique," in *La voix nue: Phénoménologie de la promesse* (Paris: Éditions de Minuit, 1990), 81–98; Claude Panaccio, "Conversation angélique, langage mental et transparence de l'esprit," in *Vestigia, Imagines, Verba: Semiotics and Logic in Medieval Theological Texts (12th–14th Century)*, edited by Costantino Marmo, Semiotics and Cognitive Studies 4 (Turnhout: Brepols, 1997), 323–35; Suarez-Nani, "Le langage des anges selon saint Thomas d'Aquin," in *Connaissance*, 185–207; Harm J. M. J. Goris, "The Angelic Doctor and Angelic Speech: The Development

particularly intrigues St. Gregory the Great, who is consequently cited several times in our question 107.[54] In Scholastic writings it was the object of extremely subtle speculations that have the good fortune today of attracting the attention of philosophers who are interested in the nature of language and, more broadly, in the theme of communication.[55] Reflection on angelic speech in fact allows for daring thought experiments, since we are dealing with a pure language, detached from the accidental, physical, and contingent dimensions that encumber human communication: inter-angelic communication does not occur through the mediation of sensible signs; it is not halted by distance.

For St. Thomas—unlike William of Ockham, who considers thought as a kind of mental speech—thought and speech are not identical. Speech adds something to thought: a certain intervention of the will. What is intelligible, Aquinas explains in article 1 of our question 107, can be in the intellect in three states. It is there, first, as something preserved habitually in the intellectual memory—in other words, without being the object of an actual consideration. It is there, second, as something actually thought or conceived. It is there, third, as something "related to something else" (*"ut ad aliud relatum"*). One passes from the first state to the second by a command of the will that moved the intellect to actualize its habitual knowledge. This is the origin of

of Thomas Aquinas' Thought on How Angels Communicate," *Medieval Philosophy and Theology* 11 (2003): 1–19; John Deely, "The Semiosis of Angels," *Thomist* 68 (2004): 205–58 [an article inspired especially by John of St. Thomas]; Olivier-Thomas Venard, chap. 8, "L'idéal d'un langage purement spirituel," in *La langue de l'ineffable: Essai sur le fondement théologique de la métaphysique* (Geneva: Ad Solem, 2004); Hanns-Gregor Nissing, *Sprache als Akt bei Thomas von Aquin*, Studien und Texte zur Geistesgeschichte des Mittelalters 87 (Leiden, Boston, and Cologne: E. J. Brill, 2006), 161–76.

54. Gregory the Great, *Morals on The Book of Job* VII.8–12 (1:370–73). In connection with the dialogue between God and Satan in the Prologue of Job, St. Gregory develops a theory of language between God and spiritual creatures (angels, demons, holy men); see John Damascene, *Orthodox Faith* II.3 (FOTC 37:206): "[The] secondary spiritual lights ... have no need of tongue and hearing; rather, they communicate their individual thoughts and designs to one another without having recourse to the spoken word."

55. John of St. Thomas, in *Cursus theologicus*, disp. 45, a. 1 (4:814ff.), proposes a classification of the various theories about the angelic language. One fundamental division is the one that separates those who think that the *medium* of this angelic language remains within the speaker (Thomas Aquinas) and those who think that it is something produced in the hearer (John Duns Scotus, Peter Auriol).

the interior speech by which the mind tells itself, thanks to a simple or complex word, what it knows. It is also by an act of will that one passes from the second state to the third: the will moves the intellect to manifest its thought to someone else. Here it is a question of speech, strictly speaking. We will say therefore that one angel speaks to another when, by an act of his will, he directs his concept toward that other in such a way as to cause him to know it.[56]

This manifestation is direct. It follows immediately from the voluntary decision to communicate. A man has no direct access to what is intelligible, and so he needs to resort to sensible signs, words, and gestures, in which he embodies the content of his thought and places it at the disposition of another person, who must also exploit this sensible data intelligibly.[57] There is nothing of the sort with an angel, who immediately reveals the content of his thought by an entirely spiritual locution. But, someone will say, physical locution has the purpose not only of communicating an intelligible content but also of drawing the attention of the person to whom the message is destined so as to establish an interpersonal connection that makes the communication possible. What about in the case of an angel? How does angel B know that angel A wants to communicate something to him? St. Thomas resorts here to the vision in God: the holy angels, because they see God, see in God the movements of will of their fellow angels, especially their will to address them. In the state of nature and among the demons, however, it is a question of a rather mysterious intelligible virtue that constitutes a sort of spiritual signal.[58]

What is the relation between speech and enlightenment? "Every angelic enlightening," St. Thomas declares, "is an angelic speech; but on the other hand, not every speech is an enlightening."[59] The cogni-

56. See *ST* I, q. 107, a. 2: "For one angel to speak to another angel means nothing else, but that by his own will he directs his mental concept in such a way, that it becomes known to the other" (Angelum loqui angelo nihil aliud est quam conceptum suum ordinare ad hoc ut ei innotescat, per propriam voluntatem).

57. This recourse to sensible signs inscribed in space and time is the reason that distance prevents communication, whereas with an angel, whose language is purely intellectual, physical distance plays no role (see *ST* I, q. 107, a. 4). If the seraphim "shout," it is not so as to be heard better (see *ST* I, q. 107, ad 2).

58. See *ST* I, q. 107, a. 1, ad 3.

59. *ST* I, q. 107, a. 2: "Omnis illuminatio est locutio in angelis, sed non omnis locutio est illuminatio." Compare *ST* I, q. 107, a. 5, arg. 3: "Enlightenment is a kind of speech"

tive activity of every creature, indeed, presents a twofold aspect: objective and subjective. Objective, because the knowing subject grasps and assimilates something of a higher truth and, in so doing, he becomes ontologically richer, more luminous, and to that extent approaches the Source of all truth who is God. Subjective, because the act of intellection by which a subject actually thinks a particular truth is conditioned by his subjective dispositions and especially the decisions of his will. The manifestation of cognitive activity can pertain to either aspect. It can, first, be centered on the objective higher truth of which the knowing creature is never just a relay. This is the case, for example, when I affirm that "the good is a transcendental property of being" or that "God is the creator of heaven and earth." This communication is then at the same time speech and enlightenment. It leads the listener not so much toward the speaker as toward the truth and toward God. But the manifestation can, second, concern the subjective dimension of the thought. This is the case when I inform my friend that "I spent the day studying the notion of good in its relation to being." We are dealing then with a statement but not an enlightenment. In fact, for St. Thomas, who in this respect proves to be diametrically opposed to the modern mindset [forma mentis], which is so attentive to the subjective and historical conditions of thought, information about the subjective dispositions is not of much interest. The accumulation of positive data does not fulfill the vocation of the intellect, at least not directly: "For to know what you may will, or what you may understand does not belong to the perfection of my intellect; but only to know the truth in reality."[60] In any case, knowledge

(Illuminatio est quaedam species locutionis). This is why later Scholastics generally invert the order of topics in the Summa theologiae: they treat language first and then enlightenment, as a particular form of language. See, for example, John of St. Thomas, Cursus theologicus, disp. 45, in which article 1 is devoted to language and article 2 to enlightenment.

60. ST I, q. 107, a. 2: "Non enim pertinet ad perfectionem intellectus mei, quid tu velis, vel quid tu intelligas, cognoscere, sed solum quid rei veritas habet." Here we have the theoretical justification of the famous statement from In Aristotelis libros De caelo et mundo, De generatione et corruptione, Meteorologicorum expositio [In De caelo] I, lect. 22, §8, ed. Raimondo M. Spiazzi (Turin: Marietti, 1952): "The study of philosophy does not have the purpose of knowing what men have thought but rather how the truth of matters may be had" (Studium philosophiae non est ad hoc quod sciatur quid homines senserint, sed qualiter se habeat veritas rerum).

of singular subjective dispositions is secondary in relation to the first aim of all intellectual life: objective universal truth. Simple informative speech is therefore secondary in relation to enlightenment.

Thus, unlike enlightenment, which is always descending, speech can be two-way.[61] A higher angel speaks to a lower angel by enlightening him, but a lower angel can speak to a higher angel to inform him of the dispositions of his will. The most appropriate form of this speech is not dialogue—a form of communication that would be out of place in such a strictly hierarchical society as the angelic world—but rather interrogation, through which the lower angels manifest their desire to know.[62] With respect to God, clearly the angels do not speak to him to inform him of what he did not know concerning the objective truth of things or even their subjective dispositions. We say rather that an angel speaks to God inasmuch as he disposes himself interiorly to receive some information from God. Here again interrogation is the privileged form of this speech. An angel tells God his astonished admiration, his praise of what he perceives as the surpassing grandeur of the Lord. He also asks the wisdom of God concerning what he has to do to carry out his will, somewhat like the disciple addresses the master, not to tell him something, but to manifest his desire to know and to dispose himself better to receive his teaching.[63]

The last article of question 107 explains that an angel chooses his interlocutors.[64] He does not speak to anyone and everyone. Enlightenment is to a great extent public since it concerns universal objective truth, which is the common good of all spirits. But a simple linguistic exchange may be private, inasmuch as it concerns the subjective dispositions of an angel. The reception of the message depends solely on the will of the speaker who directs his free intention toward this or that recipient. On this point, as Claude Panaccio has remarked, St. Thomas opposes Ockham. For St. Thomas, the speaking angel

61. See *ST* I, q. 107, a. 2.

62. Several interrogative formulas contained in sacred scripture have been interpreted by tradition as angelic questions, addressed either to God or by the lower to the higher angels; see Ps 24 [23]; Is 63:1–6.

63. See *ST* I, q. 107, a. 3. It would be interesting to develop a parallel between the speech by which an angel turns toward God and human prayer as an unfolding or "explication of the will" (*explicatio voluntatis*) in God's presence (*ST* II-II, q. 83; III, q. 21).

64. See *ST* I, q. 107, a. 5.

has the initiative in the communication and maintains control of it.[65] In fact, for St. Thomas, thought that terminates in the production of a *verbum cordis* [word of the heart] is one thing, and speech or mental locution is another—that is, the activity that consists of putting this thought into a form suitable for communication: thought and speech are separate even among the angels. In contrast, for Ockham, thought is nothing other than a kind of mental speech. As soon as an angel thinks, he speaks. The speaking angel is always uttering. The receiving angel is the one who chooses whether or not to receive the information.

THE ANGELIC HIERARCHIES (Q. 108)

This enlightening activity allows us to give an account of the internal structure of angelic society. The angels do form a society. At first glance, human sociability appears to result from the imperfection of each human being taken separately: it is a remedy, a way of mitigating the limitations inherent in a fragile being with a finite intellect. Life in society thus allows man to actualize his nature progressively. But no doubt there is more to it than that, since the angels themselves, although they may be quite perfect in the natural order, are nonetheless not simply juxtaposed monads: they form a community, a society.[66] On the natural level, this society of the angels is founded on their common genus and is expressed by the natural love that angels have one for another. It is above all inspired and energized by their common reference to God: all angels come from God and go toward God under the action of one divine government. This natural angelic society is not destroyed but on the contrary is brought to its perfection and transfigured by the vocation of all the angels to the same supernatural beatitude that makes out of their community a church, still on pilgrimage or *in via* at the instant of their choice, or else definitively triumphant with their entry into the beatific vision.

This angelic society, whether in the natural order or in the super-

65. Suarez-Nani, *Connaissance*, 251, emphasizes that this free communication of the contents of thought that defines angelic speech is at the foundation of a society of free spirits: "The angelic society is a work of pure freedom, which corresponds to the desire to show oneself to the other without expecting anything in return."

66. See Daguet, "La société angélique," in *Théologie du dessein divin chez saint Thomas d'Aquin*, 49–59.

natural order, is inegalitarian. Since each angel is a species unto himself, an intelligible type distinct from any other, the angelic world can only be a perfectly hierarchical world, like a numerical series. There is no place among the angels for any horizontal diversity (several individuals sharing the same perfection equally). All diversity is vertical, both in the natural order and in the supernatural order that perfects it.[67] In question 108, St. Thomas sets out to elaborate a taxonomy of this angelic universe.[68] The reader will note, first, that St. Thomas approaches this question from the dynamic perspective of the angels' participation in the divine government,[69] and, second, that he is perfectly aware that this work can only be approximate:

> Our knowledge of the angels is imperfect.... Hence we can only distinguish the angelic offices and orders in a general way.... But if we knew the offices and distinctions of the angels perfectly, we should know perfectly that each angel has his own office and his own order among things.[70]

In fact, St. Thomas, far from constructing an a priori system, endeavors above all to give an account of the various classes of angels that tradition had already distinguished. This grouping of angels into

67. If the reader will be so kind as to recall that in an angel, unlike the situation among human beings, there is a correspondence between the gifts of nature and the gifts of grace (the highest angel in nature is also the one most fully endowed with the gifts of grace), he will understand that the angelic hierarchies and orders depend simultaneously on the angelic nature and on the grace given to the angel; see *ST* I, q. 108, a. 4: "The orders in the angels are adequately distinguished by the gifts of grace, but dispositively by natural gifts, forasmuch as to the angels are given gratuitous gifts according to the capacity of their natural gifts; which is not the case with men" (Ordines distinguuntur in angelis completive quidem secundum dona gratuita, dispositive autem secundum dona naturalia, quia angelis data sunt dona gratuita secundum capacitatem naturalium, quod non est in hominibus).

68. See also *In ad Ep*, c. 1, lect. 7 (nos. 61–62); c. 6, lect. 3 (no. 357).

69. The hierarchical distinction of the angels, which is taken essentially from their functions in the divine government, will lose some of its pertinence at the end of history (see *ST* I, q. 108, a. 7). All that will remain then will be the social structure based on the hierarchy of being and of grace, of which the functional hierarchies were the expression.

70. *ST* I, q. 108, a. 3: "Nos autem imperfecte angelos cognoscimus, et eorum officia, ut Dionysius dicit VI cap. *Cael. Hier.* Unde non possumus distinguere officia et ordines angelorum, nisi in communi; secundum quem modum, multi angeli sub uno ordine continentur. Si autem perfecte cognosceremus officia angelorum, et eorum distinctiones, perfecte sciremus quod quilibet angelus habet suum proprium officium et suum proprium ordinem in rebus."

different orders goes back to late Judaism and was adopted by Christianity.[71] To tell the truth, some fathers, while admitting the existence of a hierarchical arrangement of the angelic world, were rather skeptical about excessively precise speculations that smacked of Gnosticism and betrayed a misplaced curiosity.[72] The fact remains that, with an exegetical sense that was sometimes debatable, commentators collected the names of the spiritual creatures in the Bible, who appear in different and varied contexts, so as to make out of them a system of angelic orders or choirs.[73] Thus, as early as the fourth century, in his *Mystagogical Catecheses*, Cyril of Jerusalem mentions, in his explanation of the Eucharistic Preface, the nine angelic orders that were to become classic.[74] The *Celestial Hierarchy* of Dionysius would popularize the more precise idea (derived from Proclus) of an organization in three hierarchies and nine orders.[75] The idea became acclimated in the West through St. Gregory the Great,[76] with several nuances later added by the shrewd harmonizing skills of the Scholastics.[77] "It is rarely permitted for anyone but a pope," Voltaire remarked satirically, "to regulate the celestial ranks in this way."[78]

The main social organization of the angelic world traditionally bears the name of hierarchy. A hierarchy is a society structured by the reference of all its members to one sacred principle; it is a sacred principality (*sacer principatus*, as when we speak about the "Princi-

71. See Michl, "Engel III (christlich)," 171–76.

72. See Ignatius of Antioch, *To the Trallians* 5, in *Letters* (ACW 1:76–77): "Just because I am in chains [for Christ], and able to grasp heavenly things—the ranks of the angels, the hierarchy of principalities, things visible and invisible—it does not immediately follow that I am a disciple."

73. Thus, for St. Thomas, the names of the nine choirs are revealed. See *ST* I, q. 108, a. 5, sed contra.

74. Cyril of Jerusalem, *Mystagogical Catecheses* V.6, in *St. Cyril of Jerusalem's Lectures on the Christian Sacraments*, edited by F. L. Cross, 73 (Crestwood, N.Y.: St. Vladimir's Seminary Press, 1986). Compare, in the West, Ambrose, *Apologie de David* V.20, introduction, Latin text, notes, and index Pierre Hadot, French trans. Marius Cordier (SC 239:96–97).

75. See Dionysius the Areopagite, *Celestial Hierarchy*, chaps. 7–9, 161–73 and the bibliography of chapter 3 of this volume.

76. Gregory the Great, *Forty Gospel Homilies*, 34.7, 285; *Morals on The Book of Job* XXXII.48 (3/2:549–50).

77. See *ST* I, q. 108, a. 6 and parallel passages.

78. Voltaire, "Ange," in *Dictionnaire philosophique*, in Voltaire, *Oeuvres complètes*, (Paris: 1821), 36:380.

pate" or Principality of Andorra) that is defined by two elements: the principle of order and the plurality that is organized in terms of that principle. St. Thomas explains at the outset that, if we consider the principle of order—namely, the one God—there is only one hierarchy, only one universe that comes from God and goes to God. In contrast, if we consider the second element—namely, the plurality ordered under one principle—we can distinguish several hierarchies depending on the differentiated manner in which the structuring action of the principle is received. For example, in France during the Ancient Regime, there was only one king (and therefore only one kingdom), but each province had its own way of depending on the king. From this perspective, it is necessary first to distinguish the angelic hierarchy and the human hierarchy. God enlightens in different ways: on the one hand, with the angels who perceive directly what is intelligible and, on the other hand, with the men who receive that same light under the veils of what is sensible—in other words, in a sacramental manner. There are two regimes and therefore two hierarchies that are distinguished in terms of this difference in regime.

But even among the angels, not all are enlightened in the same manner. Certainly, all the good angels see the Divine Essense immediately, and, from this perspective, there is no hierarchy. But, as we already mentioned, not all of them see in the same way the transcendent models (*rationes*) of the divine works. From this perspective, one can distinguish three groups or hierarchies. In the first (seraphim, cherubim, and thrones), these *rationes* are drawn from the Source; they are received directly from God, without mediation. The angels of the first hierarchy are turned directly toward God and contemplate in their Origin the plan of these divine works.[79] In the second hierarchy, the divine plans are seen in their highest created causes, specifi-

---

79. See *In ad Ep*, c. 1, lect. 7 (no. 62): "This is why the orders of this hierarchy are named by comparison with God, for the Seraphim are called fiery and united to God by love, whereas the Cherubim are called brilliant, inasmuch as they know the divine secrets surpassingly. The Thrones are so called inasmuch as God carries out his judgments in them" (Propter quod ordines hierarchiae istius denominantur per comparationem ad Deum, quia Seraphim dicuntur ardentes, et uniti Deo per amorem. Cherubim vero quasi lucentes, in quantum supereminenter divina secreta cognoscunt. Throni vero dicuntur sic, in quantum in eis Deus sua iudicia exercet). We will not get into the medieval debate about the relations of superiority maintained in this hierarchy by Cherubim and Seraphim—in other words, Dominicans and Franciscans.

cally in the thought of the angels of the first hierarchy, and, in terms of this knowledge, the angels of the second hierarchy arrange the general plan of the divine government. In the third hierarchy, these plans are seen inasmuch as they are determined in a particular way, and the angels execute them.[80]

Each of these three hierarchies is itself made up of three orders of angels. The distinction among these orders is derived from the duties that these angels perform within their hierarchy. As in civil society, and in keeping with a model that Georges Dumézil would not have repudiated, there is in every hierarchy an upper class, a middle class, and a lower class (the populace). The diversity among the angels of the three orders within a hierarchy comes from their greater or lesser ability to communicate what all the angels of that hierarchy possess in common: the angels of the higher order possess and communicate, whereas those of the lower order possess without communicating.[81] Good Dionysian that he is, St. Thomas takes care to highlight the remarkable connectedness among the nine orders: the higher order of a lower hierarchy has profound affinities with the lower order of the next-higher hierarchy.[82]

Despite what might seem to be the excessively precise and therefore arbitrary character of some of these speculations about angelic society, they are not without interest for a reflection on social life in general and on ecclesial life in particular.[83] Indeed, in angelic society, the supreme vocation of any society is accomplished: to ensure the return to God of each of its members by the generous cooperation of all.

80. See *ST* I, q. 108, a. 1.

81. See *ST* I, q. 108, a. 2, ad 2.

82. See *ST* I, q. 108, a. 2. On the precise designation of each of the angelic choirs and their respective order, see *ST* I, q. 108, aa. 5–6.

83. The church on earth finds in the "utopia" of angelic society its concrete ideal, so to speak, and Dionysius already thought of the ecclesiastical hierarchy as a reflection of this celestial hierarchy. But the analogy is a delicate one to manage, and in the past it has given rise to dubious ideological interpretations; see Yves Congar, "Aspects ecclésiologiques de la querelle entre Mendiants et séculiers dans la seconde moitié du XIIIᵉ siècle et au début du XIVᵉ siècle," *AHDLMA* 28 (1961): 34–151, esp. 114–45: "Le Pseudo-Denys dans l'ecclésiologie du XIIIᵉ siècle."

13

---·---

The Good Angels, "Ministering Spirits"

Perfect models of apostolic life, ardent to transmit what they contemplate, the angels are sent by God on a mission among men. They are servants or ministers of Divine Providence: "Are they not all ministering spirits sent forth to serve, for the sake of those who are to obtain salvation?" (Hb 1:14).[1] St. Thomas tries to give a theological account of this missionary activity of the angels in question 112. These missions aim at procuring for men who are still wayfaring favorable conditions that allow them to reach their homeland more surely. The angels therefore participate in the implementation of the general means of salvation. Thus, in the Old Covenant, the angels, like good pedagogues, prepared in many ways the coming of the One who is the Way par excellence: Jesus Christ. And no doubt they still prepare it for all those human groups in which Christianity has not yet penetrated. Once Christ was present in his flesh, the angels served him and, after his Ascension, they continue to serve him in the Christian community. But the angels also help each human person to enter into this salvific plan of God and to remain faithful to it. This is the duty attributed to guardian angels, of whom we will consider the traditional foundations and then, in the school of St. Thomas, the theology

1. On the patristic foundations of this teaching about angelic missions, see Daniélou, *Angels and Their Mission*; Michl, "Engel III (christlich)," 151–53, "Engel im Dienste der Menschen."

(*ST* I, q. 113). This charitable activity of the angels in turn calls for a cult on the part of men, and it is advisable to specify the nature of this devotion.

"MINISTERING SPIRITS" (*ST* I, Q. 112)

In order to define the very notion of mission, St. Thomas Aquinas repeats what he said about the mission of the Divine Persons in *ST* I, q. 43, so as to apply it analogically to angels. We say that someone is sent when, first, he begins to exist in a place where he formerly did not exist in that manner, and when, second, he proceeds or comes somehow from another subject and leads back to him. Thus an ambassador on mission in a foreign country fulfills these two requirements: he is mandated by his government (relation of origin) and travels so as to go to his post and reside in the foreign country where he did not live previously.

Due to the fact that his *virtus* or active power is created and limited, an angel cannot be in several places at a time: if he is in A, he cannot be in B, unless the angelic action pertains to A and B *per modum unius*, inasmuch as they are only one thing.[2] He can therefore begin to be in a place where he was not before by deciding to apply his active power to a particular localized subject. Furthermore, even though his action is free, he acts at God's command.[3] He is the minister, in other words the intelligent instrument, of decisions that come from God and are intended to lead back to God those creatures that are still wayfaring. The angelic action with respect to men corresponds therefore to the criteria that define a mission, a ministry.[4]

2. On the localization of angels, see chapter 6 of this volume.

3. Origen, who because of a univocal vision of justice always had difficulty admitting the absolute gratuitousness of the divine choices and desperately searched for the causes thereof among creatures, had imagined that the importance of the missions attributed to any particular angel had to be proportional to his merit; see Origen, *On First Principles* I.8.1 (1966), 66–68. That is not the case at all.

4. See *ST* I, q. 112, a. 1. In the ad 4, St. Thomas explains that this action of an angel in the service of man in no way impairs the angel's dignity, because in reality he is in the service of God and not directly of the creature who is inferior to him. But one can also point out, following St. Bernard, that this angelic condescension participates, in charity, in the humiliation of the Son who came to serve and not to be served (Mt 20:28); see Bernard of Clairvaux, Sermon XI on Psalm XC, 10, *St. Bernard's Sermons for the Seasons*

Are all angels sent to minister?[5] The early church fathers saw nothing wrong with that. But Dionysius, in keeping with his very structured vision of the angelic world, defended in *The Celestial Hierarchy*
the idea that only the angels belonging to the lower orders perform a
ministry among men. The reader senses here a latent conflict between
the Dionysian doctrine of ubiquitous mediation [*médiatisme*] and a
naïve reading of scripture in which, according to Hebrews, *all* angels
are sent to minister and the lips of the prophet Isaiah were purified
by no less than a seraph—in other words, an angel of the first order
who is considered to be thoroughly engrossed in contemplating God
(Is 6:6). St. Thomas Aquinas, like St. Gregory the Great before him,[6]
follows Dionysius: the missionary activity *ad extra* concerns only the
lower angels, more precisely the angels of the last five orders, whose
names moreover suggest an external activity.[7] But could we not imagine that, by some miracle, a higher angel might be sent? St. Thomas
rejects this hypothesis as absurd. A miracle has no meaning unless it
allows man to glimpse the existence of a higher order than the one in
which he lives and moves. Now, not only would man be incapable of

---

and Principal Festivals of the Year, trans. a priest of Mount Melleray (Dublin: Browne
and Nolan, 1921), 1:243, slightly emended: "When they descend, they exercise mercy in
our regard, by keeping us in all our ways. As the Apostle says, they 'are all ministering
spirits sent to minister for them who shall receive the inheritance of salvation.' They are
our servants, therefore and [not our masters]. And in this they are but imitating the example of the Only-Begotten, who did 'not come to be ministered unto but to minister'"
(*S. Bernardi opera* IV, Sermones I, ed. Jean Leclercq and Henri Rochais [Rome: Éditiones Cistercienes, 1966], 455: Cum vero descendunt, faciunt nobiscum misericordiam,
ut custodiant nos in omnibus viis nostris. Administratorii enim spiritus sunt, missi in
ministerium propter nos. Plane ministri nostri, non domini nostri. Et in hoc Unigeni-
ti formam imitantur, qui non venit ministrari, sed ministrare, qui stetit inter discipulos
tamquam qui ministrat).

5. See *ST* I, q. 112, a. 2. The problem (and the different positions taken to date) is
presented at length by Peter Lombard, *Sententiae* II, d. 10 (43–45). Petau devotes to
it a chapter of his *De Angelis* II.6 (*Dogmata theologica*, 4:21–28), where he opposes St.
Thomas while citing scripture.

6. Gregory the Great, *Forty Gospel Homilies* 34.12.292: "It is related that Denys the
Areopagite, an ancient and venerable Father, says that those who are sent forth, either
visibly or invisibly, to carry out some function, are from among the lesser bands of angels.... The higher bands never withdraw from God" (Fertur vero Dionysius Areopagi-
ta, antiquus videlicet et venerabilis pater, dicere quod ex minoribus angelorum agmini-
bus foris ad explendum ministerium vel visibiliter vel invisibiliter mittuntur.... Nam
superiora illa agmina ab intimis numquam recedunt).

7. See *ST* I, q. 112, a. 4.

perceiving this subversion of the angelic order, but, most importantly, the hierarchical structure of the angelic world depends on the order of grace, and there is nothing above that.[8]

In order to account for the scriptural passages that seem to favor the idea of a mission of the higher angels, one can, following Dionysius and Thomas, liken this mission of the higher angels to the hierarchical enlightenment that they communicate to all those who are below them, which is the equivalent of an invisible mission. But a visible mission—that is, one that directly affects the world of nature—is reserved to the lower angels.[9] As for Isaiah's seraph, St. Thomas repeats here too the substance of the exegesis by Dionysius.[10] Either this angel is not a seraph but is so called improperly because his action—purifying—suggests the etymology of the word *seraphim* (burning), or else Isaiah actually means a true seraph who then acts through the implicit mediation of the whole hierarchy of lower angels, who share in his purifying power and apply it to the prophet. In either case, the prophet Isaiah is therefore in direct contact only with an angel of the last hierarchy. As Maurice de Gandillac points out, "we have here a striking example of a 'worldview' (of a partly profane character) cited by theologians so as to reject the most obvious interpretation of a Scriptural passage."[11]

Relying on Daniel 7:10, "a thousand thousands served him, and ten thousand times ten thousand stood before him," the doctrinal tra-

8. See *ST* I, q. 112, a. 2: "The angelic order is according to the gifts of grace. Now the order of grace has no order above itself for the sake of which it should be passed over, as the order of nature is passed over for the sake of grace. It may likewise be observed that the order of nature in the working of miracles is passed over for the confirmation of faith; which purpose would receive no additional strength if the angelic order were passed over, since this could not be perceived by us" (Quia ordo angelicus attenditur secundum dona gratiarum. Ordo autem gratiae non habet alium superiorem ordinem, propter quem praetermitti debeat, sicut praetermittitur ordo naturae propter ordinem gratiae. Considerandum est etiam quod ordo naturae in operationibus miraculorum praetermittitur, propter fidei confirmationem. Ad quam nihil valeret, si praetermitteretur ordo angelicus, quia hoc a nobis percipi non posset).

9. See *ST* I, q. 112, a. 2, ad 2.

10. See Dionysius the Areopagite, *Celestial Hierarchy*, chap. 13.1–3, 176–79; Aquinas, *In Is.*, c. 6 (l.354–81); *In II Sent.*, d. 10, a. 2, ad 2; *Q. de ver.*, q. 9, a. 2, ad 2; *ST* I, q. 112, a. 2, ad 2. On this question, see also Hankey, "Dionysian Hierarchy in Thomas Aquinas, 416–24: "Thomas and Denys on Isaiah VI.6"; Hankey, "Aquinas, Pseudo-Denys, Proclus and Isaiah VI.6," *AHDLMA* 64 (1997): 59–93.

11. Denys l'Aréopagite, *Hiérarchie céleste*, SC 58:149, note.

dition has come to distinguish two angelic functions that commentators sometimes tend to attribute to two distinct categories of angels. There are the angels who serve (*administrantes*) and those who stand before God (*assistentes*). St. Thomas endeavors to justify this distinction, which is omnipresent in the writings of St. Gregory the Great.[12] He does so by resorting to a "political" analogy between the celestial world and the royal courts of this world, in which a distinction was made between those who were always in the king's presence and received orders from him directly (the *assistentes*) and those who were not present and received his order through the agency of the former (the *ministrantes*). But once again, the neo-Platonic mediation is difficult to square with a certain Christian immediacy. Indeed, the Christian theologian must hold that all the good angels see the Divine Essence: even those who are sent on a mission do not cease to contemplate the Father's face.[13] Unlike man, in whom action almost necessarily hinders the activity of spiritual contemplation because it involves the sensitive powers, the mission of such a simple being as an angel does not interrupt his contemplation of God.[14] That said, Aquinas explains, some angels—those of the first hierarchy—are more deserving of the name *assistants* because they are directly enlightened by God; in other words, in seeing the Divine Essence they perceive the secrets of the King that the others do not see directly but come to know only through those higher angels.[15]

THE TRADITIONAL DOCTRINE OF THE GUARDIAN ANGELS

The way in which the action of the angels is organized on behalf of mankind—which angels in particular assist which individual human

12. See *ST* I, q. 112, a. 3. See Gregory the Great, *Forty Gospel Homilies* 34.12, 292: "It is one thing to minister, another to stand before someone. They minister to God who go forth to proclaim something to us; they stand before him who have perfect enjoyment of their intimate contemplation, and so are not sent forth to perform actions" (Aliud est namque ministrare, aliud assistere. Qui administrant Deo, qui et ad nos nuntiando exeunt; assistunt vero qui sic contemplatione intima perfruuntur, ut ad explenda foras opera minime mittantur).

13. See Gregory the Great, *Morals on The Book of Job* II.3.3 (1:70).

14. See *ST* I, q. 112, a. 1, ad 3.

15. See *ST* I, q. 112, a. 3, ad 4.

beings?—for a long time remained rather imprecise, and only very
gradually did the Christian tradition arrive at the specific doctrine of
the guardian angel: each human person is attended, from conception
until death, by his own very special angel who is set over him.

The Bible refers to a specialization of some angels in the service
of one human community or another—for example, a nation.[16] Thus
Daniel 10:13 mentions the conflict between Gabriel, aided by Michael,
"one of the chief princes," and "the prince of the kingdom of Persia"—in other words, the angel set over the Persian nation. From the
perspective of the history of religions, these guardian angels of communities could very well assume, in a monotheistic system, the role
formerly played by the national gods. With the angels of the seven
churches, the book of Revelation adopts this idea of an angel set over
a community,[17] and in this book we also see Michael, whom late Judaism had identified as the angel protector of Israel, defending the new
people of God against Satan.[18]

But this angelic protection easily shifts from communities to the
persons of whom they are composed. Thus, within the holy people,
it is addressed especially to the just. The book of Tobit bears witness
to this, with its marvelous story of the protection that Raphael gives
to Tobias throughout his perilous journey. Similarly, Psalm 91:11–12
exalts the angelic protection with which God surrounds his friends:
"For he will give his angels charge of you to guard you in all you ways.
On their hands they will bear you up, lest you dash your foot against
a stone." Does this mean that every just man is attached to a designated angel?[19] Nothing allows us to assert that at this stage. But biblical

16. See D. S. Russell, "Guardian Angels of the Nations," in *Method and Message*,
244–49.

17. On the history of the interpretations of this figure of the Angel of the Church,
see D. E. Aune, *Revelation 1–5*, World Biblical Commentary 52a (Dallas: 1997), 108–12.

18. The status of the people of God is not exactly the same as that of other peoples,
because God watches directly over Israel; see Sir 17:17: "He appointed a ruler for every
nation, but Israel is the Lord's own portion." However, in guiding his holy people, God
can have recourse to the mediation of an angel: "Behold, I send an angel before you, to
guard you on the way and to bring you to the place which I have prepared. Give heed to
him and listen to his voice, do not rebel against him, for he will not pardon your transgression; for my name is in him" (Ex 23:20–21, a passage that serves as the First Reading
in the Mass on October 2). In late Judaism, this role fell to Michael.

19. In intertestamental Judaism, we find the idea of an angel in charge of noting the

faith in providence that employs angels so as to guide the just will very quickly encounter the widespread belief in late antiquity that a tutelary god, a "good genie" or an "invisible companion" is attached to every human person.[20] And so Denis Petau begins his chapter on the guardian angels by asserting that this belief is, so to speak, innate, and he proves it by citing several testimonies taken from pagan literature.[21] Once again, only a narrowly dialectical concept of revelation, which considers the word of God to be only that which is found nowhere but in the Bible, would be disturbed by this parallelism. A Catholic vision of revelation would rejoice in it instead.

This cultural and religious background makes comprehensible the New Testament teaching that discreetly gives us to understand that particular angels are assigned to particular persons.[22] Thus, when Rhoda, the servant girl, comes to announce to the community that Peter, who was imprisoned the previous day, is standing at the door, they spontaneously think that it is *his* angel (Acts 12:15). But is this about a personal angel committed to guard Peter or is it a sort of spiritual double, a phantom, a form of *post mortem* presence?[23] Indeed,

---

good and bad deeds of every just man so as to report them to God; see *Apocalypse grecque de Baruch* XII.3 (*La Bible: Écrits intertestamentaires*, 1162: the "angels set over the just").

20. Jb 5:1 perhaps refers to this angel in charge of defending the interests of an individual at the divine court. On the influence of the Persian religion (and especially of the *fravashis*) and of the Hellenistic religion on the emergence of the guardian angel, see D. S. Russell, *Method and Message*, 259–60. In chap. 3, "The Invisible Companion," in *The Cult of the Saints* (Chicago: University of Chicago Press, 1981 [2015]), Peter Brown showed how belief in a "spiritual double," a guardian angel or a patron saint, was common in late antiquity. From a more anthropological perspective, van der Leeuw, *Religion dans son essence et ses manifestations*, 293–94, connects the doctrine of the guardian angels to the original belief in a "double" or an "external soul."

21. See Petau, *De angelis* II.7 (*Dogmata theologica*, 4:28–30): "The pagans attributed to this genie almost everything that Christians say about guardian angels" (Huic ergo Genio prorsus omnia gentiles attribuerunt, quae de custodibus angelis christiani praedicant). Clement of Alexandria was already convinced that Plato had glimpsed the doctrine of the guardian angels; see *Stromates* V.14.91.3–4 (SC 278:176–77).

22. Concerning the guardian angel in the New Testament, see Kittel, "Aggelos: Aggelos in the NT," in *TDNT*, 1:83–87 (esp. 86–87). On the Jewish context, see Hermann L. Strack and Paul Billerbeck, *Das Evangelium nach Matthäus erläutert aus Talmud und Midrash*, Kommentar zum Neuen Testament aus Talmud und Midrasch (Munich: Beck, 1922), 781–84.

23. See James H. Moulton, "It Is His Angel," *Journal of Theological Studies* 3 (1902): 514–27; George, *Études sur l'oeuvre de Luc*, 165–68.

the essential passage here is Matthew 18:10: in it Jesus Christ begs his disciples not to despise "one of these little ones; for I tell you that in heaven their angels always behold the face of my Father who is in heaven." The purpose of this passage is first to emphasize the dignity of the little ones, but it also affirms indirectly, as a condition for the validity of the reasoning, the existence of a special connection between believers and certain angels, in this case those of the highest hierarchy who see God's face.

The patristic literature orchestrates these different themes.[24] The fathers are firmly convinced that particular angels watch over the various human communities, whether they be of a natural order (peoples, nations, cities) or of a supernatural order (local churches).[25] These angels have a very special care for those in charge of communities. Dionysius, moreover, faithful to his neo-Platonic principles of mediation, sticks by this providential action of the angels of the last order upon the heads of human communities (kings, bishops), who, in turn, exercise their oversight over the persons entrusted to them. In his writings, the idea of a guardian angel set over each person could not possibly find an echo.[26] On the other hand, St. John Chrysostom promotes the personalist idea that, although formerly the angels dealt with nations as such, now with Christianity they are set over persons.[27] In fact, most of the fathers combine general assistance to the nations and particular assistance to persons.[28]

24. See Petau, *De Angelis* II.7 (*Dogmata theologica*, 4:28–36); Bareille, "Angélologie d'après les Pères, VII. L'ange gardien," *DTC*, 1:1216–19; Daniélou, chap. 7, "The Guardian Angel," in *Angels and Their Mission,,* 68–82; Michl, "Engel III (christlich)," 154–55.

25. On the theme of the angels of the nations, see Daniélou, *Origen*, 224–38, and Daniélou, "Les sources juives de la doctrine des anges des nations chez Origène," *RSR* 38 (1951): 132–37. The political implications of this theme were the topic of a debate, the elements of which can be found in Daniélou, "Appendice: Débat sur les anges des nations," in *Les anges et leur mission d'après les Pères de l'Église* (Paris: Éditions de Chevetogne, 1952), 153–78 [not included in the English edition]. One example among many others: John Damascene, *Orthodox Faith* II.3 (FOTC 37:207): "[The angels] are set over nations and places in accordance with their disposition by the Creator. They direct our affairs and help us. Moreover, they are ever round about God for the very reason that in accordance with the divine will and command they are above us."

26. See Roques, *Univers dionysien*, 149.

27. John Chrysostom, *Homilies on the Epistle to the Colossians* III.4 (NPNF–1 13:273a).

28. See, for example, Origen, *Homilies on Luke*, Homily 12.3–6 (FOTC 94:49–51):

The fathers generally admit that every human being, or at the very least every Christian, has a guardian angel. Gregory of Nyssa sees this as "a doctrine which derives its trustworthiness from the tradition of the Fathers."[29] Origen seems to have had a decisive influence here, even though his luxuriant theology is not always perfectly coherent.[30] The Alexandrian theologian asserts outright that there is an angel alongside every individual human being: "There is present to each of us, even to the 'least' who are in the Church of God, a good angel, an angel of the Lord, who guides, warns and governs, who, for the sake of correcting our actions and imploring mercy, daily 'sees the face of the Father who is in heaven.'"[31] But he is not all that sure whether the guardian angel takes his ward under his protection at his birth or at his baptism.[32] Whatever the case may be, the destiny of these angels (which in Origen's system is not yet definitively determined) proves to be closely in solidarity with that of their protégés. They share one and the same destiny, and both will be judged in terms of the results of their tandem course.[33] Origen even mentions the idea that a

---

"I think that what Scripture says about individual provinces should also be believed more generally about all people. Two angels attend each human being. One is an angel of justice, the other an angel of iniquity" (49–50); Homily 23.8 (FOTC 94:101): "I do not doubt that angels are even present in our assembly—not only generally, to every church, but even singly."

29. See Gregory of Nyssa, *The Life of Moses*, trans. Abraham J. Malherbe and Everett Ferguson (New York: Paulist Press, 1978), 64. "There is a doctrine (which derives its trustworthiness from the tradition of the Fathers) which says that after our nature fell into sin God did not ... withhold his providence. No, on the one hand, he appointed an angel with an incorporeal nature to help in the life of each person."

30. On the theory of the guardian angel in Origen, see Bareille, "Angélologie d'après les Pères, VII. L'ange gardien," *DTC*, 1: 1216–17; Manlio Simonetti, "Due note sull'angelologia origeniana: I, Mt 18:10 nell'interpretazione di Origene," *Rivista di cultura classica e medioevale* 4 (1962): 165–79.

31. Origen, *Homilies on Numbers*, Homily 20.3.6 (ACT, 128b); see also *Homilies on Luke*, Homily 12.4 (FOTC 94:49–50); Homily 35.3–4 (FOTC 94:143–44).

32. See Origen, *Commentaria in Evangelium secundum Matthaeum* 13:27–28 (PG 13:1165–72) (ANF 9:491a–b).

33. See Origen, *Homilies on Luke* 35.3–4 (FOTC 94:144): "If I am in the Church, no matter how very little I am, my angel enjoys the liberty and the trust always to see 'the face of the Father, who is in heaven.' But, if I am an outsider ... , then my angel does not enjoy the trust of beholding the face of the Father, who is in heaven.' For this reason the angels care for good people. They know that, if they guide us well and lead us to salvation, they too will enjoy the trust of seeing the Father's face.... So too, if someone perishes through their negligence, they realize that the matter is a danger to them.... If someone who was

guardian angel could originally be a bad angel who had become good thanks to the baptism of his ward.[34]

The doctrine is more secure in the works of St. Basil, whom the *Catechism of the Catholic Church* cites, incidentally, to illustrate the church's faith in guardian angels: "Beside each believer stands an angel as protector and shepherd leading him to life."[35]

THEOLOGY OF THE GUARDIAN ANGELS
(I, Q. 113)

St. Thomas therefore inherits a long tradition of reflection on the guardian angels.[36] His intention is to get an understanding of it in faith by reconnecting it with the principles of theology. Concerning the very existence of this angelic guardian, St. Thomas deploys in his *Scriptum super sententiis* the great laws of the theology of providence. God wills to have recourse to intermediate causes in order to carry out the plans of his providence. Therefore he makes use of intermediate creatures between him and mankind, which are the angels, to bring human beings back to him.[37] Not that he could not accomplish his designs by

---

entrusted to an angel sins, the angel is disgraced. And the opposite is also true. If someone entrusted to an angel, even the least person in the Church, makes progress, it redounds to the angel's glory.... For, according to the merit of those whose angels they are, the angels will contemplate the face of God either always or never, little or much"; see also Origen, *Homilies on Numbers*, Homily 20.3.7 (ACT 128b); Homélie 24.3.3 (ACT 153a).

34. See Origen, *Commentaria in Evangelium secundum Matthaeum* 13:28 (PG 13:1167–70) (ANF 9:491a–b).

35. Basil the Great, *Adv. Eunomium* III.1 (PG 29:656B), cited in CCC 336.

36. The key text for the Scholastics is Peter Lombard, *Sententiae* II, d. 11, c. 1 (45–46). After St. Thomas, the treatise on the guardian angels was increasingly padded with curiosities. One can read the minutely detailed synthesis by Suarez that leaves no detail unmentioned; see *Tractatus De Angelis*, chaps. 17–19, 6:746–65).

37. *In II. Sent.*, d. 11, q. 1, a. 1: "According to Boethius in the *Consolation*, God implements through certain intermediate causes the providence that he exerts over all things.... Therefore, since the angelic nature is midway between God and men, and since God arranged this, according to the law of his wisdom, so as to provide for inferior realities through superior ones, the angels themselves implement the divine providence concerning the salvation of mankind by helping them to tend toward their end and delivering them from things that prevent this advance toward their end. This implementation of divine providence by the angels is called the guardianship of the angels" (Secundum Boetium in libro de Consolat., Deus providentiam suam quam de omnibus rebus habet, mediantibus quibusdam causis exequatur.... Quia ergo inter Deum et ho-

himself, yet by associating himself with the angels, he makes them participate in the dignity of causes and thus enhances his own glory.[38] In the *Summa theologiae*, St. Thomas explains that the existence of the guardian angels is more particularly in keeping with the general law of the divine government that intends that realities subject to change—in other words, those realities that do not yet possess their perfection and their end—should be guided toward that end by the activity of realities that already permanently possess their perfection. So it is, for example, that our fluctuating opinions on particular questions ought to be considered and settled in terms of several major fundamental principles that govern the whole of our intellectual life.[39] Now, inasmuch as a human being is still a wayfarer, his knowledge and his emotions lack stability; they are exposed, in the order of moral action, to many vicissitudes. It is therefore necessary for the angels, who are definitively fixed in the good, to be vigilant so as to guide correctly the advance of human persons toward that same good.[40]

Does this mean that man is insufficiently equipped to arrive safely at port by himself in an autonomous fashion?[41] It is true that a hu-

---

mines media est natura angelica, et secundum legem sapientiae suae hoc est ordinatum ut inferioribus per superiora provideat; ideo ipsi angeli exequuntur divinam providentiam circa salutem hominum, adjuvando ad tenendum in finem, et liberando ab his quae processum in finem impediunt: et haec executio divinae providentiae per angelos de hominibus, vocatur custodia angelorum).

38. Ibid., ad 1: "It is not because of his insufficiency that God implements his providence toward men through the angels, but because of an ordinance of his wisdom. In order that this dignity not be denied to the angels, it is fitting for them to be the leaders of men's return to God. In this they imitate God in a certain way, inasmuch as they cooperate with God in bringing men to their destination" (Nec est propter suam insufficientiam quod suam providentiam de hominibus exequitur per angelos, sed propter ordinem suae sapientiae. Tum quia congruit angelis, ut scilicet eis haec dignitas non negetur, quod sint duces hominum reductionis in Deum; et in hoc Deum quodammodo imitantur, inquantum cooperantur Deo in introductione hominum in finem).

39. In terms of his distinctive cosmology, St. Thomas gives as a first illustration of this law the fact that immobile immaterial substances assure the correct movement of the heavenly bodies, and the heavenly bodies, thought to be incorruptible, assure that of nature as a whole, in other words, of the corporeal substances subject to generation and corruption. One could also offer the following comparison: angels are to men what, in the Middle Ages, monastic communities withdrawn from the world were to the Christian communities engaged in the world. They represented their eschatological ideal, whose beneficial influence imbued the life of secular Christians.

40. See *ST* I, q. 113, a. 1.

41. See *ST* I, arg. 1 et ad 1.

man being can know the principles of the natural law that guide his action, but concretely, when it is a matter of drawing the practical consequences of these general principles, he finds himself at a distinct disadvantage: "For what man can learn the counsel of God? Or who can discern what the Lord wills? For the reasoning of mortals is worthless, and our designs are likely to fail, for a perishable body weighs down the soul, and this earthy tent burdens the thoughtful mind" (Ws 9:13–15). Similarly, by his freedom, man is sometimes able to avoid the evil that tempts him, but he is exposed to a permanent structural danger: the weight of the many passions that impair and falsify his moral decision-making. Man therefore needs external aid. But is God not enough for this?[42] Is it not God who, first, places in me the grace and the virtues that incline me toward the good and who, second, instructs me as to what paths to follow? Yes, but whereas the gift of grace is strictly reserved to God, who alone can act within the human will, to the exclusion of any angel, it is still fitting that this spiritual instruction should be mediated by angelic enlightenment.

Every human person who is still wayfaring enjoys the assistance of a designated guardian angel.[43] In fact, St. Thomas explains, providence is exercised in a more special manner with regard to incorruptible, permanent, lasting realities, insofar as they contribute more significantly and more directly to the welfare of the universe. Now, unlike the individuals of other animal species, who live only for the good of the species itself, each individual of the human species has an immortal soul and therefore is an end in himself: a person. If then we admit that an angel is in charge of preserving each animal species, it is necessary to acknowledge also that an angel is in charge of the destiny of each person.[44] As we see, one thing at stake in this doctrine is a correct emphasis on the eminent dignity of every human person in God's sight. Moreover this was Jesus' purpose in mentioning the little ones' angels who "always behold the face of my Father who is in heaven" (Mt 18:10).[45]

---

42. See *ST* I, arg. 2 et ad 2.　　　　　　43. See *ST* I, q. 113, a. 2.

44. Although each human person, by reason of his transcendence with regard to the communities to which he belongs, is committed to the protection of his own angel, he nonetheless benefits from the assistance of the angels who watch over those communities (the angel of France, the angel of the Garonne River Valley, the angel of Toulouse); see *ST* I, q. 113, a. 2, ad 1.

45. The *sed contra* of *ST* I, q. 113, article 2 cites Jerome's commentary on this pas-

In order to integrate the doctrine of guardian angels into a Dionysian angelology that hardly lends itself to this ministry, St. Thomas goes on to say that the angels sent to guard each human wayfarer belong to the last angelic choir, the choir of angels strictly speaking, whereas those who watch over the good of a community, which is always higher than the good of an individual, belong to the higher ranks, among those at least who are sent on a mission. Indeed, the more exalted an angel in the angelic hierarchy, the more universal his action.[46]

In order to understand what is at stake in the subsequent articles, it must be noted that, for St. Thomas, although the activity of guardian angels aims at the supernatural salvation of every human being, who in actuality is a sinner, it has a much broader reason for existing. It is also necessary for the happy outcome of any supernatural life of a human being who is still wayfaring, even in the state of innocence. More importantly, it is necessary for the government of men in its purely natural dimension. In short, angelic assistance is an external help that divine providence naturally offers to every wayfaring human being, whatever his situation may be at the supernatural level.

In article 4 Aquinas examines several significant cases in terms of these principles. Adam, before he sinned, even when he was not threatened by the interior disorder that reigns in us today, already had a guardian angel. This angel instructed him and guarded him against external dangers, especially from the devil's attacks.[47] Similarly, each of the *praesciti* (i.e., every human being who, as God knows from all eternity, will not in fact be saved) has a guardian angel, even the Antichrist. This is quite simply because, "just as the foreknown, the infidels, and even *Anti-christ*, are not deprived of the interior help of *natural reason*; so neither are they deprived of that exterior help granted by *God* to the whole *human race*—namely the guardianship of the *angels*."[48] The economy of the sufficient means of salvation, an ex-

---

sage: "Great is the dignity of souls, that each one should have from birth an angel delegated to guard him"; see Jerome, *Commentaire sur saint Matthieu* 18.10 (SC 259:54–55).

46. See *ST* I, q. 113, a. 3.

47. See *ST* I, q. 113, a. 4, ad 2. On the contrary, Gregory of Nyssa thought that the mission of guardian angels had started only after the original fall and therefore was dependent on the economy of the redemption.

48. *ST* I, q. 113, a. 4, ad 3: "Sicut praesciti et infideles, et etiam Antichristus, non

pression of God's universal salvific will, is offered to all human beings. The role of a guardian angel—if he fails to lead his ward to eternal life—is therefore to prevent him from doing all the evil that he could do (and therefore do to himself, since the sinner is the first to be harmed by his sin). The only one who had no guardian angel, after all, was Jesus. He had no need of one, already being a *comprehensor*, in full possession of the vision of God, and it would not have befitted his dignity, which was greater than that of the angels.[49]

As previously noted, Origen already raised the following question: does a guardian angel's mission to his protégé begin at birth or at baptism? It is easy to see what is at stake: is this angelic protection concerned only with the supernatural order, as suggested by some patristic texts that attribute guardian angels only to Christians, or does it already result from natural providence? St. Thomas, in keeping with his principles, replies that it starts at birth.[50]

According to the same logic, St. Thomas asserts that a guardian angel never abandons his ward, even if the latter comes to grief in sin.[51] Origen was not of the same opinion. With regard to the unfaithful servant of the parable, condemned to being "cut into pieces" (Mt 24:51), he proposed the following interpretation:

Each of the faithful, though he be the least in the Church, is we are told attended by an angel who is declared by the Saviour always to "behold the face of God the Father," this angel of God, who was certainly one with him over whom he was set, is to be withdrawn from him if by disobedience he becomes unworthy; and in that case "his portion," asunder from God's portion,

privantur interiori auxilio naturalis rationis; ita etiam non privantur exteriori auxilio toti naturae humanae divinitus concesso, scilicet custodia angelorum."

49. See *ST* I, q. 113, a. 4, ad 1. On a possible guardian angel for Christ, see, furthermore, Aquinas, *In II Sent.*, d. 11, q. 1, a. 3, ad 6–7; *In Ioan.*, c. 12, lect. 5 (no. 1663).... See also Bonaventure, *In II Sent.*, d. 11, a. 1, q. 3 (282–84): "Utrum Christum habuit angelum custodem?"

50. See *ST* I, q. 113, a. 5. What about an infant still in his mother's womb? In *In II Sent.*, d. 11, q. 1, a. 3, ad 3, St. Thomas acknowledges the guardian angel's activity from the moment of animation, but in *ST* I, q. 113, a. 5, ad 3, he thinks that since the infant "is still part of [the mother]" until birth, he is protected by her guardian angel. Suarez deems that the guardian angel goes into action from the moment of conception; see *Tractatus De Angelis*, chap. 17, no. 186:753. In fact, an ancient tradition assigns to the angels a special role in the generation and formation of the embryo.

51. See *ST* I, q. 113, a. 6.

is to be numbered with the unbelievers, seeing that he did not faithfully observe the warnings of the *angel* allotted to him by *God*.[52]

Moreover, according to St. Basil, the guardian angel flees the sinner as a bee flees smoke or a dove a foul smell.[53] Yet, for St. Thomas, even though a guardian angel can permit some evils, including sin, to befall his ward, according to the unfathomable designs of God, he never totally abandons him, no more than he abandons Divine Providence.

In what does this constant activity of a guardian angel consist? I am not speaking here about the central question, which was already addressed in chapter 4, about the possibility and the nature of angelic intervention in the life of men, but only about the more precise purposes of the guardian angel's interventions into the life of his ward. St. Bonaventure records a list of twelve effects of angelic guardianship, drawn from scripture, which circulated among the schoolmasters.[54] Suarez mentioned six of them.[55] First, the guardian angel wards off dangers to soul and body, either by intervening directly on the external reality or by acting on our psyche (a presentiment of danger). Second, the guardian angel incites the soul to good and turns it away from evil, primarily by instructing it—a decisive factor for a subject such as a human being, who directs his life by knowledge. The angel enlightens our intellect not by infusing ideas into it directly but by presenting certain truths to it under sensible likenesses, thus inspiring good thoughts.[56] Third, the guardian angel counteracts the malevolent activity of the demons. The ancients, who had a very vivid sense of the disproportion of the spiritual combat in which man finds himself engaged against the devil, often insisted on this necessary rebalancing of powers. Moreover, man's free and moral action is

---

52. Origen, *On First Principles* II.10.7 (1966), 145.

53. Basil the Great, *Homilia in Psalmos, In Ps* 33.5 (PG 29:363–64; FOTC 46:257).

54. See Bonaventure, *In II Sent.*, d. 11, a. 2, q. 1 (287).

55. See Suarez, *Tractatus De Angelis*, chap. 19, 6:760–63.

56. Clement of Alexandria, *Stromata* VI.17.157.4–5 (ANF 2:517a–b): "Besides, the thoughts of virtuous men are produced through the inspiration of God; the soul being disposed in the way it is, and the divine will being conveyed to human souls, particular divine ministers contributing to such services. For regiments of angels are distributed over the nations and cities. And, perchance, some are assigned to individuals." [The French translation of the passage concludes, "and probably some are also assigned to several detailed activities."]

largely conditioned by his roots in corporeality (think of the sometimes terrible laws of heredity). The devil prefers to act on this terrain
and must be countered there by angelic action.[57] Fourth and fifth, the
guardian angel presents our prayers to God—not in the sense that he
informs a distracted or overly distant God about our spiritual acts,
but in the sense that he supports them by his own fraternal intercession.[58] Finally, sixth, the guardian angel corrects his ward.

What about the subjective dispositions of the guardian angels?
In particular, do they suffer from the setbacks, sins, or punishments
of those who are entrusted to their care?[59] The question is not unlike the contemporary debate about the presence of possible suffering in God as he beholds the sins of mankind. But, as we already remarked in connection with the affective life of an angel, St. Thomas
aligns himself with thinking that decisively goes beyond anthropo-
morphism. Following St. Augustine, he denies that an angel experiences any passion, properly speaking.[60] Moreover, sadness, even as a
purely spiritual movement, is especially to be ruled out among the
good angels. On the one hand, it is incompatible with the perfect beatitude enjoyed by an angel. (Origen could speak about the anxiety of
a guardian angel inasmuch as he supposed that the angel's own destiny was not yet fixed.) On the other hand, sadness is impossible for
a person who, like a blessed angel, adheres unfailingly to God's will:
"Nothing happens in the world contrary to the will of the angels and
the other blessed, because [their] will cleaves entirely to the ordering of divine justice; while nothing happens in the world save what

57. So St. Thomas justified the presence of an angel beside an infant who is still incapable of moral action: it is necessary to protect him from bodily evils inasmuch as
they can harm the soul; see Aquinas, *In II Sent.*, d. 11, q. 1, a. 3, ad 3.

58. See Aquinas, *In ad Ph*, c. 4, lect. 1 (no. 158), *Lectura super epistolas s. Pauli*, edited by Raphaelis Cai, 2 vols. (Turin: Marietti, 1953): "That your prayers may be known to
those who are in the presence of God, in other words, to the angels by whose ministry
they are brought to God, not that he is unaware of them, but because they intercede for
us. 'The smoke of the incense rose with the prayers of the saints from the hand of the
angel before God' (Rv 8:4)" (Vel "innotescant" his qui sunt apud Deum, id est angelis,
per quorum ministerium deferuntur Deo, non quasi ignoranti, sed quia intercedunt pro
nobis. Apoc. VIII, 4: "ascendit fumus incensorum de orationibus sanctorum de manu
angeli coram Deo," et cetera).

59. See *ST* I, q. 113, a. 7; *Resp. de 36 articulis*, art. 29–30, in *Opuscula*, Leonine edition,
42:344–45. See also Keck, *Angels and Angelology in the Middle Ages*, 105–9.

60. See chapter 8 of this volume.

is effected or permitted by divine justice. Therefore simply speaking, nothing occurs in the world against the will of the blessed."[61] That said, St. Thomas distinguishes the antecedent will of an angel—the angel per se wants the salvation of his protégé—and his consequent will, the only real will, by which he actually wills what God wills or permits.[62] An angel therefore cannot help rejoicing that God's will is accomplished in all things: joy over the conversion of a sinner who repents, but also joy over the justice manifested in the punishment of a sinner.

The last article of question 113 attempts an exegesis of the angelic battles mentioned in Daniel 10:13: "The prince [i.e., principality] of the kingdom of Persia," the angel Gabriel declares, "withstood me twenty-one days; but Michael, one of the chief princes, came to help me." That angel was not necessarily a wicked angel. According to St. Gregory, it was a good angel set by God over the interests of Persia.[63] In fact, these disagreements among the good angels, who emphasize the real merits of their respective protégés and accuse their adversaries (not without cause), testify that conflicts are inevitable, even among the good. As long as one is dealing with multiplicity and diversity, one cannot resolve oppositions between different orders of things (between the interests of two nations, for example). In the final analysis they are resolved only in the full manifestation of the secret plan of divine providence. Hence all our philosophies or even our theologies of history remain partial and inadequate. Certainly, we must do what appears to us in conscience to be in conformity with God's stated will, yet while adhering even more deeply to the will of his good pleasure, which is impossible to deduce a priori and is manifested only in the outcome. In short, the meaning of history largely escapes us, as does the very mystery of God. If for no other reason than that, the study of controversies about angels is not uninteresting.

---

61. *ST* I, q. 113, a. 7: "Nihil autem accidit in mundo quod sit contrarium voluntati angelorum et aliorum beatorum, quia voluntas eorum totaliter inhaeret ordini divinae iustitiae; nihil autem fit in mundo, nisi quod per divinam iustitiam fit aut permittitur. Et ideo, simpliciter loquendo, nihil fit in mundo contra voluntatem beatorum."

62. On the distinction between antecedent will and consequent will, see *ST* I, q. 19, a. 6, ad 1; *Q. de ver.*, q. 23, a. 2.

63. See Gregory the Great, *Morals on The Book of Job* XVII.17 (2:290–92).

THE CULT OF THE ANGELS

The doctrine that angels intervene, through charity, on behalf of men, leads the Christian people, who are not ungrateful, to render them homage on the practical level.[64] The matter is not self-evident, however. Indeed, the New Testament testifies to a certain distrust with regard to the "worship of angels."[65] Does it not conceal a disguised polytheism? Does it not threaten to weaken faith in the uniqueness of Jesus Christ's mediation? Or even to promote the sterile speculations of the Gnostics? ... Anxious to subordinate the angels to Christ, the author of the Letter to the Hebrews forcefully insists on the ministerial role that has fallen to their lot. The angel in Revelation humbly reminds the seer that he himself is only a servant: "When I heard and saw [these visions], I fell down to worship at the feet of the angel who showed them to me; but he said to me, 'You must not do that! I am a fellow servant with you and your brethren the prophets, and with those who keep the words of this book. Worship God.'"[66]

The fathers persisted in this cautious attitude,[67] and, in the fourth century, canon 35 of the Council of Laodicea condemns even devotion to the angels: "Christians must not ... invoke angels and gather assemblies [synaxes], which things are forbidden. If, therefore, any one shall

64. On the general history of devotion to the angels, see Joseph Duhr, "Anges," in DS, 1:598–626.

65. See Col 2:18; Rv 22:9; compare Marcel Simon, "Remarques sur l'angelolâtrie juive au début de l'ère chrétienne," in Le christianisme antique et son contexte religieux (Tübingen: Mohr, 1981), 2:450–64. However, Aletti thinks the worship of the angels denounced in Col 2:18 is not worship rendered to the angels, a perspective that is foreign to Judaism, but rather the worship that the angels render to God, of which some visionaries claimed to be witnesses; see Aletti, Saint Paul, 196–97; Aletti, "Colossiens: Un tournant dans la christologie néotestamentaire: Problèmes et propositions," Liber annuus, Studium biblicum franciscanum 49 (1999): 211–36 (esp. 218ff.).

66. Rv 22:8–9. See also Rv 19:10; Loren T. Stuckenbruck, "An Angelic Refusal of Worship: The Tradition and Its Function in the Apocalypse of John," Society of Biblical Literature Seminar Papers (1994): 679–96; Stuckenbruck, Angel Veneration and Christology: A Study in Early Judaism and in the Christology of the Apocalypse of John, Wissenschaftliche Untersuchungen zum Neuen Testament 2, 70 (Tübingen: Mohr, 1995).

67. See Bareille, "Le culte des anges à l'époque des Pères de l'Église," RT 8 (1900): 41–49. Bareille knew how to respond to the article of the modernist Joseph Turmel, "Histoire de l'angélologie des temps apostoliques à la fin du Vᵉ siècle," Revue d'histoire et de littérature religieuses 3 (1898): 407–34, who maintained peremptorily that "during the first five centuries, the Doctors condemned any cult of the Angels."

be found engaged in this covert idolatry, let him be anathema; for he
has forsaken our Lord Jesus Christ, the Son of God, and has gone over
to idolatry."[68] This severity is explained by the syncretist nature of the
cult of the angels as it must have been practiced and by the general
context of paganism that was still a threat. However, the fathers do not
refuse to honor the angels or even to pray to them.[69] In order to resolve the ambiguity, it was necessary to arrive at a clear qualitative distinction between the cult reserved to God and the one that can be rendered to the angels. This was accomplished, it seems, in the writings of
Eusebius of Caesarea, in the early fourth century: "[Among the incorporeal powers], some are sent by the will of the Father to men through
a salutary arrangement; we have learned to know and to venerate them
… while reserving to God alone, who is king of the universe, the homage of our adoration (tên sebasmion timên)."[70] Along the same lines,
St. Augustine would explain that it is necessary to honor the angels but
to reserve strictly to God the cult of latria (servitus).[71] Because they desire our happiness, the angels themselves incite us to render with them
this cult to God alone.[72] That said, the borderline between cultic acts

68. Council of Laodicea, canon 35, cited in Emile Amman, "Laodicée (concile de),"
in DTC, 8:2613.

69. See Ambrose, Concerning Widows, in NPNF, 2nd series, 10: 400: "The angels
must be entreated for us, who have been given to us as guards" (Obsecrandi sunt angeli pro nobis, qui nobis ad praesidium dati sunt; De viduis 9:55 [PL 16, col. 251]). Origen
was more reserved on this point; see Contra celsum V.4–5, 266–67): in order to gain the
angels' favor, we should not pray to them but imitate them.

70. Eusebius of Caesarea, Demonstratio Evangelii [Demonstration of the Gospel]
III.3 (PG 22:193–94).

71. Book X of The City of God is largely dedicated to the necessity of opposing paganism by reserving for God a unique cult, in particular the offering of sacrifice; see also
Augustine, The True Religion 55.110 (WSA I/8:102): "We honor them with charity, but
not with servility" (Honoramus eos caritate non servitute).

72. See Augustine, City of God X.7 (FOTC 14:128): "The immortal and blessed spirits who are deservedly established in heavenly abodes and rejoice in communion with
their Creator are rooted in His eternity, certain in His truth, and sanctified by His grace.
In their compassion they love us unhappy mortals and long for us to become both immortal and happy, and, therefore, they do not wish us to offer sacrifice to them but to
God, knowing as they do that, along with us, they are His sacrifice" (Merito illi in caelestibus sedibus constituti immortales et beati, qui Creatoris sui participatione congau-
dent, cuius aeternitate firmi, cuius veritate certi, cuius munere sancti sunt, quoniam nos
mortales et miseros, ut immortales beatique simus, misericorditer diligunt, nolunt nos
sibi sacrificari, sed ei, cuius et ipsi nobiscum sacrificium se esse noverunt). Moreover,
according to St. Augustine, demons can be distinguished from angels insofar as they

reserved to God and those that result from simple veneration is some-times uncertain. The offering of sacrifice certainly pertains to latria—therefore no sacrifices are offered to the angels[73]—but St. Augustine also thought, wrongly, that building churches in honor of the angels was a blameworthy act.[74]

The fact remains that in the East, from the fourth century on, the cult of St. Michael the Archangel was full-fledged.[75] At that time the Copts celebrated no less than seven feasts each year in his honor. This cult had miscellaneous origins, since Michael was a substitute for Christ among the Judaeo-Christians; subsequently, his cult also managed to salvage several rituals that were celebrated in honor of pagan divinities. Be that as it may, the cult of St. Michael traveled from the East to the West, where it experienced a meteoric rise in sixth-century Italy, particularly with the famous shrine of Monte Gargano near Puglia.[76] In the early eighth century, a shrine in Normandy marked the beginning of a promising cult on Mont St.-Michel.

Devotion to the holy angels developed especially in the Benedictine Order, since a monk by definition was dedicated to an angelic life. It is no surprise that the great doctor of devotion to the angels, especially to the guardian angels, should be St. Bernard of Clairvaux; the church selected a passage from his works for the Office of Readings on the Feast of the Holy Guardian Angels. In his *Sermon XII*, a commentary on verse 12 of Psalm 91[90], St. Bernard thanks God for

claim sacrifices as their own instead of directing them to God; see ibid., X.16 (FOTC 14:144–45).

73. See Augustine, *City of God* X.4 (FOTC 14:122); XIX.23.4 (FOTC 24:241): "The God of the Hebrew Prophets forbade sacrifices even to those holy angels of heaven and heavenly powers whom we in this pilgrimage of mortal life reverence and love as our blessed fellow countrymen" (Sed Deus ille, quem coluerunt sapientes Hebraeorum, etiam caelestibus sanctis angelis et virtutibus Dei, quos beatissimos tamquam cives in hac nostra peregrinatione mortali veneramur et amamus, sacrificari vetat). See also *ST* II-II, q. 85, a. 2.

74. See Augustine, *True Religion* 55.110 (WSA I/8:102): "Nor do we set up temples for them, for they do not wish to be honored by us in that way" (Nec eis templa construimus: nolunt enim se sic honorari a nobis).

75. See J. Daoust, "Michel," in *Catholicisme* 9 (1982): 88–93.

76. The origin of the feast on September 29 was probably the dedication of a basilica to St. Michael on the *via Salaria* in Rome. With the liturgical reform of Vatican II, the two feasts of St. Michael (May 8 and September 29) and the feasts of the holy Archangels Raphael (October 24) and Gabriel (March 24) were combined into one.

his care for us: "And lest there should be any one at all in the kingdom of heaven unoccupied in the care of us, Thou hast appointed the blessed angels to minister for us, Thou hast charged them with our keeping, and ordered them to act as our guides."[77] From this he draws several practical conclusions about the attitude that we should have toward the angels: "'He hath given His angels charge over thee: to keep thee in all thy ways.' O my brother, with how much reverence (*reverentia*), with how much gratitude (*devotio*) with how much confidence (*fiducia*) ought not these words to inspire thee! With how much reverence for a presence so august! With how much gratitude for benevolence so great! With how much confidence in a keeping so secure!"[78] And further on: "Nevertheless, although it is God who 'hath given His angels charge over thee,' we must also show ourselves grateful to these celestial spirits.... Let us therefore make a return of gratitude, yea, and of affection to such glorious guardians; let us give them love for love, let us honour them as much as we are bound to, as much as we can."[79]

Despite the reservations of Protestants (or perhaps because of them),[80] devotion to the guardian angels flourished considerably in the sixteenth century. The Jesuits in particular, with the methodical, systematic spirit for which they are known, promoted this devotion, which is inseparable from an accentuation of the individualistic side of the Christian life. In 1575 St. Francis Borgia composed a *Treatise*

77. Bernard of Clairvaux, "Sermon 12 on Psalm XC," in *St. Bernard's Sermons for the Seasons*, 1:250; *Sermo 12 in psalmum Qui habitat* 3 (*S. Bernardi opera* IV, Sermones I, 459): "Et ne quid in caelestibus vacet ab opere sollicitudinis nostrae, beatos illos spiritus propter nos mittis in ministerium, custodiae nostrae deputas, nostros jubes fieri paedagogos."

78. Ibid., 6, 252–53: "Angelis suis mandavit de te, ut custodiant te in omnibus viis tuis. Quantam tibi debet hoc verbum inferre reverentiam, affere devotionem, conferre fiduciam. Reverentia pro praesentia, devotionem pro benevolentia, fiduciam pro custodia."

79. Ibid., 7, 254: "Verumtamen etsi ille mandavit, ipsis quoque, qui et ei ex tanta caritate oboediunt et nobis subveniunt in tanta necessitate, ingratos esse non licet. Simus ergo devoti, simus grati tantis custodibus; redamemus eos; honoremus eos quantum possumus, quantum debemus."

80. Petau devotes two chapters of his *De angelis* (II.9–10 [44–55]) to a refutation of the accusations of idolatry leveled at the Catholic cult of the angels by Protestants, in this case by Gérard-Jean Voss (d. 1649), in his *De theologia gentili et physiologia christiana sive De origine ac progressu idololatriae* (Amsterdam: 1641).

and Practice of Devotion to the Holy Angels. The liturgy confirms this infatuation. In the early sixteenth century, the feast of the guardian angels became detached from the feast of St. Michael. In 1518, by the Bull *Admonet nos,* Leo X granted the liturgical feast of the guardian angels to Blessed François d'Estaing, bishop of Rodez. In 1670, the feast was extended by Pope Clement X to the whole church and was definitively appointed on October 2.

Certainly, when there is inadequate catechesis, devotion to one's guardian angel can take childish forms, but soberly and in its place, it has the merit of fostering a very lively sense of the concrete and at the same time universal character of Divine Providence, and also of the communion of saints.

14

The Enemy's Attacks

In the treatise on the divine government in the *Summa theologiae*, the study of the holy angels' luminous activity in the service of the benevolent designs of divine providence with regard to mankind (I, qq. 110–13) is immediately followed by a question about the "attack (*impugnatio*) of the demons" (I, q. 114), in other words, about the nefarious activity that the demons deploy against human beings.[1] From the very place that this question occupies in the structure of the *Summa theologiae*, it is clear that, whatever the subjective intentions of the demons may be, demonic activity is integrated, like that of the angels (albeit according to different modalities), into the providential governance of the world. "In everything God works for good" (Rom 8:28) and to his greater glory, including the wickedness of the demons. This absolute sovereignty of God is the essential theological teaching in this question. But before examining how the activity of the demons is integrated into the divine plan in spite of them, we must first consider the internal structuring of the demonic world, which to a great extent has as its purpose the maleficent work that welds the demons together, then study the very existence, the nature, and the major laws of this permanent war that the demons wage against mankind and, final-

1. For a balanced theological synthesis concerning the question of demonic activity, see Seemann and Zähringen, "Les démons et le mal dans le monde," in *Mysterium salutis*, 8:217–30.

ly, situate this combat within the concrete theological context of salvation history and its fulfillment in Christ.

THE ORGANIZATION OF THE CITY OF EVIL

"His back is made of rows of shields, shut up closely as with a seal" (Jb 41:15 RSVC); so the Bible describes the scales that cover the body of Leviathan. St. Gregory applies this to the society of the demons.[2] The demonic world therefore is not sheer chaos. It exhibits a certain form of unity and social cohesion. Two major principles guide the reflection of St. Thomas on this theme of the organization of the demonic world. The first is that sin did not destroy the nature of the rebellious angels. Although their will is definitively perverse and rejects per se any openness to communion with others, the being that they have from God remains good. Now, to say goodness is to say order. The idea of a chaos or an absolute anarchy is as contradictory as the notion of an absolute evil. Just as evil is a parasite of the good, anarchy is a parasite of order. If anarchy were to triumph, it would immediately self-destruct. Among the demons, therefore, a certain order remains that continues, at the very heart of their chaos, to give testimony to the divine wisdom and goodness. So it is that, for St. Thomas, the demonic world remains structured according to the different angelic orders from which the demons originate. This organization is in fact initially a fact of nature, even though it attains its perfection in the full sense only in the order of grace, from which the demons have irremediably fallen.[3]

Likewise it must be admitted that by virtue of their unequal angelic nature some demons exercise authority over others: there are superiors (*praelati*) among them.[4] Contrary to any sort of political Augustinianism, the existence of a social authority is in fact a given that

2. See Gregory the Great, *Morals on The Book of Job* XXXIII.31 (3/2:585–86); Aquinas, *In II Sent.*, d. 6, q. 1, a. 4, sed contra.

3. *ST* I, q. 109, a. 1. St. Thomas can thus account for the negative use of the term *Principalities and Powers* in the writings of St. Paul; see *In ad Ep*, c. 6, lect. 3 (no. 357), where Aquinas explains why only the names *Powers* and *Principalities* are adopted to designate the demons (see also *ST* I, q. 109, a. 1, ad 3).

4. See *ST* I, q. 109, a. 2. The position was already expressed by Peter Lombard, *Sententiae* II, d. 6, c. 4 (25–26).

results from the very nature of creatures.⁵ The highest superior is the one who was already the first of the angels by nature. Satan hoisted the standard of the revolt against God, and his sin was the exemplary cause of the sin of the other angels. Consequently, "the devil … became the leader of all [who were destined] to ruin."⁶ This "headship" of Satan with respect to the demons is not based on any ontological filiation but on a purely moral causality.⁷ This is the very restricted perspective from which St. Augustine, followed by St. Thomas, develops a certain asymmetrical parallelism between Jesus Christ and the church, on the one hand, and Satan and the City of Evil, on the other. The City of Evil constitutes as it were a *corpus diaboli* opposed to the body of Christ.⁸

However—and this is the second principle—this subjection to the natural head is subjectively accepted by each demon not through political friendship (since the demons detest one another), but with the perverse intention of acquiring through their complicity a greater effectiveness in their work of destruction. In short, it is a confederation welded together by a common hatred of God and men.⁹

5. St. Thomas refuses to see in the existence of an authority a consequence of sin alone; see *ST* I, q. 96, a. 4.

6. Origen, *Homilies on Exodus*, Homily 8.2 (FOTC 71:319).

7. Concerning the expression "sons of the evil one" in the parable of the weeds (Mt 13:38), St. Irenaeus carefully distinguishes filiation according to nature and free filiation according to deeds; see Irenaeus of Lyons, *Against Heresies* IV.40.3–41.2 (ANF 1:524b): Jesus "ascribed all who are of the apostasy to him who is the ringleader of this transgression. But He made neither angels nor men so by nature. For we do not find that the devil created anything whatsoever, since indeed he is himself a creature of God, like the other angels. For God made all things."

8. See Augustine, *La Genèse au sens littéral* VIII–XII, note complémentaire 46, "La chute du diable, §3 ('Corpus diaboli')" (BA 49:551–52). In *ST* III, q. 8, a. 7, St. Thomas accounts for this idea of a *corpus diaboli* by insisting on the fundamental difference between Satan's headship with regard to the wicked and Christ's headship: Christ exercises his office of Head both by an interior influx of grace and by external governance. The devil, for his part, obviously cannot exercise any direct power over the interior of creatures, but directs them from outside, through temptation, toward the wicked end that he himself pursues. Only by dint of this activity can he be called *caput malorum*. In *ST* I, q. 114, a. 3, ad 2, St. Thomas admits that men can become "sons of the devil," even without the latter exercising causality over them through temptation, but rather through sheer imitation. Aping the mystery of the Incarnation, the devil communicates something of his headship to the Antichrist; see *ST* III, q. 8, a. 8.

9. The Arg. 1 of *ST* I, q. 109, a. 2 emphasizes that the subjection of one demon to another is a chastisement and that the higher angels (who sinned more) ought to be

The communication of information within this diabolical society can in no way claim the status of enlightenment.[10] Of course, one demon can manifest to another demon a particular truth that he himself knows and that the other does not know. Nevertheless, the intention guiding that act of informing is always perverse; its purpose comes from the wicked designs of the demon, who seeks to turn others away from God, whereas enlightenment is a communication of truth that aims to direct its beneficiary toward God.

It is a cruel irony that the diabolical society, which dreams of setting itself up as an absolutely independent anti-reality, cannot even be self-sufficient. Not only does it depend on God, who preserves it in being and utilizes the perverse organization of the demonic City for its own benevolent purposes, but it also depends, under God, on the good angels.[11] The latter command the demons and communicate to them the supernatural knowledge necessary for the role that God entrusts to them—"as in *human* affairs the judge's assessors make *known* his sentence to the executioners."[12]

These few remarks about the demonic world as a society of intelligent, wicked beings are not without interest for political philosophy. Indeed, demonic society provides a theoretical model by which to speculate about the (not always theoretical) possibility of a society that rejects or decides to abstract from any reference to the objective moral good and limits its ambition to ensuring the more or less peaceful coexistence of individuals, who incidentally are often considered to be thoroughly bad and guided solely by self-interest. Now reflection on the demonic city confirms our contemporary experience: such a society is viable! It survives precariously by dint of a certain unjust, amoral equilibrium that is established among the various subjective interests. It survives above all—and more profound-

---

punished more and therefore subjected to their inferiors. But St. Thomas subtly replies that the worst chastisement is to be able to do more evil, which is made possible for the higher demons through the subordination of the lower ones.

10. See *ST* I, q. 109, a. 3.

11. See *ST* I, q. 109, a. 4.

12. *ST* I, q. 109, ad 1: "sicut in rebus humanis assessores iudicis revelant tortoribus eius sententiam." A refinement of this punishment, imagined by pious theologians: the demons fallen from the higher angelic orders are subjected to the government of the blessed angels who belong by nature to lower orders and act upon the demons in the service of God's glory; see *ST* I, q. 109, ad 2.

ly—because the natural tendencies that urge every being toward objective good remain active, even though they are consciously denied and opposed.

EXISTENCE AND NATURE OF
DEMONIC ATTACKS

This society of demons is united in the will of each one to harm human beings. A traditional iconographic theme depicts men climbing a ladder so as to go to Heaven. Flying and fluttering all around that ladder are devils who claw at the men to make them fall.[13] This is a naïve but eloquent expression of Christian experience and of the church's constant teaching about the very reality of the nefarious activity of the demons in the spiritual life of men.[14] As we have seen, this way of understanding life as a personal confrontation between the Christian, on the one side, supported by Christ and his angels, and the demons, on the other side, has its immediate source in scripture.[15] It flourishes in the spirituality of the church fathers, especially of the desert fathers and of the monastic tradition that they founded.[16] To withdraw to the desert following Jesus Christ is to pursue the devil to his inmost strongholds, and he will do anything to thwart the monk's spiritual progress: "Now these demons, if they see all Christians and especially monks joyfully laboring and making progress, first attack by attempting to place stumbling blocks in their way. Their 'stumbling blocks' are filthy thoughts."[17]

One of the foremost sources, after the Bible, of this view of Christian life as a struggle is the doctrine of the two ways or the two spirits:

---

13. See Giorgi, *Anges et démons*, 141.

14. Besides *CCC* 394–95, see the General Audience of John Paul II dated August 13, 1986, on "The wicked angels," in *DC*, 894–96.

15. See 1 Pt 5:8; 1 Cor 16:13; Eph 6:11.

16. See the substantial article "Démon" in *DS*, 3:141–238, which, while discussing questions that are strictly speaking dogmatic, concentrates on the theme of spiritual combat. Daniélou wrote "Démon," 3:152–89, and A. Guillaumont and C. Guillaumont compiled "Dans la plus ancienne littérature monastique," in *DS*, 189–212; see also Bouyer, *La Vie de saint Antoine: Essai sur la spiritualité du monachisme primitif*, 69–98 and 132–52; Grün, *Aux prises avec le mal*; José M. Blázquez, *Intelectuales, ascetas y demonios al final de la Antigüedad* (Madrid: Cátedra, 1998).

17. Athanasius of Alexandria, *Life of St. Antony* 23 (111).

a spirit of truth and a spirit of error, a good angel and a wicked angel, urge every human being.[18] A passage by St. Gregory of Nyssa summarizes this doctrine well:

There is a doctrine (which derives its trustworthiness from the tradition of the Fathers) which says that after our nature fell into sin God did not ... withhold his providence. No, on the one hand, he appointed an angel with an incorporeal nature to help in the life of each person, and, on the other hand, he also appointed the corruptor who, by an evil and maleficent demon, afflicts the life of man and contrives against our nature. Because man finds himself between these two who have contrary purposes for him, it is in his power to make the one prevail over the other.[19]

This doctrine of the two spirits is found already in the Qumram documents,[20] as well as in several intertestamental writings such as the *Testament of the Twelve Patriarchs*.[21] It made its way into the Hellenic world, where it combined with a rather common belief,[22] and thus it led some fathers (down to Hergé!)[23] to postulate the existence of a wicked angel at the side of every human being. The first Christian document to develop this teaching is *The Shepherd* of Hermas, who relates it to the practice of the discernment of spirits:

"There are two angels with a man—one of righteousness, and the other of iniquity." And I said to him, "How, sir, am I to know the powers of these, for both angels dwell with me?" "Hear," said he, "and understand them. The angel of righteousness is gentle and modest, meek and peaceful. When, therefore, he ascends into your heart, immediately he talks to you of righteousness, purity, chastity, contentment, and of every righteous deed and glorious virtue.... Look now at the works of the angel of iniquity. First, he is wrathful, and bitter, and foolish.... When, then, he ascends into your heart, know him by his works."[24]

---

18. See Daniélou, "Les deux Esprits," in "Démon," *DS*, 3:160–68.

19. Gregory of Nyssa, *Life of Moses*, 45–46, 64.

20. *Rule of the Community* III.18–IV.26, in Charlesworth et al, *Dead Sea Scrolls*, 56–67.

21. *Testament of Judah* 20 (*Apocryphal Old Testament*, 547–48), and *Testament of Asher* 1 (577–78).

22. See P. Boyancé, "Les deux démons personnels dans l'Antiquité grecque et latine," *Revue de Philologie* 41 (1935): 189–202.

23. Pen-name of Georges Prosper Rémi (1907–83), Belgian cartoonist and creator of Tintin; for the reference, see the story *Tintin au Tibet*.

24. Hermas, *The Shepherd*, Commandment 6, chap. 2 (ANF 2:24a).

Hermas is followed by Origen,[25] who incidentally refers to him explicitly, and then by many other authors, down to Francisco Suarez, who considers this doctrine of the two angels to be probable.[26]

Along similar lines, the monastic tradition set in sharp relief the idea that devils, the "demons of the vices," are specialists in certain sins. This theme is rooted both in the soil of Qumram and in Stoic philosophical speculations. It was systematized in the fourth century by Evagrius of Pontus.[27] But already Origen wrote, "For almost every human there are several spirits stirring up diverse kinds of sins in them. For example, there is one spirit of fornication, and there is another of wrath; there is a spirit of avarice, but another of arrogance."[28]

Given this very rich spiritual tradition, the theologian's focus is situated midway between, on the one hand, the very general consideration of the activity of the pure spirits upon the world and upon mankind, and, on the other hand, the examination in unlimited detail of the demonic tactics and ways to thwart them, which comes instead from the practice of spiritual discernment.[29]

Generally speaking, the characteristic way in which a demon acts upon human beings is temptation, as attested by key passages in scripture such as the narrative of the fall of our first parents or the account of the temptation of Jesus in the desert.[30] In article 2 of question 114, St. Thomas sketches a brief phenomenology of temptation. To tempt, in the proper sense, means to examine and to put to the test. The proximate purpose of temptation is knowledge. To run tests is not per se morally bad. Indeed, the morality of a test depends on

25. Origen, *Homilies on Luke*, Homily 35.3 (FOTC 94:143); see also Daniélou, "Le combat spirituel chez Origène," in "Démon," *DS*, 3:182–89.

26. See Suarez, *Tractatus De Angelis*, chap. 21, nos. 30–32, 8:1097–98.

27. See Evagrius Ponticus, *The Praktikos*, trans. John Eudes Bamberger (Spencer, Mass.: Cistercian Publications, 1970); Jean-Charles Nault, chap. 1, "Evagre le Pontique et les huit mauvaises pensées," in *La saveur de Dieu: L'acédie dans le dynamisme de l'agir*, Studi e Ricerche (Rome: Lateran University Press, 2002).

28. Origen, *Homilies on Joshua*, Homily 15.5, trans. Barbara J. Bruce (FOTC 105:147); see also *Homilies on Numbers*, Homily 20.3.4 (ACT, 127b–28a).

29. Besides the works of spiritual theology that discuss the question, the reader will find interesting the spiritual work of C. S. Lewis, *The Screwtape Letters* (New York: Macmillan, 1952).

30. See *ST* I, q. 114, a. 2; see also *ST* I-II, q. 80: "The cause of sin, as regards the devil" (*"De causa peccati ex parte diaboli"*); Tommaso Carlesi, "La tentazione nel pensiero di s. Tommaso d'Aquino," *Sapienza* 10 (1957): 23–51, 200–25, 461–80.

the ultimate end that is proposed, provided however that the act by which one seeks to obtain the knowledge is not itself intrinsically bad, as would be, for example, the violation of a secret or recourse to torture in order to extort information.

Man tempts or tests in order to know. A zoologist, for example, puts an animal in unprecedented situations so as to understand better the behavior of its species. Man tests his neighbor in this way. He can do this for a morally good purpose, as, for example, when a physician examines his patient in order to diagnose an illness or when a professor makes a student pass an examination so as to verify that he has the qualifications required for a particular degree. But he can also do it for an evil purpose when he seeks to know someone's weak points so as to conquer him or to draw him more readily into evil. In that case, he acts as an instrument of the Tempter. It is always evil when God is put to the test, because that is in itself a sign of incredulity: "Thou shalt not tempt the Lord thy God."[31]

Scripture also says that God tempts man or puts him to the test, but, according to St. Thomas, this is a very improper manner of speaking, since God knows perfectly well what is in the heart of man. Indeed, when scripture says that God tests his people or a certain individual, it means that he instructs them. He acts in such a way that they themselves discover what they are in reality in their hearts. "The LORD your God is testing you, to know whether you love the LORD your God with all your heart and with all your soul" (Dt 13:3). This testing aimed at self-knowledge is a great good for man inasmuch as it permits him to dispel several illusions concerning himself that are so deleterious to his spiritual progress.[32]

Diabolical temptation is always evil by reason of its intention. The devil tempts only so as to lead more effectively into sin.[33]

31. See ST II-II, q. 97: "Tempting God" ("De tentatione Dei").
32. The world and the flesh tempt in a purely material way: man's attitude, when faced with the random events of his situation in the world and the solicitations of the flesh, does indeed reveal his deep-seated moral dispositions. But this temptation can be exploited by other "tempters" (a man, a demon).
33. Diabolical temptation nevertheless still has a certain noetic or theoretical dimension. Since the demons do not know the secrets of the heart, the interior dispositions of souls, their weak points and their strong points, they seek to know the angle from which a particular person is most susceptible to sin; see ST I, q. 114, a. 2, ad 2.

But what, more precisely, are the process and the modalities of this tempting?[34] The novelist Bernanos gave a fine description of it that has the advantage of noting its limits:

> As subtle as the enemy may be, his most ingenious malice can affect the soul only by way of a detour, just as one overcomes a city by poisoning its wells. He deceives the judgment, sullies the imagination, stirs up the flesh and the blood, makes use of our own contradictions with an infinite skill, leads our joys astray, deepens our sorrows, falsifies our acts and intentions in their secret relations, but when he has thus upset everything, he still has destroyed nothing. He must extract the ultimate consent from us, and he will not have it at all without God speaking in His turn.[35]

Above all, it is necessary to maintain firmly that the demon cannot act directly on man's spiritual powers—his intelligence and his free will. These form, so to speak, an inviolable sanctuary to which no creature has access. God alone, because he is its creator, can incline human freedom from within toward the good, but the demon can in no way cause sin, which would no longer be sin anyway if it were forced. On the other hand, the demon can act indirectly on man's spiritual powers by obsessing them—that is, literally, by laying siege to them. To do this he deploys the natural powers belonging to a pure spirit: by acting on the local movement of corporeal realities and cleverly exploiting by this subterfuge the resources of a physical nature of which he is not the source, the demon can, like an artisan, induce certain qualitative effects in the corporeal universe and the psychological extensions thereof. By this method he bears down on the conditions of the spiritual life. These are of two types. There is, on the one hand, the psychosomatic conditioning of an individual's spiritual activity, and then there is, on the other hand, communal, historical, and cultural conditioning.

At the individual level, the demon works to make apparent goods gleam. Iago, a master of this art, saw this quite clearly: "Divinity [i.e., theology] of hell! / When devils will the blackest sins put on, / They

---

34. See chapter 4 of this volume on the action of pure spirits in the realm of human affairs. As we indicated, this demonic action cannot ordinarily be discerned at the purely rational level since the flesh (in other words, the disordered passions) and the world are to a great extent sufficient to tempt human weakness. It can be ascertained only within the framework of a faith-based interpretation of events.

35. Bernanos, *L'Imposture* (Paris: 1927), 104–5.

do suggest at first with heavenly shows."[36] The demon presents morally bad objects to man's mind at an angle designed to make them appear, sometimes almost irresistibly, as a certain good. In this way, he solicits man to place a disordered act freely. In order to do this, he can act directly on the external objects that are presented to our senses,[37] or even on the senses themselves.[38] But his action is exerted above all on the turntable that is the imagination, at the intersection of the spiritual world and the psychosomatic world. Not that the demon produces out of whole cloth any imaginative *species*—he is incapable of that. But he does toy with the physiological conditioning of the imagination and provokes combinations of images and, by that subterfuge, associations of ideas. He can thus draw my attention to one action or another that would not have come to mind spontaneously. Or else, by exciting one or another sensible passion—desire, an-

36. William Shakespeare, *Othello*, Act II, vv. 350–52, ed., introduction Harold Bloom (New York: 1987).

37. The demon can either present to our senses objects that are ordinary in appearance but artificially produced by him or else produce false miracles aimed at leading into error. They are false because these works, extraordinary as they may seem to us, do not really transcend the power of nature: they result from the intelligent use of nature's hidden powers, somewhat as the telephone at one time could appear to be a miracle to primitive populations. Thus the devil can accomplish, if not true miracles, at least prodigies that produce astonishment in human beings and tested the sagacity of the medieval theologians. See *ST* I, q. 114, a. 4: "Whether demons can lead men astray by means of real miracles" (Utrum daemones possunt homines seducere per aliqua miracula vera); *In Ioan.*, c. 10, lect. 5 (no. 1431). The question of demonic "miracles," of which the prodigies performed by Pharaoh's magicians (see Ex 7–9) or those expected of the Antichrist (2 Thes 2:9–10) are the archetype, is discussed at length by St. Augustine: *City of God* XX.19.4 (FOTC 24:297–301); XXI.6.1 (FOTC 24:352–55).

The Christian view of the world of magic and the occult is informed by these principles. Occult phenomena (anything having to do with parapsychology) may possibly, in the rarest of cases in which they are not purely and simply trickery, employ natural forces that are not yet understood. They can also involve powers of a demonic order. Thus the church staunchly condemns divination (see *ST* II-II, q. 95), in other words, the undue search for some knowledge of the future, on the one hand because it is the sign of a lack of trust in providence, and on the other hand because it can bring into play demonic power, which can conjecture the future more precisely than man. It also condemns "all practices of *magic* or *sorcery*, by which one attempts to tame occult powers, so as to place them at one's service and have a supernatural power over others" (*CCC*, 2117). See also *ST* II-II, q. 96, and Ignatius Mennessier, "Le rôle providentiel des démons," in Saint Thomas d'Aquin, *Somme théologique: La Religion*, 2a–2ae, questions 88–100, Éditions de la Revue des jeunes (Paris: Desclée 1934), 2:451–60.

38. See Faes de Mottoni and Suarez-Nani, "I demoni e l'illusione," 77–94.

ger—that colors the object, he warps my concrete practical judgment as to good and evil. This temptation in no way abolishes the subject's moral responsibility, even though its violence can sometimes attenuate it.[39]

Demonic activity is also exerted, well in advance of personal choices, on the cosmic, social, and cultural conditions affecting the spiritual life. Indeed, the devil knows how to gain the maximum return on the personal sin of a human being. "While we men supply the occasions and beginnings of our sins, the hostile powers spread them far and wide and if possible endlessly."[40] The devil excels in scheming and conspiring—in other words, in organizing intelligently and systematically, with a view to a definite end—the consequences of men's personal sins. He works to make the partial evils that originate in our weakness converge on the greatest possible evil. (Thus the devil apes God's providence, which makes all things contribute to the good of those who love him.) This devastating activity is exercised in the personal history of the sinner, who is trapped in the snare of his own faults, but it acquires particular virulence in the social and cultural order, in which the demon works to set up structures of sin that socially objectify evil and are fearfully effective in keeping man in a state of opposition to God.[41] This theme of structures of sin as instruments of satanic domination over men adopts and updates the teaching of St. Paul about the Principalities and Powers, while shifting the accent from the cosmic realm to the cultural realm.

In the nineteenth century, French Catholics, disconcerted by the barrage of advancing secularism, liked to identify this satanic conspiracy with the presumed revolutionary and Masonic conspiracy that was destined to overturn the church by setting up a godless society.[42] Of course, this sort of explanation in purely supernatural terms too

---

39. See *ST* I-II, q. 73, a. 6, ad 2.

40. Origen, *On First Principles* III.2.2 (1966), 214. See also Hedwige Louis-Chevrillon, *Le Prince du mensonge* (Paris: Éditions Saint-Paul, 1970), 29: "In evil, the weakness is the human element, but the power is diabolical."

41. See *CCC* 1869: "'Structures of sin' are the expression and effect of personal sins. They lead their victims to do evil in their turn."

42. See, for example, Jacqueline Lalouette, "Le combat des archanges (Saint Michel et Satan dans les luttes politiques et religieuses de la France contemporaine)," in *Le Diable*, Cahiers de l'Hermétisme (Paris: Dervy, 1998), 69–85.

often is an excuse not to analyze the immanent causes of historical developments and by that very fact prevents one from reacting appropriately. But it is not illegitimate per se. In every age, Satan is able to stir up the Beasts (Rv 13)—in other words, the social, political, and cultural structures that facilitate his plans. In early Christianity the demons were credited with having invented the snares of magic, astrology, and even women's fashions.... Most importantly, Christian authors—who were not yet won over by the charms of interreligious dialogue!—broadly classified pagan religions as a whole under the category of the demonic.[43] They were convinced that the demonic powers took pleasure making human beings venerate them through the worship of the false pagan gods. This doctrine is omnipresent in *The City of God*, for example.[44] Demons were also regarded as the instigators of the persecutions conducted by pagans against Christians and the fomenters of schisms and heresies in the church. In our days, the concept of the culture of death, as developed for example in the Encyclical *Evangelium vitae*, in connection with the idea of a conspiracy against life that is embodied in the social structures that spring from sin and lead to sin, lends itself easily and legitimately to an interpretation of this type.

Some contemporary theologians insist with good reason on the depersonalizing character of diabolical action. Just as the demon himself, while remaining a person in the strict metaphysical sense, thwarts by his free choice the movement by which a person is led to fulfillment in the moral order of the interpersonal relations of communion in knowledge and love, so too his tempting aims to depersonalize human beings, to close each one in on himself and, in so doing, to dissolve them into an anonymous mass in which they are more susceptible to the influence of the collective structures of sin.

43. See Julien Ries, "Cultes païens et démons dans l'apologétique chrétienne de Justin à Augustin," in Ries and Limet, *Anges et Démons*, 337–52.

44. See Augustine, *City of God* II.24.1 (FOTC 8:117): "As I have so often suggested, and as we know from Sacred Scripture, and as the facts themselves reveal, [the *demons'*] business is to see that they are taken for gods and worshiped accordingly, that such honors be bestowed upon them as will make their worshipers accomplices in an evil cause, most damnable in God's judgment"; II.29.2 (FOTC 8:126): "They are not gods, but fiendish spirits, to whom your eternal happiness is a torment"; IV.1 (FOTC 8:189): "the false gods which pagans then worshiped in the open, and now worship under cover, were unclean spirits, malignant and lying demons."

In order to make himself imperceptible, he [Satan] practices the impersonal mode of operating, to the point of dissolving his personality. He makes himself a mass phenomenon in the sight of men—in other words, he slithers into every situation in which personal psychological awareness [*conscience*] ceases, and personal responsibility with it, in which man is no longer an "I" but a psychological conglomerate. He loves the absence of thought in men and detests it when human beings come to reflect. He loves mutism and hates speech, which is the means par excellence of revealing the person. The imprisonment of man within himself is inherently part of all phenomena of a satanic and demonic character.[45]

Besides temptation, which is the ordinary mode of demonic activity, we may note (without dwelling on them, because they are far from being the most decisive)[46] several more extraordinary manifestations of demonic activity: obsession and possession.[47] "Obsession" refers to an action of the physical order (noises, movements of objects, frightening apparitions, violent attacks, such as we find in the lives of St. Anthony of the Desert and the Curé of Ars) or of a psychological order (fixed ideas, anxieties) that show that the demon is besieging a human being or a community. But the most spectacular form is possession, of which the Gospels give several examples. Certainly, possession can be understood in the broad (but no less terrible) sense in which a person, by his free consent to sin, is alienated from himself and becomes a plaything of Satan. But in the technical sense of the term, "possession" refers to the state of a person whose body or even active sense faculties the demon seizes and masters so as to use them as a passive instrument for the purpose of accomplishing his wicked works. The demon unites himself to the faculties of movement or sensation as the mover to the moved and has his own way with them by dint of his spiritual action upon what is corpore-

---

45. Emil Brunner, *Doctrine chrétienne de la création*, 165.

46. It is interesting to note the development that leads Bernanos from a very external approach in depicting the activity of the demon to a more interiorized approach. Whereas in his early works, such as *Sous le soleil de Satan*, the devil intervenes in person, flesh, and bone, in the plot of the stories, in the later works he is no less terribly present but now acts imperceptibly through the mediation of a "possessed" being who is internally empty, such as Father Cénabre or Monsieur Ouine.

47. See Lucien Roure, "Possession diabolique," in *DTC*, 12:2635–47; François-Xavier Maquart, "L'exorciste devant les manifestations diaboliques," in *Satan*, Études carmélitaines (Paris: Desclée de Brower, 1948), 274–94; Nanni, *Il dito di Dio e il potere di Satana*, which contains a recent bibliography on the subject.

al. For example, he expresses himself through the mouth of the possessed person. It is abundantly clear that the immense majority of presumed cases of diabolical possession can be explained by more or less subtle forms of psychological disorders that result in a split personality.[48] The reader will note, however, that mental illness, like all evils, results also, more or less directly, from diabolical activity: a case of pseudo-possession does not rule out some other form of diabolical activity. Be that as it may, the church insists on several strict criteria for diagnosing true possession: the possessed person must reveal faraway, hidden things, such as concealed deeds; he must speak or understand a foreign language that is completely unknown to him; he must manifest superhuman physical strength—all this together with a marked aversion for the rituals, symbols, and teachings of the Christian religion.[49]

What is the meaning of possession? In a thoroughly religious society, one might think that the devil resorts to possession so as to create a climate of fear that facilitates sin. But in a secularized world like ours, the devil's interest in manifesting himself is not so evident. He would run the risk of making people think about God. "The devil's cleverest ruse," according to the famous remark by Baudelaire, "is to persuade us that he does not exist."[50] Indeed, forgetting about Satan leads to a sort of secularization of moral evil, which loses its literally dramatic character. Evil is reduced to a fatality of the species. It thereby becomes human, something so familiar that one easily becomes resigned to it, because worldly wisdom thinks that it can, if not justify it, then at least explain and therefore understand it: "It's only hu-

48. See Joseph de Tonquédec, *Les maladies nerveuses ou mentales et les manifestations diaboliques* (Paris: Beauchesne, 1938); J. Lhermitte, "Les pseudo-possessions diaboliques," in *Satan*, Études carmélitaines (Paris: 1948), 424–44.

49. These signs, which were already determined by Benedict XIV and the old Roman ritual, are found in the current Roman ritual of exorcisms, *Rituale Romanum ex decreto Sacrosancti Oecumenici Concilii Vaticani II instauratum auctoritate Ioannis Pauli PP. II promulgatum: De exorcismis et supplicationibus quibusdam* (Vatican City: Tipografia poliglotta vaticana, 1999), *Praenotanda*, no. 16. About this ritual one can profitably read the documents and commentaries published in *Notitiae* 35 (1999): 137–222.

50. See John Paul II, General Audience of August 13, 1986, on "The wicked angels," *DC*, 895: "Making himself unknown corresponds to his 'interests.' Satan's craft in the world is to lead men to deny his existence in the name of rationalism and any other system of thought that looks for every possible excuse not to admit his work" [translated from the French].

man!" "Silly people close their eyes to these things! Such a priest no longer dares to pronounce so much as the devil's name. What do they make of the interior life? The gloomy battlefield of the instincts. Of morality? A kind of sensory hygiene."[51] The Christian teaching about Satan, without in any way diminishing the responsibility of the human person, on the contrary sheds a harsh light on the breadth, depth, and seriousness of the combat being waged in his heart. It reveals to man at the same time his dignity as a moral subject and his not very lustrous concrete situation as a puppet, indistinctly consenting and being manipulated, in a cosmic enterprise that reaches far beyond his own intentions. It is not very clear why the demons would promote awareness of this.[52]

THE PURPOSES OF DEMONIC ACTIVITY

For St. Thomas, a theologian can and must consider this battle of the demons against mankind from two perspectives: that of the subjective intentions of the demons and that of its integration into God's plan.[53] From the demons' perspective, the sole purpose of all their activity is to harm. It depends on two motives. On the one hand, the demons are jealous of human beings, which inspires in them an active will to prevent the salvation of souls and concretely to lead them into sin, which is the supreme evil: separation from God.[54] But their jealousy toward man has its source much higher, in their hatred of God, an insatiable hatred that no success can ever alleviate. Man, insofar as he is the image of God, is what Satan wants to sully and destroy. On the other hand, "through pride [the demons] usurp a semblance of Divine power, by deputing certain ministers to assail man, as the an-

51. Bernanos, *Sous le soleil de Satan*, 232.

52. The fact remains that a certain apologetic value can be attributed to possession. God forces the devil to manifest his existence and his malice, as well as his subordination to God. For some people possession is, in this era of scientism, an argument with which to convert unbelievers and alert Christians. In any case, God is more likely than Satan to be the one who wants to manifest the existence of satanic forces.

53. See *ST* I, q. 114, a. 1.

54. See Clement of Alexandria, *Stromata* II.13.56 (FOTC 85:197): "The Lord ... has a foreknowledge from the very first ... of how [the devil] is jealous of the forgiveness of human sins and by his mischievous calculations to induce them to share in his fall will introduce other occasions for God's servants to sin."

gels of God in their various offices minister to man's salvation."[55] They
make sport of the heavenly hosts by aping them. More deeply, perhaps, their hunger for power leads them to try to establish their dominion over human beings through sin. They invent for themselves a
counterfeit of the mystery of the divine Lordship, and, as the fathers
often remarked, they have the perverse desire to divert to themselves
the adoration that belongs to God alone. "All these I will give you, if
you will fall down and worship me" (Mt 4:9).[56]

This demonic action that aims to found a City of Evil takes the
form of opposition to the establishment of the Heavenly City. Like
some maleficent ivy or ominous shadow, it somehow intimately accompanies the developments of the divine economy of salvation. Thus
Charles Journet clearly demonstrated how the hatred of God that inspires a demon takes the form of an increasingly explicit anti-Christian
sentiment in proportion as the divine mystery of the recapitulation of
all things in Christ is accomplished. The demons attack first the preparations for the Incarnation, then Christ himself, and finally his mystical
body.[57]

But how did the demons know the mystery of the redemptive Incarnation that is at the center of the plan of salvation history that they
try to thwart? Beneath its anecdotal externals, this problem of demonic knowledge of the Incarnation in reality involves a major question of fundamental theology: to what extent and in what ways are
the supernatural mysteries of grace accessible to a created knowledge
of the natural sort? Like all the angels, the (future) demons had *in
via* [while they were wayfarers] a knowledge of faith that was necessary for their supernatural vocation. They knew then that God had a
plan to establish his Kingdom, but nothing indicates that this faith

55. *ST* I, q. 114, a. 1: "et propter superbiam divinae potestatis similitudinem usur-
pant, deputando sibi ministros determinatos ad hominum impugnationem, sicut et angeli Deo ministrant in determinatis officiis ad hominum salutem."

56. See Irenaeus of Lyons, *Against Heresies* V.24.4 (ANF 1:553a): "[The devil] has set
himself ... with greater and greater determination, in opposition to man, envying his life
[with God] and wishing to involve him in his own apostate power."

57. See Journet, *L'Église du Verbe incarné*, IV, 356–69. We recognize in this the "twofold contrasting progress" that Maritain was fond of—in other words, the principle of
the simultaneous growth of good and evil in history; see Jacques Maritain, "Pour une
philosophie de l'histoire," in Maritain and Maritain, *Oeuvres complètes*, 10:649–56.

pertained explicitly to the Incarnation of the Son.[58] Since Adam's fall, the demons must have suspected that God was preparing something like a major coup. Yet, despite the prophecies, the modalities of this work of redemption largely escaped them—hence the ambiguity of their attitude toward the person of Jesus, as it emerges from the Gospels themselves. On the one hand, the demons manifest a certain knowledge of Jesus' identity—"I know who you are: the Holy One of God"[59]—but, on the other hand, they remain undecided since they tempt him and seek to know who he really is—"If you are the Son of God ..." (Mt 4:3, 4:6).

St. Thomas returned several times to this question.[60] Relying on an already existing tradition of interpretation, he thinks that the demons effectively knew that Jesus was the Christ, the one sent by God who had been announced by the prophets. On the other hand, they were in doubt and uncertainty as to his deeper identity. Certain signs—the performance of miracles—sometimes led them to conjecture and suspect that he was Son of God in the strong sense, but they were not at all sure of it, especially because of the weaknesses—such as hunger and fatigue—that they observed in him. The scandal of the Incarnation worked thoroughly against the demons.

It was only gradually, compelled by events like the Resurrection and the Ascension, that the demons were led to recognize the divinity of Jesus Christ. Certainly they cannot see it, but the signs that testify to it are evidence that is too strong to be rejected without intellectual suicide. The demons are obliged to believe that Jesus is Son of God. This faith—the famous faith of the demons mentioned in James 2:19: "The demons believe and tremble"—has no salvific value, inasmuch as it does not result from good will prompted by the attraction of the good but rather from a purely intellectual compulsion.[61]

58. See *ST* I, q. 64, a. 1, ad 1.

59. See Mk 1:23; Lk 4:34.

60. See *ST* I, q. 64, a. 1, ad 4; *ST* III, q. 41, a. 1, ad 1; *ST* III, q. 44, a. 1, ad 2; *ST* III, q. 47, a. 5; *In 1 ad Co*, c. 2, lect. 2 (nos. 94–95).

61. On the faith of the demons, as a constrained belief, see *ST* II-II, q. 5, a. 2; *Q. de ver.*, q. 14, a. 9, ad 4.

THE INTEGRATION OF THE DEMONS'
ACTIVITY INTO THE PLAN OF
PROVIDENCE

The relative ignorance of the demons with regard to Jesus' identity and the modalities of his redemptive mission led them to be infuriated with him at the hour of the Passion: "if they had [understood this], they would not have crucified the Lord of glory" (1 Cor 2:8). In doing so, their apparent victory accomplished their definitive defeat. Without knowing it, without wanting to, they worked for the salvation of the world. "On the cross, the wisdom and the omnipotence of God proved themselves by making Satan an instrument of the redemptive will."[62] This is the central affirmation of Christian theology relative to the activity of the demons in the world: it is strictly subordinated to the designs of providence and thus contributes to the good of those who love God.[63]

This must be understood correctly. No more than God willed the sin of the angels does he will their activity of tempting, which aims directly at leading human beings to something that God can by no means will: sin. However, even though he could, God does not always prevent this activity. He permits it sometimes.[64] This permission (not in the sense of authorization but of nonprevention) is a good act. It is justified by a greater good, according to the classic axiom that sums up the essence of Christian theodicy: "Almighty God ..., being Himself supremely good, would never permit the existence of anything evil among His works, if He were not so omnipotent and good that He can bring good even out of evil."[65] Let us make a comparison. Surgeons are not responsible for traffic accidents (at least not

62. Brunner, *Doctrine chrétienne de la création*, 168.

63. See *ST* I, q. 114, a. 1. The principles developed in this article govern the teaching in *ST* I, q. 64, a. 4 (see chapter 10 of this volume).

64. See Athanasius, *Life of Antony*, 29: the demons must ask God's permission, as we see when they attack Job; Augustine, *City of God* II.23.2 (FOTC 8:115): "For, though the demons have some power in these matters, they have only as much as the hidden will of Almighty God allows them" (Etsi aliquid in his rebus daemones possunt, tantum possunt, quantum secreto Omnipotentis arbitrio permittuntur); John Damascene, *Orthodox Faith* II.4 (FOTC 37:209): "[The wicked angels] have no power or strength against anyone, unless this be permitted them by the dispensation of God, as in the case of Job [Jb 1:12] and as has been written in the Gospel about the swine [Mk 5:13]."

65. Augustine, *Enchiridion* III.11 (11): "Neque enim Deus omnipotens, quod etiam

as surgeons). But once such a tragedy has occurred, they derive from the disaster the best possible outcome: the remove from dying victims the organs that are still sound so as to transplant them and thus prolong a life.[66] *Mutatis mutandis*, it is the same with God and the demons. God did not positively will the fall of Satan and the demons. He only permitted it for reasons that it is not for me to set forth here, which are the general reasons for permitting sin.[67] But now that the fall has occurred, God is powerful enough to derive from it the best possible outcome.

In fact, God in a way makes good the demonic malice that he by no means intends—he "orders" it, St. Thomas says—in other words, integrates it into an order—by making it serve his proper ends. He does this in two ways. First, according to a classic theme, God permits the demons' attacks because they contribute to the spiritual progress of the saints, to the increase of their merits, and therefore "to the glory of the elect."[68] As Origen puts it, "The reason the Lord has not deprived the devil of his dominion over this world is because there is still need of his works for the battle-training and victories of the blessed."[69] Second, God can also utilize the demons directly as an instrument of

---

infideles fatentur, rerum cui summa potestas, cum summe bonus est, ullo modo sineret mali aliquid esse in operibus suis, nisi usque adeo esset omnipotens et bonus, ut bene faceret et de malo"; see also *Enchiridion* VIII.27; XXVIII.104. The *CCC* in paragraph 311 cites this principle at the heart of its reflection on evil. *Literal Meaning of Genesis* XI.22 (ACW 42:153) makes as it were an application thereof to the very first sin, Satan's: "God, knowing this creature would be evil by his own free choice, none the less made him, not holding back His goodness but giving life and being to a will that would be depraved; for God foresaw the many good effects He would bring about from him by His divine goodness and power" (Praesciens eum propria voluntate malum futurum, fecit eum tamen, non abstinens bonitatem suam in praebenda vita atque substantia futurae etiam noxiae voluntati, simul praevidens quanta de illo bona esset sua mirabili bonitate ac potestate facturus). See also *City of God* XXII.1 (FOTC 24:415–17).

66. See a similar image in Theodoret of Cyr, *Thérapeutique des maladies helléniques* (SC 57:200): "God himself did not appoint it Satan's destiny to play the role of an enemy, but he fittingly utilizes his malice, as physicians utilize vipers to cure certain illnesses."

67. On the Thomist position concerning the theme of God's permissive will and sin, see, for example, D. Bañez, *In Iam*, q. 23, a. 3; Réginald Garrigou-Lagrange, *De Deo Trino et Creatore* (Turin: Marietti; and Paris: Desclée de Brouwer, 1943), 342–53; Jean-Hervé Nicolas, "La permission du péché," *RT* 60 (1960): 5–37 and 509–46.

68. See *ST* I, q. 114, a. 1, ad 3. In *Super Evangelium s. Matthaei lectura* [*In Matth.*], c. 4 (no. 308), ed. Raphaelis Cai (Turin: Marietti, 1951), St. Thomas lists the five benefits of temptation (which has been overcome) for the just.

69. Origen, *Homilies on Numbers*, Homily XIII.7.2 (ACT, 78a).

his justice to punish the guilty, even though the demons inflict evil for an entirely different intention from that of reestablishing the higher good of divine justice.[70] Gregory the Great wrote about Satan:

> Although they [the other angels] dispense the succours of mercy to all that labour in this present life, this one unwittingly serves the ends of [God's] secret justice, while he strives to accomplish the ministry of their condemnation.... For not alone do the good [angels] serve God by the aid which they render [to men], but likewise the wicked [angels] by the trials which they inflict; not only they [i.e., those good angels] who lift upward them that are turning back from transgression, but [also] they [i.e., the wicked] who press down those who refuse to turn back.[71]

At first glance, the church's teaching on the active and nefarious presence of the demons could be somewhat frightening. And, in fact, when poorly integrated into doctrine as a whole and Christian life, belief in demons has sometimes given rise, individually and also collectively, to an existential anguish, an unhealthy panic, as if man were passively prey to occult powers, whether good or evil, who battled inside him without his consent. This view of things is a clever victory of the demon, because Christianity, quite the contrary, has presented itself from the beginning as a message of liberation from the fatalism and fear inspired by the "Powers."

To cut short these unnatural fears, it is enough to recall that in the final analysis the demon has no power over us but what our freedom is willing to grant him.[72] Certainly, the negative circumstances of our freedom (original sin, structures of sin, vices) and the difference in nature between man and the demon may seem to make the spiritual combat an uneven match. But it is not, inasmuch as man can freely have recourse to the help of divine grace and of the angels.[73] In fact, this

---

70. See *ST* I, q. 114, a. 1, ad 1.

71. Gregory the Great, *Morals on The Book of Job* II.38 (1:93–94).

72. In *In II Sent.*, d. 6, a. 8 (137), St. Albert the Great wonders whether God is not unjust in permitting this combat of man against a much stronger enemy. Not at all, he determines, because "this combat consists entirely in consent, and the will is equally free of constraint in all rational creatures.... Here then lies the equality and the possibility of resistance" (Pugna enim haec tota consistit in consensu: et haec voluntas aeque libera est a coactione omnibus rationalibus creaturis.... Et in hoc ergo est aequalitas et possibilitas resistendi).

73. See *ST* I, q. 114, a. 1, ad 2: "In order that the conditions of the fight be not un-

teaching about the activity of the demons is not an invitation to panic but rather to a calm and peaceful vigilance over oneself and to a healthy fear of God.

In this combat, the church, following St. Paul, encourages the faithful to "put on the whole armor of God, that you may be able to stand against the wiles of the devil" (Eph 6:11). "In order to defend oneself effectively and fully against the devil, it is not just a matter of employing certain particular means, but rather of opening oneself up by faith to the power of Christ."[74] Thus the believer participates in Christ's paschal victory over the forces of evil. A vigorous life in union with Christ is consequently the best defense against demonic attacks: "The greater evidence we see of demonic power over these depths on earth, the more inseparably should we cling to the Mediator by whose power alone we can rise from the deepest depth to the heights of heaven."[75] Prayer (whether private or communal[76]—"Deliver us from Evil"), frequent reception of the sacraments, and good works are the most effective weapons of the Christian in spiritual combat.

That said, most religions have certain rituals whose immediate purpose is to drive away evil spirits and to neutralize malignant forces. The church, which includes natural religion while purifying and evangelizing it, is not without such rituals, and it too resorts to exorcisms.[77] However, already in biblical religion, exorcisms are no longer magical rites, as in ancient Babylon, but rather authentic prayers in which the victory over the demon is referred entirely to God.[78] God

---

equal, there is as regards man the promised recompense, to be gained principally through the grace of God, secondarily through the guardianship of the angels. Wherefore (2 Kgs 6:16), Eliseus said to his servant: 'Fear not, for there are more with us than with them'" (Ad hoc quod non sit inaequalis pugnae conditio, fit ex parte hominis recompensatio, principaliter quidem per auxilium divinae gratiae; secundario autem per custodiam angelorum. Unde IV Reg., Elisaeus dixit ad ministrum suum, "noli timere, plures enim nobiscum sunt, quam cum illis").

74. Zähringen, "Démons," 229.

75. Augustine, *City of God* XVIII.18 (FOTC 24:106).

76. See Egon von Petersdorf, "De Daemonibus in Liturgia memoratis," *Angelicum* 19 (1942): 324–39.

77. It is important not to reduce exorcism to its solemn and spectacular forms. Indeed, an exorcism is any rite intended to drive away demons; see Daniélou, "Exorcisme," in *DS*,4:1995–2004.

78. See Tb 6:8, 8:2–3; Mt 12:27.

is the one who will restrain Satan and his minions if we call on the power of his name.[79] Jesus himself performed exorcisms, commanding the demon to withdraw, and he entrusted this power to his disciples (Mk 16:17). And so, founded on Christ's promise, the church employs all sorts of sacramentals that manifest Christ's victory over the demon (signs of the cross, the use of holy water or blessed medals) and unceasingly prays for the final liberation.

The believer's participation in Christ's victory over the Evil One is thus an essential element of Christian hope:

What then shall we say to this? ... Who shall bring any charge against God's elect? ... Who shall separate us from the love of Christ? Shall tribulation, or distress, or persecution ... ? No, in all these things we are more than conquerors through him who loved us. For I am sure that neither death, nor life, nor angels, nor principalities, nor things present, nor things to come, nor powers, nor height, nor depth, nor anything else in all creation, will be able to separate us from the love of God in Christ Jesus our Lord (Rom 8:31–39).

79. Zec 3:2; Jude 9.

Bibliography

———:———

OLDER WORKS

Albert the Great. *Commentarii in II Sententiarum*. Opera omnia 27. Edited by Auguste Borgnet. Paris: Vivés, 1894.

Alexander of Hales. *Summa theologica fratris Alexandri*. Vol. 2. Quaracchi: 1928.

Ambrose. *De Abraham libri duo*. PL 14:441–524. 1845.

———. *De viduis liber unus*. PL 15: 233–62. 1845.

———. *De Fide ad Gratianum*. Edited by Otto Faller. CSEL 78. 1962.

———. *Apologie de David*. Introduction, Latin text, notes, and index by Pierre Hadot. French translation by Marius Cordier. SC 239. Paris: Cerf, 1977.

———. *Concerning Widows*. In NPNF, 10:391–407. 2004.

Anselm of Canterbury. Orationes. PL 158: 855–1016. 1853.

———. *De la chute du diable*. French translation by R. de Ravinel. Introduction and notes by Michel Corbin. L'oeuvre de saint Anselme de Cantorbery 2. Paris: Cerf, 1986.

———. *Pourquoi un Dieu-homme [Cur Deus homo]*. French translation and notes by Michel Corbin. In *L'oeuvre de saint Anselme de Cantorbery*, vol. 3. Paris: Cerf, 1988.

Apocryphal Old Testament. Edited by H. F. D. Sparks. Oxford: Clarendon Press, 1984.

Aquinas, Thomas. Vita Adae et Evae. Edited by Wilhelm Meyer. Munich: G. Franz, 1879.

———. *In Sent. [Scriptum super libros Sententiarum]*. Vols. 1 and 2. Edited by Pierre Mandonnet. Paris: Lethielleux, 1929. Vols. 3 and 4. Edited by Marie F. Moos. Paris: Lethielleux, 1933–47. Since this edition stops at disputatio 22 of Liber IV, for later passages we used the Parma edition, vol. 8. 1858.

———. *Summa theologica*. New York: Benziger Brothers, 1912–25.

———. *Compendium of Theology*. Translated by Cyril Vollert. St. Louis: B. Herder, 1948.

———. *Q. de pot. [Quaestiones disputatae de potentia]*. In *Quaestiones disputatae*, edited by P. Bazzi et al. Vol. 2. Turin: Marietti, 1949.

———. *In Matth.* [*Super Evangelium s. Matthaei lectura*]. Edited by Raphaelis Cai. 5th ed. Turin: Marietti, 1951.

———. *In De caelo* [*In Aristotelis libros De caelo et mundo, De generatione et corruptione, Meteorologicorum exposition*]. Edited by Raimondo M. Spiazzi. Turin: Marietti, 1952.

———. *Ioan.* [*Super Evangelium s. Ioannis lectura*]. Edited by Raphaelis Cai. Turin and Rome: Marietii, 1952.

———. *Q. de ver.* [*The Disputed Questions on Truth*]. Translated by James V. McGlynn, Robert W. Mulligan, and Robert W. Schmidt. 3 vols. Chicago: Henry Regnery, 1952–54.

———. *In ad Ro; In 1 ad Co. Lectura super epistolas s. Pauli.* Edited by Raphaelis Cai. 2 vols. Turin: Marietti, 1953.

———. *"Les Anges." Summa Theologica I,* questions 50–64. French translation by Charles-Vincent Héris. Éditions de la Revue des jeunes. Paris: Desclée, 1953.

———. *Opuscula theologica.* Edited by Raimondo M. Spiazzi. 2 vols. Turin: Marietti, 1954.

———. *In Iob* [*Expositio super Iob ad litteram*]. Leonine edition. Vol. 26. 1963.

———. *Opuscula.* [*De substantiis separatis; In Decretalem I expositio*]. Leonine edition. Vol. 40. 1967–68.

———. *Expositio super Isaiam ad litteram.* Leonine edition. Vol. 28. 1974.

———. *CG* (*Summa contra Gentiles*). *Providence.* Part I. Translated by Vernon J. Bourke. Notre Dame, Ind.: University of Notre Dame Press, 1975.

———. *Comp. theol.; Resp. de 36 articulis.* [*Opuscula*]. Leonine edition. Vol. 42. 1979.

———. *Q. de malo* [*Quaestiones disputatae de malo*]. Leonine edition. Vol. 23. 1982.

———. *In De anima* [*Sententiae libri De anima*]. Leonine edition. Vol. 45/1. 1984.

———. *Q. de malo* [*On Evil*]. Translated by Jean Oesterle. Notre Dame, Ind.: University of Notre Dame Press, 1995.

———. *Q. de anima* [*Quaestiones disputatae de anima*]. Leonine edition. Vol. 24/1. 1996.

———. *Thomas d'Aquin, De la vérité, Question 2* (*La science en Dieu*). Introduction, translation, and commentary by Serge-Thomas Bonino. Preface by Ruedi Imbach. Vestigia 17. Paris and Fribourg: Cerf, 1996.

———. *Quodl.* [*Quaestiones disputatae de quolibet*]. Leonine edition. 1996.

———. *Q. de spiritualibus creaturis* [*Quaestiones disputatae de spiritualibus creaturis*]. Leonine edition. Vol. 24 /2. 2000.

Arethas of Caesarea. *Commentarium in Apocalypsin.* PG 106: 487–786. 1863.

Aristotle. *Nicomachean Ethics.* Translated by F. H. Peters. London: Kegan Paul, Trench, and Trübner, 1893.

———. *Physics.* Translated by R. P. Hardie and Russell K. Gaye. Oxford: Clarendon Press, 1930.

———. *Metaphysics.* Translated with commentaries by Hippocrates G. Apostle. Bloomington: Indiana University Press, 1966.

Athanasius of Alexandria. *Life of Antony: The Coptic Life and The Greek Life.* Translated by Tim Vivian and Apostolos N. Athanassakis. Kalamazoo, Mich.: Cistercian, 2003.

Athenagoras. *A Plea for the Christians.* In ANF 2:129–48. 2004.

Augustine. *Sermones.* PL 39. Paris: 1845.

———. *The City of God.* Translated by Demetrius B. Zema, SJ, and Gerald G. Walsh, SJ. FOTC 8, 14, 24. 1950, 1952, 1954.

———. *Enarrationes in Psalmos I–L.* CCL 38. 1956.

———. *Enarrationes in Psalmos CI–CL.* CCL40. 1956.

———. *The Enchiridion on Faith, Hope and Love.* Edited by Henry Paolucci. Translated by J. F. Shaw. Chicago: Regnery Gateway, 1961.

———. *The Trinity.* Translated by Stephen McKenna., CSsR, FOTC 45. 1963.

———. *Sermones I-L de vetere Testamento.* CCL 41. 1971.

———. *Eighty-Three Different Questions.*Translated by David L. Mosher. FOTC 70. 1982.

———. *The Literal Meaning of Genesis.* Translated and annotated by John Hammond Taylor. ACW 41–42. 1982.

———. *The True Religion.* WSA I/8:29–104. 2005.

Averroès. *Commentarii in tres libros De anima,* in *Aristotelis libri omnes … cum Averrois Cordubensis variis in eosdem commentariis.* Vol. 6. Venice: Iuntas, 1574.

Bañez, Domingo. *Scholastica Commentaria super caeteras primae partis quaestiones.* Venice: 1602.

———. *Comentarios inéditos a la Tercera parte de santo Tomas.* Edited by Vincente Beltran de Heredia,Vol. 1, *De Verbo Incarnato.* Madrid, 1951.

Basil the Great. *Homilia in Psalmos.* PG 29:207–494.1857.

———. *Homélies sur l'Hexaéméron.* Greek text, introduction, and French translation by Stanislas Giet. SC 26. 1949.

———. *Contre Eunome, suivi de Eunome, Apologie.* Introduction, traduction, et notes de Bernard Sesboüé. SC 2. Paris: Cerf, 1983.

———. *On the Holy Spirit.* Translated by Stephen Hildebrand. New York: St. Vladimir's Seminary Press, 2011.

Bekker, Balthasar. *Le monde enchanté, ou examen des communs sentiments touchant les esprits, leur nature, leur pouvoir, leur administration et leurs opérations.* 4 vols. French ed. Amsterdam: Pierre Rotterdam, 1964.

Bernard of Clairvaux. *St. Bernard's Sermons for the Seasons and Principal Festivals of the Year.* Translated by a priest of Mount Melleray. Vol. I. Dublin: Browne and Nolan, 1921.

———. *S. Bernardi opera IV: Sermones I.* Edited by Jean LeClercq and Henri-Marie Rochais. Rome: Éditiones Cistercienes, 1966.

———. *On the Song of Songs.* Sermon V. Translated by Kilian Walsh. Spencer, Mass.: Cistercian Publications, 1971, 25–31.

Billuart, Charles René. *Tractatus de angelis.* In *Summa sancti Thomae.* Vol. 2. Paris: 1874–76.

Bonaventure. *Opera theologica selecta.* Cura PP. Collegii S. Bonaventurae, editio minor. Vol. 2, *Liber II Sententiarum.* Quaracchi: 1938.

Cabrol, Jean (Capreolus). *Defensiones theologiae divi Thomae Aquinatis.* Edited by Ceslai. Paban and Thomae Pègues. *Tours:* Alfred Cattier, 1900–8.

Cajetan, Thomas. *Commentaria in Summam theologiae.* In *Sancti Thomae Aquinatis*

Doctoris Angelici Opera Omnia iussu impensaque Leonis XIII P. M. edita. Rome: 1898–1906.

———. In *De ente et essentia D. Thomae Aquinatis Commentaria.* Cura et studio P. M.-H. Laurent. Turin: Marietti, 1934.

Chartularium Universitatis parisiensis. Edited by Heinrich Denifle and Emile Chatelain. Vol. 1. Paris: Ex typis fratris Delalain, 1889.

Clement of Alexandria. *Extraits de Théodote.* Texte grec, introduction, traduction, et notes par F. Sagnard. SC 23. Paris: Cerf, 1948.

———. *Stromateis* [Book V, Vol. 1]. Edited by Alain Le Boulluec and Pierre Voulet. SC 278. 1981.

———. *Stromateis.* Books 1–3. Translated by John Ferguson. FOTC 85. 1991.

Condamnation (La) parisienne de 1277. Nouvelle édition du texte latin, traduction, introduction, et commentaire par David Piché, avec la collaboration de Claude Lafleur. Sic et non. Paris: 2002.

Cyril of Jerusalem. *Mystagogical Catecheses.* In *St. Cyril of Jerusalem's Lectures on the Christian Sacraments,* edited by F. L. Cross, 40–80. Crestwood, N.Y.: St. Vladimir's Seminary Press, 1986.

———. *Lenten Lectures (Catecheses).* In *Works,* vol. 1, translated by Leo P. McCauley, SJ, and Anthony A. Stephenson. FOTC 61.Washington, D.C.: The Catholic University of America Press, 1969. Reprinted 2005.

Cyprian. Treatises. "On Jealousy and Envy." Translated by Roy J. Ferrari. FOTC 36:291–308. 1958. Reprinted 2007.

DBS (Dictionnaire de la Bible (Supplément). Edited by Jacques Briend et al. 13 vols. Paris: Letouzey and Ané, 1923–2002.

DEB (Dictionnaire encyclopédique de la Bible). Edited by Pierre-Mourice Bogaert. Turnhout: Brepols, 1987.

Denys l'Aréopagite. *Oeuvres complètes du Pseudo-Denys l'Aréopagite.* Traduction, préface, notes, et index par Maurice de Gandillac. Nouvelle édition avec appendice. Bibliothèque philosophique. Paris: Aubier-Montaigne, 1980.

Descartes, René. *Entretien avec Burman.* In *Oeuvres et lettres.* Bibliothèque de la Pléiade. Paris: Gallimard, 1953.

Dionysius the Areopagite. *Pseudo-Dionysius: The Complete Works.* Classics of Western Spirituality. New York and Mahwah, N.J.: Paulist Press, 1987.

DS (Dictionnaire de spiritualité: Ascétique et mystique; Doctrine et histoire. 45 vols. Paris: Éditions Beauchesne, 1932–95.

Dupont-Sommer, André, and Marc Philonenko, eds. *La Bible: Écrits intertestamentaires.* Paris: Editions Gallimard (Pléiade), 1987.

Eusebius of Caesarea. *Demonstratio Evangelii* [Demonstration of the Gospel]. PG 22.9–794. 1857.

Evagrius Ponticus. *The Praktikos.* Translated by John Eudes Bamberger. Spencer, Mass.: Cistercian Publications, 1970.

Gonet, Jean-Baptiste. *Clypeus theologiae thomisticae contra novos ejus impugnatores.* Vol. 3, *De angelis.* Paris: Vivés, 1876.

Grégoire de Nazianze. *Discours 38–41.* Introduction, texte critique, et notes de Claudio Moreschini. Traduction par Paul Gallay. SC 358. 1990.

Gregory of Nyssa. *La création de l'homme.* Introduction et traduction de Jean La-
place. Notes de Jean Daniélou. SC 6. 1943.
———. *The Life of Moses.* Translated by Abraham J. Malherbe and Everett Fergu-
son. New York: Paulist Press, 1978.
———. *Discours catéchétique.* Introduction, traduction, et notes par Raymond
Winling. SC 453. 2000.
Gregory the Great. *Forty Gospel Homilies. Morals on the Book of Job,* 4 vols. Oxford:
John Henry Parker, 1844–50.
———. Translated by Dom David Hurst. Kalamazoo, Mich.: Cistercian Publica-
tions, 1990.
Guillaume d'Auxerre (William of Auxerre). *Summa aurea.* Edited by Jean Ribaillier.
Spicilegium bonaventurianum 16–20. Paris: Éditions du Centre national de la
recherche scientifique; Rome: Editiones Collegii S. Bonaventurae ad Claras
Aquas, 1980.
Hermas. *The Pastor.* ANF 2:9–55.
Hervé de Nédellec. *In quatuor Libros sententiarum Commentaria.* Paris: 1647.
Hilary of Poitiers. *Tractatus super psalmos. In Ps. 132,* no. 6. PL 9:748–49. 1844.
Hobbes, Thomas. *Leviathan.* Edited by A. R. Waller. Cambridge: Cambridge Uni-
versity Press, 1904.
Hugh of St. Victor. *De sacramentis.* PL 176: 173–618. 1880.
Ignatius of Antioch. *Letters.* ACW 1. 1946.
Irenaeus of Lyons. *Proof of the Apostolic Preaching.* Translated and annotated by Jo-
seph P. Smith. ACW 16. 1952.
———. *Against Heresies.* In ANF 1:315–567. 2004.
Jean Buridan. *Subtilissimae Quaestiones super VIII Physicorum libros Aristotelis.* Par-
is: 1509.
Jean Cabrol. *Defensiones theologiae divi Thomae Aquinatis de novo editae cura et stu-
dio RR. PP.* Edited by Ceslai Paban and Thomae Pègues. 7 vols. Tours: Alfred
Cattier, 1900–1908.
Jerome. *Commentarii in epistolam ad Ephesios.* PL 26: 467–590. 1866.
———. *Commentarii in epistolam ad Titum.* PL 26:589–635. 1866.
———. *Commentaire sur saint Matthieu.* (Livres III–IV). Texte latin, traduction,
notes, et index par Emile Bonnard. SC 2:259. 1979.
John Cassian. *Conferences.* ACW 57. 1997.
John Chrysostom. *Homilies on Genesis 18–45.* Translated by Robert C. Hill. FOTC
82. 1990.
———. *Homilies on the Epistle to the Colossians.* In NPNF 13: 270a–75b. 2004.
John Damascene. *The Orthodox Faith.* In *Saint John of Damascus: Writings.* Translat-
ed by Frederic H. Chase Jr. FOTC 37: 165–406. 1958.
John Duns Scotus. *Ordinatio II,* d. 1–3. Opera omnia VII. Vatican City: Typis Poly-
glottis Vaticanis, 1973.
John of St. Thomas. *Cursus philosophicus thomisticus.* Vol. 2, *Naturalis philosophiae.*
Nova editio a B. Reiser. Turin: Marietti, 1933.
———. *Cursus theologicus.* Vol. 4, *Opera et studio monachorum solesmensium.* Paris,

Tournai, and Rome: Typis Societatis S. Joannis Evangelistae, Desclée et sociorum, 1946. [*Tractatus de angelis* 442–835.]

Josephus. *The Jewish War*. Books I–III. Translated by H. St. J. Thackeray. In *Josephus: Works in Nine Volumes*. Vol. 2. Loeb Classical Library. Cambridge, Mass.: Harvard University Press, 1961.

———. *Jewish Antiquities*, Books XV–XVII. English translation by Ralph Marcus. Vol. 8 of *Josephus in Nine Volumes*. Cambridge, Mass., and London: Harvard University Press, 1969.

Justin Martyr. *Dialogue with Trypho*. PG 6:471–800. 1857. Translated by Thomas B. Falls. Revised by Thomas P. Halton. Washington, D.C.: The Catholic University of America Press, 2003.

———. *The First Apology*. ANF 1:163–87. 2004.

———. *The Second Apology*. In ANF 1:188–93. 2004.

Lactantius. *The Divine Institutes*. Translated by Mary Francis McDonald, OP. FOTC 49. 1964.

L'École de Chartres, Bernard de Chartres, Guillaume de Conches, Thierry de Chartres, and Clarembault d'Arras. *Théologie et cosmologie au XIIᵉ siècle*. Translated by Michel Lemoine and Clotilde Picard-Parra. Sagesses médiévales. Paris: Les Belles Lettres, 2004.

Liber de causis. Édition établie à l'aide de 90 manuscrits, avec introduction et notes par Adriaan Pattin. Louvain, n.d.

Magnard, Pierre, Olivier Boulnois, Bruno Pinchard, and Jean-Luc Solère, *La Demeure de l'être: Autour d'un anonyme*. Étude et traduction du *Liber de Causis*. Philologie et Mercure. Paris: J. Vrin, 1990.

Maimonides, Moses. *The Guide for the Perplexed*. Translated by Michael Friedländer. 2nd ed. London: Routledge and Kegan Paul, 1956.

Mansi, Giovan Domenico. *Sacrorum conciliorum nova et amplissima collectio*. Vol. 13. Graz: Akademische Druck- u. Verlagsanstalt, 1960.

Nicolaus Medensis (Durandellus). *Evidentiae contra Durandum*, ad fidem codicum primum editae studio et cura Prospero Stella. Corpus philosophorum Medii Aevi, Opera philosophica mediae aetatis selecta. Vol. 3. Tübingen: Francke, 2003.

Origen. *Contra celsum*. Translated by Henry Chadwick. Cambridge: Cambridge University Press, 1965.

———. *On First Principles: Being Koetschau's Text of the De Principiis*. Trans. G. W. Butterworth. New York: Harper and Row, 1966.

———. *Homilies on Genesis and Exodus*. Translated by Ronald E. Heine. FOTC 71. 1982.

———. *Homilies on Luke*. Translated by Joseph T. Lienhard, SJ. FOTC 94. 1996.

———. *Homilies on Joshua*. Translated by Barbara J. Bruce. Edited by Cynthia White. FOTC 105. 2002.

———. *Commentary on the Gospel of Matthew*. In ANF 9:409–512. 2004.

———. *Homilies on Numbers*. Translated by Thomas P. Scheck. ACT. 2009.

———. *Homilies on Numbers*. Homily 20.3.4 (ACT 127b–28a). 2009.

Petau, Denis. *De angelis*. In *Dogmata theologica*. Paris: Vivés, 1864, 3:603–712, and 1866, 4:1–121.

Peter Damien. *Sermones*. PL 144: 505–924. 1853.

Peter Lombard. *Sententiae in IV libris distinctae*. Vol. 1, part 2 (Liber I et II). Edited by Collegii s. Bonaventurae. Spicilegium bonaventurianum 4. Grottaferrata and Rome: Editiones Collegii S. Bonaventurae ad Claras Aquas, 1971. English edition *The Sentences*. Vol. 2. Translated by Giulio Silano. Mediaeval Sources in Translation 43. Toronto: Pontifical Institute of Mediaeval Studies, 2008.

Peter of Poitiers. *Sententiae II*. Edited by Philip S. Moore, Joseph N. Garvin, and Marthe Dulong. Publications in Medieval Studies 11. Notre Dame, Ind.: University of Notre Dame Press, 1950.

Plato. *The Collected Dialogues*, edited by Edith Hamilton and Huntington Cairns. Bollingen Series LXXI. 13th ed. Princeton: Princeton University Press, 1987.

Règle (La) du maître II (ch. 11–95). Texte, traduction, et notes par A. de Vogüé. SC 106. Paris: Cerf, 1964.

Roland-Gosselin, Marie-Dominique, ed. *Le "De ente et essentia" de s. Thomas d'Aquin*. Paris: J. Vrin, 1948.

Rupert of Deutz. *De glorificatione Trinitatis*. PL 169:13–202. 1854.

Sophronius of Jerusalem. *Orationes*. PG 87: 3201–3366. 1865.

Spinoza, Benedict. *Tractatus Theologico-Politicus: A Critical Inquiry into the History, Purpose, and Authenticity of the Hebrew Scriptures*. Translated from Latin. London: Trübner, 1862.

Suarez, Francisco. *Commentarii et disputationes in tertiam Partem D. Thomae*. Opera omnia 18. Paris: Vivès, 1860.

———. *Tractatus de Angelis*. In *Commentarii et disputationes in primam Partem D. Thomae*. Opera omnia 2. Paris: Vivès, 1866.

Summa Sententiarum. PL 176. 1854.

Tertullian. *Against Marcion*. Edited and translated by Ernest Evans. 2 vols. Oxford: Clarendon Press, 1972.

———. *The Flesh of Christ*. In ANF, 3: 521–43. 2004.

———. *On the Veiling of Virgins*. In ANF 4:27–37. 2004.

———. Disciplinary, Moral, and Ascetical Works. "On Patience." Translated by Rudolph Arbesmann, OSA, Sister Emily Joseph Daly, CSJ, and Edwin A. Quain, SJ. FOTC 40:191–222. 1959.

Theodoret of Cyr. *Thérapeutique des maladies helléniques*. SC 57. Partial English translation, *A Cure of Greek Maladies*, in *Theodoret of Cyr*, by István Pásztori-Kupán (London and New York: Routledge, 2006), 85–108.

Voltaire. *Dictionnaire philosophique*. Oeuvres complètes 36. Paris: 1821.

Voss, Gérard-Jean. *De theologia gentili et physiologia christiana sive De origine ac progressu idololatriae*. Amsterdam: 1641.

WSA (The Complete Works of Saint Augustine in English). Edited by Boniface Ramsey. Hyde Park, N.Y.: New City Press, 1990–present.

CONTEMPORARY WORKS

Aertsen, Jan. *Nature and Creature: Thomas Aquinas' Way of Thought*. Studien und Texte zur Geistesgeschichte des Mittelalters 21. Leiden; New York: Brill, 1988.

Aletti, Jean-Noël, ed. *Saint Paul: Epître aux Colossiens*. Études bibliques 20. Paris: J. Gabalda, 1993.

————. "Colossiens: Un tournant dans la christologie néotestamentaire: Problèmes et propositions." *Liber annuus, Studium biblicum franciscanum* 49 (1999): 211–36.

Amato, Angelo. "L'Angelologia nella tradizione della Chiesa." In *Angeli e demoni.* Bologna: Edizioni Dehoniane, 1992, 105–50.

Amman, Emile. "Laodicée (concile de)." In *DTC,* 8:2611–15. 1925.

"Ange." In *DTC,* 1:1189–1271. 1903.

L'ange et l'homme. Cahiers de l'Hermétisme. Paris: 1978.

Anges, démons et êtres intermédiaires. Colloque de l'alliance mondiale des religions du 13–14 janvier 1968 à Paris. Paris: Labergerie, 1969.

Anges et esprits médiateurs. Connaissance des religions 71–72. Paris: Dervy, 2004.

Arnold, Clinton E. *Powers of Darkness: Principalities and Powers in Paul's Letters.* Downer's Grove, Ill.: InterVarsity Press, 1992.

————. "Returning to the Domain of the Powers: *Stoicheia* as Evil Spirits in Galatians 4:3, 9." *NT* 38 (1996): 55–76.

Aulen, Gustav. *Christus victor.* Paris: Aubier, 1949.

Aune, David E. *Revelation 1–5.* World Biblical Commentary 52a. Dallas: Thomas Nelson, 1997.

Barbel, Joseph. *Christos Angelos: Die Anschauung von Christus als Bote und Engel in der gelehrten und volkstümlichen Literatur des christlichen Altertums.* Theophania 3. Bonn: P. Hanstein, 1941.

Bareille, Georges. "Le culte des anges à l'époque des Pères de l'Église." *RT* 8 (1900): 41–49.

————. "Angélologie d'après les Pères." In *DTC,* 1:1192–1222. 1903.

Barth, Karl. *Church Dogmatics.* Vol. 3, part 3. Edited by G. W. Bromiley and T. F. Torrance. Edinburgh, T. and T. Clark, 1960; section 51: "The kingdom of heaven, the ambassadors of God and their opponents," 3:369–531 at 381–89.

Barton, George A. "The Origin of the Names of Angels and Demons in the Extra-Canonical Apocalyptic Literature to 100 A.D." *JBL* 31 (1912): 256–67.

Baumgartner, Walter. "Zum Problem des Yahweh-Engels." In *Zum Alten Testament und seiner Umwelt; Ausgewählte Aufsätze.* Leiden: E. J. Brill, 1959.

Benoîst d'Azy, Paul. "Le Christ et ses anges dans l'oeuvre de saint Thomas." *BLE* 44 (1943): 93–117, 121–36.

Benoît, Pierre. "Angélologie et démonologie pauliniennes: Réflexion sur la nomenclature des Puissances célestes et sur l'origine du mal angélique chez saint Paul." In *Fede e cultura alla luce della Bibbia.* Turin: Editrice Elle Di Ci, 1981, 217–33.

Bernanos, Georges. *Sous le soleil de Satan.* Paris: Plon-Nourrit, et cie, 1926.

————. *L'Imposture.* Paris: Plon, 1927.

————. *Les grands cimetières sous la lune.* Paris: Plon, 1938.

Bertola, Ermengildo. "Il problema delle creature angeliche in Pier Lombardo." *Pier Lombardo* 1 (1957): 33–54.

Besnier, Philippe. *Faute et peine chez saint Thomas d'Aquin.* Montsûrs: Editions Résiac, 1989.

Bianchi, Cinzia, and Christof Müller. "Diabolus." In *Augustinus-Lexicon.* Basel: Schwabe, 1996–2002, 2:381–96.

Blanco, Arturo. "Angeli: Il senso della fede cristiana negli angeli in una cultura scientifica e tecnologica." In *Dizionario interdisciplinare di scienza e fede*. Vatican City: Urbaniana University Press; Rome: Città Nuova, 2002, 1:71–83.

Blázquez, José M. *Intelectuales, ascetas y demonios al final de la Antigüedad*. Madrid: Cátedra, 1998.

Boismard, Marie-Émile. "Satan selon l'Ancien et le Nouveau Testaments." *Lumière et vie* 15 (1966): 61–76.

Boissard, Edmond. "La doctrine des anges chez saint Bernard." *Analecta Sacri Ordinis Cisterciensis* 9 (1953): 114–35.

Bonino, Serge-Thomas. "Le Diable dans le *Catéchisme de l'Église catholique*." *Nova et vetera* 74 (1999): 39–49.

———, ed. *Thomistes ou De l'actualité de saint Thomas*. Paris: Parole et Silence, 2003.

———. "Ángeles." In *Diccionario de teologia*, edited by Cesar Izquierdo, 7–11. Pampelune: Ediciones Universidad de Navarra, 2006.

———. *Les Anges et les Démons: Quatorze leçons de théologie catholique*. Paris: Éditions Parole et Silence, 2007.

———. "L'ange et le prophète: Un aspect de l'angélologie de saint Thomas d'Aquin." In *Le retour des anges*, Actes du Colloque tenu à Rome les 15 et 16 avril 2005. *RT* 108 (2008): 531–71.

Bonnefoy, Jean-François. *Christ and the Cosmos*. Translated by Michael D. Meilach, OFM. Paterson, N.J.: St. Anthony Guild Press, 1965.

Borchert, Bruno. "La seconde venue de Satan." *Concilium* 103 (1975): 129–37.

Botte, Bernard. "L'ange du sacrifice et l'épiclèse de la Messe romaine." *RTAM* 1 (1929): 285–308.

Bouëssé, Humbert. *Le Sauveur du monde*. Vol. 1, *La place du Christ dans le plan de Dieu*. Doctrina sacra 4. Chambéry-Leysse: Collège Théologique Dominicain, 1951.

Boureau, Alain. *Satan hérétique: Histoire de la démonologie (1280–1330)*. Paris: Odile Jacob, 2004.

Bouyer, Louis. *La Vie de saint Antoine: Essai sur la spiritualité du monachisme primitif*. St. Wandrille: Éditions de Fontenelle, 1950.

———. *Le sens de la vie monastique*. Turnhout and Paris: Éditions Brepols, 1950.

———. *Cosmos: Le monde et la gloire de Dieu*. Paris: Cerf, 1982.

Boyancé, Pierre. "Les deux démons personnels dans l'Antiquité grecque et latine." *Revue de Philologie* 41 (1935): 189–202.

Brague, Rémi. *La Sagesse du monde: Histoire de l'expérience humaine de l'univers*. Paris: Fayard, 1999.

———. *The Wisdom of the World: The Human Experience of the Universe in Western Thought*. Chicago: University of Chicago Press, 2004.

Breton, Stanislas. "Faut-il parler des anges?" *RSPT* 64 (1980): 225–40.

Briancesco, Eduardo. *Un triptyque sur la liberté: La doctrine morale de saint Anselme, De Veritate, De Libertate arbitrii, De Casu diaboli*. L'oeuvre de saint Anselme, Étude no. 2. Paris: Desclée de Brouwer, 1982.

Brottier, Laurence. *L'appel des "demi-chrétiens" à la "vie angélique": Jean Chrysostome prédicateur; Entre idéal monastique et réalité mondaine*. Paris: Cerf, 2005.

Brown, Peter. *The Cult of the Saints*. Chicago: University of Chicago Press, 1981, 2015.

Brunner, Emil. *La doctrine chrétienne de la création et de la rédemption*. French translation by Frédéric Jaccard. Dogmatique 2. Geneva: Labor et fides, 1965.

Brunner, Fernand. *Platonisme et aristotélisme: La critique d'Ibn Gabirol par saint Thomas d'Aquin*. Louvain: Publications universitaires de Louvain; Paris: B. Nauwelaerts, 1965.

Brunon, Jean-Baptiste, and Pierre Grelot. "Démons." In *VTB*, 257–61. 1988.

Bultmann, Rudolph. "New Testament and Mythology: The Problem of Demythologizing the New Testament Proclamation [1941]." In *The New Testament and Mythology and Other Basic Writings*, edited and translated by Schubert M. Ogden, 1–43. Philadelphia: Fortress Press, 1984.

Caird, George B. *Principalities and Powers: A Study in Pauline Theology*. Oxford: Clarendon Press, 1956.

Callan, Terrance. "Pauline Midrash: The Exegetical Background of Gal 3:19b." *JBL* 99 (1980): 549–67.

Caquot, André. "L'angélologie biblique: L'Ancien Testament." In *Les anges*, edited by Georges Tavard. Histoire des dogmes II.2b, 11–28. Paris: Cerf, 1971.

Carlesi, Tommaso. "La tentazione nel pensiero di s. Tommaso d'Aquino." *Sapienza* 10 (1957): 23–51, 200–25, 461–80.

Caro Baroja, Julio. *Les sorcières et leur monde*. Bibliothèque des histoires. Paris: Gallimard, 1971.

Carr, Wesley. *Angels and Principalities: The Background, Meaning and Development of the Pauline Phrase "hai archai kai hai exousiai."* Cambridge: Cambridge University Press, 1981.

Cazelles, Henri. "Fondements bibliques de la théologie des anges." *RT* 90 (1990): 181–93.

CCC (*Catechism of the Catholic Church*). 2nd ed. Vatican City: Libreria Editrice Vaticana, 1997.

Charlesworth, James H., et al, eds. *The Dead Sea Scrolls: Rule of the Community*. Multi-language ed. Philadelphia: American Interfaith Institute and World Alliance, 1996.

Chenu, Marie-Dominique. *La théologie au XIIe siècle*. Études de philosophie médiévale 45. Paris: J. Vrin, 1957.

Chrétien, Jean-Louis. "Le langage des anges selon la scolastique." In *La voix nue: Phénoménologie de la promesse*. Paris: Éditions de Minuit, 1990, 81–98.

———. "La connaissance angélique." In *Le regard de l'amour*. Paris: Desclée de Brouwer, 2000, 125–39.

Colish, Marcia L. *Peter Lombard*. Brill's Studies in Intellectual History 41. Leiden: Brill, 1994.

———. "Early Scholastic Angelology." *RTAM* 62 (1995): 80–109.

Collins, James D. *The Thomistic Philosophy of the Angels*. Washington, D.C.: The Catholic University of America Press, 1947.

Condamnation (La) parisienne de 1277. Latin text, trans., introduction, and commentary David Piché. Sic et non. Paris: J. Vrin, 1999.

Congar, Yves. "Aspects ecclésiologiques de la querelle entre Mendiants et séculiers dans la seconde moitié du XIIIe siècle et au début du XIVe siècle." *AHDLMA* 28 (1961): 34–151.

Contenau, Georges. *La Magie chez les assyriens et les babyloniens.* Paris: Payot, 1947.

Corvez, Maurice. "Chronique bultmanienne." *RT* 56 (1956): 322–52.

Cottier, Georges. "*Intellectus et ratio.*" *RT* 88 (1988): 215–28.

Courtès, Pierre-Ceslas. "La peccabilité de l'ange chez saint Thomas." *RT* 53 (1953): 133–63.

———. "Le traité des anges et la fin ultime de l'esprit." *RT* 54 (1954): 155–65.

Cunchillos, Jesús Luis. "Cuando los Angelos Eran Dioses." *Estudios Biblicos* 12 (1976): 118–38.

———. "Étude philologique du mal'ak: Perspectives sur le mal'ak de la divinité dans la Bible hébraïque." In *Congress Volume, Vienna, 1980,* edited by J. A. Emerton, 30–51. Supplements to Vetus Testamentum, 2. Leiden: Brill, 1981.

Daguet, François. *Théologie du dessein divin chez saint Thomas d'Aquin: Finis omnium Ecclesia.* Bibliothèque thomiste 54. Paris: J. Vrin, 2003.

Dales, Richard C. *Medieval Discussions of the Eternity of the World.* Brill's Studies in Intellectual History 18. Leiden, New York, and Cologne: E. J. Brill, 1990.

Daniélou, Jean. "Les sources juives de la doctrine des anges des nations chez Origène." *RSR* 38 (1951): 132–37.

———. *Les anges et leur mission d'après les Pères de l'Église.* Paris: Éditions de Chevetogne, 1952.

———. *Origen.* Translated by Walter Mitchell. New York: Sheed and Ward, 1955.

———. *The Angels and Their Mission according to the Fathers of the Church.* Translated by David Heimann. Westminster, Md.: Newman Press, 1957.

———. "Démon: Dans la littérature ecclésiastique jusqu'à Origène." In *DS,* 3:152–89. 1957.

———. "Exorcisme." *DS* 4:1995–2004. 1960.

———. *The Theology of Jewish Christianity.* Translated by John A. Baher. Philadelphia: Westminster Press, 1964.

Daoust, J. "Michel (Culte)." *Catholicisme* 9 (1982): 88–93.

Davy, Marie-Madeleine. "Le moine et l'ange en Occident au XIIe siècle." In *L'ange et l'homme.* Cahiers de l'Hermétisme. Paris: A. Michel, 1978, 107–27.

Day, Peggy L. *An Adversary in Heaven: Satan in the Hebrew Bible.* Atlanta: Scholars Press, 1988.

De Blic, Jacques. "Saint Thomas et l'intellectualisme moral à propos de la peccabilité de l'ange." *MSR* (1944): 241–80.

Deely, John. "The Semiosis of Angels." *Thomist* 68 (2004): 205–58.

De Finance, Joseph. *Être et agir dans la philosophie de saint Thomas.* 2nd ed. Rome: Presses de l'Université Grégorienne, 1960.

———. *Connaissance de l'être: Traité d'ontologie.* Paris and Bruges: Desclée de Brouwer, 1966.

Delcor, Mathias. *Le livre de Daniel.* Sources bibliques. Paris: J. Gabalda, 1971.

———. "Le mythe de la chute des anges et de l'origine des géants comme explication du mal dans le monde dans l'apocalyptique juive, Histoire des traditions." *Revue de l'histoire des religions* 190 (1976): 3–53.

312 Bibliography

———. "L'apocalyptique juive." In *Encyclopédie de la mystique juive*. Paris: Berg, 1977, 2–278.

De Libera, Alain, and Cyrille Michon. *L'être et l'essence: Le vocabulaire médiéval de l'ontologie*. Deux traités de Thomas d'Aquin et Dietrich de Freiberg. Paris: Éditions du Seuil, 1996.

Delling, Gerhard. "*Stoicheion*." In *TDNT*, 8:683–87. 1972.

De Lubac, Henri. *Surnaturel: Études historiques*. Paris: Éditions Montaigne, 1946.

Delumeau, Jean. *La Peur en Occident, XIVe–XVIIIe siècle*. Une Cité assiégée. Paris: Fayard, 1978.

———. *Le Péché et la Peur*. Paris: Fayard, 1983.

Den Boeft, Jan. "Daemon(es)." In *Augustinus-Lexicon*, Basel: Schwabe, 1996–2002, 2:213–22.

Dequeker, L. "Les *Qedôsîm* du Ps 89 à la lumière des croyances sémitiques." *ETL* (1966): 469–84.

———. "La cour céleste de Yahweh." *Collectanea Mechlinensia* 52 (1967): 131–40.

De Savignac, Jean. "Les Seraphim." *VT* 22 (1972): 320–25.

De Tonquédec, Joseph. *Les maladies nerveuses ou mentales et les manifestations diaboliques*. Paris: Beauschesne, 1938.

———. *La Philosophie de la nature*. Vol. 2. Part 1, *La nature en général*. Paris: P. Lethielleux, 1957.

De Vaux, Roland. *Bible et Orient: Les chérubins et l'arche d'alliance, les sphinx gardiens et les trônes divins dans l'Orient Ancien*. Paris: Cerf, 1967.

Dhorme, Édouard. "La démonologie biblique." In *Hommage à Wilhelm Vischer*. Montpellier: La Faculté Libre de Théologie Protestante de Montpellier, 1960, 41–54.

Dhorme, Édouard, and Louis-Hugues Vincent. "Les chérubins." *Revue biblique* 35 (1926): 328–56.

Dilschneider, Otto. *Christus Pantokrator*. Berlin: K. Vogt, 1962.

Dion, Paul-Eugène. "Les deux principales formes de l'angélologie de l'Ancien Testament dans leur cadre oriental." *Science et Esprit* 28 (1976): 65–89.

———. "Raphaël l'exorciste." *Biblica* 57 (1976): 399–413.

Dondaine, H.-F. "L'objet et le medium de la vision béatifique chez les théologiens du XIIIe siècle." *RTAM* 19 (1952): 60–130.

———. "Le premier instant de l'ange d'après saint Thomas." *RSPT* 39 (1955): 213–27.

Dondelinger, Patrick. "Satan dans la Bible." In *Encyclopédie des religions*, edited by Frédéric Lenoir and Ysé Tardan-Masquelier, 2:1463–67. Paris: Bayard, 1997.

Drewermann, Eugen. *La parole et l'angoisse: Commentaire de l'Évangile de Marc*. Traduit de l'allemand et adapté par Jean-Pierre Bagot. Paris: Desclée de Brouwer, 1995.

Duhem, Pierre. *Le Système du monde: Histoire des doctrines cosmologiques de Platon à Copernic*. Vol. 8. Paris: Hermann, 1958.

Duhr, Joseph. "Anges." *DS*, 1:598–626. 1937.

Duquoc, Christian. "Symbole ou réalité (Satan)." *Lumière et vie* 15 (1966): 99–105.

Dz-H (Heinrich Denzinger, *Enchiridion symbolorum definitionum et declarationum de rebus fidei et morum*), Quod emendavit … et edidit Peter Hünerman, editio xxxvii, 1991. French edition by Joseph Hoffmann. Paris: Cerf, 1996.

Elders, Leo. *La Métaphysique de saint Thomas d'Aquin dans une perspective historique*. Paris: J. Vrin, 1994.

Faes de Mottoni, Barbara. "'Enuntiatores divini silentii': Tommaso d'Aquino e il linguaggio degli angeli." *Medioevo* 12 (1986): 189–228.

————. "Thomas von Aquin und die Sprache der Engel." *MM* 19: 140–55. 1988.

————. "Tommaso d'Aquino e la conoscenza mattutina e vespertina degli angeli." *Medioevo* 18 (1992): 169–202.

————. "Discussioni sul corpo dell'angelo nel secolo XII." In *Parva mediaevalia: Studi per Maria Elena Reina*. Trieste: Università degli Studi di Trieste, 1993, 1–42.

————. *San Bonaventura e la scala di Giacobbe: Letture di angelologia*. Saggi Bibliopolis 49. Naples: Bibliopolis, 1995.

————. "Ange." In *Dictionnaire encyclopédique du Moyen Âge* 1:64–66. 1997.

————. "L'illusione dei sensi? Angeli e sensi in Bonaventura e Tommaso d'Aquino." *Micrologus* 10 (2002): 295–312.

Faes de Mottoni, Barbara, and Tiziana Suarez-Nani. "I demoni e l'illusione dei sensi nel secolo XIII. Bonaventura e Tommaso d'Aquino." In *Jakobs Traum: Zur Bedeutung der Zwischenwelt in der Tradition des Platonismus*. St. Katharinen: Scripta Mercaturae Verlag, 2002, 77–94.

Fernandez de Viana, Félix. "Motores de cuerpos celestes y Angeles en S. Tomas de Aquino." *Estudios Filosoficos* 8 (1959): 359–82.

Ferrer-Rodríguez, María-Pilar. *La inmaterialidad de las substancias separadas: Santo Tomas versus Avicebron*. Pamplona: Servicio de Publicaciones de la Universidad de Navarra, 1988.

Flasch, Kurt. "Die Seele im Feuer: Aristotelische Seelenlehre und augustinisch-gregorianische Eschatologie bei Albert von Köln, Thomas von Aquino, Siger von Brabant und Dietrich von Freiberg." In *Albertus Magnus und der Albertismus: Deutsche philosophische Kultur des Mittelalters*, edited by Maarten J. F. M. Hoenen and Alain de Libera, 107–31. Studien und Texte zur Geistesgeschichte des Mittelalters 48. Leiden: E. J. Brill, 1995.

Fletcher-Louis, Crispin H. T. *Luke-Acts: Angels, Christology and Soteriology*. Wissenschaftliche Untersuchungen zum Neuen Testament. Tübingen: Mohr Siebeck, 1997.

Foerster, W. "*Daimôn, daimonion*." *TDNT*, 2:1–19. 1964.

Foerster, W., and Knut Schäferdiek. "Satanas: Satan in the New Testament." *TDNT*, 7:151–65. 1971.

Foerster, W., and Gerhard von Rad. "*Diaballô, diabolos*." *TDNT*, 2:71–81. 1964.

"Foi chrétienne et démonologie." In *DC*, 72:708–18. 1975.

Fontinoy, Charles. "Les anges et les démons de l'Ancien Testament." In Ries, *Anges et Démons*, 117–34. 1969.

Forbes, Chris. "Paul's Principalities and Powers: Demythologizing Apocalyptic?" *Journal for the Study of the New Testament* 82 (2001): 61–88.

————. "Pauline Demonology and/or Cosmology? Principalities, Powers and the Elements of the World in Their Hellenistic Context." *Journal for the Study of the New Testament* 23 (2002): 51–73.

Forest, Aimé. *La structure métaphysique du concret selon saint Thomas d'Aquin*. Études de philosophie médiévale 14. Paris: J. Vrin, 1931.

Fortescue, Adrian. "Chéroubicon." In *Dictionnaire d'archéologie chrétienne et de liturgie*. Paris: Letouzey, 1913, 3:1281–86.

Frank, Karl S. *Angelikos Bios: Begriffsanalytische und begriffsgeschichtliche Untersuchung zum "Engelgleichen Leben" im frühen Mönchtum*. Münster: Aschendorff, 1964.

Fung, Ronald Y. K. *The Epistle to the Galatians*. The New International Commentary on the New Testament. Grand Rapids: Eerdmans, 1988.

Gagnebet, Marie-Rosaire. "L'amour naturel de Dieu chez saint Thomas et ses contemporains." *RT* 48 (1948): 394–446; 49 (1949): 31–102.

Galopin, Pièrre-Marie. "Ange." In *DEB*, 59–61. 1987.

———. "Ange de Yahvé." In *DEB* 62. 1987.

Galopin, Pierre-Marie, and Pierre Grelot. "Ange." In *VTB*, 58–62. 1988.

Gardeil, Henri-Dominique. *Initiation à la philosophie de saint Thomas d'Aquin*. Vol. 2, *Cosmologie*. Paris: Cerf, 1953.

Garrigou-Lagrange, Réginald. *De Deo Trino et Creatore*. Turin: Marietti; and Paris: Desclée de Brouwer, 1943.

Génies, anges et démons: Egypte, Babylone, Israël, Islam, Peuples altaïques, Inde, Birmanie, Asie du Sud-Est, Tibet, Chine. Sources orientales 8. Paris: Éditions du Seuil, 1971.

George, Augustin. *Études sur l'oeuvre de Luc*. Sources bibliques. Paris: Gabalda, 1978.

Giblet, Jean. "La puissance satanique selon l'Évangile de Jean." In Ries and Limet, *Anges et démons*, 291–300. 1989.

Gilboa, Raquel. "Cherubim: An Inquiry into an Enigma." *BN* 82 (1996): 59–75.

Gilson, Étienne. *Jean Duns Scot: Introduction à ses positions fondamentales*. Études de philosophie médiévale 42. Paris: J. Vrin, 1952.

———. *L'Être et l'essence*. 2nd ed. Paris: J. Vrin, 1972.

———. *Le thomisme*. 6th ed. Paris: J. Vrin, 1972.

———. "A New Ontology." In *Thomism: The Philosophy of Thomas Aquinas*. Toronto: Pontifical Institute of Medieval Studies, 2002.

Giorgi, Rosa. *Anges et démons*, traduit de l'italien par Dominique Férault. Guide des arts. Paris: Hazan, 2004. English edition: *Angels and Demons in Art: A Guide to Imagery*. Los Angeles: J. Paul Getty Museum, 2005.

Glorieux, Palémon. *Autour de la spiritualité des anges*. Tournai: Desclée, 1959.

Gonzalez Ayesta, Cruz. *Hombre y verdad: Gnoseologia y antropologia del conocimiento en las Q.D. De Veritate*. Filosofica 172. Pampelune: Ediciones Universidad de Navarra, 2002.

Görg, Manfred. "Keruben in Jerusalem." *BN* 4 (1977): 13–24.

———. "Die Funktion der Serafen bei Jesaja." *BN* 5 (1978): 28–39.

Goris, Harm J. M. J. "The Angelic Doctor and Angelic Speech: The Development of Thomas Aquinas' Thought on How Angels Communicate." *Medieval Philosophy and Theology* 11 (2003): 1–19.

Greene, John T. *The Role of Messenger and Message in the Ancient Near East: Oral and Written Communication in the Ancient Near East and in the Hebrew Scriptures*. Atlanta: Scholars Press, 1989.

Gribomont, Jean. "Introduction." In *Les Oeuvres du Saint-Esprit*, by Rupert of Deutz. SC 131. 1967.

Grillmeier, Alois. *Christ in Christian Tradition: From the Apostolic Age to Chalcedon (451)*. Translated by J. S. Bowden. New York: Sheed and Ward, 1965.

—. *Le Christ dans la tradition chrétienne: De l'âge apostolique à Chalcédoine (451)*. Paris: Cerf, 1973.

Grün, Anselm. *Aux prises avec le mal: Le combat contre les démons dans le monachisme des origines*. Spiritualité orientale 49. Bégrolles-en-Mauges: Abbaye de Bellefontaine, 1990.

Grünthaner, M. J. "The Demonology of the Old Testament." *Catholic Biblical Quarterly* 6 (1944): 6–27.

Grundmann, W. "*Aggelos: Aggelos* in the Greek and Hellenistic World." *TDNT*, 1:74–76. 1964.

Guérard des Lauriers, Michel-Louis. *Le Péché et la durée de l'ange*. Collectio philosophica lateranensis 10. Rome: Desclée, 1965.

Guggisberg, Fritz. *Die Gestalt des Mal'ak Jahwe im AT*. Neuchâtel: Université de Neuchâtel, 1979.

Guillaumont, Antoine, and Claire Guillaumont. "Démon: Dans la plus ancienne littérature monastique." In *DS*, 3:189–212. 1957.

Haag, Herbert. *Abschied vom Teufel*. Einsiedeln: Benziger, 1969.

—. *Liquidation du diable*. Méditations théologiques. Paris: Desclée de Brouwer, 1971.

—. *Teufelsglaube*. Tübingen: Katzmann, 1974.

Hadot, Pierre. *Porphyre et Victorinus*. Vol. 1. Études augustiniennes 32. Paris: Études augustiniennes, 1968.

Hamonic, Thierry-Marie. "Dieu peut-il être légitimement convoité? Quelques aspects de la théologie thomiste de l'amour selon le Père Labourdette." *RT* 92 (1992): 239–66.

Hankey, Wayne J. "Aquinas, Pseudo-Denys, Proclus and Isaiah VI.6." *AHDLMA* 64 (1997): 59–93.

—. "Dionysian Hierarchy in Thomas Aquinas: Tradition and Transformation." In *Denys l'Aréopagite et sa postérité en Orient et en Occident*, Actes du Collqoue International, Paris, September 21–24, 1994, edited by Y. de Andia, 405–38. Paris: Institut d'études augustiniennes, 1997.

Hazard, Paul. *The Crisis of the European Mind, 1680–1715*. Cleveland and New York: World Publishing, 1963.

Heidt, William G. *Angelology of the Old Testament: A Study in Biblical Theology*. Washington, D.C.: The Catholic University of America Press 1949.

Heising, Alkuin. "Der heilige Geist und die Heiligung der Engel in der Pneumatologie des Basilius von Cäsarea." *ZkTh* 87 (1965): 257–308.

Horn, Hans-Jürgen, ed. *Jakobs Traum: Zur Bedeutung der Zwischenwelt in der Tradition des Platonismus*. St. Katharinen: Scripta Mercaturae Verlag, 2002.

Hugon, Édouard. *Tractatus dogmatici*. Vol. 1, *De Deo uno et trino, Creatore et gubernatore; De angelis et homine*. Paris: P. Lethielleux, 1933.

Ide, Pascal. "Les anges dans la nature." *Carmel* 99 (March 2001): 33–50.

Immaculata (Soeur). "Les Anges dans la liturgie." *Carmel* 99 (2001): 19–30.

Introvigne, Massimo. *Indagine sul satanismo: Satanisti e anti-satanisti dal Seicento al nostri giorni.* Milan: A. Mondadori, 1994.

Jacob, Edmond. *Esaïe, 1–12.* Commentaires de l'Ancien Testament. Geneva: 1987.

———. "Variations et constantes dans la figure de l'Ange de YHWH." *Revue d'Histoire et de Philosophie religieuse* 68 (1988): 405–14.

John Paul II. *Catéchèses sur les anges et les démons.* DC 83, 797–98 [the creation of invisible beings; angels are free creatures]; 851–53 [the ministry of angels; angels in salvation history]; 894–97 [the wicked angels; Christ's victory over the spirit of evil].

Johnson, Lawrence. *Christ Sanctifier of the Angels.* Rome: Pontificia Universita San Tommaso, 2000.

Journet, Charles. "L'univers antérieur à l'Église." *RT* 53 (1953): 439–87.

———. "L'aventure des anges." *Nova et vetera* 33 (1958): 127–43.

———. *L'Église du Verbe incarné: Essai de théologie de l'histoire du salut.* In *Oeuvres complètes.* Saint-Maurice, 2004.

Journet, Charles, Jacques Maritain, and Philippe de la Trinité, eds. *Le Péché de l'ange: Peccabilité, nature et surnature.* Bibliothèque de théologie historique. Paris: Beauchesne, 1961.

Jugnet, Louis. *La Pensée de saint Thomas d'Aquin.* 3rd ed. Paris: Éditions de la Nouvelle Aurore, 1975.

Kallis, Anastasios. "Geister (Dämonen): Griechische Väter." In *RAC*, 9:700–15. 1976.

Kasper, Walter, and Karl Lehmann, eds. *Diavolo—demoni—possessione: Sulla realtà del male.* Queriniana 149. 2nd ed. Brescia: Queriniana, 1985. [Original German edition: *Teufel—Dämonen—Besessenheit: Zur Wirklichkeit der Bösen.* Mainz: Matthias Grünewald, 1978.]

Keck, David. *Angels and Angelology in the Middle Ages.* New York and Oxford: Oxford University Press, 1998.

Keel, Othmar. "Mit Cherubim et Seraphim." *Bibel Heute* 112 (1992): 171–74.

Kelly, Henry A. *The Devil: Demonology and Witchcraft.* London: Doubleday, 1968.

Kertelge, Karl. "Jésus, ses miracles et Satan." *Concilium* 103 (1975): 45–53.

———. "Diavolo, demoni, esorcismi in prospettiva biblica." In *Diavolo—demoni—possessione: Sulla realtà del male*, edited by Walter Kasper and Karl Lehmann, 7–44. 2nd ed. Brescia: Queriniana, 1985. Original German: *Teufel—Dämonen—Besessenheit: Zur Wirklichkeit des Bösen.* Mainz: Matthias Grünewald, 1978.

Kirchschläger, Walter. "Satan (et démons): (E) Satan (et démons) à Qumram; (F) Satan et démons dans le Nouveau Testament." In *DBS*, 12: 21–47. 1996.

Kittel, Gerhard. "*Aggelos: Aggelos* in the NT." In *TDNT*, 83–87. 1964.

Kleineidam, Erich. *Das Problem der hylemorphen Zusammensetzung der geistigen Substanzen im 13. Jahrhundert, behandelt bis Thomas von Aquin.* Breslau: G. Tesch, 1930.

Koch, Klaus. "Monotheismus und Angelologie." In *Ein Gott allein? JHWH-Verehrung und biblischer Monotheismus im Kontext der israelitischen und altorientalischen Religionsgeschichte*, edited by Walter Dietrich and Martin A. Klopfenstein,

Bibliography 317

565–81. 13. Kolloquium der Schweizerischen Adamedie der Geistes- und So-
zialwissenschafter. Fribourg: Universitätsverlag; Gottingen: Vandenhoeck and
Ruprecht, 1994.
Koloska, Alfred. *Gottessöhne und Engel in der Vorexilischen Büchern des AT und in der
Ras-Schamaramythologie im Lichte des Biblischen Monotheismus.* Vienna: 1953.
Kornfeld, Walter. "Satan (et démons): Satan dans l'Ancien Testament; Démons
dans la Bible hébraïque; Protection contre les démons; Bibliographie." In *DBS*,
12:1–21. 1996.
Kretschmar, Georg. *Studien zur frühchristlichen Trinitättheologie.* Tübingen: Mohr
Siebeck, 1956.
Kuhn, Harold B. "The Angelology of the Non-Canonical Jewish Apocalypses." *JBL*
67 (1948): 217–32.
Labourdette, Michel M. "La théologie, intelligence de la foi." *RT* 46 (1946): 5–44.
Lagrange, Marie-Joseph. "L'ange de Jahvé." *Revue biblique* (1903): 212–23.
———. *Épître aux Galates.* 4th ed. Études bibliques. Paris: J. Gabalda, 1942.
Lalouette, Jacqueline. "Le combat des archanges (Saint Michel et Satan dans les
luttes politiques et religieuses de la France contemporaine)." In *Le Diable.* Ca-
hiers de l'Hermétisme. Paris: Dervy, 1998, 69–85.
Lamirande, Émilien. *L'Église céleste selon saint Augustin.* Paris: Études augustini-
ennes, 1963.
Lang, D. P. "Aquinas' Proof for the Existence and Nature of the Angels." *Faith and
Reason* 21 (1995): 3–16.
Lange, Armin, Hermann Lichtenberger, and K. F. D. Römheld, eds. *Die Dämonen:
Demons, die Dämonologie der israelitisch-jüdischen und frühchristlichen Literatur
im Kontext ihrer Umwelt.* Tübingen: Mohr Siebeck, 2003.
Langton, Edward. *La démonologie: Étude de la doctrine juive et chrétienne, Son origine
et son développement.* Paris: Payot, 1951.
Laporta, Jorge. "Pour trouver le sens exact des termes: *Appetitus naturalis, deside-
rium naturale, amor naturalis,* etc. chez Thomas d'Aquin." *AHDLMA* 40 (1973):
37–95.
Lavatori, Renzo. *Satana, un caso serioso: Studio di demonologia cristiana.* Bologna:
Ed. Dehoniane, 1996.
Lechner, Odilo. "Zu Augustins Metaphysik der Engel." In *Studia Patristica* 9. Berlin: Akademie-Verlag, 1966, 422–30.
Lee, Jung Y. "Interpreting the Demonic Powers in Pauline Thought." *NT* 12 (1970):
54–69.
Legeay, Georges. "L'ange et les théophanies dans la sainte écriture, d'après la doctrine des pères." *RT* 10 (1902): 138–58, 405–24; *RT* 11 (1903): 46–69, 125–54.
Lehmann, Karl. "Il diavolo, un essere personale?" In *Diavolo—demoni—possessi-
one: Sulla realtà del male,* edited by Walter Kasper and Karl Lehmann, 79–111.
2nd ed. Brescia: Queriniana, 1985. Original German: *Teufel—Dämonen—Be-
sessenheit: Zur Wirklichkeit des Bösen.* Mainz: Matthias Grünewald, 1978.
Le Moyne, Jean. *Les Sadducéens.* Études bibliques. Paris: Lecoffre, 1972.
Leroy, M.-V. *Les anges* [mimeographed course notes]. Toulouse: n.d.
Lewis, C. S. *The Screwtape Letters.* New York: Macmillan, 1952.

Lhermitte, Jean. "Les pseudo-possessions diaboliques." In *Satan*. Études carmélitaines. Paris: 1948, 424–44.

Limbeck, Meinrad. "Les sources de la conception biblique du diable et des démons." *Concilium* 103 (1975): 31–44.

Ling, Trevor O. *The Significance of Satan: New Testament Demonology and Its Contemporary Relevance*. Scottdale: Herald Press, 1980.

Lipinski, Edouard. "Chérubin." In *DEB*, 264–66. 1987.

———. "Démon." In *DEB*, 340–41. 1987.

———. "Satan." In *DEB*, 1172–73. 1987.

———. "Séraphins." In *DEB*, 1192. 1987.

Litt, Thomas. *Les corps célestes dans l'univers de saint Thomas d'Aquin*. Philosophes médiévaux 7. Louvain and Paris: Publications universitaires, 1963.

Lods, Adolphe. "La chute des Anges: Origines et portée de cette spéculation." *Revue d'histoire et de philosophie religieuses* 7 (1927): 295–315.

Lohse, Bernhard. "Zu Augustins Engellehre." *Zeitschrift für Kirchengeschichte* 70 (1959): 278–91.

Lottin, Odon. "La composition hylémorphique des substances spirituelles: Les débuts de la controverse." *RNSP* 34 (1932): 21–41.

Louis-Chevrillon, Hedwige. *Le Prince du mensonge*. Paris: Éditions Saint-Paul, 1970.

Lyonnet, Stanislas. "Le démon dans l'Écriture." *DS*, 3:142–82. 1957.

———. "Satan." In *VTB*, 1196–99. 1988.

MacGregor, G. H. C. "Principalities and Powers: The Cosmic Background of St Paul's Thought." *New Testament Studies* 1 (1954–55): 17–28.

MacIntosh, J. J. "St. Thomas on Angelic Time and Motion." *Thomist* 59 (1995): 547–75.

Madec, Goulven. "Angelus." In *Augustinus-Lexicon*. Basel: Schwabe, 1986–94, 1:303–15.

Maldamé, Jean-Michel. "Les Anges, les Puissances et la primauté du Christ." *BLE* 96 (1995): 121–34.

Mangenot, Eugène. "Démon d'après les Pères." In *DTC*, 4:339–84. 1911.

Maquart, François-Xavier. "L'exorciste devant les manifestations diaboliques." In *Satan*. Études carmélitaines. Paris: Desclée de Brouwer, 1948, 274–94.

Marconcini, Benito. *Angeli e demoni: Il dramma della storia tra il bene e il male*. Corso di teologia sistematica 11. Bologna: Edizioni Dehoniane, 1992.

Marieb, Raymond E. "The Impeccability of the Angels regarding their Natural End." *Thomist* 28 (1964): 409–74.

Maritain, Jacques. *Three Reformers: Luther—Descartes—Rousseau*. New York: Charles Scribner's Sons, 1955.

———. "Le péché de l'ange: Essai de ré-interprétation des positions thomistes." In *Le Péché de l'ange: Peccabilité, nature et surnature*, edited by Journet, Jacques Maritain, and Philippe de la Trinité, 41–86. Paris: Beauchesne, 1961.

———. *Distinguish to Unite: The Degrees of Knowledge*. Translated by Gerald B. Phelan et al. Notre Dame, Ind.: University of Notre Dame Press, 1995.

Maritain, Jacques, and Raïssa Maritain. *Oeuvres complètes*. Fribourg: Editions universitaires; Paris: Editions Saint-Paul, 1982–95.

Maurer, Armand. *The Philosophy of William of Ockham in the Light of Its Principles.* Toronto: Pontifical Institute of Medieval Studies, 1999.

Mayer, Cornelius, ed. *Augustinus-Lexicon.* Basel: vol. 1, 1986–94; vol. 2, 1996–2002.

McEvoy, James. *The Philosophy of Robert Grosseteste.* Oxford: Clarendon Press; New York: Oxford University Press, 1982.

Mehlmann, Johannes. "Tertulliani liber de carne Christi ab Augustino citatus." *Sacris erudiri* 17 (1966): 269–89.

Meier, John P. *A Marginal Jew: Rethinking the Historical Jesus.* Vol. 2, *Mentor, Message and Miracles.* New York: Doubleday, 1994.

Meier, Samuel A. *The Messenger in the Ancient Semitic World.* Cambridge, Mass.: Harvard University Press, 1988.

Ménager, Daniel. *Diplomatie et théologie à la Renaissance.* Paris: Presses universitaires de France, 2001.

Mennessier, Ignatius. "Le rôle providentiel des démons." In Saint Thomas d'Aquin. *Somme théologique: La Religion,* 2a–2ae, Questions 88–100, traduction française de I. Mennessier. Éditions de la Revue des jeunes. Paris: Desclée, 1934, 2:451–60.

Merlan, Philip. "Aristotle's Unmoved Movers." *Traditio* 4 (1946): 1–30.

Meyer, Charles. "Les anges et les démons dans la doctrine de l'Église." *Concilium* 103 (1975): 71–79.

Michaelis, Wilhelm. *Zur Engelchristologie im Urchristentum.* Basel: Heinrich Majer, 1942.

Michl, Johann. "Engel III (christlich)." *RAC,* 5:109–200. 1962.

———. "Ange." In *Encyclopédie de la foi.* Paris: Cerf, 1:83–96. 1965.

———. "Satan: Histoire de la théologie." In *Encyclopédie de la foi,* 4: 191–200. 1967.

———. "L'angélologie biblique: II. Le Nouveau Testament." In *Les anges.* edited by George Tavard, 29–49. Histoire des dogmes II.2b. Paris: Cerf, 1971.

Michon, Cyrille, Olivier Boulnois, and Nathanaël Dupré La Tour, eds. *Thomas d'Aquin et la controverse sur "L'Éternité du monde": Traites sur "L'Éternité du monde" de Bonaventure, Thomas d'Aquin, Peckham, Boèce de Dacie, Henri de Gand et Guillaume d'Ockham.* Paris: Flammarion, 2004.

Milner, Max, ed. *Entretiens sur l'homme et le diable.* Centre culturel international de Cerisy-La-Salle. Paris-La Haye: Mouton, 1965.

Montagne, Ambroise. "De l'apparition de Dieu à Moyse sur le Mont Horeb (Exode, Chap. III)." *Revue biblique* 3 (1894): 232–47.

Montano, Edward. *The Sin of Angels: Some Aspects of the Teaching of St. Thomas.* Washington, D.C.: The Catholic University of America Press, 1955.

Morerod, Charles. "Le sens et la portée de la hiérarchie des vérités à Vatican II et chez saint Thomas." *Nova et vetera* 71 (1996): 15–47.

Mougel, René. "La position de Jacques Maritain à l'égard de *Surnaturel,* Le péché de l'ange, ou 'esprit et liberté.'" In *Surnaturel: Une controverse au coeur du thomisme au XXe siècle,* Actes du colloque organisé par l'Institut Saint-Thomas d'Aquin les 26–27 mai 2000 à Toulouse. *RT* 101 (2001): 73–98.

Moulton, James H. "It Is His Angel." *Journal of Theological Studies* 3 (1902): 514–27.

Muchembled, Robert. *A History of the Devil: From the Middle Ages to the Present.* Cambridge: Polity Press, 2003.

Mulder, Dirk C. "Les démons dans les religions non-bibliques." *Concilium* 103 (1975): 21–30.

Mullen, E. Theodore, Jr. *The Assembly of the Gods: The Divine Council in Canaanite and Early Hebrew Literature.* Chico, Calif.: Scholars Press, 1980.

Nanni, Gabriele. *Il dito di Dio e il potere di Satana: L'esorcismo.* Esperienza e fenomenologia mistica. Vatican City: Libreria editrice vaticana, 2004.

Nault, Jean-Charles. *La saveur de Dieu: L'acédie dans le dynamisme de l'agir.* Studi e Ricerche. Rome: Lateran University Press, 2002.

Nicolas, Jean-Hervé. "La permission du péché." *RT* 60 (1960): 5–37 and 509–46.

———. "De l'existence dans l'univers créé de créatures invisibles." In *Synthèse dogmatique,* vol. 2, *Complément.* Fribourg and Paris: Éditions universitaires, 1993, 268–76.

Nissing, Hanns-Gregor. *Sprache als Akt bei Thomas von Aquin.* Studien und Texte zur Geistesgeschichte des Mittelalters 87. Leiden, Boston, and Cologne: E. J. Brill, 2006.

O'Brien, Peter T. "Principalities and Powers: Opponents of the Church." In *Biblical Interpretation and the Church,* edited by D. A. Carson, 110–50. Nashville: T. Nelson, 1984.

Olyan, Saul M. *A Thousand Thousands Served Him: Exegesis and the Naming of Angels in Ancient Judaism.* Tübingen: J. C. B. Mohr, 1993.

Osborne, Thomas M. *Love of Self and Love of God in Thirteenth-Century Ethics.* Notre Dame, Ind.: University of Notre Dame Press, 2005.

Page, Sydney H. T. *Powers of Evil: A Biblical Study of Satan and Demons.* Grand Rapids: Baker Books, 1995.

Panaccio, Claude. "Conversation angélique, langage mental et transparence de l'esprit." In *Vestigia, Imagines, Verba: Semiotics and Logic in Medieval Theological Texts (12th–14th Century),* edited by Costantino Marmo, 323–35. Semiotics and Cognitive Studies 4. Turnhout: Brepols, 1997.

Parker, Floyd. "The Terms 'Angels' and 'Spirits' in Acts 23:8." *Biblica* 84 (2003): 344–65.

Peghaire, Julien. "L'intellection du singulier matériel chez l'ange et chez l'homme." *Revue dominicaine* 39 (1933): 135–44.

———. "*Intellectus*" et "*ratio*" selon S. Thomas d'Aquin. Publications de l'Institut d'études médiévales d'Ottawa 6. Paris: J. Vrin; Ottawa: Inst. d'études médiévales, 1936.

Pelz, Karl. *Die Engellehre des heiligen Augustinus.* Münster: Aschendorff, 1913.

Pépin, Jean. "Influences païennes sur l'angélologie et la démonologie de saint Augustin." In Max Milner, *Entretiens sur l'homme et le diable* 51–59. Paris: Mouton, 1965.

Peterson, Erik. *The Angels and the Liturgy.* Translated by Ronald Walls. New York: Herder and Herder, 1964.

Philippe de la Trinité. "Du péché de Satan et de la destinée de l'esprit." In *Satan: Études carmélitaines.* Paris: Desclée de Brouwer, 1948, 44–85.

———. "La pensée des carmes de Salamanque et de Jean de Saint-Thomas sur le péché de l'ange." *Ephemerides Carmeliticae* 8 (1957): 315–75.

————. "Réflexions sur le péché de l'ange." *Ephemerides Carmeliticae* 8 (1957): 44–92.

————. "Évolution de saint Thomas sur le péché de l'ange dans l'ordre naturel?" *Ephemerides Carmeliticae* 9 (1958): 338–90.

Philips, Gérard. *La raison d'être du mal d'après saint Augustin.* Louvain: Éditions du Museum Lessianum, 1927.

Pinckaers, Servais. *The Source of Christian Ethics.* Translated by Sr. Mary Thomas Noble, OP. Washington, D.C.: The Catholic University of America Press, 1995.

————. "Les anges, garants de l'expérience spirituelle selon saint Thomas d'Aquin." *Revue Théologique de Lugano* 1 (1996): 179–92.

Ponnau, Dominique, and Erich Lessing. *Dieu en ses anges.* Paris: Cerf, 2000.

Popper, Karl. *The Open Universe: An Argument for Indeterminism.* Totowa, N.J.: Rowman and Littlefield, 1982.

Porro, Pasquale. "Aevum." In *Dictionnaire du Moyen Âge*, edited by Claude Gauvard, Alain de Libera, and Michel Zink, 12–14. Paris: Quadrige and PUF, 2002.

Quay, Paul M. "Angels and Demons: The Teaching of IV Lateran." *Theological Studies* 42 (1981): 20–45.

Quelquejeu, Bernard. "Naturalia manent integra: Contribution à l'étude de la portée, méthodologique et doctrinale, de l'axiome théologique 'Gratia praesupponit natura.'" *RSPT* 49 (1965): 640–55.

Quillet, Jeannine. "Présence réelle de Satan dans l'oeuvre de Bernanos." In Milner, *Entretiens sur l'homme et le diable*, 271–85. 1965.

Rahner, Hugo. "*Pompa diaboli*: Ein Beitrag zur Bedeutungsgeschichte des Wortes *pompê-pompa* in der urchristlichen Taufliturgie." *ZkTh* 55 (1931): 239–73.

Rahner, Karl. "Angelologie." In *Sacramentum mundi: Theologisches Lexicon für die Praxis.* Freiburg, Basel, and Vienna: Herder, 1967, 1:146–54.

Ratzinger, Joseph. "Looking at Christ: The Figure of Christ as Reflected in the Gospel Account of His Temptation." In *On the Way to Jesus Christ.* San Francisco: Ignatius Press, 2005, 79–101.

————. "Abschied vom Teufel?" In *Dogma und Verkündigung.* Munich and Freiburg: 1973, 225–34. English translation "Farewell to the Devil?" In *Dogma and Preaching.* San Francisco: Ignatius Press, 2011, 197–205.

Régamey, Pie-Raymond. *Les anges au ciel et parmi nous.* Je sais, je crois. Paris: A. Fayard, 1959.

Rey, Bernard. *Les tentations et le choix de Jésus.* Lire la Bible 72. Paris: Cerf, 1986.

Reynolds, Philip L. *Food and the Body: Some Peculiar Questions in High Medieval Theology.* Studien und Texte zur Geistesgeschichte des Mittelalters 69. Leiden, Boston, and Cologne: Brill, 1999.

Ries, Julien. "Cultes païens et démons dans l'apologétique chrétienne de Justin à Augustin." In Ries and Limet, *Anges et Démons*, 337–52. 1989.

Ries, Julien, and Henri Limet, eds. *Anges et Démons: Actes du colloque de Liège et de Louvain-la-Neuve, 25–26 novembre 1987.* Homo religiosus 14. Louvain-la-Neuve: Centre d'histoire des religions, 1989.

Rigaux, Béda. *L'Antéchrist et l'Opposition au Royaume messianique dans l'Ancien et le Nouveau Testament.* Gembloux: J. Duculot; and Paris: J. Gabalda, 1932.

Rituale Romanum ex decreto Sacrosancti Oecumenici Concilii Vaticani II instauratum auctoritate Ioannis Pauli PP. II promulgatum: De exorcismis et supplicationibus quibusdam. Vatican City: Tipografia poliglotta vaticana, 1999.

Rivière, Jean. *Le Dogme de la Rédemption: Essai d'étude historique.* 2nd ed. Paris: V. Lecoffre, 1905.

———. *Le Dogme de la Rédemption: Études critiques et documents.* Louvain: Bureaux de la Revue, 1931.

Robert, Charles. "Les fils de Dieu et les filles des hommes." *Revue biblique* 4 (1895): 340–72.

Robin, Léon. *La Théorie platonicienne de l'Amour.* Paris: Presses universitaires de France, 1933.

Rofé, Alexander. *The Belief in Angels in the Bible and in Early Israel.* Jerusalem: Makor, 1979.

Roques, René. *L'univers dionysien: Structure hiérarchique du monde selon le Pseudo-Denys.* Paris: Aubier, 1954.

———. "Denys l'Aréopagite (le Pseudo-): La doctrine du Pseudo-Denys." *DS,* 3:264–86. 1957.

Roschini, Gabriele M. *Mariologia.* Vol. 2. Rome: A. Belardetti, 1947.

Röttger, Hermann. *Mal'ak Jahwe—Bote von Gott: Die Vorstellung von Gottes Boten im hebräischen A.T.* Regensburg: Frankfurt am Main, 1978.

Roure, Lucien. "Possession diabolique." In *DTC,* 12:2635–47. 1935.

Russell, D. S. *The Method and Message of Jewish Apocalyptic.* Philadelphia: Westminster Press, 1964.

Russell, Jeffrey B. *The Devil: Perceptions of Evil from Antiquity to Primitive Christianity.* Ithica and London: Cornell University Press, 1977.

Rybinski, J. *Der Mal'ak Jahwe.* Paderborn: Ferdinand Schoningh, 1930.

Schärf, Rosa Riwkah. *Die Gestalt des Satans im Alten Testament.* Zürich: Tschudi, 1948.

Scheeben, Matthias J. *La Dogmatique.* Vol. 3. Edited by l'abbé P. Bélet. Bibliothèque théologique du XIXᵉ siècle. Paris: Société générale de librairie catholique, 1881.

Schierse, F. J. "Satan: Étude biblique." In *Encyclopédie de la foi,* Cogitatio fidei 18. Paris: Cerf, 1967, 4:186–91.

Schlier, Heinreich. *Essais sur le Nouveau Testament.* Lectio divina 46. Paris: Cerf, 1968.

Schlössinger, Wilhelm. "Die Erkenntnis der Engeln." *Jahrbuch für Philosophie und Theologie* 22 (1908): 325–349, 492–519; 23 (1909): 45–84, 198–230, 274–315.

———. "Das angelische Wallen." *Jahrbuch für Philosophie und spekulative Theologie* 24 (1909–10): 152–224.

Schneeweis, Emil. *Angels and Demons according to Lactantius.* Studies in Christian Antiquity 3. Washington, D.C: The Catholic University of America Press, 1944.

Schoonenberg, Piet. "Osservazioni filosofiche e teologiche su angeli e diavoli." In *Angeli e diavoli.* Giornale di teologia 60. Brescia: Queriniana, 1972, 94–128.

Second Vatican Council. *Vatican Council II.* Vol. 1, *The Conciliar and Post Conciliar Documents.* Edited by A. Flannery. Northport, N.Y.: Costello Publishing; Dublin: Dominican Publications, 2004.

Seemann, Michael, and Damasus Zähringen. Chapter 11, "Le monde des anges et des démons." In *Mysterium salutis: Dogmatique de l'histoire du salut*. Paris: Éditions du Cerf, 1970, 8:139–203.

Serres, Michel. *La Légende des anges*. Paris: Flammarion, 1993.

Shakespeare, William. *Othello*. Edited and with an introduction by Harold Bloom. New York: Chelsea House Publications, 1987.

Siegwalt, Gérard. *Dogmatique pour la catholicité évangélique: Système mystagogique de la foi chrétienne*. III: L'affirmation de la foi. (2) Cosmologie théologique: Théologie de la création. Paris: Cerf; Geneva: Labor et fides, 2000, 227–353.

Simbanduku, Celestin. *Yhwh, les dieux et les anges: Permanence du polythéisme dans la religion de la Bible*. Rome: Urbaniana University Press, 2004.

Simon, Marcel. "Remarques sur l'angelolâtrie juive au début de l'ère chrétienne." In *Le christianisme antique et son contexte religieux*. Tübingen: Mohr, 1981, 2:450–64.

Simon, Yves. Chap. 2, "Cognition and Activity." In *Introduction to the Ontology of Knowledge*. New York: Fordham University Press, 1990, 39–84.

Simonetti, Manlio. "Due note sull'angelologia origeniana: I, Mt 18:10 nell'interpretazione di Origene." *Rivista di cultura classica e medioevale* 4 (1962): 165–79.

Simonin, H.-D. "La connaissance de l'ange par soi-même." *Angelicum* 9 (1932): 43–62.

Sirat, Colette. *La Philosophie juive au Moyen Âge*. Paris: Éditions du Centre national de la recherche scientifique, 1983.

Solignac, Aimé. "La connaissance angélique et les jours de la création." BA 48:645–53. 1972.

Spanneut, Michel. "Stoïcisme." In *Catholicisme*. Paris: 1996, 14:465–90.

Spicq, Ceslas. *L'Épître aux Hébreux*. Études bibliques. Vol. 2. Paris: J. Gabalda, 1953.

———. "L'existence du Diable appartient à la révélation du Nouveau Testament." In "Satan 'mystère d'iniquité,'" *Communio* 4, no. 3 (1979): 19–27.

Steinmann, Jean. *Le prophète Ezéchiel et les débuts de l'exil*. Paris: Cerf, 1953.

Stier, Fridolin. *Gott und sein Engel im A. T.* Münster: Verlag der Aschendorffschen Verlagsbuchhandlung, 1934.

Strack, Hermann L., and Paul Billerbeck. *Das Evangelium nach Matthäus erläutert aus Talmud und Midrasch*. Kommentar zum Neuen Testament aus Talmud und Midrasch. Munich: Beck, 1922.

Stuckenbruck, Loren T. "An Angelic Refusal of Worship: The Tradition and Its Function in the Apocalypse of John." *Society of Biblical Literature Seminar Papers* (1994): 679–96.

———. *Angel Veneration and Christology: A Study in Early Judaism and in the Christology of the Apocalypse of John*. Wissenschaftliche Untersuchungen zum Neuen Testament 2, 70. Tübingen: Mohr, 1995.

Studer, Basil. "Ange." In *Dictionnaire encyclopédique du christianisme ancien*. Paris: Cerf, 1990, 1:124–28. Original Italian edition 1983.

———. "Démon." In *Dictionnaire encyclopédique du christianisme ancien*. Paris: Cerf, 1990, 644–50. Original Italian edition 1983.

Suarez-Nani, Tiziana. "Angélologie." In *Dictionnaire du Moyen Âge*, edited by Claude Gauvard, Alain de Libera, and Michel Zink, 56–59. Paris: Quadrige and PUF, 2002.

————. *Les anges et la philosophie: Subjectivité et fonction des substances séparées à la fin du XIIIe siècle*. Paris: J. Vrin, 2002.

————. *Connaissance et langage des anges selon Thomas d'Aquin et Gilles de Rome*. Études de philosophie médiévale 85. Paris: J. Vrin, 2002.

————. "Les anges et la cosmologie au Moyen Âge." In *Anges et esprits médiateurs*, Connaissance des religions 71–72. Paris: Éd. Dervy, 2004, 103–15.

Sullivan, Kevin P. *Wrestling with Angels: A Study of the Relationship between Angels and Humans in Ancient Jewish Literature and the New Testament*. Arbeiten zur Geschichte des Antiken Judentums und des Urchristentums 55. Leiden: Brill, 2004.

Tavard, Georges, André Caquot, and Johann Michl. *Les anges*. Translated from German by Maurice Lefèvre. Histoire des dogmes II.2b. Paris: Editions du Cerf, 1971.

Teyssèdre, Bernard. *Naissance du diable: De Babylone aux grottes de la mer Morte*. Paris: A. Michel, 1985.

TDNT (*Theological Dictionary of the New Testament*). Edited by Gerhard Kittel and Gerhard Friedrich. 10th ed. 10 vols. Grand Rapids, Mich.: Eerdmans, 1964–78.

Thompson, Reginald Campbell. *Semitic Magic: Its Origins and Development*. New York: Ktav, 1971.

Torrell, Jean-Pierre. *Initiation à saint Thomas d'Aquin: Sa personne, son oeuvre*. Vestigia 13. 2nd ed. Paris: Cerf; Fribourg: Presses universitaires de Fribourg, 2002.

Touzard, Jules "Ange de Yahweh." In *DBS*, 1:242–55. 1928.

Trottmann, Christian. *La vision béatifique: Des disputes scolastiques à sa définition par Benoît XII*. Bibliothèque des Écoles françaises d'Athènes et de Rome 289. Rome: Ecole française de Rome, 1995.

Turmel, Joseph. "Histoire de l'angélologie des temps apostoliques à la fin du Ve siècle." *Revue d'histoire et de littérature religieuses* 3 (1898): 407–34.

Tur-Sinai, Naphtali H. *The Book of Job: A New Commentary*. Jerusalem: Kiryath Sepher, 1957.

Vacant, Alfred. "Ange: Angélologie dans l'Église latine depuis le temps des Pères jusqu'à saint Thomas d'Aquin; Angélologie de saint Thomas d'Aquin et des scolastiques postérieurs." In *DTC* 1:1222–48. 1903.

Vallin, Philippe. *Le Prochain comme tierce personne chez saint Thomas d'Aquin*. Bibliothèque thomiste 51. Paris: J. Vrin, 2000.

Van der Leeuw, Gerardus. *La Religion dans son essence et ses manifestations: Phénoménologie de la religion*. Paris: Payot, 1970.

Van der Nat, Pieter. G. "Geister (Dämonen): Apologeten und lateinische Väter." *RAC* 9:715–61. 1976.

Van Fleteren, Frederick. "Angels." In *Augustine through the Ages: An Encyclopedia*, edited by Allan D. Fitzgerald, OSA, 20b–22a. Grand Rapids: W. B. Eerdmans, 1999. See also "Demons," 266b–68a; and "Devil," 268a–69a.

————. "Anges," "Démon," "Diable." In *Saint Augustin, La Méditerranée et l'Europe (IVe–XXIe siècle)*, edited by Allan D. Fitzgerald; French edition edited by Marie-Anne Vannier. Paris: Cerf, 2005, 40–43, 436–39; 443–45.

Van Imschoot, Paul. *Théologie de l'Ancien Testament*. Vol. 1, *Dieu*. Paris and Tournai: Desclée, 1954.

Venard, Olivier-Thomas. *La langue de l'ineffable: Essai sur le fondement théologique de la métaphysique.* Geneva: Ad Solem, 2004.

Vercruysse, Jean-Marc. "Les Pères de l'Église et Lucifer." *RSR* 75 (2001): 147–74.

Vernier, Jean-Marie. *Les anges chez saint Thomas d'Aquin: Fondements historiques et principes philosophiques.* Angelologia 3. Paris: Nouvelles Éditions latines, 1986.

Villeneuve, Roland. *Le Diable dans l'art.* Paris: Éditions Denoël, 1957.

VTB (Vocabulaire de théologie biblique). Edited by X. Léon-Dufour. 6th ed. Paris: Cerf, 1988.

Von Balthasar, Hans Urs. *Le chrétien Bernanos.* Paris: Éditions du Seuil, 1956.

———. "Comment en arrive-t-on à Satan?" *Communio* 4 (1979): 4–9.

———. *The Glory of the Lord: A Theological Aesthetics.* Vol 1, *Seeing the Form.* San Francisco: Ignatius Press, 1982.

Von Ivanka, Endre. "La signification historique du 'corpus areopagiticum.'" *RSR* 36 (1949): 5–24.

Von Petersdorf, Egon. "De Daemonibus in Liturgia memoratis." *Angelicum* 19 (1942): 324–39.

Von Rad, Gerhard.. "*Aggelos: Mal'ak* in the OT." In *TDNT*, 1:76–80. 1964.

Wahlen, Clinton. *Jesus and the Impurity of Spirits in the Synoptic Gospels.* Wissenschaftliche Untersuchungen zum Neuen Testament 185. Tübingen: Mohr Siebeck, 2004.

Wartelle, André, ed., trans. *Justin Martyr: Apologies.* Paris: Études Augustiniennes, 1987.

Wawrykow, Joseph. *God's Grace and Human Action: "Merit" in the Theology of Thomas Aquinas.* Notre Dame, Ind.: University of Notre Dame Press, 1995.

Weisheipl, James. "Albertus Magnus and Universal Hylemorphism: Avicebron." In *Albert the Great Commemorative Essays*, edited and introduction by Francis J. Kovach and Robert W. Shahan, 239–60. Norman: University of Oklahoma Press, 1980.

White, Stephen L. "Angel of the Lord: Messenger or Euphemism?" *Tyndale Bulletin* 50 (1999): 299–305.

Wilder, Alfred. "St. Thomas and the Real Distinction of the Potencies of the Soul from Its Substance." In *L'anima nell'antropologia di s. Tommaso d'Aquino.* Studia Universitatis s. Thomae in Urbe 28. Milan: Massimo, 1987, 431–54.

Wippel, John F. *The Metaphysical Thought of Godfrey of Fontaines: A Study in Late Thirteenth-Century Philosophy.* Washington, D.C.: The Catholic University of America Press, 1981.

———. "Thomas Aquinas and the Condemnation of 1277." *Modern Schoolman* 72 (1995): 239–48.

———. *The Metaphysical Thought of Thomas Aquinas: From Finite Being to Uncreated Being.* Monographs of the Society for Medieval and Renaissance Philosophy 1. Washington, D.C.: The Catholic University of America Press, 2000.

Wissink, Josef B. M., ed. *The Eternity of the World in the Thought of Thomas Aquinas and His Contemporaries.* Studien und Texte zur Geistesgeschichte des Mittelalters 27. Leiden, New York, and Cologne: E. J. Brill, 1990.

Wood, Rega. "Angelical Individuation according to Richard Rufus, St. Bonaventure, and Thomas Aquinas." In *Individuum und Individualität im Mittelalter,* edited by Jan A. Aertsen and Andreas Speer, 209–29. MM 24. Berlin and New York: Walter de Gruyter, 1996.

Wright, Archie T. *The Origin of Evil Spirits: The Reception of Genesis 6:1–4 in Early Jewish Literature.* Wissenschaftliche Untersuchungen zum Neuen Testament 2. Reihe 198. Tübingen: Mohr Siebeck, 2005.

Zähringen, Damasus. "Les Démons: L'existence de Satan et des démons." In *Mysterium salutis: Dogmatique de l'histoire du salut.* Paris: Cerf, 1970, 8:204–30.

Index of Names

THOMISTIC RESSOURCEMENT SERIES

—————:—————

Series Editors: Matthew Levering
Thomas Joseph White, OP

The Trinity
An Introduction to Catholic Doctrine on the Triune God (2011)
Gilles Emery, OP
Translated by Matthew Levering

Christ and Spirituality in St. Thomas Aquinas (2011)
Jean-Pierre Torrell, OP
Translated by Bernhard Blankenhorn, OP

Introduction to the Mystery of the Church (2014)
Benoît-Dominique de La Soujeole, OP
Translated by Michael J. Miller

The Mystery of Union with God
Dionysian Mysticism in Albert the Great and Thomas Aquinas (2015)
Bernhard Blankenhorn, OP

The Incarnate Lord
A Thomistic Study in Christology (2015)
Thomas Joseph White, OP

Angels and Demons: A Catholic Introduction was designed and typeset in Arno by Kachergis Book Design of Pittsboro, North Carolina. It was printed on 55-pound Natures Book Natural, and bound by Thomson-Shore of Dexter, Michigan.